W9-CND-838

Emigrant Nation

Emigrant Nation

The Making of Italy Abroad

Mark I. Choate

HARVARD UNIVERSITY PRESS

Cambridge, Massachusetts

London, England

2008

Copyright © 2008 by the President and Fellows of Harvard College
Printed in the United States of America

Library of Congress Cataloging-in-Publication Data

Choate, Mark I., 1971–
    Emigrant nation : the making of Italy abroad / Mark I. Choate.
      p.   cm.
    Includes bibliographical references and index.
    ISBN: 978-0-674-02784-8 (alk. paper)
    1. Italy—Emigration and immigration—History.   2. Italians—Foreign
    countries—Ethnic identity.   I. Title.
  JV8131.C5 2008
    305.85'1—dc22   2007045996

For my mother and father

Contents

Illustrations follow page 100

Acknowledgments

I have accumulated countless debts in researching and writing this book, which would not have been possible without the foundational work of giants in the fields of migration studies and colonialism. My footnotes and references convey my thanks to those scholars. Here I wish to thank my friends and advisors at Yale, especially Frank Snowden, Paul Kennedy, Robert Harms, and Paolo Valesio. Other friends and colleagues also commented on the entire manuscript, in particular Donna Gabaccia, Nicola Labanca, Emilio Franzina, Jenny Hale Pulsipher, Ignacio Garcia, and Carolyn Ugolini. I owe much to the advice and criticism of Benedict Anderson, Giulia Barrera, Linda Colley, the late Peter D'Agostino, John Lewis Gaddis, Jay Geller, Akira Iriye, Roger Louis, Timothy Naftali, Wolfgang Schieder, Gaddis Smith, Jonathan Spence, Lydio Tomasi, and Hans-Ulrich Wehler. I thank Mauro Canali, Emilio Gentile, Luigi Goglia, Gian Luca Podestà, Giovanni Mutino, and Andy Sarzanini for their thoughtful assistance in Italy. Carl Ipsen, whom I knew while researching this topic as a graduate student in 1998–1999, is in his own category.

I owe the most to my family: my wife, Tova, who contributed brilliantly to every aspect of this work, and our three children, Sophie, Anne, and Jonathan. This book is dedicated to my mother and father, Gretchen and John Choate, who inspired my love of history.

A joy of this project has been working in many archives in Europe and the United States. I thank the directors and staff of the Sudan Archive in Durham, England; the Diplomatic Archive and Library of the Italian Foreign Affairs Ministry; the Italian Army General Staff Archive; the Apostolic Vatican Library and the Secret Vatican Archive in Vatican City; the Italian Central State Archive and Library; the Central Headquarters of the Dante Alighieri Society in Rome; the Italian Overseas Agricultural Institute, Florence; the Historical Archive of the Banco di Napoli; the Archive of the Italian Chamber of Deputies; the Italian Red Cross in Rome; the Sovrintendenza dei Beni Culturali, Comune di Roma; the Institute for the History of the Italian Risorgimento in Rome; the Italian State Archives of Rovigo, Venice, Palermo, and Milan; the Ambrosian Library in Milan; the Center for Migration Studies at Staten Island, New York; and the German Federal Archive at Berlin-Lichterfelde, the Public Record Office in London, the British Library, the National

Archives in Paris, the Center for Overseas Archives in Aix-en-Provence, and the United States National Archives at College Park, Maryland.

I am also grateful to the librarians in Rome, especially at the Biblioteca del Ministero delle Risorse Agricole; Biblioteca della Camera dei Deputati; Biblioteca di Storia Moderna e Contemporanea; Istituto Centrale della Statistica; Centro Studi Emigrazione, Roma; Società Geografica Italiana; Biblioteca Nazionale Centrale "Vittorio Emanuele II"; Bibliothèque de l'École Française de Rome; Biblioteca di Studi Meridionali "Giustino Fortunato," and Istituto Italiano per l'Africa e l'Oriente. I also thank Sue Roberts, Dick Hacken, and Robert Murdock at the Yale and Brigham Young University libraries.

I thank Kathleen McDermott of Harvard University Press for her encouragement and expert guidance, and two very helpful anonymous reviewers.

I also gratefully acknowledge generous support from the Smith-Richardson Foundation, the Andrew W. Mellon Foundation, the Pew Charitable Trusts, the Fulbright Foundations of Italy and the United States, the U.S. Department of Education, Yale University, and Brigham Young University. The National Italian American Foundation has graciously supported the publication of this book.

All mistakes in this work are my own. In addition, all translations are mine, unless otherwise noted.

Note: Place names are always a problem. Here I have combined historical usage with the recommendations of the Permanent Committee on Geographical Names in London, using for example Adwa not Adowa nor Adua, and Adis Abeba not Addis Ababa, but Assab rather than Aseb and Massawa rather than Mitsiwa. I have used the English names for Rome, Florence, Genoa, and Naples, but have used Italian names for other cities.

The three maps (see Appendix) are derived from Direzione generale della statistica, *Annuario Statistico italiano, 1914* (Rome, 1914). All data for figures are taken from Commissariato Generale dell'Emigrazione, *Annuario statistico della Emigrazione Italiana dal 1876 al 1925* (Rome, 1926): Figure 1.1: 8, 44; 1.2: 86–91; 3.1: 1641, 1657–1659; 3.2: 1646–1651; 3.3: 44, 689; 3.4: 667, 1542; 3.5: 689.

Emigrant Nation

Introduction:
The Program of Emigrant Colonialism

Between 1880 and 1915, thirteen million Italians emigrated to North and South America, Europe, and the Mediterranean Basin, launching the largest emigration from any country in recorded world history.[1] Italy's experience stands out as an example of the globalizing processes of international migration, as emigration created a capillary network tying Italy in an intimate way to other societies across the world. It was a circulation of individuals and families, but also of capital, traditions, and ideas. Italian emigration changed Italy and the world, with a sustained impact on economic developments, social customs, governmental institutions, and political theory: historical lessons still relevant for immigration and emigration in the twenty-first century.

As a newly united nation, Italy struggled to adapt to its mass exodus. Intellectuals and politicians debated emigration's impact and implications: Was emigration temporary or permanent, good or bad? Was it a "hemorrhage" of Italy's best blood, or did it reflect the exuberance of the Italian people expanding across the globe? Should Italy center itself as the pole of Italians scattered worldwide, or should it conquer new territories for emigrant settlement under Italian rule? Intense controversy produced radically different proposals to solve Italy's domestic and international problems. By 1900, Liberal statesmen had developed a flexible set of programs to establish a network of culture, trade, and exchange with Italians outside of Italy's territory and legal reach. This idea of Italian expatriate communities to the mother country (*la madre patria*) was opposed by anti-Liberal Nationalists in Italy and anti-immigrant bigots worldwide, yet Italy reaped tremendous benefits from its emigration during a crucial period in its economic development.

1

From Italy's point of view, emigration presented a range of political and economic challenges and opportunities. In the first major study of Italian colonialism, published in 1874, Leone Carpi observed that the Italian word *colonìa* meant not only overseas possessions, but also settlements of emigrants in foreign countries.[2] Carpi proposed, based on this definition, that emigration itself was a type of colonial expansion, though tenuous and unpredictable. And unlike colonists in Africa who profited from exploiting indigenous laborers, emigrants themselves stood to be exploited unless protected by active intervention from their native country. With enormous human resources at stake, Italy had much to lose or gain by cultivating emigration. The state had first associated emigration with criminals, draft dodgers, or irresponsible adventurers. It was a problem for the national police. But as emigration rapidly grew, restricting population movements became impossible and even dangerous. The state began to intervene actively in migration, with the aim of extending international influence and reaping colonial benefits. The foreign ministry, responsible for Italy's possessions in Africa, also developed a policy for emigration settlements in Europe and the Americas. These official policies and related private programs I have termed "emigrant colonialism." The Italian state mobilized resources and forged alliances, even with the Catholic Church, bridging the bitter gulf between church and state. Debates over emigration, and their consequences for domestic and foreign policy, shaped Italy's place in the world. Italians became pioneers in establishing a "global nation," beyond imperial control and territorial jurisdiction, held together by ties of culture, communications, ethnicity, and nationality.[3]

How could Italy reach emigrants who had voluntarily left their homes? Italian activists and theorists emphasized the extralegal and nongovernmental aspects of Italian identity, or *italianità:* formative experiences in schools and churches; taste and tradition in food, literature, and music; ties to family in Italy; patriotic celebrations and festivals; and social clubs and organizations. In the words of Bishop Geremia Bonomelli, "Language and religion are the two principal means for keeping alive and solid the ties between mother Italy and her daughter Italy, which grows and prospers in the South American Continent."[4] This sentiment was confirmed by the work of social scientists: Lamberto Loria established the field of Italian ethnography at the height of emigration, between 1905 and 1913, by studying the behavior of Italian emigrants abroad, especially their loyalty to native traditions and cuisine (which required authentic Italian food imports). Loria and his colleagues hypothesized an overarching national identity over the many inevitable contradictions among the ancient peoples on the Italian peninsula, a cultural identity tried and tested through the crucible of emigration. With a scientific approach, *italianità* could be demonstrably replicated in a variety of environments and situations abroad. Emigrants' Italian identity could be proven to resist the pressures of assimilationist "melting pots" as if in a human laboratory. In defining *italianità* abroad as a sentimental tradition, rather than legal citizenship, Italians influenced their domestic identity as well. Italy is an example of what I term an "emigrant nation," an analytical category embracing population at home and also abroad, beyond territorial borders. "Making Italy Abroad" meant not just forming an expatriate community, but changing Italy itself. Emigration's impact was fundamental, shifting the roots of society and culture in the mother country and also in Europe, the Americas, and Africa, much like the mass migrations of the twenty-first-century world. While many aspects of the Italian experience were unique to an imperialist era, the theoretical questions that Italians faced still bear comparison today.

Italy was itself a new creation, recently united as a country between 1859 and 1871 after more than a millennium of regional divisions. Italian Liberals triumphed with the establishment of a constitutional monarchy ruling the entire peninsula, but Republicans were bitterly disappointed. The King of Sardinia, Victor Emmanuel II, now King of Italy, drew upon a long pedigree from his family's rule of Piedmont but lacked a clear vision for his new possessions. The Italian Parliament too remained uncertain on how to face the future. One of the state's first challenges was a wildly expanding and fluctuating current of emigration. Though one of the most densely populated countries in Europe, Italy lagged behind its neighbors in economic productivity and development. Italian laborers had long traveled for temporary work to neighboring regions within Italy and to Austria-Hungary, Germany, Switzerland, and France. But under the pressures of industrialization and changing markets, transoceanic emigration became more attractive and more necessary. Italian workers could double or triple their wages by working abroad.[5] The northern regions of Veneto, Lombardy, and Liguria maintained emigration to Europe, and launched a growing migration to South America. From 1898 onward, however, the United States surpassed Brazil and Argentina as a destination for emigrants, and emigration to Brazil dropped off after 1901. Australia, which had hosted thousands of Italians, sharply curtailed its own immigration in 1901. In these years at the turn of the century, emigration from southern Italy began en masse, primarily to the United States. Year by year, steamships displaced sailing ships in the transatlantic passenger trade, making the crossing fast, cheap, and safe. Between 1878 and 1881, Italy's annual migration to the Americas doubled from twenty to forty thousand; it doubled again by 1886, exceeding consistently high continental migration, then doubled again in 1891 and again in 1904, with more than half a million Italians emigrating across the Atlantic in 1906 and 1913. From 1905 to 1907, one in fifty Italians emigrated each year; in 1913, 2.4 percent of Italy's resident population emigrated abroad. The national census of 1911 revealed that Italian expatriates numbered more than one-sixth of Italy's population.[6]

Such colossal numbers, and their impact, made emigration the most important issue facing Italy after unification. Italian society, culture, and politics relied upon a shifting population base, as emigrants moved between countries and continents or returned home, taking social and economic resources with them. Emigration galvanized a host of domestic concerns: ancient divisions within the recently united peninsula, regional underdevelopment in southern Italy, prevailing illiteracy, and organized crime. Why did so many choose to depart their newly created country? What did it mean to be Italian abroad and at home?

Emigrant settlement also molded Italy's international identity. Italy had been formed as a Great Power, alongside Britain, Russia, France, Austria-Hungary, and Germany. As a result, Italy's leaders felt pressure after 1882 to compete in the European scramble for colonies in Africa and Asia. Could Italy afford to fall behind the king of Belgium, who by 1885 had seized the Congo Basin? Italian emigration and colonialism developed together, joined by proposals to settle Italian African territories with emigrants diverted from the Americas. In the background loomed fears of Europe's Great War, cast in terms of the Darwinian "struggle for life."[7] The war was inevitable after Germany's annexation of French territory in 1871; it would explode in 1914, at the height of mass migration. Would Italian emigrants fight for the survival of their mother country?

Amid the many tensions resulting from emigration, two theories regarding Italian expatriates forever changed international politics: national socialism and irredentism. Enrico Corradini's national socialism characterized Italy as a "proletarian nation" whose emigrant workers were enslaved and abused by "bourgeois nations." According to Nationalists and Fascists, Italy must unite its social classes internally, and overthrow its external masters by international armed struggle. Another explosive theory was irredentism, meaning the national redemption of ethnic minorities abroad. Not all Italians had been united within the borders of the Kingdom of Italy: the "nation" of the Italian people was not yet one with the Italian "state." This missing culmination of political union fostered an enduring concern for Italians outside Italy. The term "irredentism," invented in the 1870s, evoked the redemption of Italian lands still under Austrian imperial rule *(le terre irredente)* by including all speakers of the Italian language in the Italian nation and uniting their territory to the Italian polity. Like other irredentist movements that have aimed to unite populations across political borders, Italian activists made ethnic identity, language, and religion into key weapons of political struggle across international borders.[8] The massive movement of emigrants outside the kingdom led to a union of irredentists with emigration advocates, both joining in social, cultural, and ultimately political concern for Italians abroad. Teaching the Italian language abroad was subsidized by the Italian government directly and indirectly through Italian religious, secular, and state schools abroad. Adult Italian emigrants who spoke only regional language and dialects, and their children born abroad, would learn the "language of Dante" to communicate with fellow emigrants and with the Italian state. Emigrants became part of Italy's ongoing drama of unification and Risorgimento, or resurgence, building Italy as a "global nation." The romantic fervor and dynamism of political exiles such as Giuseppe Mazzini and Giuseppe Garibaldi had earlier provided vital impetus and support for Italy from abroad. Now Italian expatriates again played an integral part in shaping the face of their fatherland, much like the roles played by Chinese emigrants in establishing the Chinese republic and Polish emigrants in creating an independent Poland in the twentieth century.[9]

An expatriate network offered clear advantages to the Italian state. To extend its reach, the government collapsed the analytical categories of emigrant, exile, expatriate, and unredeemed into the single theoretical concept of "Italians Abroad." All were part of the fatherland, without distinguishing between emigrants traveling third-class and expatriate businessmen traveling first-class. Under the banner of Italians Abroad, Italy pioneered an ethnic form of "cultural citizenship," valuing cultural belonging over formal political allegiances.[10] Beyond the idealized "nation-state" of the Kingdom of Italy, uniting all members of the Italian nation in a single state, there was the imagined "nation-superstate," a network of Italians worldwide in a supranational global nation. Drawing upon the powerful rhetoric of irrendentism, the government held censuses of Italians abroad, and sponsored congresses and expositions to showcase the accomplishments of Italians beyond the borders of Italy. Perhaps Italy could imitate the world's biggest empire. J. R. Seeley had argued in 1883 that the British empire had developed spontaneously, expanding from Britain into a "Greater Britain."[11] To forge a "Greater Italy," the Liberal Italian state deliberately treated emigration and colonial expansion as one and the same.

With a powerful resonance, Italians conflated the mass migration of workers with the expatriation of intellectual and political elites. The exile of Dante Alighieri from his native Florence, and even the emigration of Virgil from Mantua, blended rhetorically with the temporary economic exile of millions of laborers worldwide. When considering historic precedents for emigration, Liberal Italian politicians shunned the idea of "diaspora," or dispersal. The historic plight of the Jewish nation, its population scattered by defeat and decline, challenged Italy to react creatively to the dangers and risks of emigration. Before Italy's unification, the ancient nation had been regularly compared with fallen Israel. Giuseppe Mazzini characterized the divided Italian peoples as "soldiers without a banner, Israelites among the nations," and indicated that unification would remove the need for emigration.[12] Giuseppe Verdi launched his career in 1842 with the patriotic opera *Nabucco*, adapting the history of Nebuchadnezzar and the Babylonian Captivity as a parable for the contemporary oppression of Italians by the Austrian Empire. The diasporic children of Israel pine for their homes, and Verdi's chorus "Va' pensiero sull'ali dorate," based on Psalm 137, became a patriotic anthem for Italians divided under papal, Habsburg, and Bourbon rule:

> Fly, my thoughts, on golden wings,
> Go to rest on the slopes and hills
> Where breezes warm and free
> Make fragrant my native soil!
> Greet the banks of the Jordan,

> The fallen towers of Zion,
> My beautiful and desolate fatherland!
> What dear and fatal memories![13]

But once the Kingdom of Italy had united the peninsula, except for lands still under Austro-Hungarian rule, Italian subjects were no longer the slaves of foreign empires. Italy's liberal rulers believed the new home country would meet its children's needs abroad, and there would be no more diaspora.[14] Instead, the word became a politically loaded invective to attack the government of Liberal Italy. Enrico Corradini, who founded the Italian Nationalist party and rallied support for Benito Mussolini's Fascism, condemned Italy's support for emigration in 1909: "The Jews of antiquity always mourned their emigration which they called dispersion, *diaspora.* But we have become used to boasting of it. . . . this appears a sign of our blindness and meanness of spirit, from which the Jews did not suffer."[15] Some scholars today have applied the term "diaspora" to Italian emigration in this period, but unlike the Jewish and African diasporas, Italians were never stateless. Italy offered diplomatic aid abroad and support for return home. The state aimed to bring all Italians together to recreate the international prestige, power, and wealth of Italy's former glories.

Italy's history offered two very different models for achieving imperial greatness based upon population settlement. Ancient Roman legions had conquered and then settled colonies in the Mediterranean, spreading Italian language and culture by force as well as by persuasion. The vision of a reborn Roman empire in Africa promised power and influence for "Greater Italy," and was the basis of Italy's African empire in the nineteenth century. Its principal architect was prime minister Francesco Crispi, who in 1890 pioneered state-sponsored settler colonialism in East Africa along the Red Sea, with emigration as his justification:

> What is our purpose in Eritrea? Our purpose is the institution of a colony that can accommodate that immense emigration which goes to foreign lands, placing this emigration under the dominion and laws of Italy; our purpose is also to do everything that can help our commerce and the commerce of the country we have occupied.[16]

Crispi promised to Parliament to protect emigrants on conquered Italian soil in Africa. His disastrous error was to assume the African lands were blank slates awaiting occupation by Italy's surplus population of would-be emigrants.

An alternative model for imperial power and wealth recalled the medieval trading empires of Venice and Genoa. Some Liberals argued that Italy could support Italian emigrant communities worldwide in a cooperative, patriotic synergy. Instead of exploiting foreign populations by force, Italy's "colonies" of emigrants would voluntarily maintain ties with their mother country, at less expense and with much less bloodshed. To encourage this transnational relationship, Italian state rhetoric maintained that emigrants were an organic part of the nation and part of the expanded state, linked through a shared cultural background. This somewhat artificial identity was deliberately constructed, subsidized, and elaborated through a variety of channels for young and old, including schools, patriotic banquets, choirs and bands, gymnastic groups, the Dante Alighieri Society, the Italian Geographic Society, the Catholic Scalabrinian missionaries, and Italian Chambers of Commerce Abroad. Liberal Italy looked to emigrant settlements or colonies in the Mediterranean and the Americas, whether of wealthy traders in Cairo, construction workers in Tunis, or the growing Italian populations of Buenos Aires and New York, to bring territories within Italy's sphere of influence.

For Italy to gain benefits from its emigrants, the fruits of their sacrifices would have to return home. The state encouraged and welcomed all return migration, be it from patriotic loyalty, economic disappointment abroad, or visits to family at home. Approximately half of Italian emigrants returned, bringing capital and experience with them. Upon return all emigrants regained Italian citizenship automatically, even if they had previously renounced it.[17] With the support of United States regulators, Italy set up a special channel for emigrants to send home remittances, accumulating in the millions of dollars, through the nonprofit Banco di Napoli. Italian emigration provided economic returns that African imperialism could never match. As Italy transformed from an agricultural to an industrial economy, emigrant remittances steadied the Italian currency and contributed substantially to Italy's international balance of payments on the gold standard.[18] At the grassroots level, the infusion of money helped end usury in the countryside and fund new homes and new businesses. Those returning to their hometowns from overseas were called "Americans" [americani] with the stereotype of wealth, independence, and exotic mystique. Thanks to chain migration building upon family connections and local friendships, many Italian towns produced a mirror community of emigrants concentrated in a town or neighborhood overseas. But could these advantages be sustained on the national level for Italy? What were the long-term risks and advantages of developing emigration as colonial expansion?

Emigration directly affected Italy's strategic situation, just as migration shapes international security in the twenty-first century.[19] The massive numbers of male emigrants, and their male children, were all reservists or prospective soldiers in the Italian conscript army. Consuls abroad maintained records of male emigrants so they could be recalled to the Italian army. The debate over dual citizenship for emigrants turned on the military obligations of universal conscription. Even males born abroad to Italian fathers were by Italian law held responsible for military service in wartime.[20] The Italian state's eagerness to appropriate emigrants as subjects of the Italian King, and to claim emigrant settlements as Italian colonies, influenced how migrants were perceived in their new communities, even if individual immigrants had broken ties with their native land. Nations receiving Italians in North and South America and Europe, such as the "immigration-states" of Argentina and the United States, viewed Italy's designs with suspicion, as the Italian state planned for Italians in America to remain loyal to their mother country in affection, culture, and trade even during military hostilities. Italy's policies could run directly counter to emigrants' best interests.[21]

Controversies over colonialism engaged Italy's most prominent politicians, including the founder of Italian Socialism Filippo Turati, the foreign minister Antonino Di San Giuliano, and the prime ministers Luigi Luzzatti and Benito Mussolini. This crucial debate in foreign policy and societal vision proved a potent dialectic in Italian politics from 1890 through World War II. Emigration shaped history within Italy and beyond, affecting European colonialism in Africa, the international economy, the birth of national socialism, and the societies and cultures of the Americas and Africa influenced by the emigrants themselves.

Like gender, race, and class, migration affects all aspects of history, including social, diplomatic, political, economic, and cultural histories. The international history of the nineteenth and twentieth centuries must incorporate migration trends and their fundamental impact. Yet the chronology of emigration resists the standard narrative of historical turning points in sending and receiving countries. Emigration's timetable depends upon the decisions of millions of individuals, choosing to leave their homes; and the decisions of a few legislators, who set the limits of emigrants' choices. Apart from the business cycles of boom and bust, for Italian emigrants the major turning points were 1901, the date of Italy's second emigration law, with its farsighted provisions guiding the peak years of emigration; 1915, when Italy entered the Great War; and 1924, when the United States Congress all but ended Italian immigration under a harsh quota regime.

The story of one individual migrant illustrates many of the transnational issues of politics, family, economics, religion, and war connected to migration. On Columbus Day, 1905, Vincenzo Di Francesca entered New York City, after crossing the ocean aboard the steamship *Città di Napoli* and passing the federal inspections at Ellis Island. Seventeen years old, he had emigrated at the invitation of his brother Antonio, leaving the rest of his family behind in the village of Gratteri, Palermo province, Sicily. Vincenzo remained firmly within Italian spheres even as he traveled the globe. In New York City he converted to Methodism and became a pastor in an Italian Protestant congregation. In November 1914 the Italian consul notified Vincenzo that he had been called to military duty back in Italy. Vincenzo gathered his savings and returned to his homeland. When Italy entered World War I in May 1915, he began service on the front lines with his infantry regiment. After the war he returned to New York, and then was sent to Australia as a pastor to the nascent Italian community in Melbourne. He returned to Italy in 1932 and married a Sicilian. When Italy launched its imperialist invasion of Ethiopia in 1935, Vincenzo was recalled to the army. He was a civilian by the time of World War II but was nonetheless terrified by the Allied bombardment and invasion of Sicily in 1943. Afterwards, Vincenzo decided to retire to a house so remote that no invading army would ever again embroil him in fighting. Miles away from his native village, in the Sicilian interior, he lived the rest of his life in peace.[22]

Vincenzo Di Francesca's story is, of course, unique, but it reflects specific currents in the larger history of Italian migration. The date of his arrival in New York, 12 October, had recently become Columbus Day thanks to the political activity of the city's Italians. The public commemoration of Christopher Columbus, the Italian who united Europe and the Americas, signaled the coalescence of individual immigrants into an influential community, under the leadership in part of Italy and its state-sponsored organizations. Vincenzo's adoption of Protestantism was not uncommon, and this trend concerned Catholic bishops in Italy and in the United States as they mobilized missionary resources to reach out to Italians abroad. Vincenzo later returned to Italy as one of more than three hundred thousand emigrant reservists to fight in the Great War. The Ethiopian War involved him in Italy's conquest of African territory for the state-sponsored settlement of Italian emigrants. After traveling the world, Vincenzo married in his native region. Vincenzo had not abandoned his homeland, and during his absence, Italy had not forgotten him. Vincenzo was never a stateless migrant: though an immigrant coming into the United States, he was also an emigrant who departed from and returned to Italy governed by national migration policy.[23] While traveling across borders, Vincenzo remained within a network of native culture, family, and citizenship. He never ceased to be Italian.

Another biographical example illustrates how networks of emigration and colonialism connected the world's continents. The journalist Adolfo Rossi played a significant role in redefining Italian conceptions of America and Africa, and combining the two through colonial migration. Rossi chose to emigrate to New York in 1879 at the age of 21. He recounts how one night at his home in Lendinara, Veneto, he decided upon an adventure: "No, I will not stay vegetating here. The world is big, there's America, and New York is a vast metropolis."[24] Robbed while crossing the ocean by steamship in third-class steerage, Rossi arrived in New York with only four shillings. He worked first as a pastry-maker, then as a bellhop at the Metropolitan Opera. He next moved to Colorado and worked as a railroad agent before returning to New York City to edit the newspaper *Il Progresso Italo-Americano*. As he had planned, Rossi returned to Italy after five years and published two books about his experiences: *Un italiano in America* (An Italian in America) and *Nel paese di dollari* (In the Land of Dollars), both with advice and warnings for emigrants. Rossi worked as a journalist for several leading papers in Italy, and Milan's *Corriere della Sera* sent him to East Africa to report on the Italian war against Ethiopia. Expelled by the colony's military government in January 1896 for his critical reporting, Rossi returned to Italy and later became a commissioner in the new Italian Emigration Commissariat, created by Parliament in 1901 to protect and develop Italian emigration worldwide. In 1902 Rossi investigated emigrant conditions on plantations in Brazil, and his report led Italy's terminating Brazilian-sponsored immigration programs; Italians would have to pay their own passage.[25] Rossi returned to the Americas again and became the Italian consul in Denver, Colorado, assisting the Italian miners of the western United States. Finally, he served as consul in Argentina and Paraguay, and died in Buenos Aires in 1919. His career, tied to Italian settlement overseas, and his careful reports to the metropole in Italy, represented and defended Italians in Africa and the Americas over four decades.[26]

Although Italy's colonial experience does not fit the model of economic exploitation in the "scramble for Africa," its population-based approach to colonialism had many precedents. In 1584 Richard Hakluyt had called upon the British queen to settle Virginia with unemployed men and women to fortify the colony and expand Britain's sphere of trade and influence. The prospect of colonial population settlements played a significant role in the development of Germany's colony in Southwest Africa and Japan's colonies in Korea and Manuchuria. Italian politicians consciously compared their policies with the settlement colonies of Britain, France, Germany, and Japan, hoping to match or exceed their successes. Reports on colonial theory and practice circulated throughout the closed circle of the Great Powers, ultimately leading to a common colonial disaster. The colonial theorist that Italians most often cited was a Frenchman, Paul Leroy-Beaulieu, who in 1874 distinguished between European colonies of "population," such as French Algeria, and colonies of "exploitation," such as Vietnam or French West Africa. Leroy-Beaulieu argued that the success of colonization depended upon the emigration of humans or capital from the metropole to the colonies. Attempting to steer the Italian state away from French Tunisia, in later editions he called upon Italians to colonize their overflowing population by conquering Libya. The primacy of settlement colonies was taken for granted until 1902, when John A. Hobson defined a new "imperialism" following the Anglo-Boer War. Hobson argued that population settlements were no longer the basis for empires, as had been the case in British North America; rather, the new imperialism protected the economic interests of a small, powerful cabal invested in mines and plantations. Hobson's enormously influential analysis, which Lenin adapted in 1917 for a Communist audience, diverted attention from the ongoing role of emigration in colonialism.[27]

Italians claimed that their African colonies, as havens for Italian emigrants, were uniquely benign and justifiable in contrast to, for example, British Rhodesia and French West Africa. But European settlements in

Africa proved more insidious and more devastating than the new forms of economic exploitation, creating racial conflicts with deep roots. The French Algerian government stated its racial aims in 1902: "Colonization is most important, and not just for purposes of [economic] development. Its principal purpose is to assure the possession of the land by the farmers of our race, and to reinforce the French element in the colony by attracting immigration."[28] In colonial Algeria, the French pursued a racial conquest far more profound than mere economic investment. To achieve a white preponderance in the settlements, the colonizing government had to suppress and combat native cultures in a never-ending racial struggle. As one French writer observed, "What makes the situation particularly delicate for Algeria, is the example—unique in the world—of a population colony which is simultaneously an exploitation colony. Between two impenetrable races, a more or less stable equilibrium has been established. The French have the advantage of a more advanced civilization, and political predominance; the indigenous have the advantage of numbers."[29] Until losing Eritrea and Libya in World War II, Italy pursued the same course which led the French in Algeria and the Portuguese in Angola and Mozambique to long, disastrous wars of decolonization. These civil wars were the inevitable outcome of demographic colonialism in Africa. Italy had faced defeat earlier as well, as the Ethiopian Empire resisted its territorial conquests and, as the journalist Adolfo Rossi had warned, crushed the Italian colonial army at Adwa in March 1896. Yet the definition of colonialism as the settlement of Italians abroad, rather than the exploitation of conquered territories, allowed Italy to shift its resources after Adwa. Private societies and public agencies in Italy turned from Africa to the Americas as the colonial landscape for a new century.

Italy's colonial experiences illuminate a thorny debate in international historiography: were European colonialisms dictated by domestic or foreign politics? Leopold von Ranke and his historicist followers in the nineteenth century studied foreign policy (*Außenpolitik*) as history's determining factor. In their view, Germany's political decisions, including imperialism in Africa, were driven by competition with European neighbors. Eckhart Kehr, Hans-Ulrich Wehler, and many others in the twentieth century have argued for the opposite interpretation. Wehler characterized German imperialism as "social imperialism," based upon the "primacy of domestic politics" (*Innenpolitik*).[30] In this interpretation, Germany's naval arms race against England and its seizure of southwest Africa were intended to distract attention from economic problems, and to support certain interest groups at home: international competition was driven by internal influences.

Italy's case resolves the apparent dichotomy: colonialism combines foreign and domestic priorities when tied to population movements and emigration. Mass migration extended the limits of the imagined Italian nation, which was predicated upon population, both in the Romantic conception of the early nineteenth century and the Social Darwinist ideology of the late nineteenth and early twentieth centuries. Migration changed dynamics at home and abroad, relieving overpopulation and raising wages in Italy, changing Italian culture, establishing Italian economic interests abroad, and opening new possibilities for international influence. By focusing colonial policies on numbers of people settled, whether in the "free colonies" of expatriate communities in the Americas, the "demographic colonies" in Italian Africa, or the "internal colonization" of land reclamation projects in Sardinia, the Italian state disregarded international boundaries. By concentrating on extralegal attributes of citizenship, such as language, patriotic celebrations, social support networks, communications with the mother country, and even tastes in food and music, the Italian government hoped to ensure that its emigrants, or "colonists," remained loyal Italians abroad and when they returned home. Italy's nonviolent achievements in linking migrant communities bring a new perspective to rapid changes in the transatlantic world, European colonial systems, and the rise of a global community before World War I.

This book approaches Italian migration from the viewpoint of Italy: national emigration rather than immigration. What will follow is not a traditional international history, as Italians perceived colonialism and migration as intrinsically linked. After Italian colonial settlements in Africa collapsed, Italians proposed the development of expatriate settlements in Europe and the Americas as Italian colonies. Such ideas did not remain in the intellectual sphere. The Italian state achieved key successes in channeling emigrant remittances and preserving some measure of expatriate loyalty. Greater Italy existed on the interstices of political borders, and at the limits of political influence.

Emigrant colonialism remained controversial in Italy and abroad. Certainly, Italian emigrants in Europe and the Americas were not colonial oppressors of foreign peoples. Nations hosting Italian emigrants abroad resisted Italian state influence, and could force immigrant assimilation through legal regulations on employment and citizenship. Strictly limited in its actions, Italy as a sending state could only create an open, indirect, and adaptive policy for emigrants, relying upon persuasion, incentives, and sometimes deception, especially later under the Fascist regime. Italy could not intervene directly in other nations' domestic affairs, but could encourage voluntary donations from expatriates by strengthening cultural affinity and political ties. The state supported nongovernmental organizations as proxies to carry out an international economic project beyond the scope of traditional politics. Expatriate culture proved a powerful tool for building political identity and attracting international resources.

This project began as a study of Francesco Crispi's brutal suppression of labor organizations in Sicily and Tuscany. He spoke of colonialism as a natural solution to emigration and to all social tensions in his native Sicily and across Italy. Even though Sicilian emigration was small during those years, Crispi decried the oppression of Italians overseas: in 1891, eleven Italians had been lynched in New Orleans, and in 1893 some thirty Italians were killed by a mob in Aigues-Mortes, France. This drew uncomfortable parallels with the persecutions of African, Chinese, and South Asian minorities worldwide.[31] When Crispi's land reforms were defeated in Parliament, he promised to resolve the "Southern Question" of underdevelopment not through labor organization, but with state-sponsored emigration to Italian Africa, where emigrants would be free from racist persecution. I was inspired by the late Alberto Aquarone's insights that emigrant colonies and African colonial settlements were two sides of the same coin. Although Italian migration and colonialism moved in tandem, their historiographies have followed separate tracks. This book is the first to investigate thoroughly Aquarone's thesis; it also takes up the challenges of Matthew Frye Jacobson, Nancy Foner, Virginia Yans, and others to engage the histories of ethnic migrations as transnational processes related to migration today.[32]

Rather than following emigrants to their destinations, by city and by country, *Emigrant Nation* takes the perspective of "the land they left": a land that didn't want to let go. Instead of investigating individual emigrant settlements worldwide, this book will focus on Italy and its attempts to become the center of a global network of Italians. The varied efforts and programs from the Italian metropole give context and background to the Italian emigrant experience. This is an unconventional approach to migration history, but is made possible by the work of many scholars of immigration and their excellent local studies of Italian immigration in the United States, Brazil, Argentina, France, Switzerland, and Germany, as well as essential analyses of emigrant remittances and religion.[33] Economic historians, particularly Cafagna, Balletta, and De Rosa, have established the importance of emigrant remittances to the Italian economy, and historians of religion, particularly Rosoli, Brown, Francesconi, and D'Agostino, have investigated the work of Catholic Bishops Scalabrini and Bonomelli among emigrants.[34]

What this book contributes is the combined approach to emigration and colonialism, so important to Italy a century ago. Worldwide emigration and African settlement were closely intertwined within the ideology and practice of Italian colonialism, and fueled an ongoing debate over how to protect and cultivate Italians abroad, "under the Italian flag" or under foreign rule.

Other scholars have pointed to the connection between Italian emigration and colonialism. In his classic, global study of 1919, *The Italian Emigration of Our Times,* Robert Foerster condemns Italian designs for African settlement, calling for more empathetic emigration policies from Italy and better immigration policies from the United States; his work also demonstrates the racist assumptions of scholars and politicians of the time.[35] The rapid decline of Italian emigration after 1975 made its study more historical than political. Comparative approaches have appeared only recently. Donna Gabaccia's outstanding *Italy's Many Diasporas* (2000) outlines Liberal Italy's approach toward emigration in the comparative context of diasporas worldwide. Gabaccia focuses on the "diaspora nationalism" of emigrants' national sentiments outside Italy, rather than nationalism fomented from the Italian state to strengthen its power.[36] Several article-length studies in Italian and French have investigated the major debates in Parliament over emigration and colonialism.[37] Romain Rainero and Emilio Franzina have investigated the implementation of Italian colonial ideas with the pilot settlements of Eritrea, doomed to fail in 1896.[38] Much work has been devoted to Italian colonialism in Africa from the Libyan War forward.[39] But Italian colonialism between 1896 and 1912 has been neglected, even though this was the high point of Italian emigration, and a time of ideological transition crucial for later Italian imperialism.[40]

This study highlights the international context of Italy's policies, developed in comparision to and competition with other West European colonialisms and other countries' emigration policies. The great powers imitated each other and tried to improve upon each others' examples. Furthermore, Italy's innovations and new policies parallel the experiences of emigration states in the twenty-first century: India, Mexico, South Korea, and others. The conclusion presents comparisons and highlights some lessons learned from the elaboration and historical study of the Italian case.

Italy's massive emigration, and the political and colonialist effort to channel this population, were fundamental to Italian history. Emigrant settlement, though a false promise, became the rallying cry for three Italian wars in Africa; the last war would lead to Italy's participation in World War II and the country's destruction. The chronology of mass Italian emigration can be adapted as a framework of turning points for Italian society and history generally. At a local level, waves of emigration forever affected the demographics, families, and social structure of towns in Basilicata, Sicily, and elsewhere. Benito Mussolini's emigration to Switzerland from 1902 to 1904, and Enrico Corradini's experiences in South America in 1908, were key moments in the development of ideological nationalism and fascism. Emigrant remittances undergirded Italy's much studied economic "takeoff" of 1896–1908. The innovative legislation of 1901 and 1902 stands out for its pacifist, constructive Liberal spirit in protecting emigrants en route, encouraging remittances, and subsidizing Italian culture abroad. Many emigrants had sent remittances before 1902, and many would have returned home to Italy without official encouragement, but government support made such decisions much easier for emigrants.[41]

Emigration advocates proposed a role for Italy as the axle turning a vast arc of Italian population worldwide, guiding, influencing, and strengthening this virtual community by repairing broken spokes. This perspective oversimplified complex dynamics within emigrant communities, which could see themselves in a very different light. Many, no doubt, did not see themselves as the romanticized outposts of *italianità* abroad, as the Kingdom of Italy wished. But insofar as emigrants dealt with Italian consuls, or sent money to Italy through the Banco di Napoli or other channels, or worked with Italian Chambers of Commerce in international trade with Italy, they participated in the programs of emigrant colonialism. The Italian state did not screen remittances or return migration for purity of motives, whether resulting from local allegiances, nostalgia for family, or unadulterated patriotism. Italian government agencies and their subsidized affiliates worked to turn all these personal and individual motivations toward a national purpose. In the Liberal calculus, emigration would clearly benefit Italy if it yielded return migration and remittances. The Liberal state allowed free emigration, but tried to channel the flows of emigrants to benefit the "fatherland." *Italianità* might take many different overlapping or contradictory forms: anticlerical, Protestant, or Catholic; anarchist, Socialist, Republican, or Liberal; local, provincial, regional, or national. Each could contribute to an expanding Italy. More research will be required to document fully Italy's long-term impact on emigrant neighborhoods; this book will concentrate on the transnational exchanges planned and promoted by Italy.

From the beginning, the Italian nation-state was self-consciously constructed along artificial political, cultural, and linguistic lines. The dilemma of nation-building in a crowded and competitive international neighborhood was captured in Massimo d'Azeglio's famous aphorism, paraphrased as "we have made Italy, we must now make Italians."[42] D'Azeglio contributed to this cultural project instrumentally with his patriotic paintings, memoirs, and historical fiction, later duly distributed by the Dante Alighieri Society to departing emigrants.[43] The construction and development of Italian political identities, and the conscious exportation of political-cultural programs internationally, offer new insight into global history, European history, and the history of the Americas. While migration is an international phenomenon, it is played out on the national stages of emigration and immigration. The Italian state worked to nationalize its emigration by intervening transnationally, leveraging diplomatic resources to influence international travel, the dissemination of media, transnational religious activity, and ethnic economic activity abroad, to achieve specific national benefits. Host nations abroad aided Italy in its efforts to help its emigrants, as banks in the United States supported the intervention of the Banco di Napoli, and Italian schools were welcomed in rural Argentina and Brazil. These peaceful interventions ultimately benefitted societies on both sides of the migration divide.

Emigrant Nation is structured along thematic and chronological lines. Chapter 1 analyzes Italy's attempts to grapple with the mass exodus of its population, with a range of colonial theories and experimental policies. Against Francesco Crispi's grand plans to settle emigrants in Africa, Luigi Einaudi proposed a colonial vision of a "New Italy" peacefully and spontaneously established in the Americas. Chapter 2 presents the synthesis of Italian emigrant colonialism formed after failure in Africa. Irredentism, the philosophy of redeeming Italians outside the Kingdom of Italy through politics and culture, was adapted to embrace emigrants as well, and the new discipline of Italian ethnography provided theoretical support for mapping an "ethnographic empire" of emigration. Chapter 3 investigates the concrete effects of emigration economics within Greater Italy: remittances, exports, and return migration. State-sponsored Italian Chambers of Commerce Abroad were the cornerstone of ethnic niche economies and trading networks, marking Italy's expansion into emigrant markets. Return migration, demonstrated in careful statistics, concretely brought home to Italy the full impact of international migration.

Chapter 4 focuses on language and traditions fostered to bind emigrants to their native country. The Italian state broke new ground with the Italian Schools Abroad, teaching the Italian language to illiterate emigrants speaking only regional dialects, and also to their children born abroad. Chapter 5 discusses the crucial participation of Catholic missionaries in these schools. Religious and secular coordination abroad, despite strident opposition between church and state in Italy, became a way to influence millions of emigrants outside narrowly restricted diplomatic and administrative channels. Chapter 6 analyzes the new Nationalist critique of Liberal Italian foreign policy. Enrico Corradini achieved a breakthrough success in his campaign for national socialism by linking frustration with the results of emigration to Italy's imperial failures. Rehabilitating Crispi and attacking Einaudi, the Nationalists adapted debates over emigration as a platform for war in Libya. As documented in Chapter 7, the capillary network of relations between Italy and its emigrants abroad was tested by a series of disasters, as even aid relief for earthquake victims was politicized as a rallying of emigrants to the mother country. Most dramatic was the appeal for emigrant colonies to send their sons to fight for Italy in World War I.

The end results of Italian emigration were far from obvious, as the statistics climbed geometrically and inexorably, without precedent and with no end in sight. The Italian state and its allies created a multifaceted program for Italy Abroad based on limited available information, with blind guesses as to the future. Italy's experience, positive and negative, can be an example for academic and political approaches to global migrations in the twenty-first century.

From Africa to the Americas

In June 1887, the Italian government celebrated its annual Festival of the Constitution by dedicating an extraordinary monument in Rome: an Egyptian obelisk from the reign of Ramses II. The recently excavated obelisk was more than three thousand years old; the Italian state was infantile in comparison. Its constitution had been granted in 1848 by the King of Piedmont-Sardinia, Carlo Alberto. After two wars of unification Carlo Alberto's son had become the first King of Italy in 1861. Rome became Italy's capital only in 1871, with the fall of papal rule. Nonetheless, the new Italy claimed a much older tradition as the "Third Rome," following the Roman Empire of antiquity and the papal Rome of the Renaissance. Monumental obelisks were the most tangible symbol of revived global ambitions. Ancient emperors had brought them to Rome from Africa at great expense, and had ordered imitation obelisks to be carved as well. Renaissance popes had excavated and restored the huge stones, then redesigned the city around them, cutting broad new streets and placing the obelisks at the focal points. By early 1887, obelisks stood before the Italian Royal Palace, the Chamber of Deputies, St. Peter's Basilica, and the Lateran Palace. In all, eleven obelisks could be seen across the city, each topped with the religious symbol of a crucifix, a dove, or the papal arms.[1] The new obelisk, however, would carry no cross: it was topped by the Star of Italy.

Five months before the obelisk's dedication, Italy had suffered its first major colonial defeat, in East Africa. On 26 January 1887, Ethiopian forces under Ras Alula ambushed and massacred 422 Italian soldiers near Dogali.[2] Prime Minister Agostino Depretis' government resigned;

although Depretis was reappointed in April, the leading figure in the new government was the Interior Minister, Francesco Crispi. Under his leadership, Dogali became a summons for commemoration and vindication. Ramses II's obelisk had been discovered in 1883; Crispi decided to place the obelisk on the second largest piazza in Rome, in front of the main train station, and dedicate it "to the heroes of Dogali" (see illustrations). The piazza was also renamed *Piazza dei Cinquecento* ("Piazza of the 500") in honor of the fallen, whose names were inscribed on a bronze plaque at the obelisk's base.[3] The ceremony consecrated a secular, Africanist site within the geography of the Eternal City. Crispi thus exploited the shame of defeat at Dogali to bind modern Italian imperialism with ancient Roman traditions.

How Italy could fulfill an imperial role was far from clear. Italy's political philosophers had begun to raise expectations even before the peninsula had been unified in Italy's Risorgimento, or resurgence, under Piedmontese rule. The abbot Vincenzo Gioberti published a celebrated three-volume study of the "primacy of the Italian race" in 1844. After listing Italian triumphs in the arts, sciences, morals, and politics, he predicted wondrous consequences if Italy's nine small kingdoms, duchies, and Papal States were unified. Gioberti served as prime minister of Piedmont in 1848–1849, and his ideas resonated throughout the peninsula. His contemporary Giuseppe Mazzini, the apostle of Italian Republicanism, envisioned an even greater international role for Italy. He felt that each nationality in Europe had a mission ordained by God. In the eighteenth century, the French Revolution had brought the Rights of Man to the world; in the nineteenth century, Italian unification would establish something yet more important, the Duties of Man. In 1871 Mazzini called upon the newly united Italy to take part in the colonial expansion of Europe by bringing civilization to North Africa. The new Italian state would not be content with improving its own civil society, raising literacy, and developing its uneven economy. Rather, Italy would have to find a role on an international stage.[4]

Italy had distinct disadvantages in pursuing an empire. Unlike France and Britain, the new Kingdom of Italy lacked the capital resources to develop plantation colonies for economic exploitation. Instead of an expanding economy seeking new markets, Italy boasted a robust population and a glorious imperial past. The ancient Roman empire was mined for monumental symbols, like the obelisks, and an imperial ethos. The other Great Powers of Europe, including France, Britain, Russia, Germany, and Austria, also claimed to be Rome's heirs; Italy's designs were different. Italian colonialists cited the ancient Roman legions that had settled, developed, and defended imperial outposts. In this tradition, Italian political rhetoric defined colonial expansion as the development of Italy's population overseas. Each emigrant settlement was a *"colonia,"* the same term used for Italy's African colonies. To distinguish between the two types of colonies, Italian theorists called emigrant settlements "spontaneous colonies," while African possessions were called "colonies of direct dominion."[5] The ambiguous direction of Italian colonialism, and the rapid growth of Italian emigration, combined together for an incendiary debate in Italian politics and culture over how and where to build the long-sought dream of Greater Italy.

Understanding Italy's Mass Emigration

As Italy joined other European states in the "scramble for Africa" between 1881 and 1898, millions of Italians left their country in an unprecedented transatlantic mass migration, establishing their own American colonies. For Italians, America did not mean the United States, but the land named for Amerigo Vespucci: North and South America. Even more broadly, America meant migration outside Europe and the Mediterranean Basin, which had long been familiar destinations. One woman who emigrated to Melbourne explained, "I migrated to America. It did not occur to me that Australia was not in fact America."[6] Adolfo Rossi confessed, "I had read some books about the United States the previous month and had fallen in love with North America: this was the only reason I picked New-York instead of Sidney or Buenos Ayres [*sic*]."[7] "America" became a legend of employment, opportunity, and sacrifice. Hundreds of thousands of Italians traveled to the Americas for work, without ever having traveled to Rome or Florence for pleasure. One observer in Argentina noted "the word America has come to mean wealth, prosperity, fortune. To justify their hard life, the Italians say that they came to America to *do America* [*fare l'America*] and not to learn Castilian Spanish."[8] Most migrants planned to work hard, save, and go back to Italy, never becoming part of local society. America became the direct object to an action verb (as in *fare l'America*), an imagined economic site rather than a place with its own traditions, culture, and history.

Chain migration networks, fostered by American immigration law, widened the gulf between Italian migrants and their American neighbors. The United States did not allow American companies to recruit laborers abroad; migrants therefore traveled to places where they had other connections or acquaintances.[9] Through successive waves of emigration, many Italian villages developed sister communities in the Americas. Emigrants could travel thousands of miles and never leave the ambit of their fellow villagers, friends, and families. Stonecutters from Massa and Carrara in Tuscany went to and from Barre, Vermont. Emigrants from Molfetta in Puglia went to Hoboken, New Jersey; from Bagnoli del Trigno in Molise to Fairmont, New Jersey; from Floridia in Sicily to Hartford, Connecticut. Natives of Pachino, Sicily, established settlements in Toronto, Canada; Caracas, Venezuela; and Lawrence, Massachusetts. Emigrants from the other side of Sicily in Sambuca, 125 miles away, chose between *sambucese* neighborhoods in New Orleans, Chicago, or Brooklyn, New York.[10]

Emigration exposed relative hardship in "the beautiful country" of Italy *(il bel paese)*. Prefects in the Italian provinces reported in 1882 that emigrants were leaving their villages to improve their economic conditions or, less often, to escape poverty.[11] Crushed under one of Europe's highest tax burdens, threatened by malaria, isolated by a lack of roads, with their vineyards devastated by phylloxera disease, many families found a better future abroad.[12] In contrast with the Irish, relatively few penniless Italians found benefactors to pay their passage overseas. Most migrants raised money by selling or mortgaging their land and possessions, sometimes falling prey to deceitful emigration agents working on sales commissions. Author Edmondo De Amicis traveled from Northern Italy to Argentina in 1884, and reported conditions aboard his steamship, which carried 1,400 emigrants in third class:

> Many groups had already formed, as always happens, among emigrants of the same province or profession. Most of them were peasants. And it was not difficult for me to follow the dominant theme of the conversations: the sad state of the agricultural class in Italy; too much competition among workers, to the advantage of landlords and tenants; low wages, high prices, excessive taxes, seasons without work, poor harvests, greedy employers, no hope for improvement. . . . In one group, with a note of bitter gaiety, they laughed at the upper class, soon to be devoured by anger when they found themselves without workers and forced to double

salaries, or to give up their lands for a piece of bread. "When we will have all gone away," said one, "they will die of hunger too."[13]

The implications of mass emigration disturbed landlords and politicians. Italians bitterly debated what to do about the rising tide of emigration, which revealed deep conflicts over Italy's domestic and foreign priorities.

Lacking statistics, politicians couched emigration in moral terms as either "good" or "bad." Landlords condemned emigrants as adventurers, draft dodgers, and reprobates.[14] The Italian government's office of statistics began collecting emigration data only in 1876, artificially dividing emigrants' passport requests into two categories, temporary and permanent. Transatlantic migration was assumed to be permanent; migration within Europe and the Mediterranean, temporary. In reality, however, some Italians did settle permanently in France, or departed from France in search of better opportunities in Argentina. The fluidity of emigration gradually became clear, and after 1904 statisticians divided migration simply into transoceanic and European/Mediterranean.[15]

Year after year, emigration defied the predictions of social science, as high levels of migration to Europe were topped by wildly fluctuating emigration to the Americas.[16] (See Appendix, Figure 1.1.) Ligurians had emigrated overseas in large numbers since the 1840s and 1850s, following their countryman Christopher Columbus, but after Italy's unification, mass migration spread to the agricultural interior. Even industrializing regions produced a startling exodus: thousands left the valleys of Biella in northern Italy, just as others arrived to work in the Biellese textile factories.[17] The North produced more emigrants than the poorer South, but the South produced more per capita. The Veneto region led the nation between 1880 and 1915 with more than three million emigrants; Campania, the region around Naples, sent 1.45 million emigrants, Calabria sent 870,000, and Basilicata sent 375,000. Emigration from Sicily remained quite low through the 1880s, at 41,000, compared to 93,000 from Calabria and 81,000 from Basilicata, even though Sicily had more than twice the population of Calabria and five times the population of Basilicata.[18] After the Italian state's bloody suppression of the Sicilian *Fasci* trade unions in 1893–1894, Francesco Nitti, a native of Basilicata, urged Sicily in 1896 to imitate its neighbors: "Sicily is much richer than Basilicata and Calabria. . . . It is more unbalanced only because there has been no emigration."[19] Unable to change conditions at home, Sicilians emigrated abroad. Before 1914, 1.3 million left the island; the vast majority traveled to the United States and many settled there permanently.[20]

Emigration expanded so rapidly that the state struggled to manage or at least monitor the phenomenon through statistics and regulations. Nearly all Italians traveled with passports, which qualified poor emigrants for assistance from Italian consuls and, as Italian officials noted, "might be useful to them when dealing with foreign authorities."[21] Yet some continued to depart clandestinely without papers, to escape conscription or debts, for example, or to enter the United States without passing health and "moral" examinations. Unrecorded clandestine migration continued into the twentieth century. In 1913, Italy's all-time record year for emigration, inspectors found emigrants traveling in secret on almost every steamship leaving Italy, sometimes listed as crew and often not listed at all.[22] Italian consulates collected data about local Italians abroad, who were numbered in Italy's national census starting in 1871. At first the census was a matter of pride for the Italian king, who could boast of *"more than a million"* subjects abroad in 1881, but the census became a serious political and statistical tool.[23] No census was taken in 1891 for lack of funds, but the consuls' detailed responses to the 1901 international census were published in nine volumes as *Emigrazione e colonie*. This study reversed categorical thinking by describing the Italians in Tunisia as a permanent colony and in Argentina as a temporary colony, since few Italians had become Argentine citizens.[24] Consuls usually counted Italian citizens together with Italian speakers from Austria-Hungary, as well as second-generation migrants, even American citizens, if they had Italian fathers.

Statistics revealed how migration followed the trends of political competition, racial prejudice, and impersonal market forces. Emigrants were a valued labor resource for expanding economies but the first to be unemployed in depressed economies.[25] Migration from northern Italy to Argentina began in the 1870s, but Brazil surpassed Argentina as an emigrant destination by 1888. (See Appendix, Figure 1.2.) In this year slavery was finally abolished in Brazil, and its regional governments began to pay for the passage of white Europeans to work the country's coffee and sugar plantations. Italians named their new rural settlements after their home towns, founding Nova Milano, Nova Roma, Nova Bassano, Nova Vicenza (later Farroupilha), Nova Prata, Nova Brescia, Nova Trento, and

Nova Pompeia (later Pinto Bandeira) in southern Brazil.[26] Nonetheless, many Italians were treated harshly by plantation masters. The Italian government intervened in 1902 by banning subsidized migration to Brazil; emigrants would have to buy their own tickets. Emigration to Brazil rapidly declined, even as migration to the United States soared. The Panic of 1907 and another American economic crisis in 1911, coupled with Italy's Libyan War in 1911–1912, caused temporary drops in migration to the United States. Argentina drew a steady current of migration, but in 1911–1912 Italy enforced a political boycott. The Italian state blocked travel to Argentina by working-age males, by far the largest demographic group of Italian emigrants, to force the Argentines to recognize their economic dependence on this labor supply. Transatlantic migration ended temporarily with the calamity of World War I, then returned briefly after the war, before strict immigration restrictions and economic depression ended the flow. Italy's mass emigration to Australia began only after World War II, when migration to the United States and Canada also revived.

The United States played a unique role as the most attractive, yet most restrictive, country of immigration. New York City was the premier port of entry, and in 1855 the New York state government established Castle Garden in Battery Park, Manhattan, as a screening facility to receive healthy immigrants and reject unhealthy or politically subversive foreigners. After New York had processed eight million immigrants, the United States government assumed this role in 1890, and built elaborate facilities at Ellis Island in New York Harbor under the direction of the Public Health Service and the Department of Labor's Bureau of Immigration. First- and second-class travelers were not required to stop at Ellis Island for medical examinations, because they had paid much higher fares. Third-class travelers in steerage, by contrast, were considered "immigrants" and possibly unwelcome, and twelve million were processed at Ellis Island by 1924.[27] Even before they embarked from Europe, migrants were screened by American inspectors, and relatively few were rejected upon arrival in the United States. Brazil and Argentina organized similar facilities, the Hospedaria de Imigrantes at Sao Paolo and the Hotel de Inmigrantes at Buenos Aires, but these stations were smaller and less restrictive than Ellis Island.

The criteria for migrants' entry came under fierce debate in the United States and in Italy. At ports on both sides of the Atlantic, inspectors rejected immigrants according to an expansive checklist: those judged to be "idiots, insane, paupers, diseased persons, convicts, polygamists, women [immigrating] for immoral purposes, assisted aliens, contract laborers, anarchists, [or] procurers" were sent back to their homes in Europe. Contagious and "loathsome" diseases and conditions that qualified for exclusion included trachoma, varicose veins, hernia, ringworm, arthritis, anemia, pellagra, epilepsy, tuberculosis, and venereal diseases.[28] Unwed mothers, unaccompanied minors, and charity cases were refused entry, as were immigrants who had arranged for work in America before their arrival—an exclusion which defied logic, but was defended by American labor unions.[29] Anti-immigration activists proposed literacy tests as an additional restriction.

To combat mafia and organized crime, the American consul in Palermo suggested the rejection of "those who hold belief in *omertà*, [namely] an antisocial practice, based partly on the cowardice of fear and partly on a distorted sense of honor, which extends assistance to the criminal rather than to the victim of a crime, and blocks the administration of justice by refusing to testify or by giving false testimony." The consul cited the trial of an innkeeper who had silently abetted a kidnaping and murder, who told the court, "I wish the jurors to know that if I had been guilty I would have escaped to America as I had plenty of time."[30] Such stories tarnished the reputations of all Italians in the United States. To combat immigration restrictions and to improve its public image, the Italian state relied upon its Italian Chambers of Commerce in New York, San Francisco, and elsewhere. Many of the Italian members had become American citizens, and could influence American politics directly as voters rather than as outsiders.

Italy also contemplated restrictions on emigration. When Italian parliamentary committees discussed emigration for the first time in 1888, they demonstrated the personal prejudices, factual errors, philosophical divisions, and confusion surrounding emigration, even though policy changes in emigration would affect the lives of millions. A nobleman from Messina, Sicily, told his committee "he does not think the absolute freedom of emigration is a good idea"; yet a lawyer representing Alessandria, Piedmont, noted that with the completion of major railroad construction in Northern Europe, and mob hostility to Italian workers in France, "emigration to America has become a necessity. It is an inevitable evil no one can stop." Giustino Fortunato from Basilicata believed restricting emigration "would be a calamity for the Southern provinces," and a deputy from Bergamo, Lombardy, also argued that limiting emigration would raise Italy's population and lower wages. Was there another solution? A count from Forlì, Romagna, noted it would be more humanitarian to organize internal migration, rather than suppress international migration, and the Socialist leader Andrea Costa called for more study of why people needed to leave their homes. A representative of Milan proposed that the government spend several million lire "to buy land in the faraway regions where emigrants go," where they could be settled and officially protected; but a Neapolitan count argued that emigration should be "neither protected nor obstructed." Ominously, Leopoldo Franchetti from Umbria warned that limitations on emigration would undermine the foundations of public rights in Liberal Italy.[31]

The prime minister Francesco Crispi proposed that emigration could be positive, and that the state could link together emigrant communities, or "colonies," around the world for an international nation-building project. Crispi had fought for Italian unity in exile, in Sicily as a revolutionary, and in Parliament as a Republican and then as a Liberal monarchist. Massive emigration undermined the prestige of Italian unification as hundreds of thousands voluntarily dispersed in search of better opportunities. In proposing Italy's first emigration legislation in December 1887, Crispi aimed to colonize the emigrants themselves, wherever they traveled. Rather than draining the nation, emigration would expand Italy beyond its boundaries: "The Government cannot remain an indifferent or passive spectator to the destinies of [emigrants]. It must know exactly where they are going and what awaits them; it must accompany them with a vigilant and loving eye . . . it must never lose sight of them in their new home . . . to turn to its advantage the fruits of their labor. Colonies must be like arms, which the country extends far away in foreign districts to bring them within the orbit of its relations of labor and exchange; they must be like an enlargement of the boundaries of its action and its economic power."[32] Crispi believed that Italy could extend a patriotic message to emigrants worldwide, to strengthen them against the assimilationist "melting pots" of Argentina, France, and the United States. Italy could bind emigrants and their children to *la madre patria*, literally "the mother-fatherland," through language, culture, and economic ties.

As emigration increased, patriotic communities of Italians abroad did form a loyal international network, rallying in support of Italy's colonial wars. In 1888, after the Italian military disaster at Dogali, Italians in Alexandria in Egypt raised 5,000 lire for support of the wounded, with smaller amounts donated from Cairo, Rio de Janeiro, and Pernambuco, Brazil. The war ministry, however, declined the money: Italy had suffered few casualties in Africa and, optimistically, the ministry expected few in the future.[33] After Italy's defeat at Amba Alagi in December 1895, and before the debacle at Adwa in March 1896, Italians in Buenos Aires opened a subscription for the Italian Red Cross. Italians in Chicago, New York, and Tunis attempted to volunteer as recruits in the Italian army. The war ministry again refused their assistance. They insisted that only draftees could serve in the Italian army in Africa and no outside funds were needed or wanted.[34] Perhaps the war ministry resented the foreign ministry's involvement in African affairs. Nonetheless, Italians abroad felt concern for the fate of Italy's colonial campaigns, and for Italy's international reputation, which reflected on Italians everywhere.

Italy in the Scramble for Africa

Italy entered the colonial "scramble for Africa" as a late-comer. At the Berlin Congress of 1878, Italy's prime minister Benedetto Cairoli followed a far-sighted "clean hands" policy, and refused to stake claims on African territories: he believed that each nation in Europe, and across the world, had the right to self-determination. But other governments did not have such scruples. In March of 1881 the French army marched into Tunis, on Sicily's doorstep. Italians were shocked at the news. Cairoli fell from power, and his successors scrambled to catch up with France. The new prime minister Agostino Depretis appointed the lawyer Pasquale Stanislao Mancini as foreign minister. Despite his earlier legal theories in support of national independence movements, Mancini launched Italian imperialism in December 1881 by assuming control of a coaling station at Assab, a port claimed by the Ottoman Empire. Fascinated by the Suez Canal, Mancini claimed Italy could "find the key" to the Mediterranean in the Red Sea.[35] In 1882 another opportunity arose when the British government invited Italy and France to join its intervention in Egypt. Both Mancini and the French foreign minister declined the offer, fearing a military defeat.[36] Italy thus restricted its African colonial schemes to the Horn, for the time being. The Italian military expedition to Massawa in 1885 greatly expanded the Red Sea colony and sparked a lengthy debate in Parliament over the expenses. By 1889 Italy also developed claims to Asmara and eastern Somalia.[37] Meanwhile, the Congo basin went to Belgium, the vast Sahara to France, lands in southwest and east Africa to Germany, and Egypt and South Africa to Britain.

If Britain had seized the lion's share of colonial territories, to Italy was left the hyena's share. Italian ministers continually had to invent arguments for retaining and funding these colonies. Meanwhile, Italy prepared diplomatic support among the European Powers for a claim on the ancient Roman territory of Libya, ruled by the Ottoman Empire as the provinces of Tripolitania and Cyrenaica. As Italy changed ministries every few years, some politicians increased the country's commitments in Africa, but no one felt confident in retreating, as it might erode Italian prestige. Domenico Farini, president of the Senate and an anticolonialist, explained, "we cannot call back the troops unless we have a success somewhere else. Otherwise our impotence will be too manifest, our reputation too damaged."[38] There seemed no way out of Africa.

Mass migration and the possibility of settlement offered a new role for Italy's Red Sea colony as it grew in size and expense. Beginning in the 1870s, the abuse and deception of emigrants made newspaper headlines regularly throughout Italy.[39] In 1885, Mancini exploited emigration to justify colonialism. He postulated, first, that Italian emigrants should not be scattered all over the world; second, the economic success of Italians in South America suggested likely successes in Africa as well; and third, perhaps Italy should establish "agricultural colonies" for European settlement in the African interior, besides commercial stations on the coast. However, Mancini became distracted by the Scramble for Africa, not wanting Italy to lose its place in the "generous competition" to a "not great State" like Belgium.[40] He made international prestige the foundation of Italian colonialism, heralding Italy's heritage from Columbus to Vespucci as a summons to empire.

Two years after Mancini left office in 1885, Francesco Crispi proposed to fulfill Italy's international calling with a grand program combining emigration and colonial expansion. Crispi had arrived at imperialism after an odyssey of political rejection and aborted revolution. He was born in 1818 in southwestern Sicily, 130 miles from the Tunisian coast of Africa. Exiled after fighting in the 1848 revolution, Crispi returned to Sicily in 1860 as second in command of Giuseppe Garibaldi's Expedition of the Thousand. The expedition's 1,087 men and two women joined with peasant rebels to overthrow the Kingdom of Naples in a brilliant campaign through Sicily, Calabria, and Campania. After Garibaldi surrendered his gains to the King of Piedmont, Crispi abandoned the antimonarchist republican ideals of his former mentor, Giuseppe Mazzini. Crispi made Italy's unity under the new king his overriding priority.[41] He entered government in 1876, but fell from power the following year in a bigamy scandal. In impotent fury, he railed in 1881 against Cairoli, also a member of the Thousand, for his failure to secure Tunisia, and blasted Mancini for losing Egypt the next year. The Red Sea colony was no substitute for territory in the Mediterranean.

When Crispi became prime minister and foreign minister in 1887, after the Dogali defeat, he promoted an aggressive foreign policy as a way to solve Italy's internal problems, especially its unimproved agriculture, endemic unemployment, and backward social structures in the South.[42] He hoped the creation of overseas settlements would liberate Italians from the archaic great estates and tiny, scattered landholdings that polarized rural society and strangled economic development. Thus, despite his earlier opposition to Mancini's projects in the same territories, in 1889 Crispi made passionate appeals to Parliament for increased funding for Italy's colony on the Red Sea: "do you believe, o sirs, that the favors of fortune can be obtained without sacrifices? All the great conquests cost the various Powers in the beginning, and cost greatly! The benefits were gathered late. And must we, now that we are at the point of drawing profit from the money spent and the blood shed—today when we can have in Africa, at short distance from Italy, *a territory to colonize,* that permits us *to direct all that mass of unfortunates who run to America* to search their fortune—must we renounce this benefit which we are about to assure for our homeland?"[43] In Crispi's mind, Italy's overseas emigration could be turned to a direct advantage to the state. By moving the field of migration from America to Africa, Italy could establish its reputation as a world power. In 1890 he joined Asmara and the ports of Assab and Massawa to form the colony of "Eritrea" on the Red Sea. Assab and Massawa were hot, harsh deserts, but Asmara on the high plateau enjoyed a temperate climate, free of the tsetse fly, with some of the best agricultural land on the continent of Africa.[44] Crispi announced Eritrea as a haven for Italian emigration "under the dominion and laws of Italy."[45] Territorial settlements would strengthen Italy's African colony and allow masses of emigrants to thrive amid transplanted Italian customs, traditions, and society in the shadow of the Italian flag.

Crispi's vision relied upon the example of the British Empire. Britain's settler colonies in North America, Australia, New Zealand, and even South Africa captivated Italian politicians. Through spontaneous settlement in the seventeenth and eighteenth centuries, and subsidized or penal settlement in the nineteenth and twentieth centuries, Britain had established new colonial cultures and economies, overwhelming any local competitors. German imperialists hoped to accomplish the same results in southwest Africa.[46] Like Italy, Germany was a new state experiencing mass migration in the 1880s. Naval enthusiasts in both countries pointed to Britain's use of military force in defending emigration routes and settlements. The British Emigrants' Information Office, which provided information on all emigration destinations while steering attention toward Australia, South Africa, and Canada, became a model for similar Italian and German institutions.[47] Italian officials also envied the success of French colonization in Algeria, adopting the categorical worldview of Paul Leroy-Beaulieu: lands were either "population colonies" for white settlement, "exploitation colonies" for capitalist investment, or "mixed colonies" for both.[48]

Italian plans for a population colony in Italian Africa were expensive and controversial. The big newspapers of Northern Italy opposed wasting money in demographic settlements. Exploration of East Africa's resources did not satisfy the high hopes raised by the irrational Scramble for Africa. Yet Crispi's projects did find popular support, especially in the South.[49] If the Italian people could not be supported at home, perhaps they could still live under Italian protection in nearby Italian Africa. This emigration would not diminish Italy's population or bolster rivals. Following a view of population control dating to the Middle Ages, many viewed spontaneous emigration as a "hemorrhage" of Italy's best blood, assuming that the most industrious of the poor would emigrate to better themselves.[50] In the Darwinian struggle between national peoples, the Italian race would falter unless the government retained its population, the basis for national survival.

Italians agreed that emigration was unstoppable; only the destination was in question. Although large landowners complained of a shrinking workforce and rising wages, the burgeoning population on Italy's narrow territory raised fears of revolution.[51] Perhaps emigration could bring benefits. Industrialists such as Alessandro Rossi called for deregulation of emigration, arguing that restrictions only forced Italians to travel clandestinely from foreign ports. This supported Italy's competitors instead of Italy's own shipping industry and navy, and stunted Italy's possibilities of becoming a great naval power. To test his ideas, Rossi sponsored a paternalist settlement of Catholic emigrants in Eritrea.[52] In Africa Italy could redeem its reputation, its economy, and its population beyond its borders.

The Failure of Demographic Colonialism

Rossi's was not the only experimental demographic settlement. In 1890 Parliament authorized Leopoldo Franchetti, a conservative baron from Tuscany, to settle several dozen families in pilot communities. Franchetti had coauthored with Sidney Sonnino a landmark study of southern Italy and Sicily in 1876.[53] The two authors, both trained in Britain, highlighted the systemic social problems tied to the extensive cultivation of large estates, and proposed Tuscan-style sharecropping (mezzadria) as an alternative. As Liberal Italy failed to reform the South, by the late 1880s Franchetti came to see Africa as the only road to Italy's redemption. By distributing new land to Italians transplanted outside of Italy, the vicious circles in Italian agriculture would be broken. In Eritrea Franchetti created regulations for expropriating territory and distributing it among Italian settlers. With strict property contracts he meant to ensure that Italian colonists would support themselves on their own land, avoiding the establishment of large capitalist plantations and a big state bureaucracy.

Franchetti soon clashed with the colony's military government, in part because of his prickly personality. He fought at least three duels over insults to his work in Eritrea: in 1891 with Governor-General Gandolfi and with the editor of La Tribuna, and in 1902 with the Foreign Minister Giulio Prinetti.[54] Prime Minister Antonio di Rudinì naively hoped the duels of 1891 would resolve the differences between Franchetti and the colonial commander Gandolfi, but their basic goals for the colony were incompatible. Franchetti promoted a vigorous consolidation within Eritrea and rightly saw that war against Ethiopia would ruin his settlements. The army commanders, on the other hand, opposed the limitations of civilian government in the colonies.[55]

Oreste Baratieri, the longest-serving military governor of Eritrea, proposed in 1890 an alternative to Franchetti's purely secular settlement: Italian Catholic missionary work. Like Crispi, Baratieri had been one of the Thousand; but unlike Crispi, an anticlerical Freemason, Baratieri was a practicing Catholic from the Trentino, an Italian region still under Austrian imperial rule. Italian missionary establishments in Eritrea, he believed, were necessary to oppose the local hegemony of the French Lazzarists. The bishop of Cremona, Geremia Bonomelli, arranged for the support of Propaganda Fide in Rome and asked the bishop of Piacenza, Giovanni Battista Scalabrini, to send some of his missionaries from the Americas to Eritrea. Bonomelli and Scalabrini used emigration as a ground for collaboration between church and state, sworn enemies since Italy had dismantled the papal territories between 1860 and 1870.[56] The bishops' early enthusiasm for colonial settlements revealed their discreet patriotism. With the Catholic Church established in the colony, Baratieri hoped to succeed where Franchetti's godless parliamentary project might fail. As Governor-General of Eritrea in 1895, Baratieri solicited a colonization project from the National Association to Support Italian Catholic Missionaries, a group of lay Catholics who also supported reconciliation between Italy and the Vatican. Alessandro Rossi agreed to fund a pilot settlement on a site selected by Baratieri. But the land was less fertile than promised, and the colonists were in trouble from the beginning.[57]

Baratieri's and Franchetti's expropriations on the high plain provoked confrontation with Ethiopia and with Eritrean chieftains. Italy's diplomatic efforts only aggravated the nascent conflict. In 1889 Crispi had proclaimed a protectorate over Ethiopia, based upon his interpretation of vague language in the notorious Treaty of Wichale. Count Pietro Antonelli, who later became Italy's ambassador to Argentina, had negotiated the instrument with Emperor Menelik. The Ethiopians penned an Amharic text while Antonelli produced an Italian text. Both were official; a controversy arose over Section 17, thanks to the linguistic and cultural gulf between the two states. The Amharic text translates as follows: "Whenever the Ethiopian Royal King wishes to discuss anything with the Kings in Europe, he would do the necessary correspondence with the help of the Italian Government."[58] With the coded, misleading language of European diplomacy, Crispi claimed that Menelik had accepted Italian tutelage. Menelik discovered the ruse in 1890 when Queen Victoria refused to answer his letters. She replied from London that Ethiopia was an Italian protectorate, and had to communicate through Italian channels. After fighting a war with the Italians, in part over this disastrous treaty, Menelik distrusted European diplomats with good reason. They could claim that their treaty translations meant something different than what he intended. When British negotiators later arrived in Adis Abeba, Menelik insisted that the treaty points be "reduced to their simplest form." Menelik also wanted a French text of the treaty to be official, as he did not trust the English translation. The British avoided this demand in 1897, and again tricked Menelik with their treaty provisions: Ethiopia granted Britain "most favored nation" trading status, but Britain did not reciprocate.[59]

Menelik formally denounced the Treaty of Wichale in 1893, setting the stage for war with Italy. In 1894 the Eritrean chieftain Batha Agos switched his allegiance from Italy to Ethiopia, because the colonial government had expropriated all the best agricultural land for Italian settlement.[60] Baratieri embraced the war as an active role for Italy's large standing army, and achieved a political victory when Franchetti resigned his post and left Eritrea in August 1894. Baratieri was heralded with an imperial triumph when he visited Italy in July 1895.[61] He expelled Adolfo Rossi, correspondent for *Corriere della Sera,* from Eritrea in January 1896 because of his unpatriotic reports. Behind the careful propaganda, however, Italy's prospects were dismal. Baratieri had not developed a logistical base for an extended campaign, and was short of men and supplies. Yet Francesco Crispi, who had returned to power as prime minister in 1893, needed a dramatic victory to shore up his own domestic credibility. On 25 February 1896 Crispi accused Baratieri of "military tuberculosis" and goaded him into a risky attack.[62]

Italy's disastrous Battle of Adwa culminated a series of losses. By the fall of 1895 Menelik had mobilized an army of two hundred thousand soldiers from all over the Ethiopian empire. Baratieri's intelligence corps, compromised by Ethiopian spies, had estimated that Menelik could gather only forty thousand.[63] The Italian army was doomed to certain disaster. On 7 December 1895 the Ethiopians wiped out a column of indigenous Eritrean troops [*ascari*] under the command of Major Pietro Toselli at Amba Alagi. Between 1,500 and 2,000 Eritreans were killed, in addition to 19 Italian officers.[64] Italian Republicans and radicals in the industrial North rallied against the war, but Sicily was filled with war fever. On 10 February 1896 the young Gaetano Salvemini wrote to Pasquale Villari about the excitement: "Whoever visits Palermo these days cannot understand how the events of December 1893 [the *Fasci* trade union movement] took place in Sicily; all the people seem mad for Africa! they are all Africanists! they carry the portrait of [the Piedmontese Colonel] Galliano, they burn portaits of Menelik and poor [Empress] Taitu; it is a general drunkenness."[65] Crispi did win regional support for colonial warfare. But Italy's African policy was headed toward a precipice. Colonel Galliano had already surrendered the besieged fort of Makale and withdrawn his troops toward Eritrea. Troop reinforcements, and Baratieri's replacement as commander, were on their way from Naples.[66] But Baratieri could not wait; his troops were running out of food and supplies, and he had to make a decision to retreat or attack. On 28 February he held a council of war. The Italian officers voted that it would be cowardly to withdraw in the face of the African enemy. To avenge the defeat of Amba Alagi, the Italians must attack the heights near Adwa.

On the night of 29 February Baratieri sent out his troops in three columns, through unreconnoitered terrain, outnumbered six to one. The Ethiopians were renowned fighters; they were armed with thousands of rifles, donated by Italian diplomats eight years earlier, and even newer rifles and long-range machine guns supplied by Italy's enemies France and Russia. Under Generals Albertone, Arimondi, and Dabormida, the Italian columns lost their way. By daybreak the left and center columns were separated by a gap of more than four miles. The Ethiopians maneuvered for maximum superiority of forces. The Italian columns were cut apart, their artillery overrun; retreat became a rout.[67] In a single day, 4,600 to 5,000 Italian soldiers, plus 1,700 Eritrean soldiers, were killed; 500 Italians and 1,000 Eritreans were wounded; and at least 1,811 Italians were taken prisoner. A total of 268 Italian officers died, including two generals and Colonel Galliano. The Italian force had thus lost more than half its strength.[68] Of the generals, Arimondi and Dabormida were killed and Albertone captured, while Baratieri became lost in the confusion and was not found until several days later. The Ethiopian losses were estimated between three and twelve thousand dead. Because the Ethiopian chieftains divided the prisoners and buried the Italian dead, and because of the Italian force's disorganization, no one knows how many died on the battlefield.[69]

The Adwa debacle called all previous experience into question. In January 1879 the British had lost 1,300 soldiers at Isandhlwana, but sought revenge by killing more than two thousand Zulus several months later. Italy had a different reaction: the king immediately considered abdication, in the footsteps of his grandfather following military defeat in 1849. On 3 March 1896 the president of the Italian Senate, Domenico Farini, envisioned in his diary the end of Italy: "This morning I received the dispatch of the defeat at Adwa. I am dismayed. The consequences at home and abroad seem incalculable. The Crimean War [1854–1856] was the birth of the new Italy: let not the African War be its death! . . . The Piedmontese monarchy and Piedmont were supreme in Italy because they were a warrior dynasty and people: strip away this prestige, and the monarchy loses its only purpose. Take from the army its prestige, kill its soul, and the subversives will easily triumph."[70] Farini feared that Italian unity, with its shallow roots and hollow prestige, could now be toppled by revolutionary Socialists, anarchists, and Republicans. The Italian state would risk no vindication. Baratieri was tried in court martial as a scapegoat, but acquitted to save the honor of the Italian army. Francesco Crispi captured the opprobrium; it was he who had refused Baratieri's earlier requests for supplies and had called for the attack. In the end, King Umberto remained on the throne and Crispi resigned in disgrace. Although the country was filled with mourning, the debacle could not be commemorated for shame. In a single colonial battle, the army had lost more officers than in all the Italian wars of unification, from 1848 to 1870.[71] No funerary obelisks were erected in Rome, although a monument was established in Milan: Ferdinando Bocconi endowed a private university in memory of his son Luigi, lost at Adwa.[72]

Adwa cast a shadow over all of Europe. The British diplomats who traveled to Ethiopia in 1897, to renew diplomatic relations between the two empires, deplored the watershed in imperial relations: "It is difficult to overrate the evil consequences which have arisen owing to the Italian defeat at Adowa. Up to that time Europeans had always been treated with marked respect by Abyssinians of all classes; now, unfortunately, it is exactly the reverse." The British found they were insulted with "gestures derogatory to the Europeans" and rude names like "Ali."[73] No matter the background to the battle of Adwa, it became a defeat for all European empires.

Francesco Crispi divided Italian society even further by condemning aid to the Italians held prisoner in Ethiopia. Crispi lectured Countess Lovatelli, patroness of the relief effort, that Italian women had no role in Africa: "We are now a nation of 32 million people, and our method of insisting on our rights and enforcing respect is very different. Our fellow-

countrymen who were made prisoners at Abba Carima [Adwa] are anx-
iously expecting an army to set them at liberty, and Italian women
should, as in 1848 and 1860, inspire that army with valour and encourage it to conquer. Piety is a sacred thing, but in the eyes of the Abyssinians it is regarded as an expression of fear and weakness; besides, there is
between us and the enemy a barrier of barbarism, which will prevent our
aid from reaching the sufferers."[74] Crispi opposed the prisoner relief because it was led by women, and because an Austrian priest traveled to
Ethiopia in May 1896 to deliver the supplies. By insisting upon a fantasy
world of violent conquest and vindictive reprisals, Crispi further alienated himself and his country from realistic political choices.

Thanks to Crispi's excesses, Italian settlement in Eritrea became a lost
cause. Those remaining in Franchetti's communities insisted on free
repatriation to Italy, and the government eventually acquiesced. The
colonists in Rossi's small Catholic settlement experiment also demanded
repatriation, citing their disappointing terrain; Rossi yielded as well, and
brought them back to the Veneto.[75] Crispi's promise of virgin land in
Africa for Italian families, making emigration obsolete and land reform
in Italy unnecessary, had been proven a mere illusion. His policy had
united the Ethiopian empire in war against Italy, planting seeds of hatred
that would blossom for generations. If he had succeeded, Crispi would
have established a permanent racial divide between Italian settlers and
their expropriated African neighbors. His failure led the Italian army to
massacre and the Italian state to near collapse. Italians would have to
find another path to colonial greatness.

Calls for Colonialism in the Americas

The battle of Adwa was Europe's greatest colonial disaster in the nineteenth century. Ethiopia's victory, achieved with European weapons
against a strong European army, reversed a hundred years' trend. By
1896 the entire African continent had been subjected to European and
Ottoman rule, except for Liberia and Ethiopia. Emperor Menelik had
mobilized his people and thrown off the political yoke of European supremacy. Adwa became both a legend and a nightmare.

Italy's reaction was profound. When the news hit the press on 4 March
1896, Socialists and students organized mass protests all over Italy. In
Milan, ten thousand gathered to call for the withdrawal of troops from

Africa; an attack by police left many wounded and one dead. Workers in Pavia attacked the rail station and sabotaged rail lines to prevent further movements of troops toward Africa, as reinforcements continued to be reported in the newspapers.[76] Francesco Crispi's reputation, foreign policy, and political career collapsed completely.[77]

Crispi's enemies stood ready with a new vision for Italian colonialism. A coalition in Parliament ranged from Ferdinando Martini, who opposed Crispi's colonial wars and mismanagement; to Giustino Fortunato and Attilio Brunialti, who preferred Libya to Eritrea; to the Radicals and Socialists, who were entirely "anti-imperialist."[78] Crispi's close relations with Germany and Austria inside the Triple Alliance were also discredited. Domination of the Mediterranean now gave way to other concerns, such as interests in the Americas and relations with France. Italy's neomercantilist economic policy also collapsed. Demographic colonies in Africa were to provide raw materials to the home market, behind a protectionist tariff wall benefitting heavy industry, textiles, and grain producers. But Crispi's trade war with France between 1888 and 1891 had devastated agricultural exports such as olive oil and wine. The failed tariffs awakened strong Liberal support for free trade and competitive market prices. After Crispi, Italian companies in Eritrea lost their special tariff reduction in the Italian market and had to compete with all other imports on equal terms.

Schemes in East Africa simply could not compete with economic possibilities elsewhere. Spontaneous settlements of Italians in the Americas outstripped Crispi's expensive projects in Africa. Without much support from Europe, Italians had amassed wealth and influence in Argentina, Brazil, and the United States. Who could guess what might be accomplished in the Americas with some direction from Italy?

In 1896, politicians and theorists proposed developing emigration in the Americas, rather than enticing emigrants to settle in Africa. This geographical and conceptual leap across the Atlantic relied on Italy's social and economic understanding of colonies as population settlements, with or without official Italian rule.[79] Anti-Africanists urged support for Italy's "free colonies" across the world, peacefully created by Italian emigrants at no cost to the government. Liberals campaigned for a reinvention of Italian colonialism on the new frontier of Italian expansion. With a new frame of reference and new criteria for success, the Italian state ought to cultivate, not oppose, emigration abroad. Emigration must be prized as a precious economic, social, and cultural resource, and the Italian state must invest its energy in building lasting links between expatriates and the fatherland.[80]

Italians had long publicized South America's potential for growth, and they raised their voices soon after the Adwa defeat. On 3 May 1896 in Rome, activist Guglielmo Godio presented his ideas for supporting Italians in the Americas, a plan previously published as a book in 1893 and now revived in the context of the Adwa debacle. Godio contrasted Argentina's varied climate and expanding economy with Eritrea's unfriendly population and unhealthy climate. Instead of conquering a people through barbaric warfare, Italy ought to rise to the challenge of increasing its international commerce with South America.[81] Parliamentary deputy Attilio Brunialti also revived his campaign to support the "new Italy" in the Plata River Region, regretting that his advice had gone unheeded for the past twenty years. He urged the Italian state to entice emigrants to Argentina and Uruguay, away from the tropics and the desert, by exempting emigrants' children from military service. The government should "use every means so [emigrants] speak Italian, think Italian, and maintain relations of affection and trade with Italy."[82] Brunialti promised that if emigrants loved Italy and spoke Italian, Italy's exports and political influence would grow.

Others in Parliament proposed similar methods and goals for Italy's foreign policy. On 30 June 1896, the Radical deputy Edoardo Pantano called for a serious commitment to Italian emigration in North and South America. In his judgment, the most eloquent of Italy's failures in Africa was Franchetti's failed colonization attempt, which demonstrated that "it is impossible to create artificial outlets for emigration; it is time to look at the real life of the country, and to see if emigration's natural currents . . . are not worthy of serious attention, to be better protected, supported, and disciplined." Pantano proposed that these natural currents were the secret of Italy's past prosperity, "that peaceful Italian expansion" under the medieval maritime republics. Venice and Genoa's strategy used troops effectively "not to impose, but to protect Italian industry, in the name of fraternal international relations." In contrast with "the whim of affected and artificial colonies," Italy must turn its attention to emigration following "natural impulses, historical traditions, [and] commercial tendencies."[83]

Pantano hoped the historic model of Italy's maritime republics would supplant Crispi's myth of imperial Roman conquest. The new policy would be more mundane, but more practical and effective. Pantano urged restriction on emigration agents' recruitment propaganda in the countryside, and regulation of the transatlantic voyage for the speed of ships, the quality of food and water, and the space allotted to each emigrant. The government had to establish an emigration information office in Italy and diplomatic protections for Italians abroad. Most importantly, the "inane and vexatious" restrictions on emigration had to disappear, because emigration helped even those who remained behind with higher wages in "the struggle for existence."[84] These recommendations become legislation within five years. The obvious potential of American emigration, and the lack of an alternative in Africa, ushered in a fundamental shift of attention and resources.

Pantano was not the only politician to declare a new era for emigration. Francesco Saverio Nitti, a Liberal Catholic from Basilicata, had written about emigration in 1888, noting that the ongoing emigration was an economic necessity for many areas both in the South and North, and seemed to lower crime. The state limited emigration only at its peril. "It is a sad and fatal law: either emigrants, or brigands."[85] In November 1896, Nitti published another study of emigration in his journal *La Riforma sociale*. Framing the debate in terms of internal colonization, Nitti noted that Luigi Luzzatti had shown him the new "colony" of Ostia, built on reclaimed marshes near Rome. Although the settlers were well-fed, they still suffered from malaria. Nitti calculated how many settlers could colonize all the vacant lands in Italy: 375,000 people, only twice the *annual* number emigrating to the Americas. Even if the amount of land were doubled, Italy could absorb internally only four years of transatlantic emigration. He concluded that the investment return on reclamation projects in Italy would not justify the huge expense. Since the cost of settling families in Eritrea had made Africa an impossible solution, emigration elsewhere was a necessity: "It is the only potent safety valve against class hate; it is a powerful school, and the great and only salvation for a country barren in resources and fertile in manpower."[86] Emigration seemed the key to Italy's economic, social, and moral strength.

New Disappointments in Africa and Asia

While some in Parliament pointed to the promise of American colonies, Italy as a Great Power remained committed to the logic of European imperialism and the Scramble for Africa and Asia. Who could balance the contrary pressures on Italy's international course? The king chose as his new prime minister Antonio di Rudinì, who had also succeeded Crispi in 1891. Rudinì, a conservative Sicilian baron, had antirevolutionary, anticolonial, and antireform credentials. In 1891 he had proposed abandoning the Red Sea colonies altogether. Africa to him was a burden on Italy's dignity, not a promise for the future.[87]

Rudinì hoped to replace African failures with positive support for American emigration. He wrote Ferdinando Martini in August 1896 to express his feelings, though Martini, a prolific author, was an unlikely confidant. After having led Parliament's anticolonialist faction since 1887, in 1891 Martini toured Eritrea as part of a Parliamentary investigation under the Sicilian Marquis Antonino Di San Giuliano. Martini decided Italy should promote Eritrea's potential as a settlement colony.[88] Rudinì, however, wrote not to consult Martini's opinion on African affairs, but to highlight Brazil: "Brazil is one of the most important questions that Italy faces at present. The public . . . does not understand its importance. I study these issues with love, and I am aware that the question of emigration to Brazil is one of the most important for Italy's political and economic interests."[89] In the wake of Adwa, emigrant settlement remained the key to Italy's colonial expansion, but the theater had changed from East Africa to South America, and from formal to informal empire.

Before developing American colonies, Rudinì sought to stabilize Italy's war-torn African possessions. In a compromise, Rudinì sharply curtailed the colonies without abandoning them. Luigi Luzzatti's idea to lease Eritrea to King Leopold II of Belgium was briefly considered, then dropped. Italy defended Kassala against a Dervish siege in 1896, but ceded the province to British Sudan the following year. With General Baldissera back in Eritrea as the colony's last military governor, Italy pursued peace in Ethiopia. In March 1896 the Italian diplomatic mission proposed to Menelik the immediate liberation of Italian prisoners, while the Emperor insisted that Eritrea's frontier remain unfortified. Diplomatic negotiations broke off in May, yet Italy unilaterally withdrew its expeditionary force from Eritrea and dropped its firm demands. A new Italian representative negotiated the Treaty of Adis Abeba on 26 October 1896, which denounced the 1889 Treaty of Wichale and recognized Ethiopia's independence, leaving the Eritrea-Ethiopia border to be determined within a year. The Italian prisoners were liberated when Italy paid what looked like an indemnity: 10 million francs to reimburse the costs of the prisoners' captivity.[90]

Peace on such terms was immediately controversial. In April 1896, hundreds of Italians petitioned the King to continue the war and not settle a peace until after a military victory in Africa.[91] Italian Nationalists and Fascists would later vilify Italy's retreat from Ethiopia, claiming that Italy had lost a battle at Adwa, not a war.[92] Yet the treaty of 1896 was the best course for both sides. There was no justification for mobilizing a punitive expedition. Menelik, the Ethiopian king of kings, offered peace, wisely choosing not to attack Eritrea or push Italy into a corner. He ordered Ethiopia's kings to take special care of the Italian prisoners. But the Christian Eritrean soldiers who had fought for Italy at Adwa were punished as traitors, with the amputation of their right hand and left foot. The newspaper *Corriere della Sera* organized a subscription campaign in support of these mutilated troops, and they became a living symbol of barbaric cruelty down to the Fascist era.[93]

Caught up in parliamentary troubles and domestic unrest, Rudinì did not have time to invest in the colonies after peace was settled. In November 1897 he appointed Ferdinando Martini as Eritrea's first civilian governor with three short priorities: "Respect our commitments with Menelick [sic]; Give supremacy to the civilian element in the colony; and spend little. After examining the situation and the proposals you make, we will think of the rest."[94] The colonial budget was a major worry, since in 1896 Parliament had to approve 140 million lire to pay for Crispi's war. Rudinì hoped to save some money by making Eritrea a prison: "if we must have a Colony in Africa, nothing keeps us from making it a penal colony too."[95] This would have brought in funds from the Interior Ministry's budget, but Rudinì's plans never took shape. The prime minister faced pressure from Luigi Luzzatti, the Minister of the Treasury, to abandon the African colonies altogether. As governor, Martini worried that the Chamber of Deputies in Rome would turn against him, but Rudinì assured him everyone would soon recognize that civilian government in Eritrea "will save the Fatherland many sorrows and a lot of money."[96]

In the words of Renato Paoli, who later became secretary of the Italian Colonial Institute, the colonial budget swung from one extreme to the other, "from lavishness to stinginess."[97] The change from military to civilian control was slow, painful, and confusing; ten years later, most agencies of colonial government were still in pairs, with a military and a civilian office, stunting the colony's development. Paoli compared the hatred between military and civilian parties in Italian Africa to the Guelphs and Ghibellines of medieval Italy.[98]

While maintaining Italy's presence in Africa, the new colonial administration abandoned the pre-Adwa legacy of Baratieri and Franchetti. Although Martini had admired Franchetti's efforts, he now regarded them as a failed experiment. Franchetti still stridently opposed large concessions for plantations, because they would forever close the door to the settlement of individual colonists and their families.[99] Martini, however, was convinced that the colony had to be reorganized for capitalistic exploitation. He sought high-capital investments for Eritrea, including cotton and coffee plantations. A swelling colonial bureaucracy also ran against Franchetti's principles. But Martini's most shocking innovation was a virtual ban on immigration from Italy, including spontaneous migration. Italians who could not support themselves in Eritrea were shipped back to Italy at the colony's expense. After paying for a few passages, Martini ruled that all immigrants who came to Eritrea had to put down an expensive deposit, which would cover the cost of a return passage. No prospective immigrants could present such a sum, so immigration from Italy ceased altogether. This budgetary measure also affected the relations between Europeans and Africans. In Martini's words, "we could not permit impoverished Italians to make a spectacle of themselves in the colony, perhaps even asking the natives for help. One can imagine what impression this would make on our subject peoples."[100] No Italians in Africa would live in conditions of grueling labor and deprivation, as millions did in Italy and abroad in North and South America. But the ban caused further economic problems. Italians already inside Eritrea were granted, in effect, a monopoly on skilled labor.[101]

To the Parliament in Rome, Martini's course seemed profligate and misguided. In 1901 he provoked heated antagonism by proposing a new colonial statute to replace the regulations of 1890. The foreign minister Giulio Prinetti presented the bill to the Chamber of Deputies, and Leopoldo Franchetti was appointed president of the examining commission, which also included Di San Giuliano. Without consulting Prinetti, the commission made significant changes to the bill in their report of 7 June 1901, reducing the governor's independence and calling for renewed, subsidized emigration to Eritrea. Franchetti's report claimed that if Italians did not immigrate to the colony, Ethiopians would cross the border in massive numbers, fill Eritrea's population, and make the colony ungovernable. Prinetti declared the report "disgusting" (schifoso) and Franchetti challenged him to a duel the next day. Franchetti emerged with a sword cut on his head. In May 1905 he again attacked Martini for blocking the immigration of small property owners.[102] Martini ignored Parliament and delayed a regulation for land grants, relying instead on his authority as governor to assign large estates to individuals. Grantees usually failed to follow their contracts; instead of improving the land, they simply leased it to indigenous farmers.

After creating a new Eritrea, Martini was disappointed by Italy's lack of interest. His administration ran against the popular idea of what role Italian colonies perform. Crispi had established that Eritrea's value lay in population settlement. With the failure of colonization, Eritrea's importance for Italy was vastly circumscribed. The discovery of gold might have redeemed the colony's growth, as in Australia and the western United States, but the much-sought precious metals were never found.[103] It was useless to ask Parliament to subsidize Eritrean coffee and cotton, and private capital did not flow to Eritrea without official guarantees. There were plenty of safer and more promising opportunities for investment within Italy. Africa never caught Italians' imagination as an arena for plantations, railroads, and trading concessions. Eritrea, and later Libya, became popular insofar as they showed promise for settlement and development, as extensions of Italy, not as subject foreign lands. Mussolini would later carry out his conquest of Ethiopia in a much different context, and with much different motives.

Eritrea wasted away. Pressed for funding, the Liberal Italian government closed its schools for Eritreans and left open only a primary school for Italians. Eritrean education was left to Protestant missionaries from Sweden, who of course did not teach the Italian language.[104] Martini had long mocked the idea of a "civilizing mission": "Do not talk to me about civilizing. Whoever says Ethiopia must be civilized is either lying or talking nonsense. One race must be substituted for another: this or nothing . . . The native is a hindrance to our work; like it or not, we will have to chase him down and help him disappear, like the Redskins elsewhere, with all the means that civilization, which he hates instinctually, furnishes us: the machine gun and hard liquor. It is sad to say so but unfortunately that is the way things are."[105] As colonial governor, Martini did not hunt and kill Africans out of spite, as Mussolini would order the Italian army to do in 1935–1936.[106] But he felt no imperative to improve the Eritreans' condition. Indigenous education was only the first casualty of the colonial budget. The Italian colony never developed anything along the lines of an indigenous civil service. Even Martini bemoaned the lack of Italian investment in Eritrea's infrastructure. Railroad construction was delayed indefinitely, and the port at Massawa remained unimproved, even as the British constructed Port Sudan to the north and the French built up Djibouti to the south. These ports and their railroad networks shut Eritrea out of commerce on the Red Sea.[107]

The popular vision of a demographic colony persisted, even though conditions in Eritrea precluded its reality. Martini regularly received requests and petitions from individuals and groups in Italy and North Africa seeking permission to settle in Eritrea. The petitioners seem to have disregarded the colony's near-collapse at Adwa. If Italy still owned Eritrea, they wanted to live there. A miner writing from Tunisia in 1897 required little: "It is enough if you can tell me that there is sufficient work to survive."[108] Though all were denied, the requests kept coming. Some petitioners asked for free passage; others offered to pay their own way. Some had served as soldiers in Eritrea and wanted to return.[109] The colonial government's firm answer was "no," in every case. But as Franchetti had stated, the fertile plains of Eritrea would be profitably occupied by someone. Italian immigration in Eritrea was soon replaced by Ethiopian immigration. Ironically, Italy was creating an "America" for Ethiopians, while Italians still traveled to the United States and Argentina.[110]

Martini lectured the Italian Parliament in 1908 to end their role as the Hamlets of colonial policy, always asking "to be or not to be."[111] But the governor demanded colonial development on his own terms, and faced inevitable disappointment. Those Italian politicians who cared about Africa, such as Franchetti and Di San Giuliano, refused to abandon their vision of demographic colonialism, with its tangible domestic benefits. Economic exploitation of Eritrea seemed bleak. From Italy's perspective, money was better spent on the Italian mainland. Administered by the

Colonial Office of the Foreign Affairs Ministry, Eritrea and Somalia were nearly forgotten in Italian society after 1896. If unfit for Italian settlement, these colonies had no meaningful future. The official collection *Emigrazione e colonie,* published in seven volumes to document Italian settlements on every continent, omitted Somalia and Eritrea as colonies "because their territories are considered part of the national territory and they have no diplomatic or consular agents."[112]

Yet Rudinì as prime minister proved incapable of pursuing a new, American colonialism because of discontent in Italy. A poor harvest, high tariffs, and high prices for American grain imports because of the Spanish-American War raised the price of bread and sparked riots all over Italy. In May 1898, riots in Milan were put down by the army, leaving at least 80 dead and 450 wounded. Insurrection in Italy's economic capital doomed Rudinì's ministry. King Umberto replaced Rudinì with an army officer in June 1898, as Europe's Scramble for Africa came to a climax. General Luigi Pelloux made no commitment to renounce colonial expansion, as Rudinì had vowed after Adwa. Rather, Pelloux hoped Italy would claim a share of the changing world map. Britain and France approached war over the Sudan in the Fashoda Crisis of September 1898. At the same time, the Great Powers rushed toward new conquests in China, following its recent defeat by Japan in 1894. It appeared that the Chinese coast might be entirely partitioned, as Russia took a lease on Port Arthur (Dalian), Germany took Qingdao, France took Zhanjiang, and Britain claimed Weihai. Not to be left behind, Italy mobilized an expedition to occupy San-Mun Bay (Wangpan Yang), south of Shanghai. Supported by Britain, on 2 March 1899 Italy requested a lease of the bay and influence over most of Zhejiang province. The Chinese government, however, had decided against further European concessions and refused Italy's request. The Italian government recalled its diplomat and grumbled about an ultimatum, but dropped its demands in late 1899. Italy was the only European power that missed a piece of the Chinese pie.[113]

Even before it collapsed, Italy's adventure in China attracted broad opposition in Italy. Anticolonialists called for careful studies to see if the bay could actually attract commerce, "that is, doing for China what was not done for Eritrea."[114] Italy had no established trade with China and would face entrenched competition from Shanghai and British Hong Kong. Most importantly, China was unsuitable for Italian colonialism because there was no room for Italian emigration: "Unfortunately the only capital that Italy can export—its large emigration—is useless in China, where the population is overabundant and wages are extremely low!"[115] For Italy, colonialism meant emigration; where emigration was impossible, so was a colony.

Italy's failure in China was soon overshadowed by profound developments at home. In February 1899 Pelloux revived proposals to limit freedoms of assembly and the press. To block a filibuster by Radicals and Socialists, in June Pelloux announced he would enact the laws by royal decree. But when the Speaker of the Chamber cut off the parliamentary debate, two Socialist deputies overturned the voting urns in a dramatic scene. Parliament was closed for three months, yet in February 1900 Italy's high court ruled Pelloux's censorship decree unconstitutional, returning the question to Parliament. Pelloux called for new elections in April 1900, then lost votes dramatically to the Left. In June 1900 King Umberto asked Senator Giuseppe Saracco to form a new ministry to replace Pelloux. Within a month the king would be dead. On July 29, 1900, the king was assassinated in Monza by Gaetano Bresci, an anarchist expatriate who had returned from Paterson, New Jersey, to take revenge for the casualties at Milan of 1898. Bresci's sponsors in New Jersey hoped this would launch a revolution, but all of Italy joined together in mourning Umberto's death.

After this tragic intervention by Italian emigrants, the tension in Italian politics subsided, and the Left Liberals came to power without much opposition. In February 1901 Giuseppe Zanardelli was appointed Prime Minister, with Giovanni Giolitti as Minister of the Interior. In 1903 Zanardelli died and Giolitti took his place, launching a controversial decade of political stability and economic growth. Two landmarks shifted the politics of Italian emigration in this period: Luigi Einaudi's Liberal manifesto *A Merchant Prince: A Study in Italian Colonial Expansion* and the emigration legislation of 1901 which Einaudi helped inspire.

Einaudi's Vision of "Greater Italy"

Luigi Einaudi was a new voice in the era after Adwa. When he wrote *A Merchant Prince* in the spring of 1899, he was 25 years old and a junior professor of economics in Turin. The work made him famous and launched a long and illustrious career. After World War II, he became the first President of the Republic of Italy, leading the postwar reconstruction of Italian entrepreneurship, exports, and economic success, Einaudi's triumph with *A Merchant Prince* lay in the book's brevity, clarity, and enthusiasm.[116] For a decade it was cited by virtually every Italian writer and politician who addressed emigration.

Einaudi's inspiration was the Exhibition of Italians Abroad at the Italian National Exposition in Turin. As a member of the prize jury for the Emigration and Colonies section, Einaudi studied all the entries, from Australia to India, from Argentina to Tunisia to New York (see illustrations). To communicate the proud excitement of Italy's worldwide expansion, particularly in South America, Einaudi constructed a narrative around the vision and experience of one "merchant prince," Enrico Dell'Acqua, chosen from among many charismatic "self-made men." Einaudi aimed to revive the glory and prestige of Italy's medieval past, comparing Dell'Acqua to the princes of Genoa and Milan: "the living incarnation of the intellectual and organizational qualities destined to transform today's 'little Italy' into a future 'greater Italy,' peacefully expanding its name and its glorious progeny in a continent more vast than the ancient Roman Empire."[117] Like Pantano, Einaudi replaced the image of ancient imperial Rome with the mythic wealth of medieval Italy, replicated in Latin America.

In Einaudi's hands, Dell'Acqua's business decisions become an epic tale. In 1885 Dell'Acqua thought to link Italian exports to long-term emigration, and chose Argentina and Brazil as his target markets. He avoided the United States with its high tariffs and racial prejudices, which subordinated the Italian immigrants to exploitative "vampires."[118] Dell'Acqua worked from Milan and nearby Busto Arsizio to rally capital behind the export of textiles to South America. When Argentina entered a depression in 1889, Dell'Acqua incorporated his business; when Brazil raised a tariff against imported cloth, he built a factory there for weaving imported thread. Economic downturns cleared away much of his competition, and by 1899 Dell'Acqua had hundreds of sales representatives all over South America. Einaudi concludes triumphantly that after a decade of effort, Dell'Acqua had proven that "Made in Italy" could beat out "Made in Germany."

Einaudi frames his story as a national struggle for economic survival: Italy had to attack Britain and Germany's domination of foreign markets. Dell'Acqua is a brilliant general making plans, rallying resources, and choosing his battleground. Italy's emigrants change from an illiterate rabble into "a disciplined army which moves as one, under the leadership of captains and generals in the conquest of a continent . . . From the anonymous mass rise the elect, who stamp a new life and potential, earlier unknown, on the mass." These captains open workshops and warehouses by dint of hard work and savings. Einaudi refers to the popular Victorian author Samuel Smiles and the tenacious power of self-help: "will is power." Soon Italy would furnish architects and managers, not common laborers, in the global division of labor: "We continue to furnish soldiers, but we have already begun to export 'captains of industry.'"[119]

Inspired by the success of Italy's expatriates, Einaudi assaults the economic principles of European imperialism. He denies that "trade follows the flag," citing the anemic development of Eritrea. Rather, "trade flows must follow the currents of emigration from Italy; free colonies, not official colonies, must attract merchants who want to create an outlet for industrial products of the fatherland." The infusion of Italians, and Italian goods, into Argentina would supercede the prestige of Anglo-Saxon imperialism: "On the banks of the Plata River, a new Italy is rising, a people is forming which, though Argentine, will preserve the fundamental characters of the Italian people and will prove to the world that the imperialist ideal will not remain only an Anglo-Saxon ideal. We are showing the world that Italy can create a more perfect and evolved type of colonization . . . The peaceful conquest of the English settlers was always accompanied, even if weakly, by military domination, and old England is now trying to strengthen political bonds with the colonies; but Italian colonization has always been free and independent."[120] By peaceful means, Italy was creating a new people overseas, rather than subjecting African nations under a short-sighted and expensive military occupation. Einaudi appeals to Italy's ruling classes to understand the true meaning of imperialism, and to turn from "pompous and lazy vexations and dilapidations at home, and African insanities, Chinese adventures, and the guilty negligence of the spontaneous colonies abroad, where new Italies are maturing, greater than the old."[121] True imperial grandeur lay in supporting Italian expatriate colonies, not chasing after concessions in Africa and Asia left behind by the other European powers.

Einaudi's upbeat appeal stemmed from his assertion that the battle had already been won; Italy needed only to preserve its victory. The story of Dell'Acqua disproved accusations that Italians lacked initiative or a sense of solidarity. Nor should Italy fear competition from established expatriates, for example, from Italian vineyards in California or Dell'Acqua's textile factory in Brazil: "It is the logic of little minds to believe that every factory established by our compatriots, every piece of cultivated land, every hill planted with vines in America represents a subtraction from our activity, a net loss for Italian exports. In reality, those local products accredit Italian brands and awaken latent desires, and as tastes become more refined, the market turns from imitations made by Italians to genuine Italian products."[122] Einaudi asserted that vineyards in California aroused an interest in Italian wines "which otherwise would not exist."[123] Nor could Italian expatriate products ever replace authentic merchandise from Italy. True to his Liberal principles, Einaudi saw no need to fight economic development within what he termed "greater Italy." Rather, the Italian government needed to establish trade treaties and reinforce cultural bonds in the Americas, perhaps even establishing an Italian-American university.

The year 1900 seemed to introduce not only a new century but also a new era for Italian opportunity and success. Einaudi's accomplishment lay in his appreciation of the invaluable human capital in international migration. The vision of peaceful colonial expansion captured the imagination and enthusiasm of Liberal Italians, and established an ideological foundation for Greater Italy's political framework.[124]

The fusion of emigration and expanding exports spawned the monthly journal L'Italia coloniale, published from 1900 to 1904 in support of free trade and commercial treaty reform.[125] Luigi Luzzatti, who in 1898 had successfully negotiated a trade treaty with France, contributed regularly. Under the direction of Giacomo Gobbi Belcredi, the journal blurred the distinction between emigration and traditional colonialism, equating colonial expansion with exports. Gobbi Belcredi aimed to study "the wealth and greatness of the Fatherland, and everything regarding maritime transportation, to satisfy the needs of our colonists and prepare new centers for exportation and emigration."[126] Uruguay's ambassador in Rome, Daniele Muñoz, wrote a polite but firm protest indicating that the colonial era in Latin America had ended. Italian expatriate settlements could not be called "colonies" because, unlike Europe's colonial enclaves in China, they lacked special privileges. Gobbi Belcredi replied to Muñoz with a political, social, and cultural definition of emigrant colonialism: "Italy, as is well known unfortunately, has no territorial colonies except for Eritrea; instead it has agglomerations of its children in the two Amer-

icas and the south shore of the Mediterranean . . . A colony is constituted of [expatriates] not participating in local politics, not joining the
local militia, having hospitals and banks and mutual aid societies and
schools; while certainly not a *collective organization,* the colony marks a
separation between the natives and children from other countries."[127]
Articles in the journal often addressed the legal bases for preserving
these emigrant colonies, including controversies over double citizenship, military service, and protectionist tariffs. The group behind *L'Italia
coloniale* was firmly convinced that if Italian emigrants could keep their
Italian cultural identity abroad, they and their American neighbors
would buy Italian olive oil, textiles, industrial products, and even luxury
items. This colonial model was so convincing that Italians applied it to
Eritrea: "these peoples . . . in contact with Italian colonists, acquire new
needs, start to appreciate our products, learn European customs. . . ."[128]
Even Eritrea, under Italy's political control, fell into the economic ideology of informal emigrant colonialism.

The Future of Empire

Semiprivate organizations often proved more effective than government
agencies, and a wide variety received annual government subsidies. In
the late 1890s, key groups adapted to Italy's new colonial focus in the
Americas by shifting their activity away from Africa. A dramatic example
was Milan's Society of Commercial Exploration in Africa, which since
1879 had been the country's most prestigious proponent of economic investment in Africa. The society's founder, Manfredo Camperio, proposed
in March 1897 to the members' assembly that the Society drop "Africa"
from its title, because the organization ought to focus its energy in the
Americas. The group changed its name the next year to the Italian Society of Geographical and Commercial Explorations. The Italian Geographical Society also abandoned its African projects, after a costly
debacle connected with the battle of Adwa. The Society had been sponsoring the popular explorer Vittorio Bottego's expedition in Somalia and
Ethiopia, with a subsidy from the Italian government. After Bottego left
for the interior in July 1895, he never received news of Italy's Ethiopian
campaign. He was killed in an Ethiopian ambush on 17 March 1897,
twelve months after the army's defeat at Adwa. The Geographical Society

quit sponsoring major African expeditions, until Ardito Desio's explorations of Libya in 1932. Instead, the organization continued its studies of emigration, and called on the government to protect Italians abroad.[129]

The Dante Alighieri Society also reoriented its geographical focus, from the Austrian Alps and the Adriatic to the Americas. The society had been founded in 1889 as an heir to two irredentist groups which hoped to "redeem" Italian territories still under Austrian rule (le terre irredente) by making them part of the Kingdom of Italy. The challenge for irredentists lay in preserving local Italian culture and traditions in Trent and Trieste against German or Slavic encroachment, while acting outside of politics. The Austrian and Hungarian governments suppressed irredentist politics abroad, even as Francesco Crispi boosted his alliance with Austria by arresting irredentists within Italy. To marshal resources in support of Italians outside Italy, Ruggero Bonghi founded the Dante Alighieri Society to practice "multiform action" under a cultural and literary cover, rather than "political irredentism."[130] The Society's second president, inaugurated in 1897, was the Neapolitan scholar Pasquale Villari. Villari refused to limit the Society's focus to Austria-Hungary, and reminded members that Trent, Trieste, and irredentism were not mentioned in the Society's statute. For the good of the Italian race, emigrants speaking Italian dialects around the world needed to learn standard Italian, "the language of Dante." Villari declared the Society's mission extended to Tunisia, the Americas, Switzerland, and Egypt: "Are not these also unredeemed lands? Are not these our brothers?"[131] Under Villari's leadership, the Dante Alighieri Society endorsed the 1901 emigration bill and, supported by many Italian consuls, founded 73 Dante Alighieri committees abroad, besides 214 inside the Kingdom of Italy. The local Dante committees subsidized schools to teach the Italian language to adults and children, and provided lending libraries aboard emigrant ships.[132]

As Italy's political pressure groups turned towards emigration, new colonialist organizations also embraced American expansion in their mission statements. An Italian Colonial Institute was created in 1906, following Ferdinando Martini's Colonial Congress in Asmara in 1905. Based on his own conversion from anticolonialism in 1891, Martini reasoned that if Italians became well-informed about Eritrea's conditions and potential, they would become enthusiastic Africanists. Despite Martini's intentions, the Italian Colonial Institute was conceived to promote not just Eritrea and Somalia but all Italian colonies around the world. The prospectus of 1906 explained that the Institute planned "to make public opinion knowledgeable of all Italian colonial activity, whether under direct management of the State in our colonies or in spontaneous penetration in the dominions of other States . . . [and] to construct a permanent bond with our compatriots who live abroad, whether in our colonies or in other countries."[133] This broadened the Institute's supporters far beyond the narrow interests served in Africa. Martini himself later admitted that the expatriate colonies were "so much more important" than Eritrea and Somalia, the "colonies of direct dominion."[134]

To draw attention to Italian expatriates, the Colonial Institute sponsored the First and Second Congresses of Italians Abroad in Rome in 1908 and 1911. By 1911, the Institute had established permanent organizations in New York City, Philadelphia, Sao Paolo, Vienna, Constantinople, Alexandria, and Cairo. Likewise, the Italian Agricultural Colonial Institute, founded in 1907 in Florence, with Leopoldo Franchetti as president, declared its intent to "promote the study of the agriculture of non-European countries, with the purpose of making our colonial activity more industrious and profitable, whether in the Italian overseas possessions, or in countries where most of our emigration travels."[135]

The Italian colonialists' focus on emigration paralleled the concerns of French and British imperialists. In 1887 the Prince of Wales proposed an Imperial Institute to commemorate Queen Victoria's Golden Jubilee and to spread information on emigration and the colonies' progress. Like the Italian Colonial Institute, Britain's Institute sought a role in emigration and struggled under contrasting pressures. But Italian colonialists' limited success in Africa paled in comparison with the French colonialists, who enjoyed greater resources, energy, and clout. French Algeria, founded in 1830 and colonized with French exiles and settlers in the 1840s, was legally a part of the French metropole, quite different from Italy's colonial possessions in East Africa. The French Algerians in the Paris Parliament formed a strong foundation for a *parti colonial,* an organized party of colonial interests. The Algerians stood to gain directly in business and in influence from any further French expansion in Africa. With all the shifting political winds in the history of France's Third Republic, this compact and consistent kernel of colonial interests exerted a weighty leverage of influence, under the leadership of Eugène Etienne. The Italians, by contrast, entered the twentieth century in an entirely different international position. The Colonial Institute comprised politicians and businessmen (and excluded all women) concerned with Italy's worldwide expansion and development not just in Africa, but also in the expatriate colonies of the Americas. The Italian colonialists also lacked the tenacity, focus, and purpose of the Algerian political lobby in Paris.[136] Faced with failure in Africa, Italians naturally looked elsewhere.

The promise of expansion in the Americas, heralded by economic and social developments in mass migration, captured patriotic imaginations and spawned new colonial theories to escape the wreck of Italian Africa. Nitti, Einaudi, and even Martini advanced a free-market imperialism, with the Italian state supporting emigrant settlers wherever they chose to go. The government would inform, guide, and assist emigrants, especially in safeguarding their precious savings. But after redefining Italy's colonial environment, Italian politicians needed to find ways to wield influence not through military intervention and direct bureaucratic rule, but through culture and civil society. How would expatriates remain, or become, "Italian"?

2

The Great Ethnographic Empire

Italy was a nebulous construction. Realism and romanticism regularly clashed in the elaboration and development of the "Italian" national idea. Was Italy a kingdom based on dynastic concerns of the royal House of Savoy, and relations with other kingdoms and empires? Was Italy a nation uniting all Italian speakers, as Mazzini had envisioned? What non-Italian speakers would be included within the country's borders? Answering these theoretical questions was complicated by the pressure of emigration and by recent history. Italy had expanded in stages in its Risorgimento or "resurgence," making different promises along the way to the states of the peninsula, but eventually subsuming all of them under Piedmontese rule. The capital of the new Kingdom of Italy shifted three times in ten years, from Turin in 1861 to Florence in 1865 to Rome in 1871. Yet after these initial stages of territorial expansion, Trieste and Trent remained outside Italy, under Austrian rule. Irredentists would later call Italy's World War I the "third war of the Risorgimento" to redeem these territories with Austria's defeat and dissolution. Other Italian-speaking territories outside Italy included Corsica under French rule, Dalmatia under Hungarian rule, and Canton Ticino in Switzerland. But with the spread of Italian emigrants worldwide, the geography and meaning of *italianità* were recast, both in theory and in practice.

What did this phrase mean: Italians abroad? Traditionally, it had meant the Italians still under Austrian and Hungarian rule. But with mass emigration, more Italians lived in the Americas than lived in the unredeemed provinces of Austria-Hungary. To incorporate Italians thousands of miles away would require a more flexible definition of belonging to Italy and participating in Italy's development. National ideas for Italians abroad, expounded by Italian writers and politicians in the metropole, moved in stages from the romantic irredentism of Mazzini, to the scientific study of ethnicity by Italian ethnographers, and later to the messianic fervor of Enrico Corradini's Nationalist Party. Representations of Italians abroad, in maps, censuses, and exhibitions, coalesced these ideas in unitary packages of triumphant numbers, trends, text, and illustrations, for audiences at home and abroad.

Because of its central importance to Italy, emigration iself became a framework for the organization of time and space. Emigration produced a new ethnic geography of population, displacing the traditional political geography of borders and states. To chart the expansion of Greater Italy, the Italian state produced a series of world views based on the rapidly changing distribution of Italians across the globe, similar to the ethnic world maps produced by British and German geographers. Each country of the world is shown in a color linked to the density of its Italian population (see illustrations). In this optic, a geography of emigrant food, culture, and ethnicity replaces the physical geography of emigrant destinations. Italy could be anywhere.[1]

Creative approaches to Italians abroad bore fruit after 1896 because of the colonial debacle of Adwa and the political collapse of Francesco Crispi. Crispi had counted on support from Germany and Austria-Hungary for his colonial schemes in Africa, and he had suppressed irredentist activity to win their favor. This support never materialized, and Crispi's foreign policy disintegrated with military defeat. After Crispi, colonial policy focused on Italian interests in the Mediterranean and the Americas, instead of power politics in East Africa. While Italy remained a partner in the defensive Triple Alliance, British and French influence gradually outweighed the German and Austrian partnership in Italian foreign policy. This precipitated a return to irredentist support for those Italians still under the Austro-Hungarian empire. Freed from the constraints and expenses of Africanist policies, Italy could support constructive national identities beyond borders. The phrase most commonly repeated by theorists of emigrant colonialism was *tutelare l'italianità*, holding many meanings: tutelage, guardianship, schooling, education, and protection of the essence of what it means to be Italian. The project of making Italy Abroad would not remain a theory. New laws and state organizations would build upon semiprivate cultural initiatives. By design Italians abroad would learn of their Italian identity, but, more broadly, *italianità* itself would be deepened, defined, and elaborated for Italians at home.

The 1901 Law on Emigration

Led by Liberal social scientists in Parliament, the Italian state adopted a broad mandate to build Italy Abroad. After many years of debate, on 31 January 1901 the Italian Parliament enacted a far-sighted emigration law, better in many respects than the statutes of other European countries.[2] The ideology and theory of emigrant colonialism now took a political form. The Italian government set up an independent bureaucracy, with broad powers and practically unlimited funds, to guide and protect emigrants across the world. This legal and administrative apparatus would remain basically unchanged until 1925.

The 1901 law marked a radical shift in the Italian government's attitude toward emigration. Responsibility for emigrants moved from the interior ministry to the foreign ministry, marking emigration as an international expansion instead of an internal hemorrhage. Before 1901 the Italian government had associated emigration with crime. The interior ministry policed the problem by restricting the work of emigration agents, accused of tricking gullible emigrants and trafficking in human flesh. The ministry's first emigration regulation, the Lanza circular of 1873, was so restrictive that it encouraged clandestine emigration from ports outside Italian control. Its successor, the Nicotera circular of 1876, loosened limits on passports but restricted the activity of speculators and emigration agents. In 1889 Parliament enacted its first law on emigration, sponsored by Francesco Crispi. Despite a guarantee for the freedom to emigrate, the bill again concentrated on controlling emigration agents. Emigration remained under the jurisdiction of the interior ministry, which naturally considered domestic problems ahead of Italy's international affairs. Italian police had a direct incentive to send problematic criminals, who perhaps could not be convicted, out of the country as emigrants. This laid the basis for Italian criminal organizations abroad. Not until 1901, when the management of emigration was transferred to the foreign ministry, was this disastrous course reversed, in consideration of Italy's international reputation.[3]

To reverse these negative trends, Liberals in the Italian Parliament hoped to change emigration's function in Italian culture, society, and economy. In presenting the bill on 3 July 1900, Edoardo Pantano and Luigi Luzzatti promoted a positive image of Italian emigrants, who demonstrated by nature "a miracle of the immortal genius of our race, which finds resistance amid undeserved suffering" by still remembering "the faraway fatherland." Emigration was an urgent opportunity awaiting Italy's attention: "Emigration, made necessary by overwhelming population density, by want, by the vocation of our history, does not tolerate any obstacle and, though caused by misery, resolves itself in wealth, honor, and glory benefitting our country, because without an ambition of political domination our natural colonies are establishing themselves in Latin America; emigration currents are determined by the great law of vital competition and their final results are wiser than any art of Government."[4] By protecting emigrants, Italy would earn their good will; by managing the investment of human capital, Italy would gain immense international returns. Pantano and Luzzatti called upon Parliament to rise above party politics to move humane principles into political and social action.

Under Luzzatti's plan, a model for other migration laws in Europe, Italy assumed direct management of its transatlantic emigration. The law banned independent emigration agencies and subagencies, notorious for deceiving and defrauding emigrants; only steamer companies could obtain licenses for agents to sell tickets. Emigrants received refunds if they missed a voyage because of late trains or a sickness in their family, room and board if the voyage was delayed, and more rights in disputes with the steamer companies. Such direct intervention went against traditional Liberal principles, and the new Italian social legislation proved just as controversial as the British Passenger Acts regulating emigration in the 1820s and 1840s.[5] In the end, Luzzatti's vision of state intervention for the individual and collective good triumphed over other protests. As a warning for foreign governments, the law's first article specified that "the Minister of foreign affairs can, in agreement with the Interior Minister, suspend emigration toward a determined region, for reasons of public order, or when the life, liberty, or property of emigrants may be in grave danger." The Italian state thus promised international intervention to protect expatriates' interests, and first used this power in the following year by blocking subsidized passage to Brazil.[6]

To regulate the foreign and domestic aspects of emigration, the law of

1901 created an independent emigration commissariat, reporting directly to the foreign minister.[7] The commissariat was responsible for the well-being of overseas emigrants before, during, and after their journey. Its agents inspected the Italian ports of Genoa, Naples, and Palermo, and traveling inspectors went to foreign ports and expatriate settlements. The emigration commissariat set maximum prices for third-class fares, and enforced strict regulations for safety, hygiene, food, water, air, light, and living space aboard passenger ships. Italian naval physicians inspected hygienic conditions aboard every emigrant ship, at the carrier's expense. The commissariat organized hospices in Italy for departing emigrants, and subsidized charities, cultural groups, and hospitals for Italians abroad, to promote their patriotism and economic success. All of these activities were funded by a new tax of eight lire ($1.60) per third-class berth, levied on steamer companies but paid by emigrants themselves. The fund grew enormously, much faster than the commissariat could spend it, as transatlantic emigration surpassed every expectation between 1902 and 1914. These burgeoning resources created a new touchstone of debate, as writers proposed, or opposed, using the fund for new attempts to settle Eritrea.[8]

As a separate measure, Luigi Luzzatti proposed to protect emigrants abroad by establishing a direct, secure conduit for emigrant remittances. To demonstrate its multifaceted importance, the measure was sponsored by the interior ministry and the ministries of treasury, foreign affairs, posts and telegraphs, and finances. Under the law, approved in February 1901, the nonprofit Banco di Napoli established an agency in New York City and made arrangements with seventy correspondent banks across the United States, South America, Europe, and North Africa, so emigrants could transfer money to Italy safely and reliably, at reduced rates. Emigrant Italians in the Americas soon transferred millions of lire through the Banco di Napoli.[9] The Banco became the Italian government's principal means of measuring the flow of emigrant remittances.

Luzzatti's twin laws, and the institutions they created, radically altered the politics of emigration and colonialism. Many politicians became directly involved in discussing emigration's successes and failures. The commissariat was governed by an emigration council that included Pasquale Villari, Luigi Luzzatti, Edoardo Pantano, Francesco Nitti, and the Socialist Filippo Turati; the emigration fund was ruled by a parliamentary oversight commission and subjected to an annual debate. The statistician Luigi Bodio served as the first commissioner of emigration, hiring talented inspectors such as Adolfo Rossi and Luigi Villari, son of Pasquale Villari, and establishing the commissariat's monthly bulletin, the voluminous *Bollettino dell'emigrazione*.[10] With energetic support from the Italian state, the nebulous theory of emigrant colonialism took a very concrete, quantifiable form, measured in the amount of remittances, exports, and return migration, and the number of Italian-language publications, Italian cultural associations, and Italian schools abroad. The foreign ministry administered Italy's African colonies and developed the economic and cultural resources of "free colonies" in the Americas. While the emigration commissariat concentrated on the emigrants' voyage and arrival, Italian consulates were responsible for most official aspects of Italy's informal colonialism. They also became a lightning rod for any dissatisfaction with Italy's expansion in the Americas. Consuls' responsibilities included monitoring men eligible for military service, caring for the indigent, boosting Italian imports and exports, and assisting local Italian hospitals, schools, mutual aid societies, music groups, literary circles, and athletic associations.[11] Emigrants would be united through culture, religion, and economics, not as fugitives, but heroes; not in a diaspora or "scattering," but in a consciously created, global community of Italians, under the umbrella of the Italian state.

Cultural Strategies of Italian Irredentism

Irredentist support for Italians worldwide was one of the most consistent aims of Italian foreign policy, expanding the Kingdom of Italy at the basic level of people and territory. The Italian government had already "redeemed" millions of Italians from Austrian rule, acquiring Lombardy after the Franco-Austrian-Italian war of 1859 and the Veneto and Western Friuli after the Austro-Prussian-Italian War of 1866. But the neighboring Italian-speaking regions of Trentino and Venetia Julia remained under the Austro-Hungarian dual monarchy. With Italian language as a label for definition and categorization, these "unredeemed" Italians came to be included in the newer political and cultural category of Italians Abroad, together with Italian emigrants worldwide. The Italian government intended to dissolve the distinctions of nationality and citizenship: Italian speakers from Austria who had never been part of the Kingdom of Italy, and who had never carried an Italian passport, were grouped alongside emigrants born under Italian rule but living outside of Italy. Thanks to the Dante Alighieri Society, the Italians of Trent, Trieste, and Fiume (present-day Rijeka, Croatia) began to appear in expositions and congresses featuring the accomplishments of Italians abroad.[12] The conjunction of Italian irredentism and emigration strengthened the symbolic and political weight of both movements.

Irredentism provided the developing ideology of emigrant colonialism with an established rhetoric and historical framework. Italy's unification, its modern Risorgimento, had been heralded by Italian intellectuals since the time of Dante and Petrarch. Napoleon Bonaparte's conquest of the Italian peninsula revived Italian patriotism and made unification seem a real possibility. His defeat, and the subsequent extension of Austrian rule, crushed Liberal hopes and led to a series of increasingly significant conspiracies and rebellions. The visionary Republican conspirator Giuseppe Mazzini called for the unification of Italy within her "sublime" frontiers ordained by God, meaning the entire peninsula up to the Alps. Mazzini admonished, "Your Country is one and indivisible. . . . you should have no joy or repose as long as a portion of the territory upon which your language is spoken is separated from the Nation."[13] During the 1848–1849 revolutions, which stretched from Venice to Palermo, Italians fought for unification under the green-white-red tricolor flag, in honor of the French Republican tricolor. Though these popular revolutions were defeated, the King of Piedmont-Sardinia managed to bring Italian regions under his rule in 1859, 1860, 1866, and 1870. But the process was abruptly cut short by Bismarck's formation of the Triple Alliance in 1887. The remaining Italians in Austria and in Hungary would have to wait to enjoy the benefits of Liberal Italian rule. Unification was postponed indefinitely, creating a seething discontent underneath the Italian political order.[14]

Trent and Trieste were valuable not only for their symbolism, population, and wealth, but also because of their strategic location. Italy's "natural frontiers" were also its most defensible frontiers. The Trentino/Südtirol region would complete the ring of mountains on Italy's northern border, and Venetia Julia would bring Italy to the Julian Alps in the east. Africanist politicians hoped to shift Italy's interests away from these European borders, claiming that distant Eastern Africa held a comparatively strategic value. They argued that Italy needed to acquire the territory along Eritrea's borders, to consolidate the colony as a site for Italian emigration. Antonino Di San Giuliano wrote Ferdinando Martini that "the [Ethiopian] plateau is a part of our national territory no less important than Trieste and Trent; in fact the true comparison is with the Trentino region."[15] This reasoning never really took root in Italian politics. In 1915, Italy enthusiastically entered World War I against Austria-Hungary in order to win Trent and Trieste in the "third war of Unification," without even thinking to ask the Entente for more territory in Africa.[16]

After Italy's African setbacks in the 1890s, the unredeemed Italian territories enjoyed a special place in the country's colonial projects. In an article on Italian schools abroad, the journal *L'Italia coloniale* noted, "we have special interest . . . in the study of our language in those provinces of the Austro-Hungarian Empire that ethnographically belong to Italy."[17] Cultural belonging, rather than political borders or legal citizenship, was the guiding principle of Greater Italy. Lackluster territorial possessions in East Africa now took second place to glowing Italian successes in the Americas and in the Adriatic. At the Milan Exposition of 1906, the Pavilion of Italians Abroad was divided threefold: "[first], regions of Italian language politically separated from the Kingdom of Italy: Canton Ticino, Corsica, Dalmatia and Fiume, Grisons and S. Bernardino, Malta, Nice, S. Marino, Trentino and Alto Adige, Venetia Julia (Eastern Friuli, Trieste and Istria); [second] Italian Territorial Colonies; and [third] Italian Communities in Foreign Countries."[18] In the organizers' design, the Eritrean exhibit booth was placed between exhibits on Italians in Argentina and the Italian Schools Abroad.[19] Thus Italy's costly "firstborn colony" was placed on an equal level with territories to which Italy laid no claim but cultural affinity. Moreover, Eritrea was clearly eclipsed by its colonial peers. The wealth displayed by Italians outside of East Africa had more visual impact than the samples of seeds and the collections of spears and hides sent from Eritrea. Above all, the pavilion's organizers planned to recreate Italy's lost glories in the unredeemed Adriatic sea: "The crowd, as soon as it entered, seemed to understand the epoch of our history, from when Italy dominated the seas, which are no longer ours, to the present longing for liberty, by looking at the copious collection of photographs of the monuments of our glorious maritime republics, built as a testament to their prosperous traffic, or the thoughtful profile of our martyrs, our thinkers, our artists and poets, eternal pilgrims of the Beautiful across the world."[20] The irredentist section completely overshadowed the colonial section, to the dismay of Eritrea's governor, Ferdinando Martini. King Victor Emmanuel III even refused to enter the pavilion, because he thought the exhibitors from Trieste might stage a political demonstration.[21] Irredentist demonstrations raised particularly thorny issues for the Italian government, which had to balance its foreign and domestic reputations. The Italian king could not disown the Italian Risorgimento, nor did he want an international incident with Italy's ally, Austria-Hungary. Two years afterwards, when the Hungarian-ruled Italians of Fiume organized a local committee to attend the First Congress of Italians Abroad at Turin and Rome, the king gave his official support to the Congress and, indirectly, to the inclusion of *fiumani* among his subjects abroad.[22] Seven years later, Italy would declare war on Austria-Hungary to redeem Trent and Trieste. Fiume too would eventually become part of Italy in 1924, bringing Mussolini one of his first successes in foreign policy.

Far from the loud publicity of Europe, American migration provided an ideal forum for the Italian government to carry out irredentist politics before World War I. Italian consuls in America provided services to all Italian speakers who came to them, whether they were citizens of the Kingdom of Italy or the Austro-Hungarian Empire. All Italian speakers formed part of the census of Italians abroad. As the consul of Florianopolis in southern Brazil explained, "it is difficult to make an exact count of those who have kept their nationality and those who have lost it, and those Italians belonging to unredeemed provinces, or Austrians and Dalmatians who speak Italian."[23] All were included, no matter the dialect, province, or passport. Italian mutual aid societies often included members from Austria-Hungary, although sometimes the groups fractured along these political lines.[24] The Catholic organization *Italica Gens*, supported by the Italian government and the National Association to Support Italian Catholic Missionaries, made a point of assisting all Italians, both Italian subjects and Austrian Italians. One of the group's priests boasted in 1915 that Italy's declaration of war on Austria "only confirms our labors and crowns them with an official sanction. . . . for the diffusion of *italianità* through peaceful but effective penetration, to make the fatherland ever more united and great, making worthy of Her those children she conceded to other nations, as conductors of energy and civilization."[25]

Emigration provided a political foil and a cultural opportunity for irredentist activity outside Italy.

Unredeemed Austrian Italians faced obstacles in assuming their identity as Italians abroad. To avoid anti-Italian discrimination in South America, some *triestini, trentini* and *friulani* claimed they were Austrians, to the horror of Italian patriots.[26] These emigrants carried Austrian passports, and set their legal identity against an ethnic hatred which targeted not their countrymen, but their fellow Italian speakers. Italian writers worried that the Austrians' example would divide the Italian community and dilute the cultural, super-political meaning of *italianità* abroad. Pan-German advocates also opposed the practical dissolution of the Austro-Hungarian Empire overseas. German merchants boycotted Austrian Italians in Brazil who asserted their Italian identity.[27]

Italy's obsession with Italians abroad gave irredentism a new focus and new political tools. The Italian language gained increased prestige as the defining label of Italian identity. Irredentism escaped its political ghetto and emerged in a broader political and cultural context. The unredeemed territories were raised to the same level as Italy's territorial possessions overseas, as if they were already a living part of Italy. It appeared only a matter of time before this cultural reality would become a political reality.

The Idea of Ethnographic Colonialism

In the early twentieth century, *italianità* gained a concrete scientific meaning through the discipline of ethnography. Italian writers and government officials began to label all Italian-speaking expatriate communities "ethnographic colonies," and attached to Italian ethnicity all of the unique cultural diversity of the Italian peninsula. Measuring Italy's international influence required a legitimate definition of "Italian" versus "foreign" cultures. Ethnography, the study of popular traditions and folk culture, provided the necessary cultural compass for Italy's colonial expansion.

Like their colleagues in Western Europe, Italian ethnographers began by specializing in "exotic" cultures, and their first triumphs were closely connected with European imperialism.[28] The Italian government supported the collection and exhibition of African art, musical instruments, and weapons, and Italian museums traded objects with the other European imperial museums. Artifacts from Ethiopia and Eritrea provided collections for the Ethnographic Museum of Florence, founded by Paolo Mantegazza in 1869, and the Italian National Ethnographic Museum in Rome, directed by its founder Luigi Pigorini from 1875 to 1925. Mantegazza later represented Italy at the Berlin Conference of 1884; the diplomatic negotiations there proved decisive in Europe's Scramble for Africa.[29] State-supported colonial ethnography was closely tied to the ramifications of imperial power. European study of East African "races" and cultures promised easier conquests and more effective colonial management. Ethnography also portrayed Africans in convenient terms: immature, different from Italians, retarded in their progress, but thriving under Italian rule. African ethnographic exhibits were featured in the Colonial Exhibitions at Turin in 1898 and 1911 and at Genoa in 1914; in 1911, Turin hosted Somali and Eritrean villages, while Genoa later sported Bedouin tents from Libya, imparting the illusion of complete colonial control.[30]

In the late nineteenth century, the lure of the exotic had distracted Italian social scientists from subjects at home. Italian geographers, for instance, endeavored to explore Africa, leaving much of Italy's interior unsurveyed and unmapped until after Italy's disastrous defeat at Adwa in 1896.[31] But with the decline of Italian Africa, scientists began to renounce their imperial topics in favor of local Italian studies. In 1905, the ethnographer Lamberto Loria was invited by Ferdinando Martini to the Colonial Congress in the Eritrean capital of Asmara. Loria made the voyage to Africa, but what he found in Italy fascinated him more. En route he stopped at Circello del Sannio in Campania and was struck by the originality of the local crafts, traditions, and psyche. The middle class complained of receiving only 15 percent in usurious interest for loans, while their fathers had taken in 30 percent before mass emigration and the influx of remittances. Upon his return from Africa, Loria came upon a group of emigrants in traditional dress, on their way to the port of Naples. He realized that while he had studied the cultures of Papua New Guinea and Eastern Africa for many years and at great expense, he had missed a lifetime's worth of research in Italy's own rich traditions.[32] Loria became a member of the Italian Colonial Institute and served as councilor on the Institute's Central Council from 1909 to 1912.[33] But his passion for colonial cultures had given way to the study and preservation of Italian cultures and societies, at home and abroad.[34]

To raise the prestige of Italian ethnography, Loria attempted to link his studies to more traditional anthropology. He condescendingly portrayed rural Europeans as prehistoric semisavages, but also brought a genuine respect for Italy's cultural diversity. He worried that "the leveling of progress" would destroy Italy's unique local cultures before they were scientifically documented.[35] In a patriotic project, Loria raised Italian folklore to a science, at the level of archeological anthropology and exotic ethnography: "we will understand the national thought and feeling in their fullness; not only from elect spokesmen, or the literature and art officially recognized as Italian, but from the raw and spontaneous flowers among the millions and millions of our brethren, still far from civil culture, but not unworthy of being heard, and no less Italian than us."[36] Using ethnographic examples, Loria argued for special laws to promote more effective development of the South, and other regions of Italy. He believed that Italy could achieve unity only by appreciating its regional diversity.[37]

Like Loria's, Ferdinando Martini's career illustrates the political eclipse of African colonialism by Italian emigration. After ruling Eritrea as governor for ten years, and failing to implement his major development projects, Martini returned to Italy in 1907. Still a representative in Parliament, Martini remained a colonial expert but was assigned to a different hemisphere. In 1910, under direct appointment by the king of Italy, Martini traveled to Argentina, Uruguay, and southern Brazil to promote connections between the Italian colonies and the Italian government, and to search out opportunities for Italian capital. At a banquet in Buenos Aires, Martini boasted of Italy's colonial prowess in ancient, medieval, and modern times, without mentioning Eritrea: "today the labors of Italians in Argentina also testify to the tenacious genius, the agile and diverse spirit of our race."[38] After a decade of labor in Italian Africa, Martini looked to the Americas for Italy's successful colonial expansion.

Martini worked directly with Lamberto Loria to rescue his Museum of Italian Ethnography, founded in 1907 in Florence as a radical departure from traditional ethnography. While Mantegazza's ethnographic museum in Florence displayed skulls from around the world to show mankind's supposed physical development, Loria collected folk art, music, lace, woodwork, utensils, and other cultural artifacts from all over the Italian peninsula. Loria became worried when the nobleman sponsoring the museum soon faced bankruptcy, threatening the future of the collection. Martini was serving on Rome's committee to organize the fifty-year anniversary celebrations of Italian unity, especially the National Exposition planned for 1911. Martini had previously promoted Eritrean Exhibitions, but he turned his attention to ethnography and emigration. In 1908 he invited Loria to display his collection in Rome as part of the 1911 festivities. Thanks to Martini and the funds of the Exposition, the Italian ethnographic museum was permanently established in Rome.[39]

Loria had found stable financing for his museum but still faced challenges in establishing exhibits that would represent Italy's rich culture without reinforcing regional divisions, prejudices, and competition. A National Ethnographic Museum documenting the peninsula's diversity might atomize an already elusive Italian national culture. At the First Italian Ethnographic Congress in 1911, scholars hotly debated whether to organize the museum by regions or by themes. Francesco Baldasseroni, who had worked closely with Loria in setting up the Exhibition in Rome, made a passionate plea for Italy's cultural unity and against imposing regional divisions upon a convoluted cultural map: "Is Italy nothing more than a political unity? Permit me my doubts. . . . The regional framework in Italy no longer exists, and one cannot expect a museum director to recreate it."[40] Baldasseroni aimed to "make Italians" culturally, with a united cultural identity to reinforce and reflect the country's political solidarity. He contended that Italy's regions had changed at different periods of history and that a geographical focus was better suited to isolated, primitive cultures. Despite the opposition of Pigorini and others, who favored a more traditional regional framework for the museum, in the end the museum was organized by occupations, crafts, and artistic genres.[41]

Italian ethnographers immediately applied their scientific studies to emigration, studying the exportation of a scientifically established Italian cultural identity. Baldasseroni called for a broad, complex, and thorough study of Italian expatriate cultures, investigating links to the emigrants' native communities and the influence of host societies. This would provide a cultural cartography for solving the problems of "Greater Italy":

We must ask ourselves: how far do the millions of Italians who abandon the Fatherland preserve their customs and traditions, or at what point do they accept foreign traditions? Where is the adaptation of emigrants the easiest? And when do the changes happen? Are Northern or Southern Italians more tenacious in maintaining their customs and habits? . . . this

ebb and flow of population, that goes abroad and returns home periodi-
cally, how does it change and when does it destroy local traditions? These
men in a continual double relationship between their civilization and a
foreign civilization: what elements do they most tenaciously preserve of
their culture and what do they accept of the other?[42]

Although important, such questions proved too difficult for Italian
scholars to answer. Amy Bernardy, professor of Italian at Smith College
in Massachusetts, reported on the ethnography of Italian colonies in the
United States. She noted that although Italians of the United States had
abandoned much of their regional dress and domestic crafts, they had
preserved their pastimes, such as bocce and puppet shows, and their regional culinary traditions.[43] Fortunately for Italy, food offered the most
important economic aspect of ethnographic colonialism. Authentic Italian cooking required imported preserves, cheeses, wines, vinegar, and
other ingredients and presented a substantial opportunity for Italian exports. In the United States, Italian cuisine first became established in a
secure immigrant niche, then expanded into the national market.[44]

Ethnography provided a powerful scientific basis for Italy's colonial mission. As envisioned by colonialists, Italy's cultural identity would triumph
over subject peoples in Africa and hold together against assimilationist
pressures in the Americas. In 1915 the president of the Italian Colonial
Institute, Ernesto Artom, distinguished between Italy's "colonies of direct
dominion" in Africa and her widespread "ethnographic colonies." He emphasized that the Colonial Institute had committed itself to both forms of
colonialism, on several fronts in Italy and abroad:

> promoting within our country that intense colonial movement, from
> which all civilized peoples draw prosperity and wealth, and to which
> Italy is called, by its traditions, geographic position, and demographic
> development; constituting an organization among the population
> colonies in the *great ethnographic empire*, which our people could have
> in the world, replacing the divided Italic members with a powerful vi-
> tal organism, pulsing with the heartbeat of a vigorous national life;
> [and] preparing our country for colonial life in the colonies of direct
> dominion, addressing the principal problems of our possessions of
> Libya, Eritrea, and Benadir.[45]

Artom employed organic metaphors, historical mandates, and natural
law in defining Italy's colonial mission. An international commitment to

Italians abroad would bring vigor and life to Italy itself. With the proper incentives, the Colonial Institute hoped to promote unity, solidarity, and synergy within Greater Italy, through a worldwide organization. Not only would colonies organize on a local level, but they would trade with each other in exports and imports. Applying the theory of ethnographic empire would thus bring wealth both to the emigrant colonies and to Italy.

3

Migration and Money

In Greater Italy, culture and economics were two sides of the same coin. Transplanted Italian men, women, and their families in emigrant colonies, if loyal to Italian social traditions and food culture, required extensive resupply. Italian exporters and shippers relied upon emigrants to purchase Italian products, and Italians abroad relied upon commerce for contact with their native land. When Italian trade failed to flourish in an expatriate colony, emigrants lost vital ties with their mother country. Brazil, Argentina, and the United States provide contrasting examples in the early twentieth century. The decline of Italian migration and exports to southern Brazil led to the social and cultural isolation of rural Italian-Brazilian settlements, as they lost regular communications with Italy. At the same time, growth in Italian exports to the United States and Argentina injected capital into the port cities of New York, Buenos Aires, Genoa, Naples, and Palermo. Part of this capital funded charities and cultural initiatives on both sides of the Atlantic. The frequent arrival of Italian ships in the Americas made return migration inexpensive, strengthening intercontinental ties. Those expatriates who sold Italian goods became natural leaders in developing "Italian" communities. Promoting an Italian identity was in their economic interest. Opportunities in Italian trade also provided a strong incentive for second-generation emigrants to learn standard Italian. From the perspective of Italians in the Americas, economic relations substantially justified their Italian identity. Vague ideas of *italianità* translated into concrete economic gains. Remittances and trade from emigrants became the keystone for the Liberal vision of emigrant colonialism.

Economic advantage underpinned the life of flourishing Italian communities abroad. Among many other concerns, trade with Italy was the fundamental tenet of the "New Ten Commandments of Italian Emigrants," published in May 1913 by the leading Italian newspaper of Argentina, *La Patria degli italiani:*

1. There is only one Fatherland, and your Fatherland is Italy. You shall love no other country as much as Italy.
2. You shall never name your fatherland without reverence. Exalt the glories of your Italy, which is one of the most ancient and noble nations in the world.
3. Remember the national holidays, wherever you might be. On these occasions, at least, forget your political party and religious faith; remember only that you are Italian.
4. Honor the official representative [consul] of your fatherland, and respect him as a symbol of the faraway fatherland, even if sometimes he displeases you.
5. You shall not kill a citizen of the Fatherland by erasing in yourself the Italian consciousness, feeling, and citizenship. You shall not disguise your name and surname with a barbaric transcription.
6. You shall not attack out of envy the authority and prestige of your compatriots who hold honorary appointments.
7. You shall not steal citizens from your fatherland, letting your children squander their *italianità* to become absorbed by the people among whom you have emigrated.
8. Be proud to declare yourself always, everywhere and on every occasion, Italian in origin and in sentiment, and be not servile, be not despised by those who host you.
9. *You shall always buy and sell, consume and distribute goods and merchandise from your fatherland.*
10. You shall marry only an Italian woman. Only with this and by this woman shall you be able to preserve in your children the blood, language, and feelings of your fathers and of your Italy.[1]

The widely circulated decalogue united the cultural and economic fears and desires of Greater Italy, as the leaders of Italian colonies in the Americas who distributed the commandments worried at length about the acculturation and integration of newly arrived immigrants. Fresh currents of immigration revitalized Italian communities abroad, but untutored independent newcomers could also undermine and fragment their local community and change the colony's relationship with host societies. Fragile emigrant communities needed careful cultivation to grow and thrive. The prestige and material success of well-established Italians abroad depended upon a thriving, patriotic, influential, and active community: hence the intense pressure and religious fervor attached to Italian colonial mores. Immigrants were enjoined always to exalt Italian culture, Italian industry, and especially Italian imports, before their fellow countrymen and in the eyes of non-Italians, with a civic religion of expatriate ritual, confession, and obeisance. Addressing male readers, *La Patria* ordered immigrants to preserve the Italian blood line with marital fidelity to the Italian race. This familial bond would uphold obedience to the previous nine commandments and prolong immigrants' Italian connections. The newspaper linked immigrants' ethnic "responsibilities" to the ancient biblical injunctions against murder, theft, and adultery, while urging them to rise above any particular religion or other division, "remembering only to be Italian." Far from a disinterested appeal, the decalogue reveals the economic motives of Italian importers.

Economic gain provided a fundamental motive for promoting Italian culture among expatriates. Dante meant dollar signs, in the crude formula of Giuseppe Prezzolini, the Fascist director of New York City's Casa Italiana at Columbia University: "as Dante and the Italian language become better known, more Italian products will be sold; in fact, as the prestige of Italian art, history, and literature increases, so much will increase the number of Americans who travel to Italy, who start using Italian products, who become used to Italian tastes and who, after returning home to America, will remain clients of Italian cooking and fashions."[2] Other Italian writers were more subtle. In his 1913 textbook on Greater Italy, Pierto Gribaudi urged the merchants and industrialists of Italy to "create, with the help of the political and ethnographic Greater Italy of which we have spoken, also a commercial Greater Italy. . . . Italian trade must follow the emigrants. . . . Let us set up *made in Italy* against the well-known *made in Germany;* this will not only be patriotic, but also extremely useful for our commercial expansion."[3] From Italy's perspective, the expatriate colonies offered vast economic and commercial opportunities. Gribaudi noted that the nearly six million Italians abroad sent half a billion lire into Italy every year.[4] A Socialist newspaper in Feltre, Veneto, printed the Emigrants' Ten Commandments from Buenos Aires and added an eleventh, calling on emigrants to help end migration by building up their homeland: "Work and contribute with all your strength so that Italy develops its economy to support industry and commerce and gradually lower its emigration."[5] Besides representing Italy effectively abroad, the emigrants could help at home by sending remittances and by buying Italian products. Italy came to rely upon its ethnic expansion overseas to sustain its domestic economy.

To understand, harness, and exploit the economic dimension of migration, the Italian state deployed an extensive statistical apparatus. Italy's expertise in demography and statistics is still reflected in scientific censuses worldwide, through the "[Corrado] Gini coefficient" and "[Vilfredo] Pareto interpolation." With migration, Italian statistics achieved a political and institutional apotheosis.[6] Italy's leading statistician, Luigi Bodio, became Italy's first General Commissioner of Emigration in 1901, to widespread acclaim. Under the guidance of Bodio and his successors, the Italian Emigration Commissariat approached emigration as a statistical phenomenon. In contrast, Britain and Germany followed a more interventionist policy, tied to political and imperial considerations. The Emigrants' Information Office in London and the *Zentralauskunftstelle für Auswanderer* in Berlin published pamphlets directly for emigrants, warning them away from certain countries and consistently recommending that they go to British or German territorial possessions, rather than taking their chances elsewhere.[7] The Italian Commissariat's official *Bollettino dell'emigrazione,* published from 1902 to 1927, reflected emigration's central economic importance for Italy, transcending Italy's territorial empire.[8] Rather than a periodical produced for Italian migrants themselves, the *Bollettino*'s thousands of pages addressed the needs of statisticians, economists, Italian state agencies, consulates, and other organizations serving migrants. This orientation freed the commissariat from articulating a unified, coherent policy for Italian emigration, which would have aroused divisive controversy. The *Bollettino* specialized in providing statistical, legislative, and anecdotal material from Italy and a wide array of foreign countries. Migration statistics were rehashed monthly, quarterly, annually, and by decade. Consuls wrote detailed academic reviews of the situation for emigrants in their locality. These lengthy dissertations were reworked and distributed to emigrants by Italy's Catholic and Socialist charities. With the voluminous *Bollettino,* the Italian state also distributed annual reports on the operations of the commissariat and the spending of the migration fund, built through the sacrifices of so many emigrants.

A developing network of financial and commercial exchange defined Greater Italy in ways more quantifiable and often more successful than Italy's cultural expansion. Trade and remittances provided Italy its most tangible benefits from emigration in the prewar period. Migrants sent home hundreds of millions of lire each year, in bank channels supported by the Italian state, contributing directly to Italy's industrial "takeoff" in the crucial years before World War I. Expatriate colonies, guided by official Italian Chambers of Commerce Abroad, provided Italian exports a crucial boost in certain markets. Although later criticized sharply by Italian Nationalists, the growth of remittances through emigration proved enormously important for Italy's economic development.

Remittances in the Italian Economy

In retrospect, the long period of peace from 1870 to 1914 stands out as a pivotal period in Europe's economic history. The technologies of the Second Industrial Revolution allowed nations to reinvent their economies on an unprecedented scale; only the computer revolution of the late twentieth century is comparable. Italy's crucial growth spurt began in 1896, which marked the end of an international depression and the liquidation of Italy's Ethiopian war, and lasted until 1913, following Italy's new war in Libya and the Mediterranean. Italian industrial production doubled in these seventeen years, growing on average between 4.3 percent and 5.4 percent annually. Italy's labor force turned increasingly to industry: between 1901 and 1911, 54 percent of the increase in the population of males over age ten was absorbed by the growth in manufacturing jobs. The power of Italy's industrial plant doubled between 1903 and 1911, reaching 1.17 million horsepower. In this period Italy entered the ranks of the world's wealthiest industrial nations.[9]

Emigrants' remittances were crucial in steadying this historic economic boom, just as remittances have benefitted economic development in the early twenty-first century.[10] Industrializing countries usually face a paradox: building up their technological and industrial base requires extensive imports, but these imports must be matched by exports or foreign loans to maintain the country's balance of payments in the international economy. Faced with a trade deficit, and forced to maintain their balance of payments, most developing countries suffer a devaluation of their paper currency on the international market, which forces a rise in interest rates and price inflation. Remittances allowed Italy to escape this financial dilemma. In the years before World War I, Italy's exports matched only 60–80 percent of its imports, yet the country enjoyed a steady currency and low interest rates. Before 1890, Italy had financed two-thirds of its trade deficit with foreign loans, but after 1900, remittances balanced out foreign loans, and counterbalanced Italy's spending on imported foreign goods. From 1901 to 1913, against Italy's commercial deficit of 10,230 million lire ($2 billion) stood an "invisible credit" of 12,291 million lire ($2.45 billion). More than half the credit came from remittances, more than a third from tourism, and the rest from shipping. The credit turned Italy from a debtor nation into a modest creditor nation. Directly through remittances, and indirectly through exports and shipping, migration became a decisive factor in Italy's favorable balance of payments, by balancing Italy's internal consumption with external inputs. Thanks to its international credits, Italy was able to industrialize without relying extensively on foreign loans, without serious price tensions, and without lowering real wages.[11]

Remittances flowed through a variety of channels, and included money sent through banks, money donated to the Italian Red Cross and other Italian charities, and money carried home by returning migrants. Up to the end of the nineteenth century, Italian emigrants usually sent money home by postal money orders. For the period 1901–1915, 41.0 percent of Italy's net gain in money orders came from the United States, and 51.6 percent came from Europe and the Mediterranean Basin (see Appendix, Figure 3.1).[12] But even as Italy received tens of millions of lire annually through banks and the postal system, these money transfers presented widespread abuses. Emigrants in the Americas could not normally speak the language of their host country and could not use local banks, which insisted upon English, Spanish, or Portuguese. Especially in the United States, many Italians fell prey to *padroni* or bosses who arranged for immigrants' food, work, housing, and banking, all at exploitative rates. Many bosses in New York City enjoyed international connections to the criminal *camorra* in the port city of Naples. These bilingual bosses were recommended to immigrants by dishonest fellow Italians in the colony, or by emigration agents in Europe. The bosses' greatest opportunity for profit was in banking services, offered conveniently through saloons, grocery stores, and even shoe-shining stands. When sending remittances to Italy, small-scale *banchisti* usually delayed the transfer of funds to allow time for speculation, often resulting in bank failure. From time to time these "bankers" absconded to Europe with the banks' funds. These tragedies are reflected in the song "Se n'è fuiuto 'o banchiere" (The banker has fled), recorded in New York City in the 1920s:

> Cursed neighbor, why did you come to my house,
>   to get me in this mess
> My wife Maria was right, who told me,
> "Oh, watch out for this banker, he is a big scoundrel."
> Friend Antuone told me, "You know, this banker is honest,
>   he has millions" . . .
> Ah, ah, ah, the banker has massacred me! Ah, ah, ah,
>   my neighbor has deceived me!
> My wife was a dishwasher, earning thirty cents a week . . .
> We ate dry bread, to save money.
> Now I am worn out and ruined.[13]

While many immigrant bankers were honest, scoundrels gave all Italian bankers a bad name. Immigrants had little redress, for the same reason they went to the illegal bank in the first place: local officials did not understand their dialects. Bank fraud among immigrants was very difficult for local governments to prosecute, since absconders usually fled the country and immigrants rarely testified before authorities. Italians in large colonies at least enjoyed a competitive choice between bankers, but Italian bankers in small settlements usually exercised a monopoly, often controlling even the local post office.[14]

The Italian state became directly involved in emigrant banking to rescue migrants from fraud and to protect the financial gains of emigrant colonialism. Legislation for "tutelage of remittances and the savings of Italian emigrants abroad," enacted in Parliament on 1 February 1901, was born as a twin to the emigration law of 31 January. The renowned Banco di Napoli, founded in 1539 as a charitable credit institution for southern Italy, contracted with Parliament to transfer remittances from the Americas to Italy at special rates. Inexpensive "emigrant money orders" could be cashed at all local offices of the Banco di Sicilia, Banca d'Italia, all Italian post offices, and of course at the Banco di Napoli. To limit the competition between the nonprofit Banco di Napoli and private banks, and to focus the Banco on money transfers, Parliament did not allow the Banco to extend loans or issue currency overseas. The bank did offer special rates for currency exchange at the port of Naples and at all its branches, and opened its own agency in New York City after a wave of American bankruptcies in the Panic of 1907.[15]

Even though the Banco di Napoli was a nonprofit institution, its involvement in emigration provoked widespread protests and controversy. Bankers and moneychangers in Italy and the Americas faced enormous reductions in their exploitative profits and speculations; after all, this was Parliament's objective. Italian-American newspapers sympathetic to the bankers claimed that the project was a tax-accounting scheme, to find out exactly how much each emigrant earned and carried home. Sicilians resisted the Banco di Napoli because of ancient regional antagonisms; the bank had been excluded from business in Sicily since 1848. In contrast to the United States, South American governments opposed Italian intervention as unwanted competition against local businesses. The Banco di Napoli organized a publicity counteroffensive, to appeal to emigrants and to reassure legitimate bankers that the Banco intended only to oppose dishonesty and fraud. Bank examiners in New York and New Jersey welcomed Italy's aid against private, unregulated banks.[16] To limit popular opposition, the Banco selected local bankers within the Italian American community to act as its corresponding representatives overseas, such as the Banco de Italia y Rio de la Plata for Argentina and the Banca Italo-Americana of San Francisco for the Pacific United States. This latter bank competed within the Italian community against A. P. Giannini's Bank of Italy, later Bank of America. Nicola Miraglia, director of the Banco di Napoli, specifically rejected American Express's application to handle remittances in the United States or worldwide: "we would end up placing ourselves entirely in their hands, perhaps without benefit, certainly raising immense difficulties and uproar . . . it is not intended for this service to be entrusted to foreigners."[17] Instead of American Express, the correspondent for the eastern United States was the Italian American Cesare Conti, whose institution went bankrupt in 1914. Despite delays and setbacks with correspondent banks, the Banco di Napoli streamlined its services and processed hundreds of millions of lire in remittance orders.

Thanks to centralized remittances, the Italian government could now transparently gauge the flow of money from emigrant colonies. Emigrants had always sent money home, but after 1902 the Emigration

Commissariat relied heavily upon the Banco di Napoli's statistics to justify the importance of migration for Italy. Remittances held pride of place in the most exhaustive compendium of Italian emigration statistics, *Annuario statistico della Emigrazione Italiana dal 1876 al 1925*, published by the Emigration Commissariat in 1926. In 1902, its first year of activity, the Banco processed 9.3 million lire in remittances. Volume nearly tripled to 23.6 million lire in the following year. Prewar levels of remittances held at 84 million lire. After 1916, because of wartime inflation and currency fluctuations, remittances soared to a peak of 980 million lire in 1920. For the period 1902 to 1915, a full 70.4 percent of the remittances came from the United States (see Appendix, Figure 3.2). The United States Federal Immigration Commission reported that in 1907 alone, 52 million dollars were sent back to Italy through 2,625 private banks.[18] The Italian Parliament had intervened to fight injustice, but the Banco created a smooth system for remittances just in time for an unprecedented boom in Italian migration to the United States, and an unprecedented capital transfer into the Italian economy.

Other channels contributed to the inexorable rise of remittances. Many emigrants carried money home on their person, especially the "swallows" who migrated seasonally to Argentina. These funds did not appear in Italian state statistics. Remittances sent as international money orders were overshadowed by commercial money orders from imports and exports, while money sent in the regular mail was untraceable. An indirect measure of remittances came from deposits held in Italian postal savings banks by Italians living abroad. Thanks to higher wages abroad and a favorable exchange rate, the percentage of savings deposits in Italy held by emigrants increased geometrically from 0.02 percent in 1890 to 31 percent in 1909. Deposits held by expatriates dropped precipitously to 6.5 percent in 1910, due to the Panic of 1907 in the United States, the resulting unemployment among immigrants, and return migration. The percentage of emigrant-held deposits increased again with revived migration and the emigration wave of 1913 after the Libyan War, rising to 12.3 percent by 1914. When the Italian lira and other European currencies collapsed at the end of World War I, the expatriates' share of deposits in Italy soared to 41 percent in 1919, 61 percent in 1920, and peaked at 63 percent in 1921. Hundreds of millions of dollars, reis, and pesos poured into Italy and revolutionized economic life in towns and villages across the peninsula. The injection of capital cut local lending rates, permitted the construction of new homes, allowed for richer pageantry at the feasts of local saints, financed tax payments, and raised the value of land, allowing investment in orchards and intensive agriculture.[19]

Immigrant remittances aroused the worst fears of American nativists. Without loyalty to their adopted home, and without long-term plans for their future in America, temporary migrants appeared unwilling to invest their money in America and less likely to join strikes. Nativists feared cheap competition in labor markets and the importation of immigrant strikebreakers. In 1897, a sponsor of restrictive legislation before the United States Congress viciously attacked all temporary migrants: "Those whom it is the universal sentiment to exclude are the paupers, imbeciles, criminals, and other off-scourings of Europe, together with alien-contract laborers, and the 'birds of passage,' who, retaining domicile and citizenship in other lands, fatten on the substance of our own."[20] Ironically, Italians felt the same way about "alien" immigrants to their own colonies. Like nativists in the United States, Renato Paoli, the secretary of the Italian Colonial Institute, hurled racist insults against the Greeks and Indians who sent home remittances from their shops in Eritrea: "Both races are the most irreducible and the least assimilable. . . . As soon as they gather enough money, [they] go back to Greece and India, and turn their businesses over to a compatriot. They lack any patriotic feeling toward the colony that hosts them: they seek to exploit it, often in the most unfair way, without giving anything back. This is the most dangerous class, in my judgment, for the future of the colony. . . . Silent, disciplined, calm, parasitic, they attach onto the colony's vital parts and slowly suck its living blood, that is, its capital."[21] Although Paoli nicknamed Eritrea "the Abyssinians' America," an immigrant magnet rumored in Africa to be "a fantastic land of inexhaustible wealth," he opposed immigration from any place but Italy.[22] This imperialist antipathy, even as millions of Italian emigrants relied on the acceptance of other countries, shows the two-faced bias of the emigration/immigration dichotomy: approval of the former, hatred and mistrust of the latter.[23] Yet nativist fears of immigrant labor were misplaced. Both temporary and permanent migration served a vital role in developing economies in the nineteenth century, as in the twenty-first century. Despite opposition, mass immigration provided an essential labor supply to the growth of industry in the United States and agriculture in South America.

The Italian Chambers of Commerce Abroad

Emigration offered new opportunities for Italian industry, as optimistic Italian expansionists hoped to link the export of Italian goods with the export of Italian people.[24] The fatherland's industry and agriculture stood to gain or lose a great deal in international markets, particularly in Argentina and the United States. If expatriates did not buy Italian products abroad, but produced their own Italian-style goods overseas and dumped them at cheap prices back in Italy, their competition could ruin entire sectors of the national economy. Italy needed to maintain a strong, competitive export presence among expatriate colonies, or any temporary economic gains from emigration could backfire.

Far too important to be left to the invisible hand of laissez-faire ideology, the economics of Italy's expansion were coordinated through the Italian Chambers of Commerce Abroad. Unlike U.S. Chambers of Commerce, which are independent and sometimes highly critical of the United States government, the Italian Chambers were actual representatives of the state, entrusted with the nation's export interests. The Ministry of Foreign Affairs first established the international network in 1883 and ordered consuls to establish and support chambers of commerce wherever possible; they were maintained by the Ministry of Commerce, which sought their advice and gave them lavish subsidies.[25] The Chambers aimed to evoke patriotism throughout Italy's emigrant colonies, as when the Italian Chamber of Montevideo, Uruguay, was founded in 1883:

> We are revindicating our Nation's colonizing traditions, which made it great in all ages, especially in the great history of the Republics— especially Venice which made her flag wave gloriously in the most distant seas. England and France impose their civilization with cannon shot, but Italy presents itself with a peaceful mission, seeking only to expand its vitality in distant countries. . . . Let no one be distanced from the moral and material benefits, which our Fatherland carries to far-off lands. We do not want the Chamber of Commerce to be a caste; we want it to unite all laborers who love the Fatherland and want to honor it. . . . No one can say that Italy is imposing itself, when its means of battle are for the profit of civilization.[26]

Like Einaudi, the Chamber envisioned the peaceful colonialism of economic expansion uniting all Italian communities abroad. Italy's cultural superiority was linked with tangible products for export. As noted by a French newspaper, the Montevideo Chamber displayed vermouth (including Martini), mortadella (bologna), earthenware, hams, and pastas "perfectly arranged with everything necessary for its purpose, thanks to the subsidy which the [Italian] government has granted this useful institution."[27] The Chambers united the colonies' notables, who served their own economic interests and Italy's interests by boosting trade with the mother country. At every turn they encouraged their fellow Italians to buy Italian products and send deposits to Italian banks.

The Italian Chambers of Commerce Abroad exerted local influence in their communities and international influence through a worldwide network. By 1911, chambers were established in Buenos Aires and Rosario in Argentina; Montevideo, Uruguay; Sao Paolo, Brazil; and Mexico City. In Europe, chambers represented Italian commerce in Berlin, London, Paris, Marseilles, Brussels, and Geneva; in the Mediterranean Basin, there were chambers in Constantinople, Smyrna (Izmir, Turkey), Tunis, and Alexandria, Egypt. In the United States, Italian chambers were formed in San Francisco, New York City, and Chicago, and later in Boston, New Orleans, and San Antonio. These organizations overseas were the crowning jewels of the *Unione delle Camere di Commercio* in Rome, which also represented more than forty chambers in Italy. Italian chambers abroad published bulletins of regulations, tariffs, and trading contacts, and maintained public museums of Italian industrial and agricultural samples, on display for local importers and retailers to taste, touch, and feel. The chambers also sent local products to Italy's commercial museums in Milan, Turin, and Venice, to encourage Italy's international trade.[28]

To coordinate their strategy and tactics, the Italian Chambers Abroad organized a series of international congresses, in cooperation with the chambers of the peninsula. Rome hosted the first conference in 1901, followed by Paris in 1911, Brussels in 1912, and Naples in 1913. The outbreak of war in 1914 shattered the chambers' cohesion, as each chamber rallied to the cause of its host country. Before the war, the united chambers called upon Italy and other countries to lower tariffs, establish Italian credit unions abroad, improve shipping and communications, and make other changes to benefit international commerce. The Chambers Abroad worked to break down administrative barriers within Greater Italy, proposing that the Italian postal service reduce postage rates for foreign mail to domestic letter rates. This measure would have erased national boundaries for postal communications; wherever an Italian sent a letter, the price would have been the same. Postage between Italy and Eritrea was already at domestic rates. The proposed resolution would have extended the postal regime for Italy's formal colonies also to Italy's expatriate colonies, just as Italy had negotiated in French Tunisia. Although this proposal failed, the Chambers of Commerce advised the Italian government on all its trade policies by offering an independent, on-site perspective and providing crucial information and representation for Italian interests abroad.[29]

One example of a successful chamber, with an elaborate political and social agenda, was the Italian Chamber of Commerce in Tunis. France's establishment of a Tunisian Regency in 1881 had thwarted Italy's own hopes for dominating the territory. Tunisia was less than a hundred miles from Sicily, and Italians had built up an influential community in the Bey's court. Four years after France established its protectorate over Tunisia, the Italian middle class of Tunis created a Chamber of Commerce to defend its interests, and Italy's interests, under the new regime.[30] The Chamber became a lynchpin of Italian resistance to French assimilation. Thanks to continued immigration, by 1900 Italians made up seven eighths of the colony's European population of eighty thousand people. Tunisia was supposed to be a settlement colony, like its neighbor Algeria, but the settlers were Italian, not French! France's leading colonial theorist, Paul Leroy-Beaulieu, changed his definition of "settlement colonies" to make Tunisia a "colony of exploitation," as in central Africa; the Italians, and other Tunisian residents, were meant to be exploited. The French administration barred immigrants from employment on public works or in the colonial government, unless they adopted French citizenship. Even after 1902, when the governments of Rome and Paris made a diplomatic rapprochement, the Italians and French in Tunis continued to feud.[31]

Despite harassment and persecution, the Italian community rallied around its Chamber of Commerce. Subsidized by the Italian Foreign Ministry, the Italian chamber published a weekly (and later daily) newspaper, *L'Unione: Organo della Colonia e della Camera Italiana di Commercio ed arti,* to inspire the Italians of Tunisia.[32] The chamber united the Italian elites and projected a permanent Italian identity in Tunis. Attacking this chamber, the French colonial paper *La Quinzaine coloniale* revived discussion of "the Italian peril" in 1905, even while noting that attention had turned to the "black peril, red peril, yellow peril . . . what a dreadful polychromy!"[33] Colonialists agreed that the Sicilian immigrants from Palermo and Trapani were necessary to build Tunisia's infrastructure, but their compatriots posed a problem for France: "Above the workers and farmers, organizing them and trying to lead them, there is an Italian bourgeoisie at Tunis of industrialists, merchants, lawyers, doctors, engineers, professors, and architects. . . . Shorn of political influence, and excluded little by little from all public functions, they wanted to form and have attempted to maintain an Italian group, impenetrable to French influence. To accomplish this aim they have gathered themselves in a Chamber of Commerce, intended to guard their common interests, and have created numerous educational and welfare services."[34] The French colonialists complained of the bourgeoisie's celebrations of an Italian civil religion, using ceremony and ritual to mobilize the Italian community: "to support the cult of *italianità,* the Italian bourgeoisie in Tunis does not miss any occasion to manifest its faithfulness to the Mother-Fatherland *(la Mère-Patrie).* All the patriotic anniversaries are pretexts to deploy Italian processions, with flags and banners, in the streets of Tunis."[35] Ominously, the Italian workers of Tunisia celebrated Italian holidays rather than Bastille Day. Why did the Italians of Tunisia resist assimilation, while the Italians of Algeria became naturalized Frenchmen? French colonialists replied, "it is the presence of bourgeois leaders, long established in the country and who, through a flexible resource of credit institutions, mutual aid societies, and schools, strive to maintain the mass of their countrymen in a spirit closed to French influence and alive in the cult of *italianità.*"[36] Despite the annoying independence of the Italian community, the French government decided not to label Italian immigration as undesirable, as the United States authorities had done, but instead looked for new ways to profit from the immigrants' labors.

    To limit the political and social influence of the Italian Chamber, officials in Paris ordered the creation of a French Chamber of Commerce in Tunis. Like Italy and other European countries, France had begun to create its own network of foreign chambers of commerce in 1883. To France's embarrassment, however, the plan was thwarted because almost all the "serious" French merchants in Tunis refused to participate in a French chamber of commerce under the French protectorate. They felt that opposing the Italians openly would be bad for their business. The consul noted that "the creation of a French Chamber would in effect justify the Italian Chamber and revive the conflict between the two colonies [French and Italian]" within Tunisia.[37] The best France could do was to organize an "International" Chamber of Commerce in friendly allegiance with the Italian Chamber. For France, Tunisia remained a foreign country, administered under the French Foreign Ministry instead of the Colonial Ministry. Although France exercised a formal protectorate over Tunis, the Italian expatriate colony exerted a stronger influence. Tunis appeared more Italian than French.

After Crispi's fall from power in 1896, Paris and Rome ended their tariff war and steadily developed friendly ties. Italy recognized France's possession of Tunisia; France guaranteed the protection of the Italian schools in Tunis, Bizerte, Goletta, Sfax, and Susah (Sousse), and set letter postage between Tunisia and Italy at twenty centimes, the same price as Italian domestic mail, instead of the standard twenty-five centimes for international mail. In 1905 Italy lowered the cost of its domestic mail to fifteen centimes, and in turn requested France to lower the cost of postage from Italy to Tunis.[38] The French government was mortified to contemplate the Italian ambassador's request:

> There are two kinds of problems with accepting the Italian proposal: First, we would give the impression to the Italian population of Tunisia, and we would help strengthen the feeling among Italians in Italy, that Tunisia, from a territorial point of view as well as a postal point of view, is in some way an annex of Italy. The consul has pointed out a very convincing example of this: the day after the new [lower] Italian domestic tariff went in force, almost all the letters brought to Tunisia by the Palermo courier on 6 September 1905 were stamped 0f.,15 instead of 0f.,20. Indubitably, whatever we do to facilitate exchanges between the Italians of Tunisia and those of the peninsula will strengthen the already close ties between the immigrants and their country of origin. This would voluntarily slow down and complicate the work of assimilating the Sicilian colony into the Regency, to which all the incessant efforts of our policy must lead.[39]

The French Foreign Ministry emphasized that Tunisia's economic base was its Italian population, numbering one hundred thousand in 1906. If France lowered postal rates on the 860,000 letters sent each year from Tunisia to Italy, the colonial administration would lose 43,000 francs annually and become insolvent. Exploiting these poor Italian immigrants therefore remained a state priority. The French prime minister rejected the Italian request in 1905 and again in 1907, noting that "the Italian government does not conceal its ardent desire to gain a concession that would represent an important benefit for its policy and influence in the Regency."[40] Emigrants' correspondence with their families and friends provided a critical link between the Italian colony and the Italian metropole, and French colonial authorities aimed to tax, exploit, and attenuate this connection as far as possible.

Affection for Italian expatriates, however, could also hurt Italian industry. Italians were slow to realize that their expatriate cousins could become potent trading rivals, favored by high American tariff barriers that put European products at a disadvantage. At the first exposition of Italians abroad, the Italo-American Exposition in Genoa of 1892, the generous and short-sighted jury gave special honor to wines made by the heirs of Columbus in "the young Latin America." The jury gave Brazilians and Argentinians official praise and validation, even when Italian competitors were more deserving: "if in some cases the prize appears greater than merited, this is because we wanted to encourage, and extend a helping hand, to those who are pioneers on new or unknown paths. . . . We desire to and must aid our compatriots . . . [out of] feelings of brotherhood and gratitude."[41] The Italians saw the Americans as an economic alter ego: "all in all, they are flesh of our flesh, and blood of our blood; but it is easy to see they have a great and almost indestructible supremacy over us. They can begin where we end; to the intact and unchained forces of primitive nature they unite the power of our civilization, which we inherit with the burden of many old traditions and troublesome fetters."[42] The Genoese jury viewed Italians in America not as rivals, but with the same mystical confidence and condescension as Luigi Einaudi. He insisted that expatriate industries never competed against their fatherland and would at worst acquaint Americans with Italian products.[43]

By contrast, the Italian Chambers of Commerce in the United States fought for support within the Italian community and for recognition outside the Italian community. The Italians of San Francisco had created a chamber in 1885, but the Italians of New York could not agree how to organize themselves until 1887. The New York chamber's greatest fear was that Italy and things Italian would hold a poor reputation in North

America. At first the chamber only provided information about Italian exports and displayed product samples, but soon the organization adopted an activist role in opposing restrictions on immigration, supporting the commemoration of Columbus Day in the State of New York, and lobbying for customs reform and cheap transportation to better distribute Italian goods throughout the country.[44] The group lobbied the Italian government to set up an affiliate of the Banco di Napoli in New York City, to fight against the illegal Italian bankers.

The chamber of New York also fought strenuously against the distribution of adulterated and false Italian products, which could give *made in Italy* a bad name. In the United States, American products could be legally labeled "Florentine" or "Italian," even if they did not come from Florence or Italy. Bars sold "martinis" without a drop of Martini vermouth and cheesemongers sold "Parmesan" cheese that did not come from Parma province. Oil wholesalers sold "pure olive oil" that was a third, a half, or two-thirds cottonseed oil; wine sellers refilled the distinctive Chianti wine flasks with bad American wines and sold them as Italian. The New York chamber sought to awaken Italy to the threat of American competition. It urged a ban on bottle-makers' export of empty Italian wine bottles and convinced the Italian government to ban the export of rennet *(caglio)*, essential to the manufacture of Italian cheeses. The chamber reserved a special invective for the "blind" Italian industrial expositions that had given prizes to American wines produced in direct competition with Italian wines.[45] Cheap products were falsely labeled "Italian" in the United States, but in Britain Italian exports suffered the opposite problem. Some British retailers did not allow Italian products to be judged on their own merits. Italian furniture was marketed as English, silk from Como marked as from Lyons, and Biellese wool sold as Manchester cloth.[46] Einaudi's vision of Italian products conquering the world faced the obstacles of misrepresentation, prejudice, and outright fraud. Only community organization among expatriates, and the consistent defense of their social and economic interests, could improve the reputation of an embattled ethnic minority.

The long-sought link between emigration and increasing exports proved tenuous. Nonetheless, certain Italian industries saw a dramatic rise in exports to countries receiving Italian migrants, especially Argentina and the United States. Even as domestic wine and pasta production increased in these two countries across the Atlantic, they imported more and more Italian pasta, wine, vermouth, cheese, and sweets. Adolfo Rossi had noted in 1882 that Italian wines were practically unknown in the western United States, but the Italian vineyards of California persevered in creating a new market for wine in the United States and raising demand for Italian wine imports, as Einaudi had predicted.[47] Other principal Italian exports of the period included cotton cloth and thread, marble, dried fruits, and citrus fruits. Piero Gribaudi noted that Italian American glove makers in the United States took advantage of high tariff protection to beat out Italian imports, but "we should not be so pessimistic to believe that emigration will be more dangerous than useful to Italian exports." Italy had benefitted from a sudden new demand abroad for Parmesan and pecorino cheese, canned tomatoes, salted fish, vegetables, and olive oil.[48] Italian exports to the United States almost doubled between 1901 and 1914, reaching 272 million lire in 1909. This achievement was tightly linked to population migration; importers concentrated almost exclusively on the Italian immigrant market, without reaching out to a broader national market until after World War I.[49]

Emigration and the Italian Merchant Marine

Italy's export industries benefitted indirectly from migration, but the shipping industry reaped direct profits. Even Italy's royal family joined in the business, forming the Lloyd Sabaudo line and naming ships after various princes. Economists claimed that migration secured the survival of Italy's merchant marine during a period of intense competition from Britain and Germany, as sailing ships became obsolete and were replaced by steamships.[50] The expensive new ships carried smaller crews and reduced transatlantic passages from two months to two weeks, but required supplies of iron and coal not plentiful in Italy. In the early twentieth century, emigration's new consumer market offered the solution to an impending shipping crisis. Italy's leading ports, shipping companies, and naval construction yards rapidly specialized in migrant transportation during the emigration boom of 1905–1914, under the regulation of the Emigration Commissariat.

When Italy's mass migration began in the 1880s and 1890s, crude speculation and complete deregulation led to horrific conditions for emigrants. Independent emigration agents, condemned as "traffickers in human flesh," recruited clients in the countryside for struggling and

poorly equipped Italian shippers. Agents lied to their clients and connected them with the shipping line that paid the highest bonus, not lines
that were fast, safe, or even routed to the emigrant's chosen destination.[51] Small shipping companies speculated on each voyage by combining emigrants and cargo in the hold. Emigrants were more profitable than
grain or other cargo, but competition was so keen that the emigrants' fare
of 60 lire ($12) did not cover the cost of emigrants' food for the voyage.
Writing in 1894, Ferruccio Macola condemned these "slave-traders of
1893," who rented old ships built for coal transport and loaded them with
human cargo: "With the knife blade of competition they pare down the
conditions of emigrants stowed in the cargo hold, like anchovies in tin
cans, because their sheer number compensates the expenses [of the spec-
ulation]. The steamers rigged by these greedy people become sinister
ghost ships, which mark their slow path across the sea with a line of cadavers."[52] Slow sailing ships could take forty to sixty days to cross the
Atlantic, and could easily run out of fresh water. Macola noted that a
single voyage could lose two or three dozen children to disease, because
500 passengers were packed into 500 cubic meters.[53]

These disastrous voyages were halted by the Emigration Commissariat, established by the Emigration Law of 1901. The commissariat
regulated all ships carrying emigrants from Italian ports and from Le
Havre, France. Shipping lines operating from other ports were not allowed to sell tickets or recruit passengers in Italy; the Emigration Commissariat assumed that agents would misrepresent these voyages and
cheat their customers. Italian inspectors and doctors traveled on each
emigrant voyage at the shipper's expense, with full powers to enforce the
commissariat's regulations. Such interventionism went against Liberal
scruples and became the hallmark of truly historic social legislation. To
preserve a free market in emigrant transportation, the Italian government allowed foreign shippers to compete freely with Italian lines in Italian ports, even if Italian shippers were denied the same privilege abroad.
Lobbyists argued to ban foreign shippers from the Italian market, claiming this would work wonders for the Italian merchant marine. Likewise,
some British shippers called on their government to exempt them from
the Italian regulations.[54] The Italians rejected all such proposals, in the
interests of Italian emigrants.

Shippers became most agitated when the commissariat banned their
unsafe or unseaworthy ships from emigration service. In 1907 the com-

missariat withdrew permission for the *Sicilian Prince* and *Neapolitan Prince* to carry Italian emigrants. The Prince Line combined emigrants, grain, and other cargo in the hold; poorly laden, one of the two ships "rolled forty-two degrees in a calm sea."[55] To increase its profits, the Prince Line exploited the most vulnerable of emigrants, those who had failed mandatory health inspections. In Italian ports, authorities inspected each passenger according to the same criteria as the American processing station at Ellis Island, verifying emigrants' health, sanity, morality, and ability to work. The United States required this inspection to spare emigrants a rejection at immigration centers and a round trip home at the expense of the shipping company. However, the Prince Line and other shippers took rejected passengers on as "crew," for a sizeable sum. This "crew" would conveniently "desert" on the other side of the ocean. This reduced the real crew to a minimum and compromised the ship's safety.[56] The Prince Line was supposedly an Italian company renting English ships, but the Italian operators were actually a front for an English company. The company appealed to the British ambassador for help, but he refused to support the claims. Another British company, the Anchor Line, complained of unfair discrimination in 1903, claiming that their aging but "strong" ships had been blacklisted by Italian inspectors who "are not infrequently doctors who may never have been to sea and are totally ignorant of the surroundings as well as of the natural exigencies and discomforts to be expected on board ship." The British ambassador sided with the Italian inspectors, most of whom were surgeons in the Italian navy, and reported that the Italian government welcomed the traffic of honest and efficient British shippers.[57]

By restricting operators like the Prince and Anchor Lines, the Emigration Commissariat dramatically increased the safety, reliability, and decency of Italian emigration after 1901. This encouraged more people to emigrate and expanded the industry as a whole. The pressure of foreign competition quickly led to faster, safer, and better ships. Between 1904 and 1909 nearly the entire Italian transatlantic fleet was replaced with new ships constructed in Italy and in England.[58] Tragedies continued, nonetheless; on 4 August 1906 the Navigazione Generale Italiana's fine ship *Sirio,* en route from Genoa to Brazil, shipwrecked off the coast of Portugal and more than 150 people drowned. The passenger lists were not in order, and for several weeks the Emigration Commissariat could not determine who had perished.[59]

For politicians of this period, emigration's boost to the Italian merchant marine carried a direct link to Italy's international power. Shipping was considered an adjunct and a coefficient for the navy: from 1860 until 1946 the Italian "merchant marine" and the "military marine" (Italian Navy) were governed together by the *Ministero della Marina*. A former undersecretary of this ministry, Admiral Leone Reynaudi, became the second Commissioner for Emigration in 1904, following the statistician Luigi Bodio, with a mandate to build up Italy's international power through migration.[60] Italian writers often invoked the *marina,* including the Navy and merchant marine, as the partner and protector of expatriate expansion overseas. Shortly after the brief Anglo-German-Italian blockade of Venezuela, in 1903 the journal *L'Italia coloniale* reminded Parliament of the importance of Italian ships calling in foreign ports: "Until the Italian Parliament realizes that Italy needs a rich and powerful navy, it will be useless to aim for good policies . . . without ships the credit of the fatherland cannot be maintained. The Italians abroad . . . cannot be protected without ships. Ships carry the Italian flag to wave frequently in faraway ports, they prevent disorders, give peaceful admonishments, succor [*ricuorano*] our own . . . It takes a good, strong *marina,* and money spent on it is anything but unproductive."[61] Shipping, commerce, and naval construction thus blurred together in the nexus of mass migration.

The Impact of Return Migration

Italy's tremendous economic advantages from emigration largely depended upon return migration. Regarding remittances, Parliament noted that "it is notorious that no savings are usually sent in the year of departure, and in the third or four year the emigrant either returns home [with savings] or brings his family to join him in the newly adopted fatherland."[62] Although plans could change, truly "permanent" emigrants thought they would never return to the mother country: they invested all their time and money in affairs abroad. The Banco di Napoli faced this reality in 1908, as the Italian consul of Florianopolis, Brazil, explained why no bankers would process the Banco's remittances: "Our compatriots in the State of Santa Catarina are all small landowners, definitively established here. They no longer send their savings to the fatherland because not only are their meager earnings sufficient only for survival, but most of them no longer have relatives in the fatherland." The Italian consul of Salonica (Thessaloniki), Greece, also apologized: "I will certainly support the development of remittances in this region. But I think it will be difficult here, because there is no real emigration, but a stable colony with only two or three hundred workers. Also there is now an Italian post office which sends money at a minimal cost."[63] Temporary migrants, by contrast, sent or carried their life savings home to Italy for retirement. Nearly half of all Italian emigrants returned home, a much higher rate than other national emigrations of the time.[64]

The reality of return migration, however, only gradually became clear. In 1882, Italian statisticians posited that "emigrants intend never to return to their fatherland."[65] As late as 1905, the famous economist Vilfredo Pareto argued that emigrants were "lost" to their mother country and subtracted from its capital. The national cost of children's education and upbringing would not be "reimbursed" if the grown children emigrated to work elsewhere as adults. According to Pareto's argument, Italy subsidized foreign economies by paying the overhead costs of workers' development from infancy, and then sending the workers away in their productive years. Pareto estimated that Italy lost between 400 and 450 million lire a year through emigration in this way. His critics replied that the unavailability of jobs in Italy made the loss of "surplus" workers purely hypothetical.[66] But only the careful collection and rigorous analysis of statistics could resolve the debate.

Statistics revealed a crucial trend: striking return migration, from American destinations as well as European. Migration across the Atlantic, measured annually by third-class passenger lists in ships bound for Italy, showed a *net return* to Italy during years of recession in the United States and at the beginning of World War I (see Appendix, Figure 3.3). Another record was taken at the municipal level, of the numbers of people marked in municipal registers as emigrating permanently or returning permanently from migration (see Appendix, Figure 3.4). For the decade 1901–1910, an average of 119,749 persons every year emigrated permanently, above the number of those who returned. However, the decade 1911–1920 produced an average *net return migration* of 23,311 persons a year.[67] The greatest numbers returned to Italy at the beginning of World War I and at its end, when it was again safe to cross the seas.

Return migration from the Americas varied drastically by country. This reflected general trends in Italian emigration: entire Italian families settled in Brazil, while male workers migrated temporarily in North America and Argentina. Between 1905 and 1915, the Italian government found that three-quarters of emigrants returning from the United States, and two-thirds of repatriates from Argentina, traveled alone. From Brazil, however, between half and three-quarters of the returning Italians traveled with their families. Women returning to Italy comprised between a tenth and a fifth of return migration from the United States and Argentina but more than half of the return migration from Brazil, in the years 1905 to 1915. These characteristics of American migration changed only in 1922, when anti-immigration legislation in the United States reduced Italian immigration to a trickle.[68] Because immigrants who left the United States would not be allowed back into American ports, return migration to Italy virtually ceased. Italy's cyclical and temporary transatlantic migration became a diminutive one-way migration.

Why such high rates of return before 1922? To the genuine surprise of Americans, many Italians left their villages intending to return. For them, America was "the land of the dollar," a place to make money but not a place to live with one's family.[69] Strong ties to extended family networks brought many people back home. Also, Italy's impressive economic development between 1890 and 1920 doubtless persuaded many Italians in South America to return home. If instead the Italian economy had collapsed, or if Brazil and Argentina had outperformed Italy over the long term, more Italians would have remained on their lands in South America. In the twentieth century, however, the *bel paese* lured its migrants back home with favorable citizenship laws, flattery from the government, a strong economy, and the ties of individual emigrants to their local communities' traditions, landmarks, and fair weather. Return tickets were inexpensive, as passenger steamers crisscrossing the ocean usually had plenty of room for the voyage to Italy.

Drawn by ties to their homeland, migrants were also pushed back across the ocean by business cycles of boom and bust. Immigrants to the United States worked in the growing sectors of the industrial economy and were the first to be unemployed with economic downturns. Some officials argued that Ellis Island "is a more sensitive and accurate thermometer of the country's economy than Wall Street."[70] After the Panic of 1907 and the resulting depression in the United States, Italians returned in record numbers from the United States, while the numbers returning from Brazil and Argentina remained more steady (see Appendix, Figure 3.5).

This sudden return of Italian laborers provoked worry and consternation in the Italian Parliament, but brought important long-term benefits. Return migrants brought back their cash savings, social experience, and job training to Italy's developing economy.[71]

Thanks to return migration, Italian emigrants were not "lost" to their native country as many Italian politicians had feared. On the contrary, migration effectively expanded Italy's labor market beyond the limits of Italy's resources. Remittances contributed to building up Italy's capital and industrial plant so future laborers could find work within Italy. Many Italian writers and politicians hoped that emigration would provide money and manpower for future national emergencies, especially a long-expected European war. In fact, migration proved a crucial resource for Italy in World War I. Italy gained population during the Great War, in contrast to every other combatant power in Europe. Hundreds of thousands returned to Italy from Europe and the Americas at the war's outbreak, and over 300,000 more returned as reservist soldiers to fight after Italy entered the conflict in 1915. In the 1930s and 1940s, Italy's Fascist government hoped for a similar return migration to fuel its wars of aggression. This mass return did not take place.[72]

After extensive statistical analysis, Italians realized that emigration was not draining population on a national level. In Europe, only Ireland faced this threat. Elsewhere, emigration rates stayed below the natural population increase of births subtracted by deaths.[73] The Italian statistical yearbook of 1895 revealed that, despite a surge in emigration the country's natural increase of 326,563 far outnumbered total emigration (225,346), divided into permanent emigration overseas (101,207) and temporary emigration to Europe (124,139). But at a provincial level, permanent migration decimated Catanzaro, Potenza, Campobasso, Salerno, Rovigo, and Turin.[74] Temporary migration, especially to France, Austria, Germany, and Switzerland, brought less damage. The single province of Udine, on Italy's northeastern border, supported more than a third of the entire country's temporary migration, but migrants would return from across the border within a few months.[75]

By 1897 the demographic situation had changed significantly. In the north, Udine continued to grow and Turin also gained in population, as growth in the city balanced population losses in the alpine hinterland. Rovigo also reversed its population decline. For the South, however, the statistics revealed a mass exodus, clearly depleting local populations in

Campania and Basilicata.[76] After 1900 Italy's statistical yearbooks no longer directly compared natural increase in births and deaths with permanent migration at the provincial level. Local depopulation had moved from cold statistics into desperate reality.

The Italian census of 1901 documented severe depopulation in small villages with massive emigration, analyzing those relatively few municipalities (*comuni*) that lost population between 1 January 1882 and 10 February 1901. (To save money, Francesco Crispi had canceled the national census of 1891.) Over twenty years, 613 municipalities in Piedmont had lost 83,758 people, while only 176 villages in Campania had lost 52,389 persons. Most strikingly, 93 villages in Basilicata had lost 59,682 persons.[77] Across Italy, seventy-one municipalities had declined in population by 800 or more; twenty-four of these were in Basilicata. Nationwide, Italy's population increased so rapidly that any local decrease was unusual; yet Basilicata continued its massive emigration from a tiny population base. Hundreds of thousands sold their small plots of land to start a new life in the Americas, especially the United States. The 1901 census also listed villages that had lost at least 20 percent of their population: thirty-two villages in Basilicata were included. Potenza itself had lost 20.6 percent of its people, falling to 16,163 residents; it was the only provincial or regional capital to have lost a fifth of its population.[78]

Ten years later, the 1911 census confirmed the trends. Piedmont lost 108,095 people from 873 municipalities, while Sicily's loss was even worse: 108,909 people from 116 towns. Other regions in the South continued to lose population: Campania lost 55,126 persons from 249 municipalities; Abruzzi-Molise lost 30,715 people from 173 towns; Calabria lost 24,331 from 101 towns; and Basilicata lost 21,153 from 76 communities. This census listed municipalities that had lost 10 percent of their population between 1901 and 1911: Potenza province registered 23 municipalities, and neighboring Salerno province registered 33 municipalities that had lost a tenth of their population. Turin province led the list with 87; Novara province, which included Biella, followed with 64 villages that lost more than 10 percent. Temporary migration, however, had not led to depopulation. Only one village in the province of Udine had lost a tenth of its population, although 2.7 percent of the entire province was "temporarily absent" on the day of the census. This was by far the largest absentee rate in the country, due to widespread temporary migration, and contrasted sharply with Basilicata. In the thirty years from 1881 to 1911, Basilicata had lost 10 percent of its population.[79]

These dry numbers reflect heartache and fear. Although emigration brought the benefits of remittances and trade to Italy as a whole, the local impacts of excessive emigration threatened to destroy the fabric of traditional society. Some towns would never recover from such rapid population loss. Yet many emigrants would return home. The bonds of religion and family tied Italians to their native country; the Italian state labored to forge cultural and economic bonds as well. Return migration soon gained its own dynamic and raised a separate debate.

Debates over Depopulation and Degeneration

Giuseppe Zanardelli was the first northern Italian Prime Minister to tour the South, and was shocked by what he found. On a visit to Moliterno in Basilicata in September 1902, the mayor greeted him saying, "I salute you in the name of my 8,000 fellow villagers, of whom 3,000 have emigrated to America and 5,000 are preparing to join them."[80] In 1910 a Parliamentary inquest into conditions in the South reported "abandoned houses, orchards transformed into thorny thickets, families reduced to women, children, and a few old people . . . like an empty village that had been stricken by the plague."[81] Emigration seemed to have become a never-ending part of southern Italian society. Alternatives to emigration were unthinkable. Giustino Fortunato wrote "in the name of all Southerners, I pray to God that the United States of America never decides to close its doors to the surging torrent of our miserable countrymen!"[82]

Just as bad as population loss, or even worse according to Italian nationalists, was the return of migrants with broken health and broken lives. While American opponents of mass immigration tried to block the arrival of diseased travelers, Italian opponents of mass emigration tried to limit the departure of healthy workers. They drew upon anecdotes and health inspections to claim that Italians went to the Americas healthy and returned sick and dying. Southern Italians discovered hard liquors and whiskey only in the Americas, and emigrants who returned as alcoholics shocked Italian moralists.[83] Tuberculosis, the curse of urban poverty, had been unknown in rural Italy before mass return migration. Between 1903 and 1925, shipboard doctors were shocked to find 9,678 cases of tuberculosis among migrants returning to Italy, compared with only 356 cases among the millions leaving Italy. Even malaria, a typical Italian disease, was present in return migration: 2,701 emigrants departed with malaria, and 1,013 returned with malaria, often to die.

Venereal diseases were found in 626 returning Italians versus 225 departing. All of these statistics were certainly underreported, yet of the 3.3 million who returned to Italy in these years nearly all were healthy.[84] Opponents of emigration nevertheless claimed that migrants returned with disease and despair, not wealth and prosperity.

Some of those returning to Italy had been barred entry at the ports of the United States. Inspectors screened prospective immigrants for moral, civic, political, and medical health and fitness: "idiots, insane, paupers, diseased persons, convicts, polygamists, women [immigrating] for immoral purposes, assisted aliens, contract laborers, anarchists, [or] procurers" were rejected under U.S. law. Immigrants with certain contagious diseases, even if contracted during their voyage, could be excluded; those with varicose veins and arthritis were also denied.[85] Between 1902 and 1925, on average 0.87 percent of Italian male emigrants were rejected at ports of immigration; 0.48 percent of women and children under age ten were rejected. All these migrants returned to Italy at the expense of the shipping companies. Many more prospective emigrants were turned away at Italian ports, since shipping companies performed their own inspection before embarkation, as required by the U.S. law of February 1907. By the Italian regulation of 1914, shippers reimbursed the rejected emigrants for their lodging expenses and travel between their home and the port city.[86] America's emphasis on immigrant health slanted Italy's debates over the advantages of emigration. Italian nationalists claimed that only the most physically fit and economically productive emigrants left their country, while imbeciles, cripples, and other rejects stayed in Italy. With ominous overtones from Darwinistic theories, opponents of mass migration predicted that this "reverse selection," and the imported diseases of return migration, would cause the decline of the Italian race.[87]

Besides failed health, many returned to Italy with failed finances and broken dreams. Italian officials tracked how many could not afford their own tickets home to Italy and returned at the expense of local consuls or Italian charitable societies abroad. Between 1902 and 1925, 1.6 percent of Italians who returned from the United States, and 3.1 percent of the Italians traveling from Argentina and Uruguay, returned as indigents. From Brazil, however, an astonishing 12 percent of migrants coming home to Italy traveled in poverty. Why such a difference? The Emigration Commissariat explained that Italian charities in the United States were no better than those in Brazil, but that the richer and healthier Italian emigrants chose to go to North America instead of South America.[88] Many migrants who would have been rejected by United States inspectors emigrated to South American ports instead, only to find more miserable economic opportunities than back in Italy. They eventually returned home, broken and disgraced. Critics reasoned that if migration to the Americas had infected and ruined so many lives, without providing the wealth which emigrants sought, surely emigration itself represented a national disaster.

Emigrants' best interests, and Italy's best strategic interests, were vehemently debated. The Catholic group *Italica Gens* hoped to steer emigrants toward Brazil and Latin America because of greater possibilities for Italian political influence, even when the United States offered more opportunities for workers.[89] Some imperialists still hoped to limit American migration to help the development of Eritrea and Somalia.[90] Another controversy, which pitted emigrants' economic interests against foreign policy, was the debate over rural or urban colonization. Emigrants made higher wages in cities and in mines or factories, gathered together in tightly-knit communities; but was this in their best interest? American politicians railed against the crowding of foreigners in big cities and called for immigrants to settle and cultivate the Great Plains. Adolfo Rossi, as inspector for the Emigration Commissariat and later as Italian consul in Denver, Colorado, obliged American authorities by encouraging Italians to settle in the West rather than on the eastern seaboard. In 1905 and 1906, during an official tour, Rossi emphasized to the American press that Italy did not encourage emigration, did not advise Italians to congregate in cities, and did not oppose emigrants' Americanization.[91] Rossi personally believed this to be the best policy, and it was certainly what Americans wanted to hear. Some Italians cited the colony of Tontitown, Arkansas, as a model Italian settlement under the leadership of Father Bandini, a Scalabrinian priest. Far from the evils of urban tenements filled with disease and immorality, here Italians worked the fields under the watchful care of their parish priest. Most emigrants ignored this official advice and settled in Italian American urban communities, rallying together against religious and ethnic prejudice. In the long run, this was a wise economic decision. Because Italian immigrants concentrated on the east coast and in metropolitan areas of the United States, their children and grandchildren inherited valuable property in dynamic economic centers, earning higher wages than the national average.[92] The descendants of Italians in New York City enjoy much more material wealth today than those who remained in tiny Tontitown, Arkansas.

The clash of perspectives and interests carried over into relations between immigrants and indigenous residents. Because of racial and religious prejudice and competition for labor, many Americans could not see beyond the newcomers' immediate poverty. Despite the collusion of interests between Americans and the Italians, there stood a tragic gulf of misunderstanding. Some Americans thought the immigrants were money-grubbers, ruining themselves for Mammon; many Italians felt the same about America and its culture of infinite monetary gain, without regard for the human spirit. After arranging an art exposition for immigrants in Chicago, Jane Addams noted that "an Italian expressed great surprise when he found that we, although Americans, still liked pictures, and said quite naïvely that he didn't know that Americans cared for anything but dollars—that looking at pictures was something people only did in Italy."[93] Both sides accused the other of unbridled avarice in America, the "land of dollars."

Much of the misunderstanding and controversy over immigration and emigration stemmed from different interpretations, economic, cultural, ethnic, and political, applied to the same phenomenon. Simple "push-pull" economic indicators and income differentials were tempting as an easy explanation, but emigration brought with it much deeper implications. The human costs and liabilities of mass migration, most painful on a personal level, upset the calculation of emigration's tangible assets, including remittances, exports, profits, and industrialization on a national scale. Mass emigration, with high return migration, combined the problems and opportunities of foreign and domestic policy through the local and international consequences of population movement. Italy's involvement with emigration thus moved far beyond economics. The population on the move brought cultural identities and social customs which would become the centerpiece for building a global nation.

Dogali Obelisk, Rome, erected 1887 on Piazza dei 500; relocated 1924.
Photo: Mark I. Choate.

The Italians of Argentina, Album for the 1898 Exposition of Italians Abroad in Torino. The daughter of Italy salutes the Star of Italy shining over the sea. From the Biblioteca del Ministero delle Risorse Agricole, Alimentari e Forestali, Rome. Photo: Mark I. Choate.

Postcard pastiche for emigrants: Mt. Vesuvius smoking over the Bay of Naples and a lighthouse guiding a steamship toward a Banco di Napoli remittance money order, on the rock-solid Castel dell'Ovo. From the historical Archive of the Banco di Napoli, Naples. Photo: Mark I. Choate.

Rocco Gualtieri's shop, Rome, New York, 1912: Correspondent of the Bank of Naples, and Importer. Credit: Center for Migration Studies of New York, Inc.

Italian schoolboys in Tripoli performing gymnastics on mobile ladders. From Ministero delle Colonie, *La Mostra coloniale di Genova 1914* (2d ed., Rome: G. Bertero, 1914).

The Lighthouse of the Fatherland, Janiculum Hill in
Rome, constructed 1911. Photo: Mark I. Choate.

"The Heroes of the Italian Trenches in New York." From *Il Carroccio:
The Italian Review* (November 1918).

Descendants of Columbus return for the Great War: Monument to Italian American war dead, Royal Palace Courtyard, Turin, 1923. Photo: Mark I. Choate.

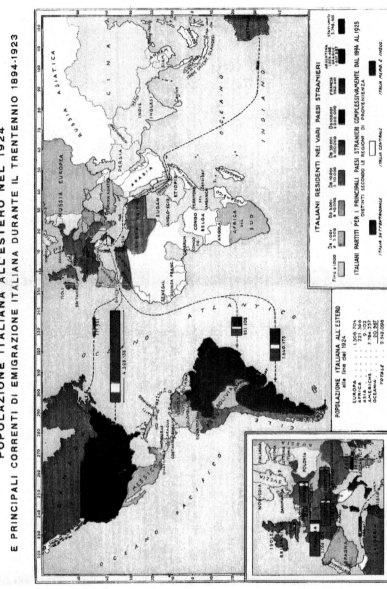

Map of the world according to Italian population, showing emigration to each continent from North, Central, and South Italy: Commissario Generale dell'Emigrazione. *L'Emigrazione Italiana dal 1910 al 1923* (Rome, 1926).

4

The Language of Dante

In 1867, Massimo d'Azeglio captured the dilemma facing the new Italian state with his epigram, "unfortunately we have made Italy, but are not making Italians."[1] Mass emigration complicated the problem with a related challenge: can a state invent a national identity for transnational emigrants? The Italian government worked at the limits of politics, relying on culture and religion to brand emigrants as Italian. The success of any emigrant colonialism depended upon an enduring ethnic identity, even if subsidized and somewhat artificial, which emigrants could carry with them abroad, and back home to Italy upon their likely return. While American governments encouraged assimilation, Italian politicians searched for the essence of *italianità,* which would not dissolve in any immigrant melting pot no matter what pressures were applied. The main ingredient in this theoretical compound of insoluble Italian identity became the Italian language, the binding element of international Italian life. Giuseppe Prato argued, "Language is the most solid defense of threatened nationalities, the only salvation and hope of oppressed peoples, the most effective means of expansion for the strongest races and superior peoples."[2] In the words of Ferdinando Martini, "the soul of the fatherland is in language."[3] If first-generation migrants speaking dialects learned standard Italian, the Italian community could unite instead of falling into regional divisions. If second-generation Italians also spoke "the language of Dante," they would be moored to Italian culture and society no matter where they lived. Retention of national language and culture, especially by emigrants' children and grandchildren, became the Holy Grail of emigrant colonialism.

Forming a strong Italian identity above traditional regional loyalties was the goal of Italian education both at home and abroad. Emigration's didactic role had already been explored in *Cuore* (Heart: A book for boys, 1886), a school textbook that became Italy's first bestseller. Edmondo De Amicis structured the book as a young schoolboy's journal, featuring patriotic readings assigned monthly by the boy's teacher. The longest chapter, "From the Apennines to the Andes," records a thirteen-year-old's search for his lost emigrant mother. He travels alone from Genoa all over Argentina, encouraged by a fellow Italian: "Go, and do not worry; here you have compatriots *(compaesani)* all around you—you will not be alone." Genoese sailors later rebuke him, saying, "What the devil! A Genoese who cries because he is far from home! The Genoese travel the world glorious and triumphant!" A Lombard in Rosario helps him raise money among Italians at a tavern, who welcome him: "A fellow patriot! Come here, little one. We are here, the emigrants!" They raise enough money to send him up to Córdoba and Tucuman, where he saves his delirious, dying mother by finding her medical care.[4] Lessons in this melodrama are clear. Italians from all regions stand as one; they can and must rely upon each other; family loyalties blend seamlessly with nationality. De Amicis used emigrant solidarity abroad as a model for national solidarity at home. His bestseller inspired schoolchildren in Italy, but also reached expatriates, as his book was distributed on emigrant ships and in Italian schools abroad. This nation-building project successfully conflated domestic and foreign Italian identities: to be meaningful at home, *italianità* must also be meaningful abroad.

Cultural expansion had always been a cornerstone for Italy's foreign policy. True to its Romantic foundations, the Italian government established its program for Italian schools abroad shortly after unification, in 1862. Francesco Crispi expanded the program in 1889 to parallel his ambitious foreign policy goals in the Mediterranean. Teaching and education were vehicles for grandiose political designs. A writer sympathetic to Crispi later noted that "he sent out uneducated but enthusiastic teachers, who accepted their calling as a noble mission."[5] His government imposed strict regulations on religious schools that desired a subsidy and in the end financed anticlerical schools in direct competition. After Crispi fell from power, Rudinì and Giolitti curtailed the expensive subsidies, but also expanded the school program's focus from the Mediterranean to the Americas, and collaborated fully with religious institutions.[6]

Italian support for schools abroad, with a focus on basic language instruction, stands out from other European cultural policies of the time. The Alliance Française, founded in 1884, aimed to consolidate the prestige and influence of French culture abroad by interacting with upper classes and cultural elites.[7] The more democratic Italian literacy project hoped to spread Italian influence from the grassroots, in primary schools and in adult evening schools. Italy's emphasis on literacy and popular culture offered a model to the German Empire. In 1896, shortly before Italy's defeat at Adwa, the German Colonial Council discussed how best to develop the potential benefits of German emigration. The council believed that traditional tools of diplomacy could not protect emigrants once they had established themselves abroad. More nuanced organizations, such as churches and schools, would have to nurture the identity of transplanted Germans. The committee recommended changes in Germany's proposed emigration law, to follow Italy's example in educating emigrants:

> It makes no difference whether Germans gather in villages or small cities, or establish communities in larger cities; if they prolong their residence in a foreign land, they will assume obligations which will restrict displays of their Germanity [*Deutschthum*]. We must employ means that preserve the character of the Folk, through the influence of public and private life, so that affiliation to the Fatherland might remain protected for the coming generation. The Church and, above all, the school must take the lead. The State cannot do much about the Church, but it can do something about schools. *Italy, despite its less favorable financial situation, spends many millions annually for the establishment and support of schools abroad. The Reich should do likewise.* Through schools, we will preserve our language; through language, our customs and family solidarity; and through these, our national character [*Volksthum*] will survive.[8]

Schools could make the difference between loyalty and apathy abroad. As recommended, Germany embarked on a serious campaign to support emigrant culture. Ironically, the empire marshalled wealth and resources to deploy Italy's methods more effectively than Italy could.[9] German churches and community schools in the Americas enjoyed an advantage over newer, less stable Italian communities. Italy's state-subsidized Dante Alighieri Society viewed its German counterpart, the Universal German School Union, as a mortal enemy in the quest for "informal empire," particularly in Brazil and in the Italian-speaking regions of Austria.[10] Supporting emigrants' language and culture became another battle in the struggle for international influence.

Italians abroad did not wait for direction from the fatherland to organize themselves into a myriad of regional, religious, political, and social groups. But their very diversity weakened the Italians' overall influence. One observer noted pessimistically in 1902 that "the Italians of the Plata are united in about three hundred different associations: which means they are perfectly divided."[11] The impressive number of Italian associations betrayed a lack of synergy and the weakness of infighting. Italian mutual aid societies often split along regional lines, and then sometimes split along provincial lines, dividing their resources. Groups formed around their own political and religious colors, celebrating their own heroes and holidays. With consuls' support, monarchists celebrated the king's and queen's birthdays; September 20, the date when Italian troops entered papal Rome; and the anniversary of Italy's Constitution of 1848, the Statuto.[12] Italian republicans opposed monarchists by honoring Garibaldi and Mazzini. Pious Catholics, on the other hand, countered Garibaldi and September 20 with commemorations of Pope Pius IX.

In relations with their fellow Italians, emigrants often reproduced in the Americas the same divisions they had known in Italy. When presenting themselves to Italy or to other national groups, however, the expatriate communities did construct a more coherent common identity. For example, the Italian Workers' Association of Buenos Aires organized an Italian Industrial and Artistic Exposition in 1881 that involved most of the Italian community. The organizers hoped to establish the prestige of Italians in Argentina, for clear social and economic benefits. They dedicated the exposition to the Italian worker: "to You, O noble child of labor, with the faraway fatherland long fixed in your mind, when you pause for an instant from your daily hard labor. . . . to You O fellow citizen, who has long given glory with your labor to the faraway fatherland, and to the land that hosts you."[13] The President of Argentina, General Julio Roca, served as patron of the two-month exposition, which hosted 48,500 visitors and brought in $784,000. One day's receipts were dedicated as a fundraiser for the Italian Hospital of Buenos Aires. In a special ceremony, children from the local Italian schools recited such poems as "The two fatherlands," "The primacy of Italy," and "To my flag," and the two local Italian bands played the Italian and Argentine national an-thems.[14] The exposition's organizers were justly proud of their success, especially because the Italians were the first expatriate colony to orga-nize such an event in Argentina: "The idea of an Italian Workers' Expo-sition in Buenos Aires, hailed from the beginning as a chimera, opposed, derided by the apostles of laziness—became a reality, leaving in Ar-gentina an indelible mark of esteem and sympathy for the Italian."[15] This success was a precursor to expositions in Italy by expatriate communi-ties from around the world, such as the International Exposition of 1898 in Turin and the Exposition of 1906 in Milan.[16]

By the early twentieth century, Italy's cultural migration policies ral-lied a broad range of patriotic interests. The "Dante Alighieri Society for Italian Language and Culture outside the Kingdom" was heavily Masonic and enjoyed excellent Liberal connections. From the opposite corner of Italian politics came the Catholic missionary orders that min-istered to emigrants, including the Scalabrinians, Salesians, and the *Opera Bonomelli*.[17] Through the Emigration Fund, Italy could enlist the open support of Catholic clergy who had no other connections with the normally anticlerical, Liberal state. Humanitarian organizations of reformist Socialists also drew upon state funding, as the Italian govern-ment coordinated a rich variety of programs to bolster the cultural vital-ity of Italian migration.

Expatriate Italian communities were constructed through tenuous networks of transatlantic correspondence, economic interest, cultural bonding, and ad hoc social associations. Small groups of political exiles pioneered vibrant communities in the 1870s and 1880s, while Italy itself was still undergoing unification. Despite the state's interest in emigra-tion, the peninsula's fractured regional history challenged any idea of a single "Italy." No Italian expatriate community would be identifiable without a common nationality, yet emigrants usually built this common background from scratch. Emigrant Italian culture had to be invented immediately, without waiting for a united Italian society to develop. With extensive public, private, and ecclesiastical support from Italy, this fragile cultural expansion developed into an international *italianità*, often more cogent and convincing abroad than at home. This transna-tional nationalism, grafted into a variety of foreign contexts, became the backbone of Greater Italy and encouraged the development of national unity at home.

Italianità and the Language of Italians Abroad

The Italian language became the glue of expatriate Italy, for reasons both practical and romantic. Like the other European nation-states formed in the nineteenth and twentieth centuries, Italy was a geographical expression of its language. The existence of a single Italian tongue, however, was itself both a cultural and political development. After the peninsula's political unity was shattered in the eighth century, a bevy of separate languages developed in geographical and cultural isolation. In mountainous areas, each village developed its own idiom. Minor Romance languages in Italy include *lombardo, veneto, napolitano, piemontese, friulano, siciliano,* and *toscano,* each with its own literature. The difference between these languages compares to the difference between Spanish and Romanian. Dante, Petrarch, and Boccaccio would make the Tuscan dialect Italy's most prominent literary language from the 1300s forward, and the Crusca Academy in Florence began publishing its *Dictionary* in 1612. This became the standard Italian language. But for nearly all Italians, the Tuscan dialect read like a foreign tongue, far removed from normal expressive speech. Even in the year 2007, more than half of Italians spoke in dialects with their families and friends. Not surprisingly, Tuscans spoke "Italian" most often, out of all the regions of Italy.[18]

Literature, writing, and language thus became inseparable from the Italian nation-building project. To support Italy's unification in the nineteenth century, the Milanese novelist and poet Alessandro Manzoni spearheaded a campaign for the nationwide use of a standardized Italian. He revised in 1840 his novel *I promessi sposi* (The Betrothed, 1827) using Florentine and Sienese words, even though his characters were from seventeenth-century Lombardy. Manzoni deliberately made his historical fiction a *patriotic* fiction of cultural unity, prefiguring political unity. Mazzini and Gioberti likewise postulated the cultural, geographical, and linguistic unity of the Italian nation, while it was still split into nine different states. Romantic visionaries glossed over divisions in the Italian peninsula and insisted that the country must incorporate regions up to Italy's "natural" Alpine frontier. The crowning of a King of Italy in 1861 and his invasion of Rome in 1870 did not complete the unification of Italians; if anything, plans for the nation's expansion became more ambiguous, as the new kingdom was deliberately open-ended. Depending on their bias, Italian politicians still hoped to win Italian-speaking Malta from Britain, Nice and Corsica from France, or Trent and Trieste from Austria. Strengthening the Italian language in these geographic areas, and among emigrants and their children worldwide, carried a full freight of competing dreams for Italian greatness.[19]

Beyond a romantic vision of "Italian," a standard language was necessary to administer any kind of colonial policy. Illiterate emigrants speaking local dialects could hardly communicate with Italian consuls or any other Italian officials, if they came from different regions. Without a common language, Italian representatives could not hope to bridge the natural divisions between Italian communities in the Americas. In 1888, the archbishop of New York sought Italian clergy to minister to Italian immigrants, but was dismayed to find that the Scalabrinian fathers brought in from northern Italy could not communicate effectively with southern Italians. The archbishop had to specify what kind of Italian missionaries he wanted to supplement the Scalabrinians: specifically, Jesuit priests who could not speak English and who were familiar with the dialects and religious customs of southern Italy. Language divided families as well. If husband and wife were from different regions of Italy, they spoke Spanish at home in Argentina, or English in the United States. If instead the emigrants learned to speak and write standard Italian, expatriate Italy would take a more concrete shape.[20]

The campaign against emigrant illiteracy exposed larger difficulties in building a united Italy. Although many emigrants were illiterate, most also came from the most literate group in the country: young males, who perhaps had learned Italian in primary school or in military service. This, of course, hurt efforts to expand literacy on the peninsula. Illiteracy among Italians aged six and over ran 68.8 percent nationally in 1871, falling to 37.9 percent in 1911. But populations in the South with high emigration still suffered from high illiteracy in 1911: 58.0 percent in Sicily, 65.3 percent in Basilicata, and 69.6 percent in Calabria.[21] Chain migration into regional American neighborhoods also reinforced dialects at the expense of standard Italian. In Chicago, the Italians divided themselves into sixteen separate neighborhoods, each speaking different regional dialects.[22] Whether in Europe or America, speaking dialect was the epitome of local tradition, unintelligible to foreigners and interlopers. The comfortable insularity of an intact local identity made transatlantic migration more liveable and successful. Regional expatriate units formed small economic niches and eased the uncertainties of return migration.

By contrast, the study of written, standard Italian provided no immediate rewards and often appeared superfluous. Standard Italian lacked words for familiar, everyday situations; for example, the Italian word for "grandson" is the same as for "nephew." Only Tuscans *spoke* Italian; for others, Italian was a sterile, artificial language. The Neapolitan professor Pasquale Villari, President of the Dante Alighieri Society, painted a bleak picture of the results: "The Italians in the Americas have become the only people forced to divide itself into separate groups of Piedmontese, Lombards, Neapolitans, Sicilians, etc. This is not only because of different customs and traditions; it also stems from the ignorance of Italian, and the great diversity of dialects, which make it almost impossible for the emigrants to understand each other. So they learn the indigenous language and rapidly lose their nationality."[23] If an Italian emigrant learned to read and write a new language in the Americas, it was usually the local language—English, Spanish, or Portuguese—rather than standard Italian.

Could political reinforcements reverse this cultural disintegration? Language schools were just a part of a holistic program for expatriate colonies. To boost Italian influence in the valleys of southern Austria, Bonaldo Stringher, governor of the Bank of Italy and vice-president of the Dante Society, expected as much benefit from Italian tourism as from Italian language schools in southern Austria. He called upon the Italian Alpine Club to compete against the German-Austrian Alpine Society for local influence.[24] The government-subsidized Dante Society financed hospitals, libraries, and hospices, and coordinated local festivals worldwide to unite all Italian emigrant groups. Italian patriots viewed language acquisition not as the primary goal of Greater Italy, but rather as the glue that would hold its many parts together.

With a mix of banquets, recitals, music, and sport, expatriate societies created communal rituals for Italians of all ages. In Morteros, Argentina, the Italian Society "Union and Benevolence," which "also admitted Italians from the unredeemed [Austrian] provinces," owned a theater for "patriotic commemorations," where Italian schoolchildren gathered to "recite and sing patriotic verses and hymns."[25] In Tunis, the Italian community held patriotic exercises in the hall of the Pro-Patria Gymnastic Society, accompanied by their 57-piece musical band "Star of Italy." The local Italian gymnastics society practiced fencing and juggling and competed in Italian national gymnastics competitions.[26] The Italians of Buenos Aires also supported a musical band, "Lake of Como," and a sharpshooting team.[27] Italian schools in Tripoli offered their colonial students the same regimen of gymnastics, military marching, singing, marksmanship, and a brass band.[28] The Italian colony of New York was extremely proud when its National Target Shooting Society, founded in 1888 by Giuseppe Garibaldi and local Italians, won the United States national championship: "before, the Americans treated our marksmen with irony, as something negligible. Afterwards, there was a remarkable change of attitude."[29] Such displays of Italian sports, fine arts, and military training gave the Italian expatriate colonies pride in themselves and earned respect from outsiders.

To cement their connection to the Italian state, Italian cultural groups usually made the local consul a president or chairman *ex officio,* guaranteeing the groups' political loyalties under the symbol of the Italian royal arms. Local mutual aid societies, formed in parallel to the spread of mutualism in Italy, worked at concrete, practical self-improvement.[30] Italian literary societies and competitive athletic groups aimed to build their reputations as Italians abroad. Speaking standard Italian, and naming their societies "Italian," gave their cultural activities a political meaning. The society Juvenes Carthaginis of Tunis, which sponsored drama, dancing, and concerts, began as an "International Society" in 1883, but dropped the "International" to become "Italian" in 1894.[31] The Italian National Target Shooting Society of New York refused to join the National Rifle Association of America, until the NRA made membership a requirement to participate in competitions in the 1890s. The Italians then joined the NRA only after their local consul gave permission; their allegiance remained with Italy.[32]

The Italian sharpshooters were also patriotic in their charity. Though they were proud of the medals they had won in Paris, Rome, and New York, they were just as proud that they had raised money to support Italian soldiers wounded in the African wars, Sicilians displaced by the floods of 1903, and Calabrians harmed in the earthquake of 1905.[33] The United States' own disasters during the same period, such as the Spanish-American War of 1898 and the San Francisco earthquake of 1906, provoked no such response. The charters of many Italian expatriate groups stated an intent to support the fatherland in time of war or natural disaster. Some groups, particularly self-help groups for Italian veterans, even promised subsidies to the families of members who volunteered for service in the Italian military during wartime. When the societies' members died for Italy, their widows and families would receive a pension.[34]

Striking similarities between Italian groups scattered across the world stemmed in part from a common emigration experience, carefully regulated by the Italian government. Between 1900 and 1910 the voyage from Naples to New York took about two weeks, and passengers were a captive audience. Voyages to South America were longer still. These weeks of travel and transition would frame a first course of education and acculturation, presented by the Dante Alighieri Society.

Challenges for the Dante Society

Illiteracy created opportunities to touch emigrants' lives and shape their feelings for Italy. Under the leadership of Pasquale Villari, the Dante Alighieri Society spearheaded efforts to use government resources, economic influence, and moral suasion to teach standard Italian to Italy's emigrants. The Society proudly announced that its "patriotic charity" [carità di patria] "does not aspire to vacuous ideals; it helps our schools abroad raise up new generations in love for Italy, and binds to the fatherland many useful scattered strengths."[35] With high ambitions and creative programs, the decentralized Dante committees combined literature, patriotism, and literacy to forge expatriate italianità amid rapidly changing social landscapes.

Emigration ports became a centerpiece of efforts for emigrant assistance and influence. In Naples and Genoa, the local Dante Society committees set up information offices to distribute pamphlets and help third-class travelers write or dictate personal correspondence. Subsidized by the emigration commissariat, by 1909 the Naples committee had created more than forty lending libraries for passenger ships. The books were entrusted to the Italian inspectors and naval doctors who accompanied every emigrant voyage from Naples, whether the ship was Italian or not. The doctors could distribute books during daily visits, or emigrants could check them out from the infirmaries on board the ships taking them farther and farther from their homes. A similar library from the Bologna committee provided reading for Italians traveling by train to work in Switzerland, coordinated by the Italian consulate in Basel.[36] Donated books and propaganda were divided in three categories: "books for elementary education: primers, easy arithmetic, natural and physical sciences, agriculture and hygiene"; "books especially chosen to boost feelings for the fatherland: stories of our unification, notes on Roman history, geographical manuals"; and "books of travels and adventures, of [Samuel] Smiles, [Massimo] d'Azeglio, [Tommaso] Grossi, [Edmondo] De Amicis, as well as the Royal Family of France and the History of Guerin Meschino."[37] These works of self-help and popular patriotism were for lending only, as were the dictionaries, but the patriotic tracts were free for emigrants to take with them to their new homes. Dante, Petrarch, and Manzoni were absent from the libraries, and even "popular" Italian literature was not popular enough. The Dante committee asked the emigration commissariat to encourage Italian writers and publishers to produce more books that emigrants would enjoy. Reading could protect and redeem emigrants as they traveled from their homes: "Perhaps for some, reading is a simple pastime, an innocent diversion, a defense against other possibilities, such as gambling, gossip, and quarrels; for everyone, the 'Dante book' is a memory of the Italian language and fatherland."[38]

Once emigrants arrived at their destinations, local Dante committees hoped to school them in Italian grammar and literature. They supported Italian schools abroad with prizes, scholarships for poor students, and heavy subsidies. Italy's Foreign Ministry helped by supplying patriotic books, such as "Moral Tales in Italian" and "Biographies and Tales of Our Fatherland's History."[39] The Ministry also provided patriotic textbooks to 128 Berlitz Schools teaching Italian in Europe and the Americas.[40] Working through the Dante Alighieri Society, in 1903 the government also established two thousand libraries for Italian schools, of two hundred books each.[41] Yet this was insufficient to support fully the tenuous existence of Italian schools. Nor did the Italian government provide pensions for schoolteachers in private Italian schools abroad, even though they often taught very poor migrants for little money.[42]

Like the schools, many of the sponsoring Dante Society committees led short lives, despite the consulates' support. The Society's exasperated headquarters in Rome expressed surprise that any committee survived a change of its presidency. As President Villari mourned in 1903, "constant and utter instability is our fiercest enemy. When we think we have established things well, everything changes suddenly and we have to start over again from the beginning."[43] Vice-president Bonaldo Stringher confessed that the Dante Society in the United States had lost its popular mission.

In Chicago, the Dante group was "elegant and academic," while the Boston committee had become "a notable academy of Italian studies, of gentlemen and ladies who feel affection for Italy" but did little besides charity visits for the Italian colony on the North End.[44] Compared to the Germanistic Society of America and the Alliance Française, Dante committees in the United States suffered a mercurial record: "disagreements, personal jealousies, lack of general interest, cultural deficiency in the public, put their existence in constant danger."[45] The concern for poor, uneducated immigrants often succumbed to petty social squabbles.

A signal defeat for the Dante Society was its failure in Marseilles, France. In 1903 Pasquale Villari, as Italian senator, overcame Parliamentary opposition to secure an initial subsidy from the emigration commissariat of ten thousand lire, for a primary school and Dante committee in this Mediterranean port city, where more than one hundred thousand Italians of all ages lived. But under the influence of Jules Ferry, the French government blocked the creation of an Italian primary school in Marseilles, allowing only a kindergarten or an evening school for adults.[46] As education minister and later premier, Ferry declared that the French Republic must strengthen itself through patriotic children's schools. Despite Italian political pressure, primary education remained exclusively in the hands of the French state. Similarly, France did not allow Italy to open more schools in Tunisia, although the Italian population had tripled in size since the treaty of 1896.[47] Villari argued in vain that Switzerland had helped establish schools for Italian immigrants, and some German towns on their own had established Italian schools. Southern France, however was the target of some irredentist claims: the city of Nice (Nizza), birthplace of Giuseppe Garibaldi, had passed from Italian to French rule only in 1860. In the end, the French did allow a charity in Marseilles to operate boys' and girls' schools. But the Dante Society leadership confessed that they faced difficulties in even forming a local committee there. Stringher blamed the delays on disloyal priests and class divisions that alienated the mass of Italian emigrants from the few expatriate intellectuals.[48] Such complaints revealed the Society's underlying Liberal political orientation, and mounting frustrations with emigration. If they could not organize a chapter amid the world's largest concentration of Italian emigrants (in 1904), and only a hundred miles outside the Italian border, how could they hope to change the course of Italian migration in the Americas?

Debates over geographic orientation divided the Dante Society, dissipated its efforts, and strained government funds. There was not enough money to subsidize schools on every continent. Should Italy concentrate on Europe, South America, North America, or the Mediterranean? Following Crispi's focus on Mediterranean schools, in 1901 only one-tenth of the foreign schools budget went to subsidies for American schools, while nine-tenths (900,000 lire) funded the Italian state schools in Tunisia, Tripolitania, Egypt, Greece, and the Ottoman Europe, including Albania.[49] By 1910 five-sixths paid for the 93 state schools with 16,721 students; one-sixth of the budget went to subsidies for 545 nongovernment schools with 55,877 students.[50] The government in Rome administered state schools directly and inefficiently. The consul in Tunis, for example, sent a telegram in 1889 to the Italian foreign minister requesting urgent authorization for a toilet in the Crispi nursery school.[51] Although expensive, schools along the southern and eastern Mediterranean coasts generally did not aim to teach Italian emigrants, who did not live there, but rather the children of local notables. This would build up Italian prestige in the area among local Arabs and Jews, Greeks, Turks, or Albanians, in preparation for the day when Italy would seize political control.[52] Tunisia was an exception within the Mediterranean, as the large Italian community filled the Italian schools to overflowing.

Pasquale Villari criticized the government's priorities in financing schools for Italy's Mediterranean neighbors rather than for its "unredeemed" American emigrants:

> It has been said, in defense of this policy, that teaching Italian to foreigners is useful as well. This may be true, and sometimes it can serve commendable political purposes. But to flood the world with illiterates, to our harm and shame, whom we have not been able to give the most elementary instruction, for want of money, and then on the other hand to teach Italian to the Turks, Arabs, and Germans in the Orient, may not be the most logical and practical system.[53]

Not all of the Dante Society agreed with Villari's opposition to state-run schools. The Italians of Tunisia relied on the state schools as proof of Italian support for their colony under the French Regency. The Dante committee of Tunis opposed reductions in state funding for any of the Mediterranean schools and adhered to Crispi's criteria of what schools Italy ought to support: "not so much by the number of local Italians who would probably attend the schools, as much as by the stature and importance of Italy's traditional interests in these countries: it seems to us that Italy should spread the essential ideas of her modern civilization along with her language, by teaching those populations that sooner or later will undoubtedly escape the current political regime [of Ottoman Turkey]."[54] While Italy awaited the fall of the Turkish empire in the Mediterranean, geographic priorities dictated that American schools would receive only subsidies.

Crispi's program favored foreign policy over domestic interests, teaching Italian to everyone but Italians. But the root of migrant illiteracy lay at home, and money could be better spent on emigrants' education before and after departure. To improve the quality of Italian emigration, emigrants needed to study reading and writing before leaving Italy. Then they would earn more money and better escape exploitation and degradation overseas. The domestic roots of emigrant illiteracy were hotly debated in the Dante Society Congress of 1904 in Naples. Napoleone Colajanni, president of the Neapolitan committee and a Socialist deputy, presented a long report on poverty and illiteracy. He then urged the Society to resolve that the Italian government triple its contributions to Italian schools abroad, while treating Catholic schools "in an attitude of benevolent diffidence, because they can spread the Italian language and give the appearance of *italianità*, but will falsify the Italian soul."[55] Colajanni's analysis of how to decrease illiteracy was muddied by his attack on Catholicism. Anticlericalism appealed to only part of the Dante Society. Its Italian-Austrian members came from urban, secular, Masonic Trieste, but also from rural, Catholic Trentino.[56] After a debate over Catholicism and illiteracy, the Congress in Naples passed a truncated resolution. Another delegate called on the Society to fight illiteracy throughout Italy by calling attention to this plague in Italian society, supporting overburdened local schools, and campaigning for better funding from the national government. The Society's president at the time, Luigi Rava, condemned the motion and ensured its defeat "because it would completely alter the nature of the Dante Alighieri Society."[57] This Congress marked the end of the Society's involvement in the social issues surrounding illiteracy.

Despite its disputes over priorities and methods, the Dante Society agreed that abandoned emigrants would lose their heritage. Emigrants quickly developed a bastardized jargon of Italianate dialects mixed with the local language of their new homes. To the chagrin of Dante scholars like Villari, Italians in New York produced hybrid expressions such as "Il capitano ha stoppato la stima [The captain stopped the steamer]," "vischio [whiskey]," and "ai don ché [I don't care]."[58] Ridiculed for this nonsense vernacular, the New York paper *Il Progresso Italo-Americano* retorted that Italians in America were only speaking "the language of money [*lingua del guadagno*]."[59] Jargon, if ugly, was useful in communicating with Americans and other Italians. The emigrants had come to America to earn money. Cultural groups in Italy therefore promoted commerce as a cultural tool: strong trade relations between Italy and the Americas might persuade emigrants that speaking good, standard Italian served a utilitarian purpose.[60] Material interests provided the most reliable foundation for allegiance to a cultural community. The émigré middle class of lawyers, bankers, pharmacists, and doctors rallied the Italian community together in part to organize a natural clientele.[61] Where migration consisted only of laborers, who perhaps had no reason to refer to Italy except to bring their family to the Americas, the memory of Italian culture and traditions could quickly dim.

Bilingualism as Battleground for Informal Empire

Italy's educational project for emigrants faced deliberate opposition abroad. Just as Italy turned to schools to build an Italian identity for Italian emigrants, nations across Europe and the Americas began to use state schools as nationalist laboratories. Language training was only part of a cultural program for young pupils, to etch a national identity in their minds. Anticlerical governments closed or seized Catholic schools so that teachers would promote an unquestioning loyalty to the state. In 1882, the French Parliament enacted Jules Ferry's legislation to make secular education free and compulsory for boys and girls, ages three to thirteen. Schools would produce literate and loyal citizens, binding them to a civic religion. The closure of Catholic schools cemented clerical opposition to the French Republic, even as many nuns and priests stayed on to teach in secular schools.[62] In the German Empire, Bismarck's *Kulturkampf* against the Catholic Church established state supervision of all schools by 1871, to train German nationalists, not Catholic or Socialist internationalists.[63]

In the United States, education adopted a new political role. Nativists worried that immigrants would cling to their European roots and weaken the country's American identity. The Committee on State School Systems of the National Educational Association (NEA) reported in 1891 that foreigners were "destroying distinctive Americanism" by spreading a "system of colonization with a purpose of preserving foreign languages and traditions."[64] This was, in fact, the cherished dream of Italy and Germany, and American nativists organized a disproportionate backlash. Henry Ford made attendance of his factory schools mandatory for all immigrant employees, and the first sentence they learned was "I am a good American."[65] The NEA resolved to make compulsory public education a weapon against European influence. State schools would pressure children to turn against their immigrant families and heritage. In 1890 George Balch composed a special pledge for immigrant children in the New York City primary schools: "We give our Heads! and our Hearts! to Our Country! One Country! One Language! One Flag!"[66] Every day, young children promised to forget their parents' language. None would carry dual loyalties. Francis Bellamy's Pledge of Allegiance became famous at the NEA-sponsored Public School Celebration of Columbia in 1893: "I pledge allegiance to my Flag and to the Republic for which it stands: one Nation, indivisible, with Liberty and Justice for all."[67] The Pledge of Allegiance bolstered a nationwide campaign to install flagpoles with American flags at every schoolhouse in the country. In Bellamy's words, the flag possessed "as great a potency to Americanize the alien child as it has to lead regiments to death."[68] Schools institutionalized a daily pledge to their (new) flags, a tradition that began to fade only in the 1980s.

Patriotic rituals such as the Pledge of Allegiance reforged American public schools as assimilationist melting pots. By contrast, Italian schools abroad flew Italian flags and celebrated Italian holidays to promote a civic religion for emigrants, bringing national themes onto a transnational stage. Italy's schools in South America, Europe, and the Mediterranean used the Italian royal seal as official representatives of the government. To counter assimilation, Italians carefully developed participatory political culture for their expatriate schools across the world. The Second Congress of Italians Abroad in 1911 resolved that Italian pupils must develop "feelings of respect and attachment to the national flag—a symbol of the ideals of our race—raising the flag at the beginning and withdrawing the flag at the end of each school day." Against an American Pledge of Allegiance, the Congress called for a poetry competition to create "a brief and fervent 'Invocation to Italy,' synthesizing the faith and aspirations of our risen nation, to be sung in every Italian school class, at the beginning and end of each school day."[69] Yet in United States public schools, Italian children would celebrate Memorial Day instead of 20 September, Washington's birthday instead of the king's birthday, and American independence instead of the Italian Statuto. Immigrant children, and their parents, learned the language, customs, and holidays of their adopted homeland.

Italians attended the public schools of the United States not because of their rhetoric but because they were compulsory and free. The success of Italian schools was a question of market forces. Free state schools were unbeatable, but Italian schools in rural South America faced no local competition. This made South America seem a better place to build Greater Italy. Ranieri Venerosi, editor of *Italica Gens*, noted that Italian schools in North American cities "bear modest fruits because they are overcome by the competition of local indigenous schools." He called for increased subsidies to the Italian schools of southern Brazil, "the most intact remnants of our ethnic expansion in America."[70] On the remote frontiers of Brazil and Argentina, Italian schools flourished as the only option for Italian and many non-Italian families, who willingly paid for their children's education. By 1905, the Italian government subsidized 32 Italian schools in Argentina and 155 schools in Brazil.[71] However, the United States had already overtaken Brazil as the preferred destination among emigrants. After Italy banned free emigration to Brazil in 1902 to stop the exploitation of emigrants on former slave plantations, Italians stopped arriving and communications with Italy ceased. Because Italian shipping companies relied on profits from emigration to support all their routes, no Italian ships called in the ports of southern Brazil. If no Italian emigrants came, few Italian goods arrived either, because Italian merchants would have to ship their products on British or German vessels through Hamburg. This gave German goods an advantage in costs and prices, and stifled Italian exports to Brazil.[72] Without communications from Italy, the frontier settlements became completely isolated from their mother country, as the immigrants preserved their original dialects and traditions. After a hundred years, a profound cultural gap still divides these rural colonies from their modern, cosmopolitan cousins in Italy.[73]

Neither rural isolation nor urban concentration of Italian emigrants could reliably preserve their *italianità*. When emigrants scattered across the frontier of southern Brazil, in towns of less than a thousand people, the efforts of Italian consuls and traveling inspectors were too diffuse to be effective.[74] When emigrants concentrated in cities, Italian schools and charitable institutions were quickly overwhelmed. By 1899 the Italian schools in Buenos Aires enrolled four thousand pupils but needed space for eighteen thousand Italian children.[75] Immigrants in cities were hard pressed to maintain their Italian culture, let alone learn standard Italian, because "they have greater contact with the indigenous peoples, out of necessity."[76] The situation only worsened with time. Many Italian politicians had preferred South America to North America for Italian migrants, in part because the Latin languages were less alien than English. For immigrants in South America, however, Spanish or Portuguese would be easier to learn than standard Italian, and much more useful.[77] Efforts to promote the Italian language could fare as well, or better, in English-speaking countries.

Teaching Italian was not an end in itself but served as the vehicle for reinforcing an Italian cultural identity abroad. The same attitude prevailed in the United States concerning English. Educators attacked bilingualism, claiming that it confused children and made them slower learners. In 1889 Wisconsin and Illinois made English the only language of elementary school instruction for all private and public schools. After World War I, fifteen other states passed similar laws, until the Supreme Court ruled them unconstitutional in 1923.[78] Theodore Roosevelt condemned bilingualism on political and social grounds. He insisted that immigrants abandon their mother tongue: "We have no room for any people who do not act and vote simply as Americans, and as nothing else. . . . We believe that English, and no other language, is that in which all the school exercises should be conducted. . . . whether the good or the evil [of immigration] shall predominate depends mainly on whether these newcomers do or do not throw themselves heartily into our national life, cease to be European, and become Americans like the rest of us."[79] Mixing accusations with false sympathy, Roosevelt aimed to sever all connections between American immigrants and their European families, starting with language. Italian colonialists, who could not help but admire Roosevelt's bold foreign policy, had to agree that the United States had the "right to demand" that all immigrants "become thoroughly Americanized."[80] Roosevelt shrewdly blamed immigrants themselves for any misunderstandings:

> where immigrants, or the sons of immigrants, do not heartily and in good faith throw in their lot with us, but cling to the speech, the customs, the ways of life, and the habits of thought of the Old World which they have left, they thereby harm both themselves and us . . . though we ourselves also suffer from their perversity, it is they who really suffer most . . . The immigrant cannot possibly remain what he was, or continue to be a member of the Old-World society. If he tries to retain his old language, in a few generations it becomes a barbarous jargon; if he tries to retain his old customs and ways of life, in a few generations he becomes an uncouth boor. He has cut himself off from the Old-World, and cannot retain his connection with it.[81]

Despite Italian attempts to maintain an open relationship with Italian immigrants in the United States, foreign languages and customs became so stigmatized that many American children could not communicate with their own immigrant grandparents.

The stakes in this struggle went far beyond language, as Theodore Roosevelt knew. For Italian nationalists, literacy and language were secondary to patriotic themes of grandeur. The Dante Alighieri Society used its namesake as a patriotic symbol, not as a literary icon. The Italian government revealed its priorities after a diplomatic negotiation over Italian education. In 1916 when Argentina reformed its foreign language programs in the public schools, the Italian foreign minister Sidney Sonnino pressured the Argentine government into retaining Italian as an obligatory course. Sonnino reported with pride to the Dante Society that Argentina had decided that "in the national colleges, instead of teaching grammar, the study of Italian literature will be obligatory, as this is considered more appropriate for communicating the glories of Italy."[82] The aim was not to speak Italian well, but to speak well of Italy. Language could be the lynchpin of informal empire.

Preserving Ethnic Expansion

Despite all progress, emigrant colonialism never developed into a self-assured success. The Dante Alighieri Society continually tried to win new recruits and sources of funding. From a sense of frustration and a high moral mission, many writers interested in Greater Italy became self-appointed apostles to publicize Italy's responsibilities to her children abroad. Pietro Gribaudi emphasized Italy's moral imperative to support its emigrants in his high school textbook on "Greater Italy": "There is no country on earth where some Italian does not live. This thought, while it must arouse in us the feeling of great and high destinies to which the Italian nation is called, must drive us to forget not our faraway brothers, who, with their honest labor, powerfully advance a knowledge and appreciation of Italy in every corner of the globe. These our brethren merit all of our affection and, in case of need, our assistance."[83] The international reach of Italian emigration was shadowed by domestic neglect; a sense of triumph combined with guilt and fear for the future. This could be seen most readily at the expositions and congresses organized to display the achievements of Italians abroad and to document the spread of Italian culture. The 1892 Italian-American Exhibition in Genoa and the 1898 pavilion of Italians Abroad at the National Exposition in Turin, which had so impressed Luigi Einaudi, were followed by the 1906 Exhibition of Italians Abroad in Milan, in conjunction with the city's International Exposition.[84] The First and Second Congresses of Italians Abroad, sponsored by the Italian Colonial Institute in 1908 in Turin and Rome and in 1911 in Rome, offered new representation for emigration.[85] These congresses became forums not only for heralding expatriate accomplishments, but for complaining about insufficient support and the insurmountable obstacles facing emigrant colonies.

The exhibitions of Italians abroad also played an important role in creating a national Italian identity and image for those who had remained at home. Most Italian national expositions inevitably highlighted individual industries and regions, reinforcing the divisions and rivalries which had bedeviled the peninsula's history. The exhibits in the pavilions of Italians abroad, however, usually could not be traced back to a particular region; they were presented as the triumph of Italian genius abroad. Visually and rhetorically, emigration was truly a national project. Outside of Italy, observers could note the special characteristics and achievements of the Italian "stock," in competition with all other "races," according to the pseudo-scientific concepts so dear to the late nineteenth century which defined ethnicity by comparison and contrast.[86]

In celebrations of Italy's expansion abroad, the international Italian-language press took pride of place. The Milan Exposition of 1906 arranged a special exhibition hall to honor the 472 Italian periodicals abroad, including 60 daily papers, written mostly or entirely in Italian. The United States alone counted 135 Italian periodicals, including 11 dailies and 89 weeklies: "many times more periodicals, and usually far superior ones, than any other Italian colony."[87] These numbers had multiplied almost fourfold since the Ministry of Commerce in 1893 tallied 130 international Italian publications, with 82 in Europe, 17 in North America, and 27 in South America. For the Milan Exposition, Giuseppe Fumagalli categorized the Italian press into news service bulletins; literary reviews; advertising supplements; publications of the Italian Chambers of Commerce; information bulletins for emigrants; revolutionary papers opposing the Italian government, which he compared to the exiled Risorgimento press of the 1840s; religious papers, published by the Salesian order; and trade journals, published for Italian construction workers, stonemasons, carpenters, and miners. Whatever its content, if a periodical was published in Italian, it promoted literacy and association in Italian communities abroad. Even the anarchist newspaper *Questione sociale* of Paterson, New Jersey, sent to the Milan Exhibition a copy of its issue from 29 July 1905, celebrating the fifth anniversary of King Umberto's assassination by Gaetano Bresci. The newspaper had sponsored Bresci's fateful voyage from Paterson to Monza. As Fumagalli later noted, President Roosevelt suppressed distribution of the paper in 1908.[88]

Italian newspapers were crucial in perpetuating emigrants' Italian identities. The metropole charged the colonial newspapers with a lofty mission: "to defend Italian language and culture from invasion by foreign races . . . [such newspapers] are attempts to defend and diffuse *italianità*."[89] In this view, Italian migrants were not invaders crossing borders, but were themselves defenders against the cultural attack of "foreign races." In the words of Guglielmo Marconi, the inventor of radio, emigrant newspapers "held high the spirit of *italianità*" abroad, helping emigrants better to remember Italy.[90] At their best, the newspapers provided important news from Italy, united the local Italian colony in charitable causes, and provided a useful economic and cultural forum. New York City's *Il Progresso Italo-Americano*, the oldest Italian daily in the United States, boasted a long list of subscription campaigns: building monuments to Garibaldi in 1888 in Washington Square Park, to Columbus in 1892 on Columbus Circle, to Verdi in 1906 on Verdi Square, and to Dante in 1912 (dedicated in 1921 in Dante Park); defending Giovanni Verrazano as discoverer of the Hudson River and Antonio Meucci as inventor of the telephone; ensuring that Columbus Day was not named Discovery Day in New York State; and building a pantheon over Garibaldi's house on Staten Island.[91] The paper also tried to defend Italians condemned to death by the American judicial system. Awash with Italian patriotism, most Italians in New York were mortified when an Italian anarchist from New Jersey assassinated King Umberto. As penance, *Il Progresso* commissioned a bronze relief sculpture and wreath for the royal tomb in the Roman Pantheon; the daily newspaper also produced a memorial for President William McKinley's tomb after he was shot by Polish anarchist Leon Czolgosz.[92] The newspaper demonstrated and consolidated the status of an Italian community in New York. More subtly, it directed its readers toward Italy, reporting extensively on Italian politics, news, and affairs.

Despite the quantity of Italian international periodicals, their quality was notoriously uneven. Papers appeared and disappeared "like mushrooms."[93] Fumagalli calculated that one out of fifteen Italian periodicals folded between 1905 and 1907, or at least 31 of a total of 472.[94] The plethora of periodicals lowered profits and prevented the establishment of Italian newspapers with national circulations and a weighty voice. At their worst, emigrant newspapers survived on blackmail payments, by threatening to ruin reputations within the Italian community. Luigi Villari, who assisted emigrants at the Philadelphia consulate, called Italian American papers "a parody of journalism," but Giovanni Preziosi defended them as "the only ideal bond that the emigrant has with his country of origin."[95] When Italian schools and churches collapsed under nativist pressure, capitalistic newspapers became the last bulwark of Italian language in America. Newspapers built up an Italian language readership abroad, broadening the market for Italian cultural production. The Second Congress of Italians Abroad in 1911 also praised the colonial press as "a very effective means, and almost the only means, so that our emigrants do not lose the notions of Italian language they learn at school, and their interest for things in the faraway fatherland."[96] Noting the large number of Italian American papers, the congress hoped for attrition. Survivors might rise above petty personal hatreds to form quality publications, as had happened in the German American community.

Another powerful Italian medium influencing expatriates and promoted heavily in the ethnic press was silent film. Italy stood at the vanguard of cinema up until the disastrous Great War, releasing the first blockbuster feature films, grossing millions worldwide, and attracting a very broad audience. In its silence, film was uniquely suited for international distribution, as gesture and spectacle communicated the films' full meaning, supplemented by translated intertitles but not hampered by the dubbed or subtitled discourse in the later "talkies." Italian films emphasized nationalizing themes consonant with the nascent international Italian community. *L'Inferno* (1911), the first Italian feature-length film and the first feature distributed in the United States, closes with a final shot of the monumental Dante Alighieri statue in Trent. The retelling of Dante's elaborate religious epic immediately transformed into a manifesto for Italians abroad, exiled and oppressed, especially under Austrian rule in Trent but, more generally, anywhere outside Italy. Gabriele D'Annunzio's ancient Roman epic *Cabiria* (1914) introduced the character Maciste, a mighty hero punished by his country's enemies, chained to a millstone on a foreign shore and concentrating in his person the entire saga of noble Italians oppressed abroad. The Maciste figure became a kind of Everyman, and his character went on to star in more than fifty feature films, including two films as a soldier during the Great War. Short subjects also played an influential role for emigrant audiences, as Italians abroad formed loyal markets for regional films from Naples and Venice, especially local dramas and the dramatic retellings of the legends of local patron saints. Transplanted Italian communities also commissioned footage of their native towns to celebrate, remember, and consecrate their group identity with a unique visual record.[97]

Italian newspapers and movies proliferated in the early twentieth century, but Italian language education dwindled in schools abroad. Italian colonialists realized that even in Argentina, the most idealized Italian American colony, Italian children were steadily losing their cultural heritage. The Dante Society secured a major victory in 1899, when Argentina made Italian language instruction mandatory in the public schools, supposedly "proving Argentina's deference to Italy."[98] In 1910, Argentina also established a chair for Dante Studies at the National University in Buenos Aires.[99] But after fifteen years of labor, even the Dante Society had to admit defeat. The Italian language courses were a mere five hours a month for eight months, hardly enough for schoolchildren to learn the language well. In 1912 Luigi Rava, the Society's former president, concluded that the Italian government had become involved too late and that the Dante Alighieri Society lacked the means to change the mind-set of a generation:

Let us be frank: we fooled ourselves for a long time about the conditions of Italians in Argentina, and we believed that the children of our emigrants, born in prosperity or blessed by the hard work of their parents, would feel a love for Italy. . . . The emigrant fathers have kept alive, and strengthened, the love of their native land! But this affection has often failed in their children. The schools have taught them to consider Argentina as their only fatherland. They have never learned of Italy; they know nothing of Italy's glories, economy, art, and beauties; they do not know the miracles and sacrifices of our political resurgence, nor the condition of our civilization. Our universities have not received them, and Paris has replaced Rome.[100]

The children of Italian emigrants felt that if Italy were so wonderful, their parents would not have left. Furthermore, many emigrants remembered the provincial, poverty-stricken Italy of the late nineteenth century and knew nothing of Italy's recent progress. Rava felt it just as well that Italian emigration now went to the United States, although Argentina had been touted as the ideal destination for thirty years. Italian nationalism simply could not encompass Italy abroad in its second generation.

To survive, Italian schools had to be an organic part of a larger Italian community. As a disillusioned Dante Society organizer in Argentina observed in 1901, Italian elementary schools rested on a faulty educational premise: "What influence can the brief, incomplete, and almost always ineffectual notions of Italian language and history exercise on Italian children born abroad, when their youthful tendency is to assimilate the life, language, and customs of the environment in which they live and love, not in school, where they sadly pass hours of . . . boredom. . . . When [a student] reaches puberty, the age when character and indelible tendencies form, the Italian school abandons him."[101] The Italian schools program concentrated too much on primary education, without any secondary vocational or professional training. The writer called for an increase in bourgeois and professional Italian immigration to organize the humble and hard-working laborers and raise community prestige. Italian professors, lawyers, and doctors could dedicate themselves to the Italian colonies' survival, if only to guarantee their livelihood and leaven the lump of mass migration.

But proposals to export Italy's educated professionals became very controversial. Opponents of emigration in Italy decried the loss of capital which professionals took with them, and charged that the country had invested too many resources in the education of these doctors and lawyers to encourage them to go.[102] Pasquale Villari argued that the Italian government should tolerate emigration but never promote or encourage it.[103] Supporters of expatriate colonies, however, replied that without an Italian middle-class leadership, illiterate and unskilled emigrants would assimilate in the Americas. Italy's unemployed "intellectual proletariat" could arguably find work abroad more easily than in overstaffed Italy.[104] Britain and Germany stood as models: by sending trained merchants, bankers, and engineers to South America, they had developed an "informal empire" of railroad companies, mines, and port facilities.[105] To match these successes, Italy would have to build up its skilled and professional emigration. But Argentina, the country with the highest percentage of Italians in the Americas, resolved the dilemma by blocking the immigration of professionals. Beginning in 1890, the Argentine government refused to grant licenses to lawyers, pharmacists, and doctors, unless they had studied in Argentina. With the number of Argentine professional students climbing rapidly, foreigners were simply ruled unfit to practice their profession in Argentina.[106] Only manual workers could emigrate to Argentina and find employment. This doomed any balanced class structure in Italian communities, making it impossible to replicate Italy inside Argentine society. Italians became "worker bees," laboring for the profit of others instead of managing their own careers.[107]

Even as educated migration proved controversial in South America, uneducated and illiterate migration aroused opposition elsewhere. In 1901 the Commonwealth of Australia enacted a harsh Immigration Restriction Act, using a literacy dictation test to exclude "undesirable" groups. To restrict emigration in the United States, Congress four times approved bills requiring immigrants to pass a literacy test in any written language; these nativist measures were vetoed by Presidents Grover Cleveland in 1897, William Taft in 1913, and Woodrow Wilson in 1915. In 1917 Congress finally gathered enough votes to override Wilson's veto and the literacy test became law, with further restrictions on immigration enacted in 1921 and 1924. During the long gestation of the anti-immigrant literacy test, Italian colonialists closely followed debates in the United States. In 1903 a former emigration inspector in Genoa noted that only Turkish immigrants to the United States had higher rates of illiteracy than Italians. He concluded that a literacy test would become law sooner or later and that Italy ought to direct its emigration away from North America into South America.[108] At the First Congress of Italians Abroad in 1908, delegates debated what to do about a possible American literacy test. Nicola Mariani pointed out that migrants' illiteracy "is the cause of the low opinion which Americans hold" toward Italians. He argued for Italy to block illiterate emigration as a matter of pride. While other delegates agreed, the Socialist deputy Angelo Cabrini, who had helped establish the Humanitarian Society in Milan for temporary emigration, opposed all literacy tests for emigration and immigration, and urged that Italy enforce mandatory elementary education to combat illiteracy, "especially in the South."[109]

Writing from the United States, Luigi Villari blamed Italy's Liberal government for allowing illiterates to emigrate. He argued that such conditions worked against emigrants' own interests; only with an education could they defend themselves against rampant fraud and exploitation.[110] At the same time, Villari romanticized illiterate workers as representing the true genius of Italy abroad, in contrast to exploitative bankers, saloon keepers, and emigration agents.[111] Established Italian Americans were suspect because many frauds against new Italian immigrants were perpetrated by their own countrymen. Luigi Villari wrote his father Pasquale from the Philadelphia consulate to decry the First Congress of Italians Abroad as a "farce":

> The idea is to bring to Italy the "prominent leaders" from the Italian colonies in America to obtain their views on the best way to protect emigrants. Precisely these "prominent leaders" are the ones who live by exploiting and swindling the newcomers! The "prominent leaders" of these colonies, instead of being asked their opinion and "enlightened guidance," should instead be put in jail or hanged.[112]

As a legal advisor to Italian immigrants, Villari was jaded and disillusioned by endless cases of exploitation that ruined immigrants' health, morals, and finances. Villari blasted the short-sightedness of Liberal governments which inevitably protected the wealthy over the poor and weak and relied upon emigration as a crutch for the country's social and economic problems: "one of the worst consequences of emigration is that it leads the government to neglect serious social problems, believing it can rid itself of them by making people emigrate; real solutions are thus postponed." He proposed internal reform and the end of emigration to America as the only moral solution.[113]

Nonetheless, many colonialists looked to build a permanent structure in the Americas upon the shifting tides of current emigration. New emigrants were uncorrupted and untainted by American society and provided hope for resolving the future of the "spontaneous colonies." Illiterate Italian immigrants interacted less with their American neighbors. This made them less likely to assimilate and more likely to return to Italy after earning money for their retirement. The *Italica Gens* argued that the most effective way to preserve Italian communities in the Americas would be "to feed them with new Italian blood, which is the element most adapted to understand and further our patriotic intentions. It is necessary, before the emigration currents cease, to concentrate and consolidate from the national point of view the many percolating Italian colonial nuclei, and in them establish *italianità* on solid bases."[114] This reliance on continual immigration, on "new Italian blood" instead of established interests, proved to be a fundamental weakness in plans for Greater Italy. Supporters of emigrant colonialism always hoped for more stable colonies to evolve out of flux, but to build these communities they based their hopes on the unpredictable flow of transnational migration. Changes in migration wrought widespread havoc. After the Italian government sharply limited emigration to Brazil, for example, expatriates were cut off from Italian trade, culture, and society. The Italian colonies of southern Brazil, established over three decades, suddenly became an ethnic backwater.

States, groups, and individual actors worldwide mixed together in a free migration dynamic that none could control, though each had a wide range of action. As a result, *italianità* represented a rich collection of social, cultural, and economic meanings, teeming with complexity, competition, unity, and division, but strengthened by transnational institutions and the science of Italian ethnography. Italians abroad united in a broad range of societies for both practical and lofty purposes, forming charities to support hospitals and repatriation for indigents; associations for recreation and athletics; mutual aid societies and cooperatives; and circles for drama, music, and poetry. The names of Italian societies reflected the diversity of Italian experience, including the namesakes Count Cavour, Giuseppe Mazzini, Giuseppe Garibaldi, his wife Anita Garibaldi, Dante Alighieri, place names in the North and South, various royal princes and princesses, "Union and Fraternity," Christopher Columbus, the Virgin Mary, and 20 September, the date in 1870 when the papacy lost power over Rome. These societies represented the practical application of Italian culture in new immigrant settings. In 1911 the Italian Colonial Institute counted 1,467 Italian societies abroad, with 430 in the United States, 316 in Argentina, 277 in Brazil, 49 in Chile, 46 in Uruguay, 79 in Switzerland, and 69 in France.[115] Numbers did not mean strength; as Luigi Barzini commented in 1902, "the Italians of the Plata are united in about three hundred different associations: which means they are perfectly divided."[116] But despite their bitter divisions and infighting, outside of the Italian peninsula these migrants were hailed as "Italians" by Brazilians, Americans, Argentines, and Frenchmen. The uprooted and transitory nature of emigration furthered the development of an Italian identity, codified with the development of Italian ethnographic studies.

Mass migration opened a new frontier of Italian experience, full of possibilities. Together with new initiatives in publishing, expositions, and irredentist politics, emigration presented a unique opportunity for charitable and educational projects. The church, like the state, sponsored ministries to aid Italian emigrants both spiritually and temporally. This cooperation would link Catholic traditions to Italian ideologies, with immediate and enduring consequences.

5

For Religion and for the Fatherland

As hundreds of thousands left Italy for harsh working conditions abroad, Catholic clerics and government bureaucrats in Rome worked together to assist, encourage, and proselytize Italian emigrants. Emigration became a missionary field for winning expatriates' patriotic loyalties to Italy and cementing their fidelity to Catholicism. Church and state found common ground and used similar methods to anchor their flock to the traditions of their mother country. In the absence of a national culture, the ancient, active, and well-defined Roman Catholic identity became a key element of *italianità*, especially as cultivated abroad. Limited in its political reach, the Italian state collaborated with the Catholic Church's increasing social and cultural commitment to Italian emigrants.

By focusing on emigration, one could forget about the bitter legacy between the Italian king and Catholic pope. The papacy did not officially recognize Italy's existence until 1929. The Liberal government of Piedmont-Sardinia had united the Italian peninsula between 1859 and 1870 by expropriating territories from the pope, the Austrian emperor, the king of Naples, and other Catholic rulers. The final act came on 20 September 1870 when Italian troops attacked the city of Rome, defended by papal troops. Pope Pius IX retreated to the Vatican Palace, and the new King of Italy settled into the papal palace on Quirinal Hill in Rome.[1] Though sworn political enemies on the Italian peninsula, church and state joined forces abroad to help emigrants for practical reasons and with positive results. At first, the Vatican decried emigration as yet another failing of the Italian Liberal state; under papal management, Italy would certainly do better. But after the fall of Crispi in 1896, the Italian government began subsidizing hundreds of Catholic schools and hospitals abroad that served Italian migrants. Catholic intervention reached where the Italian state could not, particularly in the United States, and Italy's leaders were willing to pay for the Church's help. Common goals abroad thus ushered in a new era of cooperation at home.

Charitable assistance made a world of difference for emigrant Italians. They labored on the fringes of harsh, raw capitalist economies, hired at low wages in a boom cycle and discharged immediately in a bust cycle. Italian men, many without their families, worked in factories and construction projects in cities but also worked around the clock building railroads, digging mines, and cutting tunnels in remote locations. Even when families emigrated together, they worked without a social safety net. An Italian woman returning from the frontier of Brazil confessed her pathetic conditions there to the bishop of Cremona, Geremia Bonomelli: "One day I and my husband and children left our hut and went to plow. After cutting a few furrows, my husband stopped, put his hand to his forehead as if he felt something, and called us to say, I have counted the days and today must be Christmas Day. I have never worked on Christmas. Let's go home. We went home silent and then sat down next to each other, and I was crying. Then my husband stood up and said, we cannot go forward like this. We will go home [to Italy], and we did."[2] Besides the distance from extended family and native towns, emigrants could be even further removed from their cultural and religious heritage. These traditional identities could mix easily with national consciousness; Bishop Bonomelli concluded that the anecdote "shows who our peasants are and how for them the fatherland and religion are very closely linked."[3] With political and religious initiatives, Bonomelli hoped to divert the uprooted mass of emigrants away from Socialism and toward a transnational Italian Catholicism, with a single supportive network at home and abroad.

Religion and Ethnic Separatism in the Americas

While opposed to the idea of a united Italy, the Vatican strongly supported an Italian identity among the country's emigrants. Many in the hierarchy believed that Italians were intrinsically Catholic. Furthermore, the best way to keep Italy's emigrants Catholic would be to strengthen their ties to the fatherland.[4] Only as united Italians, and Catholics, could they withstand assimilationist pressures in their new homes. To the chagrin of Irish Americans, Rome still considered the United States a Protestant nation. Until 1908 Canada and the United States remained missionary fields, under the jurisdiction of the prefect of Propaganda Fide in Rome. From this perspective, Italians were migrating en masse to a land of infidels. Anticlerical Italian Liberals, anarchists, and Socialists dominated many Italian communities in the Americas, and Protestant Italian American missionaries won many converts.[5] Return migration reflected this political and religious influence abroad, decreasing the Catholic Church's strength within Italy itself. But from an American perspective, the flood of impoverished Italian immigrants threatened to overwhelm the archdiocese of New York, and strained relations between the American church hierarchy and the Vatican. The situation demanded a religious and social response coordinated on both sides of the ocean.

The plight of Italian emigrants inspired exemplary missionary efforts addressing migrants' cultural, social, educational, and spiritual needs. The pioneer was Monsignor Giovanni Battista Scalabrini, the Bishop of Piacenza, who favored a collaborative reconciliation between church and state to resolve Italy's most pressing problems. Scalabrini, born in 1839 near Como in Lombardy, became famous as a seminary rector for his work in teaching the catechism. Pius IX appointed him bishop in 1876 and called him "the apostle of the catechism," and more than a hundred years later in 1997 he would be beatified as "the apostle of emigrants." In both fields, Scalabrini viewed education as a solution to social problems. Pius's successor, Leo XIII, asked Scalabrini in 1885 to write an anonymous pamphlet on the harmful divide between the papacy and the Italian state, which skewed Italy's social, religious, and political life. Intransigent clerics, who opposed any discussion of compromise with the Italian reconciliation, attacked the pamphlet viciously, and Leo never allowed Scalabrini to acknowledge his authorship. But Scalabrini continued to find ways to bridge divisions within Italian society.[6]

As transatlantic emigration grew through the 1880s, Scalabrini realized that a tenth of his congregation in Piacenza had emigrated from Italy. He turned to the Americas as a missionary field, to assist emigrants and to build Italian patriotism upon a foundation of Catholicism. Drawn to emigration by his concern for individual families in his diocese, Scalabrini intervened more than a decade before the Italian state. In 1887

Scalabrini wrote to Propaganda Fide and began to organize a network of priests and nuns to aid Italian emigrants in Italy and the Americas. Scalabrini also published his most famous work, *Observations on Italian Emigration in America,* publicizing his ideas and plans. He significantly altered reigning preconceptions of emigration by presenting the phenomenon as a necessary consequence of economic want and an invaluable social safety valve, which demanded the attention and protection of the Italian church and state cooperating together: "Religion and fatherland, these two supreme aspirations of every good heart, become intertwined, become complete in this work of love, which is the protection of the weak, and fuse together in a marvelous harmony. The miserable barriers, erected by hate and anger, disappear . . . every distinction of class or party withdrawn. . . . May Italy, sincerely reconciled with the Apostolic See, emulate its ancient glories and add a new, undying glory, setting even its faraway children on the shining paths of true civilization and progress."[7] Scalabrini urged broad support for emigrants' cultural identities as both Catholics and Italians. Petty politics on the peninsula should not obstruct the protection of the vulnerable Italian emigrants abroad. Pope Leo XIII specifically approved Scalabrini's call for reconciliation with Italian state officials if they took the first steps.[8]

Over the next thirty years, Bishop Scalabrini's projects for emigrant schools, charities, and worship services became a reality. In 1887 he established the Christopher Columbus Missionary Institute in Piacenza to honor the Italian "who first brought Christianity to the Americas."[9] This became the seat of the Missionary Congregation of St. Carlo Borromeo. The first ten missionaries left Piacenza in July 1888, traveling to New York City and Brazil. Following the example of the German Raphaelsverein, Scalabrini also helped organize a supportive lay St. Raphael Society, founded in 1889 by the Marquis Giambattista Volpe Landi. By 1895 Scalabrini had organized an order of sister missionaries as well. The Vatican created additional institutions, culminating with the Pontifical College for Italian Emigration, founded by Pius X in 1914 as a specialized seminary, and the Prelate for Italian Emigration, established by Benedict XV in 1920.

Bishop Scalabrini received wholehearted support from the Church hierarchy in Italy. The Jesuit journal *Civiltà Cattolica* (Catholic Civilization) praised Scalabrini's efforts to care for Italians fleeing their homeland in conditions of famine. The journal mourned that even though they "emigrate from the most Catholic land in the world," "many, many

Italians pervert themselves completely" in the United States. Scalabrini's patriotic aims also received a full endorsement. If migration continued along its present course, "soon [the emigrants] will lose, along with their faith, even the national character of Italians, and every principle of patriotic sentiment and decorum."[10] Support of emigrants' national consciousness was as important as humanitarian aid: "This sacred work mixes together the dearest and most noble feelings that can warm the heart of a man and a Christian: the love of God's glory, the love of our poor brethren, the love of Christ's church, and the love of the common fatherland [*patria comune*], which is greatly wounded when its limbs are torn away, passing to other countries as the jetsam of faith and of nationality."[11] The emigrants' identities as Italians and Catholics needed to be cherished, buttressed, and promoted by Italian and American prelates. In December 1888 Pope Leo XIII issued the Apostolic Letter *Quam Aerumnosa,* based on a draft by Bishop Scalabrini, in which he called on American bishops to support Scalabrini's program.[12] The letter specifically addressed the evils of Italian emigration, noting that emigrants often fled Italy to even worse situations abroad. The pope welcomed Scalabrini's efforts to send Italian missionaries "to console their fellow citizens in their own tongue."[13] The Italian language was fundamental to redeeming emigrants in their new homes.

While Bishop Scalabrini worked to build Italian patriotism within Catholic social programs for emigrants, his younger brother Angelo worked within the Italian government to build alliances with Catholicism. After 1896 Angelo worked as inspector general, and later director, of the Italian Schools Abroad Program, arranging state subsidies for the Dante Alighieri Society and for Catholic institutions working with emigrants. This politicization of Catholic migration brought greater support from Italy but caused increased tension in the Americas.

The papacy's plans for Italian emigration irritated the Catholic hierarchy in the United States. In their view, America was not a Protestant country and not a land for missionary work. Struggling against Protestant nativists, American Catholics labored to define themselves as Americans, not alien imports. They felt the papacy's direct intervention was unnecessary and undesirable: immigrants' problems stemmed from their European background, not from a failure of the American clergy. One Irish author claimed that the only hope for Italian Catholics was to Americanize their children: "somehow the duty of even rudimentary instruction and training in the principles and practices of the Christian religion has been grossly neglected by large numbers of parish priests [in Italy]; the state of ignorance among this people cannot otherwise be accounted for. . . . The fact is that the Catholic Church in America is to the mass of the Italians almost like a new religion. . . . It is not likely that the old folks will ever be readjusted. They must tag after the Irish, and little by little their children will do great things for God in America."[14] Italian clergy did not appreciate this sentiment. In the end, many Italian priests ignored the American hierarchy; Franciscans, Capuchins, Servites, and Augustinians reported directly to their orders in Rome. The Vatican persisted in treating America as a mission field, and Leo XIII appointed an Italian Cardinal as a new Apostolic Delegate to the United States in 1893, over the protests of American bishops. Leo also decreed the coronation of beloved statues of the Madonna in New Orleans and in Italian East Harlem, New York City.[15] The papacy took a special interest in Italian migration, which was becoming Europe's largest, was almost entirely Catholic, and carried unique political importance for the Vatican. By contrast, the American Catholic Church received emigrants from all over the world and viewed Italian immigrants as one group among many others, including Catholic Poles, Slovenes, Slovaks, Greeks, Lebanese, Syrians, and French Canadians. In 1884 the Third Plenary Council of American bishops and archbishops in Baltimore had recommended a general Catholic approach to migration, not split along the lines of nationality. Leo XIII's apostolic letter disappointed the bishops by mentioning only Italian immigrants.

Far from the American position, Scalabrini defended Italian emigrants' culture and argued that a rapid Americanization would destroy their religion. In 1899 Bishops Scalabrini and Geremia Bonomelli presented public lectures in Turin as part of the National Exposition. Scalabrini called for Italians to militate against the melting pot: "Not many years ago, in the United States there were enormous efforts to Americanize . . . the emigrants of the various European nations. Religion and Fatherland mourned for millions of their lost children. Only one people knew how to resist this violent attempt at assimilation: the people with this motto on their flag: our church, our school, our language. Let us not forget this fact. Let us also work, each according to his strength, so that all Italians abroad possess the same motto, the same steadfastness, the same courage: for Religion and for the Fatherland."[16] He argued for a continuity in emigrants' intimate relations with God, family, and culture as individuals and families moved from Europe to America.

European migrants' Catholic traditions, however, had caused a raging debate in the United States.[17] Worried about the opposition of Protestant nativists, the "liberal" Catholic party, led by Archbishop John Ireland in St. Paul, Minnesota, called for immigrants to become Americans immediately upon arrival, worshiping in strictly geographic parishes with sermons delivered in English. The more "conservative" party, under Archbishop Michael Corrigan of New York, held that foreign-language parishes could help immigrants' transition into American Catholicism without destroying their culture and faith.[18] Scalabrini tried to avoid controversy by ordering his missionaries strictly to obey their local American hierarchy. He became personal friends with Archbishop Ireland and with Archbishop Corrigan, who donated a thousand lire to Scalabrini's Congregation.[19]

Yet Scalabrini unwittingly became involved in the controversy over American Catholic identity through the infamous "Lucerne Memorial" of 1891. The Memorial or memorandum, a letter to Pope Leo XIII about emigration ministries, was drafted by the Lucerne Congress of the St. Raphael societies of Germany, Austria, Belgium, and Italy, together with delegates from Switzerland and France. Bishop Scalabrini approved a draft and the congress voted on the final text. The bishop then arranged a papal audience for Peter Paul Cahensly, the wealthy German merchant who had founded the Raphaelsverein, and the Marquis Volpe Landi, president of the Italian St. Raphael Society, to present the resolutions, but Volpe Landi fell ill and could not attend. Thus, Cahensly alone became associated with the memorandum, which became a lightning rod for ethnic conflicts between Irish-American and German-American bishops. In support of immigrants in the United States, the letter called for special parishes for each national migrant group, together with parish and catechistic schools in their language, and priests and even bishops of their nationality. This last suggestion angered both conservative and liberal bishops in the United States. The liberal prelates Dennis O'Connell, Rector of the American College in Rome, and Archbishop Ireland of St. Paul falsified the text for the American press, adding that "Irish bishops in the United States only nominate Irish priests, who do not know the languages spoken by the immigrants."[20] Liberals in the American hierarchy took the opportunity to attack German Catholic traditions, German-language parishes, and unassimilated German-American bishops, all associated with "Cahenslyism." Even President Benjamin Harrison became involved, as worries about pan-German infiltration in the United States escalated. Archbishop Corrigan, who had helped organize the St. Raphael Society in New York City, wrote a scathing letter to Cahensly, blasting his tactless ignorance.[21]

Scalabrini's reply to Corrigan, written on behalf of Volpe Landi and Cahensly, sheds some light on the purpose of the memorandum. The Italian bishop explained that the resulting affair was "a tempest in a tablespoon. . . . Their plan was very simple: that the various European nationalities would have a representative in the American Episcopate, and not a foreigner, but an American citizen."[22] The St. Raphael Societies had meant to support migrants' ethnic cultures within American Catholicism, not create isolated ecclesiastical jurisdictions. They wanted to preserve ethnicity, regardless of legal citizenship. But the memorandum had become a springboard for polemics about European invaders in American society and culture. The Vatican quickly rejected the memorandum and reassured the American bishops that it would not implement Cahensly's suggestions. Scalabrini's prestige was damaged. In 1897 the Propaganda Fide refused to let him visit the United States for fear of the local bishops' reactions.[23] This was probably an overreaction; when Scalabrini later visited the United States in 1901 and Brazil in 1904, he was well received by local hierarchies.

The controversy over immigrants' best interests persisted.[24] Should the church help immigrants learn English, and improve their prospects for success in their new homeland? Or might immigrants avoid church services in a language they did not understand and turn to Italian Protestants or Italian Socialists and anarchists for solidarity? One of Scalabrini's missionaries, Giacomo Gambera, resigned from the order when the bishop insisted he teach emigrants Italian instead of English.[25] Mother Frances X. Cabrini (1850–1917), who in 1946 became the first United States citizen to be canonized as a saint, also disagreed with Bishop Scalabrini on the best approach to language instruction. Cabrini was born near Pavia as the youngest of thirteen children. After two convents refused to accept her because of her ill health, in 1880 she founded the Missionary Sisters of the Sacred Heart near Como, planning to travel to China. Bishop Scalabrini persuaded her to change her focus and work with Italians in the Americas, and Leo XIII supported her new mission.

Mother Cabrini and her seven companions arrived in New York City in 1889, but the working relationship with Scalabrinian missionaries there deteriorated. The disorganized fathers were unable to provide Cabrini with housing and eventually went into partial bankruptcy, to the horror of Archbishop Corrigan.[26] Corrigan recommended that Cabrini return to Italy, but instead she remained and found a place for her sisters and six Italian orphans. In 1892, on the four hundredth anniversary of Christopher Columbus's voyage, Mother Cabrini successfully founded the Columbus Hospital for Italians in New York. Cabrini explained that only the symbol of Columbus could unite the Italian community, split by royalist and anticlerical factions.[27] Over time, she created schools, orphanages, and hospitals in New Orleans, Chicago, Seattle, Buenos Aires, and Paris, and in Nicaragua, Panama, Spain, and England. Mother Cabrini insisted on bilingual education in her orphanage schools: "Purely Italian schools are contrary to common sense and contrary to the interests of the Italians themselves, who have to seek their livelihood by speaking the language of the country." In the New Orleans orphanage all classes were in English, with one hour of Italian language a day, in "poetry or some dialogue in history."[28] Mother Cabrini concentrated on improving the lot of Italian American immigrants in their new homes rather than preparing Italians for a likely return to Italy. She became an American citizen in 1909 in Seattle, and condemned the Italian patriotism of the Scalabrinians in New York: "it would please me more to go where the Missionaries from Piacenza are not present because I am not too well pleased with their spirit which seems to be more attached to the tricolor flag rather than to the Pope."[29] Bishop Scalabrini, by contrast, hoped to resolve Italy's political divisions, as well as emigrants' problems, by building an international support network for migrants with the combined, unique resources of both church and state.

Missionaries in Italian Africa

Bishop Scalabrini warned against settlement colonialism but eventually collaborated with the Italian government in the East African colonies as well as in the Americas. In his pamphlet on emigration, published shortly after the Dogali defeat in 1887, Scalabrini noted that "Italy does not have colonies, unless one counts the two strips of occupied land on the banks of the Red Sea, and cannot get any colonies without bloody contests in patent violation of international law."[30] He called for Italy to abandon the pursuit of population colonies in Africa and cited a lack of territorial emigration outlets as a reason to support emigrants in the Americas. But by the 1890s, Scalabrini's friendship with Bishop Geremia Bonomelli led him to expand his American missionary work into the Italian settlements of Africa.

Bonomelli was bishop of Cremona, neighboring Scalabrini's diocese of Piacenza, and he also opposed the intransigent Catholic stance in Italian politics. He worried that the Vatican's abstentionism would lead to the victory of Catholicism's true enemy, atheistic Socialism. Bonomelli thought of organizing a missionary order for emigrants at the same time as Scalabrini, but let Scalabrini put the idea into action. Bonomelli was close friends with Oreste Baratieri, a pious Catholic from the Trentino region, who had left Austria in 1860 at the age of eighteen to fight for Garibaldi's Expedition of the Thousand. In 1890, when Baratieri was a colonel in Massawa, he asked Bonomelli if Italian priests could replace the French in Eritrea. The new Italian colony was under the Vicariate of French Lazzarist missionaries in Ethiopia, and the Vatican would have to negotiate any transfer of authority. Bonomelli presented the idea to Scalabrini and reported back that Scalabrini "embraced the idea enthusiastically and is ready immediately to dedicate a session for our Eritrea Colony in his College for American Emigrants. He is a man of action and very broad ideas. And the means? This is the problem for him too." Bonomelli asked Baratieri if the Italian government could pay for the missionaries if they went to the colony.[31] In Eritrea the missionaries could serve both as military chaplains for the Italian army and as parish priests for the planned settlements of Italian emigrants. Scalabrini hoped that through this cooperation the Italian government would release Catholic priests nationwide from military conscription so they could instead work as missionaries to emigrants for three years of service.[32]

However, the Vatican was in no hurry to offend the Missionary Institution of Lyon, France, by endorsing the Italian colony. Missionary work remained an important connection between the church and the secular French Republic because France relied on colonial missionary work as a political tool: for example, after Tunisia became a French protectorate in 1881, the Italian missionaries there were replaced by French missionaries.[33] Changing the missionaries in Eritrea would certainly offend France because Britain had sponsored Italy's colony there to cut off any northern expansion by the French colony of Djibouti. In 1893, after be-

coming the general in command of Eritrea, Baratieri renewed the negotiations to replace the French missionaries with Italians "because with
the identity of the language the [native] populations would better persuade themselves that Catholicism is the religion of the rulers."[34] Baratieri was concerned that Eritreans perceived the French missionaries as
foreigners and that the colony's rulers and missionaries ought to share
the same language and identity. Bonomelli and Baratieri agreed this was
"in the interest of Religion, in the interest of Civilization, in the interest
of the Colony and of Italy, in the interest of the Propaganda [Fide]."[35]
However, Scalabrini made no headway beyond the Propaganda Fide's
double refusal in 1890 and 1891.[36] Baratieri's disastrous defeat at Adwa
in 1896, which ruined the Italian settlements and led to the withdrawal
of Italian troops, made the proposal obsolete.

Cooperation and Competition between Church and State

In 1900 Bishop Bonomelli created a new missionary organization to assist Italian emigrants in Europe, the Middle East, and the Mediterranean
basin, under the aegis of the National Association to Support Italian
Catholic Missionaries. Bonomelli was a natural ally for the National Association. Based in Florence, the group supported patriotic initiatives to
reconcile church and state and to promote Italian and Catholic faith and
culture: "to succor Italian Catholic missionaries, and to promote, under
their direction or vigilance, the establishment of new schools and the
diffusion of the Italian language, especially in the Orient and in Africa,
and to keep alive the love of country and the faith of the numerous Italians who find themselves in faraway regions."[37] The association had donated seven thousand lire to establish Scalabrini's congregation in 1887
and had organized a Catholic Italian settlement in Eritrea in 1896.[38]
Bonomelli agreed with the association's political goals and joined with
them despite the pope's preference for social involvement through the
intransigent *Opera dei Congressi* (Work of Congresses). With the pope's
blessing, these congresses intended to raise Catholic involvement in Italian society while keeping alive the papacy's claim to sovereignty over
Rome. But in Bonomelli's opinion, the church needed to adopt new tactics to oppose political atheism. The rise of Socialism in Cremona, under
the leadership of Leonida Bissolati, infuriated the bishop: "[Bissolati]
has perverted, in the broadest sense of the word, a great number of poor

peasants. . . . I could not be more disgusted."[39] Bonomelli worried about the Socialist propaganda targeting Italy's temporary emigrants to Germany and Switzerland, and feared that the Catholic Church needed to respond with a new organization and political mobilization. This took form with his *Opera di Assistenza* (Work of Aid) for Italian Emigrant Workers in Europe and the Near East.

Scalabrini disappointed Bonomelli by distancing himself from the new congregation. In April 1900 Bonomelli pressed his case to Scalabrini for two separate Catholic organizations in support of emigration: "the public will understand that between our two institutions lies not even a shadow of opposition. You help permanent emigrants in America; I, temporary emigrants in Europe, with different means: you, independent, I as an appendage of the Association for Italian Catholic Missionaries. . . . You distrust the lay element, and have your reasons; but I want a lay component in the *Opera,* because it is doubly profitable and because the material and moral means will be more secure. I have the intimate conviction that all the famous Congresses can do is make a hole in the water."[40] Bonomelli turned to the lay National Association for funding and personnel and put the *Opera dei Congressi* at arm's length. By contrast, Scalabrini accepted donations from the National Association and also the Propaganda Fide in Rome. He supported the papal congresses in his diocese and addressed their national meeting in 1899, even though he disagreed with their intransigent politics.[41] Scalabrini warned Bonomelli about joining a lay organization: "I do not distrust lay cooperation either, but in strictly religious matters, I do not love lay initiators, because it is difficult for them to abandon secondary aims, especially regarding politics."[42]

Nonetheless, Bonomelli became president and Ernesto Schiaparelli secretary in the new "*Opera Bonomelli,*" bringing together clerical and lay leadership in what proved an unstable relationship. Schiaparelli had founded the distinguished Egyptian Museum in Turin and was also secretary of the National Association in Florence. But Leo XIII refused to give his blessing to the new *Opera* in 1900, because he did not approve of the progovernment National Association as sponsor. The *Opera* accomplished early successes: in 1901 it published an inquest on the traffic in child labor between Italy and France, and it opened churches, lending libraries, and evening schools in the Italian workers' communities of Switzerland and southern Germany.[43] These temporary villages, hastily clustered around the major construction sites of tunnels, railroads, and bridges, had already drawn assistance from Italian Socialist groups, especially the Humanitarian Society in Milan. Bonomelli's group intervened to fight divorce, alcoholism, and Marxist propaganda. But the tension between lay and religious elements tore apart the *Opera Bono- melli*. Ernesto Schiaparelli resigned as secretary in 1907, splitting the *Opera* from the National Association. Leo XIII's successor, Pius X, blessed the *Opera* in 1909 under new management.[44]

After losing control of the *Opera*, the National Association was ex- cluded from the 1908 Congress of Italians Abroad, but in 1909 it founded a new endeavor: "*Italica Gens*, Federation for the Assistance of Transoceanic Emigrants," again with Schiaparelli as general secretary.[45] The *Italica Gens* hoped to unite missionaries and clergy in Italy and the Americas "in a vast Federation, with the patriotic intent of helping in all their power all Italian emigrants, without distinction of faith or party, if they are honest and need assistance." More ambitiously, the group planned to direct emigrants away from urban strongholds of anticleri- calism into rural, conservative, and traditional "colonies": "[We will] counsel the Italian emigrants to avoid the dangers of crowding in big cities, guiding them into compact and homogeneous colonies, in which a prosperous and independent economic condition is easier to achieve and where, thanks to the willing help of Italian parish priests, in the Church and school, they can *preserve the ancestral faith,* and the national language and character."[46] Like earlier organizations, the new group conflated Roman Catholicism with Italian culture, hoping to minimize the social adjustments of emigrating from Italy to the Americas and else- where. If emigrants later returned to Italy, hopefully they would come home at least as devoted, or perhaps more devoted and patriotic, than when they had left. While the *Opera Bonomelli* subsidized Italian Cap- uchins, Salesians, and Minorites in France, Romania, and the Near East, the *Italica Gens* created networks with individual Italian Salesians, Scal- abrinians, Franciscans, Servites, Jesuits, Augustinians, and parish priests serving emigrants throughout North and South America.[47] The Emigra- tion Missionaries of Monsignor Coccolo, the Sisters of the Sacred Heart of Mother Cabrini, the Daughters of Mary, and the *Opera Bonomelli* all supported the *Italica Gens,* but the headquarters of the Scalabrinian Or- der did not.

Like the secular Dante Alighieri Society, the Catholic *Italica Gens* made Italian language education its central mission. Besides writing letters and translating documents for emigrants, the group planned to boost Italian patriotism directly through schools. South American governments allowed foreign governments to establish national schools, but the United States deliberately banned such schools. Here the *Italica Gens* proposed to meet Italy's patriotic needs through religious schools. Inexpensive parish schools, with self-sacrificing Italian priests and nuns as teachers, were the only viable competition against state-funded schools in the United States. *Italica Gens* proudly cited the opinion of Pasquale Villari's son Luigi, Italian vice-consul for emigration in Philadelphia: "parish schools are the best means for maintaining Italian language and feelings among emigrants, because the Priests have influence on the children and families outside school. I can certify from experience that the parish schools really teach Italian and establish patriotic sentiments. The results are certainly more profitable than the products of any other schools or lay institutions, which have the life cycle of mushrooms."[48] The Second Congress of Italians Abroad in 1911 also reported that parish schools had done more than anything else to preserve the Italian language in the United States.[49] Private Italian schools charging tuition simply could not compete with free American schools. The *Italica Gens* concluded that "[parish] schools, more than any other institution, must be entrusted with fostering the feeling of *italianità*."[50] By subsidizing Catholic schools and other activities, the group hoped to preserve something of "*italianità* and the Italian language [in America] for fifty or a hundred years" into the future.[51]

Beyond education, however, the *Italica Gens* unabashedly allied itself to a belligerent Italian monarchism and nationalism. The cover of the monthly *Italica Gens* magazine, published beginning in 1910 at the group's headquarters in Turin, featured the arms of the House of Savoy in red and white. Photographs from the Italian Naval League of Italy's new dreadnought battleships, the *Dante Alighieri, Giulio Cesare,* and *Vittorio Emanuele,* appeared wherever there was space on the page. *Italica Gens* published these photographs in the hope that they would be circulated widely among emigrants, promoting "the memory and the knowledge of the grand and good things the fatherland is doing. . . . The Navy is one of the highest manifestations of the spirit and the strength of a people."[52] Warships and schoolchildren became the organization's twin symbols. Religion thus took second place to nationality. The *Italica Gens* urged priests to follow the example of German priests by withholding the sacra-ments from parents who did not send their children to Italian schools.[53] With animosity towards the Germans, the *Italica Gens* harbored an anti-Austrian irredentist agenda. The federation's journal editor, Count Ranieri Venerosi, also welcomed the Libyan War with the bellicose rhetoric of racial struggle: "a country with such an army, exponent of the virile attitudes and high patriotic spirit of its people, can look with pride to the future, because it has in itself the vital germ of the superior races."[54] The group would later work closely with Mussolini's government to "fascisticize" Italian communities abroad.

The *Italica Gens'* political activism diverged from the Catholic missions who continued to oppose the Liberal monarchy and its nationalistic belligerence. While Catholic Italian patriotism sometimes paralleled Liberal Italian patriotism, the two often conflicted because of their separate goals. The Vatican and the Italian monarchy competed for fundraising dollars after the devastating Calabria-Messina earthquake of 1908. Italians abroad had to choose their loyalties and donate either through their parish or through the secular Red Cross.[55] But beyond such competition, the involvement of the Catholic Church in emigration directly influenced the Liberal government's approach. Bishop Scalabrini helped frame the political debate over emigration through his publications, speeches, and lobbying efforts and was instrumental in creating the watershed emigration law of 1901. Cooperation in emigration reform helped ease the mutual fear and distrust between Liberals and Catholics regarding imagined Masonic and Jesuit conspiracies. Pasquale Villari, for example, persuaded the Dante Alighieri Society to disavow its anticlerical Masonic origins in order to attract Catholic support in Italy and abroad.[56]

Through subsidies and coordination, the Italian state and church achieved a practical reconciliation in the field of emigration, despite persistent disagreements. The Emigration Fund exemplified the neutral ground which both clergy and government could occupy. Created through a tax on third-class emigrant fares, the fund was administered according to terms set by Parliament. Mother Cabrini, who was a personal friend of Leone Reynaudi, emigration commissioner from 1904–1908, rationalized how she could accept Italian state money in good conscience to build the Columbus Hospital of Chicago: "You know that the Emigration funds are a private company, although under the auspices of the government, but one does not have to have recourse to the government.

If it were government money, I would not take it."[57] By setting conditions on funding, the Italian state subtly controlled and coordinated the effort to propagate Italian culture.

Combined efforts over several decades produced outstanding results. In 1911, the Italian Colonial Institute carefully documented the success of Italian language schools in its *Yearbook of Italy Abroad and of Her Colonies*. In 1910, the Italian government had spent 1.65 million lire on Italian schools abroad. Three-quarters of the budget went to the ninety-three Italian state schools, and one quarter to nongovernmental schools: L270,000 for lay schools and L130,000 for religious schools. The 244 subsidized religious schools were all Catholic (under Salesians, Benedictines, Carmelites, Sisters of the Sacred Heart, and other orders) except four schools: an Italian Episcopal school in New York City; an Italian Baptist school in New Haven, Connecticut; and Evangelical schools in Trenton, New Jersey; and Asuncion, Paraguay. The 301 lay schools received twice as much in subsidies as the religious schools, but the religious schools had nearly as many students: 27,786 in religious schools compared with 28,091 in lay schools. The Colonial Institute also noted that 1,667 other schools taught in Italian outside Italy without a government subsidy. Of these, 1,553 were lay and 114 religious, primarily of the Jesuit and Franciscan orders. Only three schools in the Americas had refused the Italian government's subsidy.[58] Under the direction of Angelo Scalabrini, the Italian Schools Abroad program had succeeded overwhelmingly in recruiting religious schools to its banner.

Especially when combined with language schools, religion offered one of the most important participatory forums for any immigrant group's national identity. Ancestral rites bound migrants to the Old Country, while local churches fostered ties within New World compatriot communities. In South America, national parishes were vital for stabilizing German and Italian colonial settlements. The cooperative effort of establishing a congregation and attending regular services provided the necessary cement for new and growing emigrant communities. Catholic intervention from Italy was crucial in sustaining the Italian language overseas. By contrast, the Protestant colonies of Italian Waldenses, who emigrated from the Alpine valleys of Piedmont to South America, communicated in Spanish, never learning standard Italian.[59]

The ethnic identity of churches resonated among immigrants in the Americas. Greeks, Russians, and Ukrainians gathered in distinctive

Orthodox churches, creating a remarkable social and economic cohesion around a common faith and language.[60] Roman Catholic liturgy, however, was celebrated in Latin with only the homily in the local language. National separatism within the Church had been specifically condemned as a heresy under the papal Syllabus of Errors of 1864.[61] Yet the special needs of Catholic immigrant groups led to stress and schism within American Catholicism. In 1897 Polish immigrants in Pennsylvania split from the American Catholic hierarchy, contesting the control of local church properties and complaining that no Polish American bishop had been appointed. The schismatic Polish National Catholic Church of America, established in 1904, joined with Old Catholic congregations in Europe who had dissented from Rome in 1873 after the First Vatican Council.[62] Italian Catholics, in comparison, enjoyed the strong advocacy of Italian bishops, cardinals, and popes from across the ocean to overcome obstacles from some unsympathetic American priests and bishops. For many emigrants, this support proved crucial in their new lives in parishes and communities overseas.

Yet church involvement in Italian nationalism came at a price. With time, the moral costs of associating with the Italian state would eclipse the ethical compromises missionaries had faced in colonial Africa. After the collapse of Liberal Italy in 1922, the papacy felt free to deal with its successor. Benito Mussolini's upstart Fascist movement was not tainted by a long anticlerical history, and in 1929 Cardinal Gasparri negotiated a Concordat and the Lateran Treaty to create Vatican City as an independent country and make Catholicism the state religion of Italy. Pope Pius XI praised Mussolini as "a man that Providence introduced to us," an endorsement soon regretted.[63] Mussolini, an atheist, undermined the church's social programs long before he launched devastating wars in Africa and Europe and brought the Holocaust to Italy. In the 1920s, Fascists infiltrated the secular leadership of the *Opera Bonomelli* to coordinate its missionaries with the Italian Fascists Abroad. Pius dissolved the *Opera* in 1928 to recognize its spiritual collapse.[64] Bonomelli's brand of political Catholicism had failed to adapt to rapid changes within Italy and abroad.

Before World War I, Italian Catholic missionaries with critical Vatican support eased the transition of emigrants into the disorienting religious and social climate of the Americas. Though bitter enemies at home, the Catholic Church and Italian state were able to work together to "make Italians," and Catholics, in emigrant colonies abroad. Scalabrini's and

Bonomelli's efforts demonstrated the common colonial approach to Italian settlers in Africa and the Americas, and Liberal governments subsidized their missionaries as cultural ambassadors of *italianità*. But the Italian state had much broader goals for Italian expatriates than their salvation in the afterlife. Emigrants were to be an integral part of the Italian nation, economy, and military. Italy's interests, and the best interests of Italian emigrants, often came into conflict. Writers and politicians debated the merits of helping emigrants assimilate into their local American economies and societies or encouraging them to remain as close as possible to Italian society in anticipation of their return from the Americas. Should Italians form new cultures and communities, and "new Italies," or should they remain faithful to their European Italian heritages?[65]

The Catholic Church framed questions differently, with more sensitivity to emigrants' long-term needs and with more support for assimilation. Receiving countries of immigration also afforded more latitude to Catholic missionaries than to representatives of the Italian state. Coordination between church and state played an integral role in the success of a cultural Greater Italy beyond Italy's borders and beyond diplomatic channels. Sadly, the inevitable confrontation between fascism and the church would bring Greater Italy to an early death.

6

Emigration and the New Nationalism

Emigration from Italy was so massive and widespread that it became a fundamental factor in both foreign and domestic policy. But the Liberal government's analysis of emigration's economic costs and benefits ignored a critical issue: the question of glory and prestige. Emigration rewarded millions of Italians with better wages and a better standard of living, especially in North America, but it hurt Italy's international reputation. Observers in Italy were shocked and infuriated to find that in the eastern United States, Italians were associated with crime, mafia, and the infamous "Black Hand." Emigrant Italians were more like "international camels" and "worker bees," under English and German managers, than the "merchant princes" that Einaudi had admired.[1] What had happened to Italy's grand international mission, prophesied by Mazzini and Gioberti?

Enrico Corradini provided new answers for anyone disaffected or embarrassed by Liberal Italy's compromises and shortfalls. Giuseppe Mazzini had dreamed of nations united in a peaceful Europe, but Corradini formulated a new, militarist nationalism. After a tour of South America in 1908, he seized upon emigration as the sign of Liberalism's failed mission. Corradini used emigration as an archetypical symbol, with resonance for all Italians, to translate his arcane, literary theories into a political program of social unity and belligerent national transformation. In his novels and plays, Corradini depicted miserable, frustrated emigrants, cut off from their families and from their native land because of Liberal policies. He opened his novel of 1910, *La Patria lontana* (The Faraway Fatherland), with a debate between the Nationalist and Liberalist visions of Italian expansion. The liberal economist Luigi Einaudi had claimed that trade with Italian expatriates constituted a Greater Italy, but Corradini's protagonist, the imperialist character Piero Buondelmonti, condemns the complex loyalties of an Italian-Argentinian wine producer:

—So, you hope to ruin the sale of Italian wine in Argentina?
—Of course.
—Last night you told me you sent all your children to school in Italy, and you feel you must return to Italy at least every other year.
—That is true.
—But it is also true that you have no right to boast of your *italianità* like you did last night.
—Why?
—Simply because you are a wine producer in Mendoza, and therefore an enemy to the importation of Italian wine in Argentina. You said this yourself.
—But you forget that in Argentina I give work to many Italians, and the more my business grows the more work I will give to my compatriots.
—Yours, but not mine. . . . These [expatriates] have placed themselves outside *italianità*: because they no longer belong to the Italian concentration camp. Maybe they are still patriots, if you give this word a sentimental meaning, but they will no longer be our co-nationals in the practical, active sense of this word. For them to remain Italians, nationally speaking, the land on which they labor and enrich themselves would have to become Italian. If you don't want to trap the nation in a blind alley, the only way to become nationalists, or patriots, is to be imperialists.[2]

For Corradini, a Greater Italy based on emigration amounted to self-serving hypocrisy: it atomized Italy's national energies and left each emigrant prey to exploitation and disillusionment. The image of an ethnic concentration camp, invented by the British in their scorched-earth campaign against the Boers of South Africa, captured Corradini's concept of national struggle. Against destructive individualism and class conflict he preached a new gospel of national unity, strong government, and imperial conquest: a "national socialism." In 1911 Corradini founded the Italian Nationalist Association, an elite group with broad political influence. By the time they merged with the Fascist Party in 1923, the Nationalists had overturned the standard reference points of Italian foreign policy.[3] But emigration's central role in the creation, development, and rise of

Nationalism has not been widely noted. Emigration was a key to the Nationalists' success in crystallizing their rhetoric and attracting a broad audience. The pressure of mass politics and manipulated public opinion, beginning with the issues of migration and war, crushed the Liberals' world of secret diplomacy and patient negotiations. Bold dynamism and warfare became ends in themselves.

The Italian Nationalists scored their first success by campaigning for the conquest of Libya. In the 1870s, Italian governments had begun diplomatic negotiations over Tripolitania and Cyrenaica, anciently joined as the Roman province of Libya. One by one the European powers signed notes of support: Germany in 1887, Britain in 1902, France in 1900 and 1902, Austria-Hungary in 1902, and Russia in 1909. Each agreed that if the *status quo* changed in the Mediterranean, Italy would inherit Libya from the decrepit Turkish Empire.[4] In 1911–1912, Italy did acquire Libya, but not through a diplomatic conference. The Italo-Turkish War over Libya launched a new phase of European imperialism and revolutionized Italian politics. Italy had not fought since the battle of Adwa in 1896; spurred by the Nationalists, the Libyan War became Italy's chance to prove its strength in battle, vindicate the Adwa defeat, and reinvent itself as a colonial power.

Emigration as a Test of Liberalism

Many intellectuals chafed against the restrictions and shortcomings of "small Italy," or *Italietta,* whose civic affairs were a series of backbiting, bickering, and sordid compromises. The father of Italy's petty politics seemed to be Francesco Crispi's old rival, Giovanni Giolitti. He first became prime minister in 1892 but quickly lost his post to Crispi over the Sicilian *Fasci* and a series of scandals. When Crispi fell from power after the battle of Adwa, his successors tried to rule through conservative, repressive policies, but also failed. By 1901, this allowed Giolitti back into government as Interior Minister, where he developed a political system of corruption, intimidation, and reform that would dominate national politics in Italy for more than a decade. Giolitti governed as Prime Minister from 1903 to 1905, 1906 to 1909, 1911 to 1914, and finally 1920 to 1921. While in power, Giolitti would arrange the national elections, using his authority over the police to fix vote counts and blackmail members of Parliament. Opposition candidates in the South were violently suppressed by the police and by hired *mafiosi*. Many southern deputies were notoriously loyal to the graft of the ruling government, whoever that happened to be. In the North, Giolitti wooed Radicals, Liberals, and the Socialists to create a progressive alliance in Parliament. Giolitti excused his manipulative cynicism by comparing himself to a tailor who must sew misshapen clothes for a hunchback client (Italy).[5] He concentrated his attention on peace, industry, and rising wages, but neglected unresolved issues of irredentism, disparities between North and South, and a lack of international prestige. These issues were Giolitti's blind spot. Oblivious to their popular appeal, he saw them as outmoded and impractical. But under Nationalist leadership, the unfulfilled Risorgimento became a platform for conservative and revolutionary opposition. International politics and warfare would polarize Italian domestic politics and tear Giolitti's system apart.

The stifling political atmosphere of post-Risorgimento Italy inspired opposition from the political Left and Right, and from highest spheres of Italian culture. The Italian state had long relied upon leading artists and writers to lend their prestige and respectability. The great novelist Alessandro Manzoni served in the first Italian Senate, along with Giuseppe Verdi. Giosuè Carducci became Italy's first "national poet," by playing a prominent role in Italian unification and extolling Italy's ideals in memorable anthems. Yet subversives also appeared, threatening the prestige of Liberal Italy. One of Italy's most influential writers, Gabriele D'Annunzio, entered the Chamber of Deputies in 1898 on the Extreme Right. Frustrated with parliamentary politics, in 1900 he moved dramatically to the Extreme Left, joining the anticonstitutional Republicans and Socialists. At the political center remained the ruling ministries, who, since the time of Cavour in the 1850s, had transformed political opponents from both directions into loyal followers.[6] Dissatisfied with mundane political compromises, Italy's intellectual elite now wanted more noble and more imaginative results from the Italian state.

After Adwa, the poet Giovanni Pascoli began to formulate a new nationalist rhetoric, a synthesis of Italy's humiliation, resentment, and discontent from colonial failures and emigration. In 1904 Pascoli had inherited Carducci's mantle by succeeding him in the chair of literature at the University of Bologna. Like Carducci, Pascoli composed hymns to Rome and Garibaldi and poetry and speeches for solemn commemorations. His best works are his poems in Latin and his lyrics of peasant life, which blended his interests in emigration and contemporary politics. Pascoli felt keenly the shame of Italy's defeat at Adwa and commemorated the dead soldiers with several Italian verses. In 1899, when Messina dedicated a monument to its artillerymen lost at Adwa, Pascoli wrote "For the Sicilian batteries," footnoting Ferdinando Martini's observations of wild, inhuman Ethiopian warriors.[7] With his lyric "To Ciapin," named for an Italian red wine, Pascoli pledged undying hatred and thirst for revenge after the defeat at Abba Garima (Adwa):

> that vintage which fermented in shock
> all from a dark emotion on the first
> night of March, like the red wave of Abba Garima;
> that now holds in its robust glass
> as in a strong and silent heart, confining
> the anger of the past and the long black thought of revenge:
> . . . . .
> Preserved for that day, resolved at heart
> with our cannons, which to the savage ghebì
> are like dogs, and with our honor, which acts as messenger.[8]

Italy had been humiliated, but would take its revenge in time.

With his sense of Italy's international mission of vindication and civilization, Pascoli came to deplore internal divisions at home. In 1900 he proposed a unifying "patriotic socialism," that would overcome the Socialist doctrine of class struggle between rich and poor:

> One problem is to avoid the concentration of wealth in the hands of the few and eventually in a single Moloch. The other problem is to prevent all peoples from being absorbed by the strongest until they become a single empire. . . . [L]ogically, those who oppose the wealth of the few must also oppose the smaller and weaker peoples' falling prey to the greater and stronger; and, as they support the workers against the owners in the economic struggle . . . so in the political struggle they must support nations against empires, and single and unique traditions against absorbing ambitions. . . . As a man, and as an Italian, I wish for . . . the coming of a "patriotic socialism"; a religion . . . announced with a long series of deeds, sacrifices, and intimate martyrdoms . . . in which burns but one fire: the perpetual flame lit by a single love.[9]

Such was Pascoli's conception of national socialism: the precedence of national struggle over class struggle, and the necessity of all Italians to unite under a new civil religion, to fight against the overwhelming multinational empires of Austria, Britain, and France. Pascoli called Italy the world's "most impoverished and most menaced nation."[10] Under siege and cornered by rapacious enemies, Italy needed to lash out and assert its own imperial strength.

Beyond the shame of colonial defeat, Pascoli wrote often of the shame of Italian emigration. In his collection *Nuovi poemetti* (1909), Pascoli dedicated one poem "Sacred to Wandering Italy" and another "Sacred to Italy in Exile." The first poem, "Italy" (not "Italia"), included lines of the bastardized Italian-English from a migrant family in Cincinnati, Ohio: "Trova un *farm. You want buy?*" The second, "Pietole," incorporated the glossary of a manual for Italian emigrants, listing useful phrases for life abroad: *I am Italian I am hungry. Soy Italiano Tengo hambre. Ich bin Italiener Ich bin hungrig.*[11] Pascoli had taught in the Italian secondary schools for many years, and constantly stressed the importance of education as a necessary preparation for emigrants' success. His poems are among the most moving literature commemorating Italy's mass migrations. But a political agenda lay behind Pascoli's lyrics. In 1912 he wrote a hymn, to be set to music, for the monument to Dante built by Italian emigrants in New York City. With its first line, "Exile to whom everyone was cruel," Pascoli developed the theme of exile located in Dante and Virgil, contrasting Italy's past greatness to Italian emigrants' present misery. He used the anti-immigrant slur *"dego"* several times in his poetry, explaining to his European audience its association with crime and mafia.[12] Pascoli turned his eulogy for Giosuè Carducci into an attack on the Italian political system: "The third Italy [after ancient Rome and Renaissance Italy] has emerged inferior in every way to the aspiration of its apostles. . . . The third Italy is for the most part as poor as before, and where it appears rich, alas! the work, yes, is always Italian, but the wealth is almost always foreign. And the farmers abandon the bounteous land [*la terra saturnia*] en masse . . . The third Italy has lost its battles."[13] Emigration was positive proof of united Italy's failures. Italians served foreign masters at home and abroad. According to Pascoli, the country needed new rulers, new policies, and new ideas to achieve its national destiny.

Poets and politicians mourned especially the plight of Italians in South America. Italy's policies toward Argentina became a catalyst for opposition to Giolitti and the Left Liberals. Although Einaudi's thesis became official government policy, his vision of economic growth through emigration attracted criticism and derision. Argentina, which had seemed the most promising place for Italian designs, refused to cooperate. Shortly after Einaudi's path-breaking work, Luigi Barzini traveled to Argentina for the Milan paper *Corriere della Sera*. Barzini reported that Einaudi, who had never visited Argentina, painted too rosy a picture. "Our emigration, as it is now, is like the exportation of a raw material to be processed and transformed. It undergoes this process without protest because it is ignorant, and therefore weak; impoverished, and therefore disarmed. Under these conditions our emigration barely enters the new society, occupying the lowest place, the most despised." Barzini's reports were a "revelation" to himself and to others: "this fact condemns us. . . . Our crime is called indifference." Before departing, emigrants needed to be prepared and armed with education, orientation, facts, and figures, so they could secure the best future for themselves and their families. Still, Barzini despaired that the situation would change, as the evils facing Italian emigrants were "so vast, deep, and ancient."[14]

One problem seemed to be Italy's ineffectual diplomacy in South America. To secure goodwill concessions for its emigrants, the Italian state was forced into ever more gracious, unilateral, and unrequited capitulations. The director of the Italian Schools Abroad program, Angelo Scalabrini, explained for the Dante Alighieri Society his policy of inaction rather than advocacy:

> The centers of a future Italy are there and have formed spontaneously. What could they not become, if aided by the mother-fatherland's organized and intelligent action? However, I am equally convinced that this action will be much more effective if it is silent. . . . Those peoples [of South America] are dark and distrustful: they have a boundless national pride, like the size of their countries. . . . Silent activity is the maxim that I have adopted . . . I hope to show you that silence does not mean inertia. . . . Given the state of things, the less one speaks of Argentina and our aspirations there, the better, and if one talks of Argentina it should only be to praise it or maybe admire it. In this way we will get what we want. The peoples of Latin America must be treated a little like women and spoiled children: one must caress them and praise them; in reality, the Argentines especially have good qualities so the caresses are not thrown away and the praises are not always mere adulation.[15]

Based in condescension and dissimulation, Scalabrini's silent plot to change hearts and minds was ill-conceived and unlikely to succeed. The lack of publicity in Italy did not help; instead, the Italians of Argentina were simply forgotten. When Pasquale Villari, speaking in the Italian Senate, criticized Argentina's stance against teaching Italian in the public schools, Scalabrini begged him to strike his comments from the public record.[16] The Italian Colonial Institute pursued a similarly obsequious course for Argentina, hosting a major festival near the Roman Forum to celebrate Argentina's centenary.[17] Rather than negotiating with Argentina, Italy was reduced to supplicating for cultural concessions, always fearing that the situation for emigrants could grow worse. What grand designs for the Americas could Italy ever accomplish?

The Question of Underdevelopment

Emigration's internal impact on the regions of Italy proved as problematic as its international consequences. By exporting the country's population, Italian politicians had hoped to resolve key, divisive domestic problems: especially the "Southern Question," or why southern Italy was underdeveloped in relation to northern Italy after unification in 1860.[18] Even as conditions in the South improved, the North progressed much more rapidly in its employment levels, wages, and industrial development. Government spending in the South lagged behind the North, and often dissolved in graft and corruption. Most southern deputies in Parliament supported whatever ministry was in power, in exchange for legal and illegal aid in their reelections and protection from uncomfortable social reforms.[19] The relative disparity between northern and southern Italy only grew. Emigration seemed to magnify this cycle. As remittances built up the industry of northern Italy, southern Italy saw depopulation and social decay. Fewer good investment opportunities led to wasted remittances. The North continued to lead the South.

Italy's deep regional disparities stemmed from a myriad of causes. The southern peninsula and Sicily suffered from the effects of malaria, deforestation, enormous landed estates under absentee management, uneconomic smallholdings, poor roads and communications, and, in some areas, *mafioso* criminal influence in indifferent local governments. The climate of the Mediterranean Basin had changed since the ancient era when Sicily and Libya were famous "breadbaskets" for the Roman Empire, but the extensive cultivation of wheat, without irrigation or fertilizers, continued to dominate the agricultural landscape. Intensive cultivation of olive gardens, vineyards, and citrus groves faced disproportionate taxes. Philosophers in the Risorgimento had assumed that the South's problems stemmed from Bourbon rule and would disappear under Liberal government. Although from the late 1870s onward it became clear that the social and political roots of stagnation were more complex, still the national government in Rome failed to enact effective reforms. Overpopulation seemed the simplest explanation and emigration the easiest solution to all problems, even though Basilicata demonstrated high emigration rates from a sparse population base. In fact, regional emigration varied widely even as fertility remained comparable across north, central, and southern Italy through 1911.[20]

After the failure of land reform and political change, the South's mass emigration appeared as the most dramatic social force in centuries. Individual families decided their own fate, attacking penury and subjugation at the grassroots. Basilicata started the trend of mass migration in the 1870s, followed by Calabria, then Abruzzo and Campania, and Sicily in the mid-1890s, while Puglia produced instead a violent, successful struggle of syndicalist unions against large landlords.[21] Southern Liberals hailed emigration, not violence, as the solution to the South's structural backwardness. In 1897 Giustino Fortunato forcefully stated migration's importance for his native Basilicata: "Rather than dreaming of empires and colonies in Africa, let us think of how to protect and defend, in their departure, voyage, and arrival, the thousands of our brothers, who, no longer resigned to hunger as their inheritance, voluntarily cross the treacherous seas, go ashore at New York, at Rio de Janeiro, at Buenos Aires, and send to Italy every year, by dint of toil and deprivations, between one hundred fifty and two hundred million lire. It is these millions, and not others, that save entire provinces of our Mezzogiorno [southern Italy] from starvation."[22] The promise of African settlement had shattered. Abandoned by government, the peasants themselves found a way to solve their problems. Francesco Saverio Nitti seized upon Fortunato's aphorism "either emigrants or brigands": migration was the peaceful alternative to futile armed rebellion, which had plagued southern Italy in the 1860s after unification. Emigration would reduce the labor supply and raise wages, breaking down the gulf between sharecroppers, wage laborers, and the owners and managers of great estates. Remittances for the South's economy would inject the capital needed to create a middle class of successful farmers working their own land.[23]

Despite Nitti's enthusiasm, emigration did not solve the Southern Ques-

tion. The social and economic divisions between northern and southern
Italians were replicated in their colonies overseas. After a tour of the
United States in 1905, the Sicilian politician Antonino Di San Giuliano remarked, "the Southern Question crosses the Atlantic," claiming that
southerners were poorer and less literate than their northern compatriots. "The Southern Question reappears, painful and threatening, compli-
cating and aggravating all national problems at home and abroad."[24] Di
San Giuliano could not suppress his anger that the United States Immigration Commission labeled northern and southern Italians as separate
races, the one "desirable" and the other "undesirable." These American
criteria were patently absurd: the Dillingham Senatorial Commission
took pains to explain that "North Italians" were "Keltic" and "South Italians" were "Iberic," but reasoned that "even Genoa [in northwest Italy]
is South Italian."[25] The Americans cited northern Italian scientists, such
as Cesare Lombroso, to prove that southern Italians were biologically
inferior.[26]

Barriers of law and prejudice between North and South were reinforced by the North's rapid industrialization. The southerners did not
fall behind in their efforts or savings. More remittances poured into the
savings banks of the South, but northern Italy benefitted from its natural
resources, developed infrastructure, investment opportunities, and favorable location for international trade. The emigration commissariat
commented that "remittances rose considerably progressing from the
north to the south of the Kingdom, which is yet another testimony to the
greater sobriety and greater tendency to save among the southern populations."[27] The influx of fresh money did end usury in the southern
countryside, but the capital which migrants brought home did not re-
vivify the South's stagnant economy and society. Returning emigrants,
called "Americans," usually preferred to buy a plot of land and build a
new home in or near their native town. Wealthy landowners and speculators took advantage of them by charging outrageous prices for the
land, forcing the "Americans" into mortgages on harsh terms. Many de-
faulted on their property and returned to wage labor in the Americas
cursing their broken dreams. Leopoldo Franchetti attempted to prevent
such tragedies by forming an association to purchase large tracts of land,
to be sold to "Americans" in parcels at good prices. The emigration commissariat refused to fund the scheme, and it persisted only as another of
Franchetti's frustrated visions. In Basilicata, much of the money sent

home went to paying taxes so the family could retain its small plots and avoid prison. This was a boon to the Italian state but did not advance family fortunes. While the port of Naples benefitted immensely from mass migration, organized crime also gained in strength, levying a contribution from every item and person passing through the city. Migration thus encouraged the Neapolitan camorra to establish itself overseas in the Americas and to exploit and criminalize all aspects of the emigrants' travel. Mass migration did not raise southern Italy to the prosperity achieved by the North because remittances invested in land and real estate in the South bore fewer returns than money injected into the North's growing economy.[28]

When emigrant remittances failed to reconstruct the South's economy, Luigi Einaudi's famous economic analysis of emigration began to appear misleading or wrongheaded. Einaudi had praised a single entrepreneur, Enrico Dell'Acqua, as a model "merchant prince." Mass migration doubtless benefitted a handful of individuals, but what of the masses? The celebratory volume *Gli italiani negli Stati Uniti d'America,* published in New York for the 1906 Exposition of Italians Abroad, claimed to "demonstrate how many 'self made men' have risen from humble conditions to notable fortunes. An Italian bootblack today owns in New York a stable of racehorses, a deckhand is worth millions of dollars; from the amorphous mass, dozens and dozens of intelligent and tenacious men have emerged and will emerge."[29] How many "self made men" were commemorated in 1906, out of the more than two million Italians who had emigrated to the United States? Only several dozen.

As transoceanic emigration reached new heights, eclipsing emigration to Europe, its political acclaim began to erode. Although Pasquale Villari had pioneered the study of the Southern Question and the potential benefits of emigration, his son Luigi turned against emigration politics on two grounds: prestige and morality.[30] He rejected the debate which Einaudi had framed in terms of remittances and exports; his new arguments against emigration were neither objective nor quantitative. Villari concluded that Italy must first earn the respect of the United States before sending its emigrants overseas: "Our true economic interest is to promote our exports of merchandise rather than men. The Americans will admire us more when they see a large increase in our exports, and our emigrants will be respected more when everyone knows they come from a rich and productive country. . . . In the final analysis, the best protections for our emigrants are *dreadnoughts* and great battalions. In the United States, as in Argentina and in Brazil, the English, Germans, French, and Japanese are respected because the Americans know that England, Germany, France, and Japan have powerful fleets and would not hesitate to use them if necessary."[31] Villari appealed for Italy to rebuild its navy, which had recently been the second largest in the world, and to develop its army and industrial might, so the country could force its way into international prestige instead of infiltrating foreign lands with poor emigrants, cap in hand. No longer should Italy be identified with illiterate ragpickers and street urchins, nor with the infamous "Black Hand" mafia and camorra which had captured America's imagination.[32]

Villari's second antieconomic argument was that remittances were not the most significant outcome of emigration. He claimed that the Americas corroded the moral health of emigrants and undermined the bases of Italian society: "We hear a lot about emigrants' remittances, but we do not think of the myriad cases of emigrants who, after a year or two of America, lose all interest in their family remaining in Italy, and, though already married, take a new wife in the new world. The wife who stayed at home cannot imitate her husband, because our laws prohibit bigamy, but she consoles herself with other loves, so there are two scandals instead of one. . . . Morality is in general lower in America than in Europe, and in the colonial environment it is even more scarce. . . . The bad seed returns to the fatherland."[33] Villari blasted Italy's mass migration without proposing an alternative. He relied on anecdotal evidence to claim that emigration destroyed Italian families and that incoming dollars were outweighed by social decay. In reality, most marriages survived the separation and displacement of emigration, but children suffered from a lack of education as they had to work on the land in their father's absence. The Parliamentary inquest of 1910 also conceded that "frequently among repatriates there is a special form of crime, which is almost always forgiven in the popular conscience: the vendetta of marital honor." Some husbands who emigrated only a few days after their weddings, with their passage paid by their wives' dowries, would return in several years to kill their unfaithful wives.[34] Emigration may have raised infanticide rates as well. Certainly, remittances were earned at tremendous personal sacrifice and family hardship.[35] While the Italian state and Italian industrialists might profit from emigration, thousands of emigrants suffered.

Emigration and National Socialism

The novelist and playwright Enrico Corradini provided radical solutions for the contradictions of Italian emigration. Like Pascoli, Corradini chafed under the uninspired, mediocre social regime of fin-de-siècle Italy. His mystical vision for renewal of the nation seemed out of place. After founding and editing several short-lived cultural reviews, Corradini reached a turning point when he visited Italians in South America. Emigration, he discovered, could be a metaphor for Italy's individualistic malaise. This breakthrough marked the beginning of Corradini's confident, successful course to establish an Italian Nationalist party. With his talents for rhetoric and organization, Corradini moved beyond Pascoli to craft a powerful and effective political message.[36] Emigration was Liberalism's problem; Nationalism would be the solution. The international embarrassment of emigration attracted broad attention to Corradini's wide-ranging solutions. He had found his audience.

Corradini retold his experience of emigration in his autobiographical novel, *La Patria lontana* (The Faraway Fatherland, 1910). The protagonist, Pietro Buondelmonti, is a rustic Tuscan native who is the passionate, selfless, and sincere apostle of Italian nationalism and imperialism. Frustrated that no one will hear his message in Italy, Pietro accepts his friend's offer to travel with her and her bourgeois husband to Rio de Janeiro to study the conditions of Italian emigrants. The hero is Corradini's idealization of himself. Born in Samminiatello di Montelupo Fiorentino in 1865, Corradini had studied literature in Florence and founded a literary review, *Germinal*, in 1891. Italy's debacle at Adwa in 1896 became a defining moment in his life. Corradini later wrote, "I was a convert to the faith of the Fatherland. Like other converts from socialism later, I converted from 'literature,' in which I wandered, dissolute and blind. And my conversion came because of the Adwa defeat."[37] Indeed, Corradini struggled with a series of ventures. After *Germinal* failed in 1893, he helped found the Florentine review *Il Marzocco* in 1896 and was its editor from 1897 until 1900, when he was forced out by the journal's owners. Corradini became chief editor of *Gazzetta di Venezia* for six months, then correspondent in Florence for *Corriere della Sera* for a short time. Besides producing novels and plays, in 1901 he began giving public lectures throughout Italy. In 1903 Corradini founded the nationalist paper *Il Regno* (The Kingdom) in Florence but quit as director in 1905; the paper failed in 1906.[38]

In 1908 and 1909 Corradini, like his character Buondelmonti, escaped his disappointments with a tour of Brazil, Argentina, Tunisia, Dalmatia and Istria, as a correspondent for *Corriere della Sera* and *Il Marzocco* and as a representative of the Dante Alighieri Society. This long voyage resuscitated Corradini's career. He gained a new aura of authority in foreign affairs, displayed in his conferences and publications across the peninsula. Besides finding new readers, Corradini found a new confidence in his ideas: "on the spot it is easy to gather documents and facts; intuition becomes observation and documentation; only on location can one really experience how bad Italy's policies are."[39] Drawing upon his experiences in Latin America, Corradini created a new rhetoric and reception for his nationalist arguments.

In his last two novels and his last play, Corradini developed nationalist themes before a backdrop of mass migration. Like Pascoli, Corradini used emigration to criticize Italy's lost greatness and failed potential. When his hero Piero Buondelmonti arrives in Rio de Janeiro in *La Patria lontana* (1910), he discovers a myriad of petty divisions within the local Italian colony. Among the notable figures is a wealthy, patriotic Italian who had emigrated from Abruzzo at age twelve. Piero also meets the founder of the local Dante Society, who in 1896 had killed an Italian for shouting, "Long live Menelik!"[40] This literary patriot bore a scar on his cheek, the "sign of Menelik," from his brawl in defense of Italy's colonial honor. Corradini devoted much space to the character of Giacomo Rummo, the local revolutionary socialist leader in exile from Italy. Piero becomes convinced that his nationalism has much in common with Rummo's radical syndicalism; both men hate the decadent reformist socialists. The novel's plot is secondary and entirely predictable: after a long period of flirtation and distraction, Piero's friend flees to him from her brutal, Liberalist husband; the husband then kills her and severely wounds Piero, who is cared for by the syndicalist Rummo. The end of the novel carries a prophetic twist. As Piero plans to return to Italy, news arrives that Europe is on the brink of the long-anticipated Great War. The Brazilian colony raises two million cruzeiros in donations for the fatherland, and Piero encourages all eligible young men to return to Italy as volunteer soldiers: "if you live through the war, you will see the beautiful cities! Rome, Florence, Venice."[41] The wealthy patriot is sad that he is too old and too tied to his business to go with Piero. The syndicalist Rummo plans to ruin Piero's patriotic speech to the colony but, overcome by love of the fatherland and stirred by the news of Italy's declaration of war, instead joins Piero and four hundred other volunteers in sailing to Italy to join the army.

Corradini faced much criticism for the thin plot of *La patria lontana*. In the sequel, *La Guerra lontana* (The Faraway War, 1911), Corradini included an apologetic preface explaining the moral of both novels: "*La guerra lontana* transcends nationalism more than *La Patria lontana* did. Certainly it contains a nationalist and imperialist moral, but it also transcends this. In any case, I hope critics stop saying that I write novels to spread propaganda for nationalism."[42] The second novel is indeed a more complex and successful work, incorporating mystery, intrigue, and a twisted romance. The action takes place in Rome and Lazio in 1896, previous in time to *La Patria lontana*. Meanwhile, the Italian army fights its war in Africa, far away both physically and spiritually from the mainland's petty politics. The protagonist is a gigantic Roman, Ercole Gola, who was inspired by the Poet (Giosuè Carducci) in his youth but has squandered his talents as a newspaper editor in lust, vice, and blackmail. Gola falls madly in love with Carlotta Ansparro after raping her; she had tried to persuade him to oppose publicly the Minister (Francesco Crispi), but instead Gola endorses him. In revenge, Ansparro marries a young, wealthy deputy in Parliament, who becomes an anticolonial demagogue and starts an antiministerial newspaper. This is all for base personal motives: the Minister's nephew had broken Ansparro's heart. Gola wants to kill Ansparro but the Poet dissuades him; the character Lorenzo Orio, based on the writer Alfredo Oriani, makes a cameo appearance, railing against Italy's dissolute behavior during the colonial war. Gola hires as a correspondent Piero Buondelmonti, who is motivated by a pure love of the Fatherland. Piero tries to volunteer for the African war but is rejected. Gola and his newspaper find redemption in supporting the Minister wholeheartedly, even after the Adwa defeat. However, Ansparro's husband challenges Gola to a duel and Gola kills him. Everyone turns against the murderer, and he must emigrate with his peasant mother to Brazil in disgrace. Corradini thus contrasts "emigration, Italy's present, which scatters Italians across the world in servitude on foreign soil; [and] war, which is now far from Italy, but through which one day Italy will become master."[43]

Emigration became the axis of Corradini's thought and a vehicle for making his politics engaging, dramatic, and concrete. He claimed that "emigration . . . forces Italy to 'have a foreign policy'. . . . Emigration is one of the points of departure for nationalism, and perhaps its most important basis."[44] In his last play, *Le Vie dell'Oceano* (The Paths of the Ocean, 1913), Corradini addressed emigration and Italian politics during the years 1911–1912. The protagonist, Giuseppe Carrera, is a wealthy builder in Mendoza, Argentina, who had emigrated from Calabria at age twelve. In Act I he celebrates his fifty-seventh birthday by dividing his fortune between his four sons. His cousin, newly arrived from Italy, is an Italian patriot who proudly announces that Italy has banned emigration to Argentina. This is a turning point for Carrera, who for the first time is proud of his Italian roots. Clearly, Italy no longer needed to rely on emigration to feed its people. In Act II Italy has declared war in Libya, and Carrera raises a large sum in contributions which he wants to bring to Italy in person. The more humble Italian families in Argentina send their sons to join the Italian army, and Carrera wants his sons to go also. Yet the three older sons, born in Argentina, are friends of the anti-Italian Gallegos family and want nothing to do with their father's new patriotism. The older boys kidnap the youngest son, and in the resulting fracas Carrera kills one of his children. In Act III Carrera has returned to Calabria with his cousin and youngest son. He meets a group of departing emigrants and promises to pay them to stay in Italy, but he no longer has money. The son wants to go home to see his mother; Carrera sends him back to Argentina with the cousin and then commits suicide. The somber outcome illustrates Corradini's conviction that emigration was an irreparable disaster and that emigrants were literally "lost to the fatherland." While making money in America, Carrera had neglected his patriotic obligations to raise his children as Italians. His tragic mistakes destroyed him and his family.[45] Corradini concluded that emigration must be eradicated, with an imperialist nationalism planted in its place.

In his widely circulated speeches Corradini mustered his literary talents to lead Italian Nationalists into a new doctrine of "national socialism." Corradini made the "nation" a holy object of secular worship. The Nationalists were called to lead the nation, because the Socialist, Liberal, and clerical parties all pursued narrow interests.[46] Like Pascoli, Corradini adopted a rhetoric of unity in the face of international hostility. Besieged in a swamp of emigration, Italy had to strike out in conquest:

> The circle of conquering nations, this economic and moral circle, has tightened around us while we nourished ourselves with sacrifices of philosophical utopianism, of general blindness, and of bourgeois cow-

ardice. Can we break this circle? We now overflow it. How? With emigration.

Ladies and gentlemen, whatever you think about emigration, and whatever you have heard, think again! Emigration is a dispersion of our people in all parts of the world, on foreign soil, among foreign populations, under foreign legislation. Do not judge only by the enrichment of a few individuals, nor by how many millions the emigrants send home to the Fatherland. Judge in national terms and consider that emigration is, if I may use the expression, an anti-imperialism of servitude. This condition of emigration, of the need of so many millions of Italians to search for bread and work across the ocean, and the condition of foreign nations pressing on us from all sides, leads me to call Italy, by analogy, a proletarian nation.[47]

Emigration became more than an emotive vehicle for criticizing Italy's failures; it now justified Italy's special status in an international class struggle. As a proletarian nation, Italy represented the deserving majority, presently oppressed but soon to be redeemed through revolutionary war. Using Marxist language, Corradini described the emigrant as "a tree uprooted from its native soil and dropped across the ocean with its roots in the air. No longer a citizen, that is, not belonging to a civilization, he is reduced to a man of labor and production."[48] The emigrant's tragic alienation from both his native culture and the culture of the host nation demanded a radical solution. With its workers trapped in a feudal existence on the *fazendas* of Latin America, Italy needed to rise to a higher stage of economic development: the demographic colonialism of imperial conquest. Uniting themes from Mazzini's nationalism and from Social Darwinism, Corradini called for "changing the old Italian spirit of emigration into the spirit of superior peoples living in a superior stage of their existence: the colonial imperialist spirit. In that day, Italy will have the will and strength to redeem itself from its feudal bondage . . . [with] the liberty of being active in world history, and adding its own creation and civilization to the civilization of other peoples."[49] Corradini's national socialism framed emigration and imperialism in dramatic terms: either international prestige or transnational mendicancy; domination or subservience, empire or poverty.

Imperial expansion was the culmination of Corradini's nationalism. In his vision, imperial warfare would completely change Italy's internal dynamics, unite her disparate resources, strengthen her economy, and discipline her spirit: "The national conscience, as nationalism conceives it, can and must be a school of discipline and duty. . . . The citizen forms a new soul, believing that he obeys an order from above, and that he collaborates in a great work; a work so great as to be outside the limits of his strength and vision, but which needs his collaboration. The citizen feels a new satisfaction, he feels something religious growing in himself, and starts to believe that he is obeying something divine. He begins to act willingly according to this religiosity of his national conscience. Gentlemen, in the day when this religiosity exists for many, the trains will finally run on time."[50] Corradini's phrase would become the infamous boast of Mussolini's regime, whose trains always "ran on time." The new religion preached by Corradini appealed to many. Not only would Italians find a personal role in the national social mission, as the proletarian nation asserted itself, but industrialists would profit handsomely. Italy needed to follow the examples of Germany, France, England, and the United States in "an industrial imperialism which appears to be the modern definitive form of imperialism, but tomorrow will be only the first step of the new military, political, and general imperialisms."[51] Corradini thus appealed to big business, the bourgeoisie, and conservative interests, while speaking highly of the dynamism of Socialism and syndicalism. This strategy garnered financing for Corradini's newspaper from Cogne Mining, FIAT, and the Milan Machine Corporation in 1914, as well as the support of syndicalists Arturo Labriola, Angelo Olivetti, Paolo Orano, and Libero Tancredi for the Libyan War.[52] Benito Mussolini's newspaper and party would seek the same constituents after World War I.

Liberals, however, failed to comprehend Corradini's imperialist worldview. Corradini opposed the calculations of Liberal policy with emotional novels, fiery speeches, and historical allusions. The statistician Luigi Bodio, who served as Italy's first emigration commissioner, complained in July 1911 that "the nationalists, with their extremist expansionism, would like to converge all the country's strengths toward the goal of their dreams. They obviously do not understand what a marvelous force our emigration has become, what an enormous net benefit, not only financial, but civil, and social, it brings to Italy every year, and how it is in the interest of everyone to protect its peaceful development."[53] Bodio could not fathom Corradini's contempt for Liberal economics. The Nationalists' dynamic appeal had moved outside the Liberal frame of reference. Corradini cited Francesco Coletti's contention that "we must pose the problem in this way: if emigration had not occurred, what would have happened to Italy?" Corradini replied, "In truth, anyone who tries to combat our nationalist view of emigration begins by not grasping our nationalist thought. We are sadly astonished to realize that [our opponents] praise emigration, because they see only two alternatives: either emigrate, or stay in Italy and die of hunger. . . . But our nationalist thought, gentlemen, is very different. . . . Italy must have its own colonies which, in the worst way we can define them, are also a form of emigration, but an emigration not of individuals in dribs and drabs, abandoned to themselves, but of the entire nation in the fulness of its strength."[54] This charismatic message trumped statistics. In place of emigrant colonialism, with its diplomatic compromises and patient influence, Corradini heralded the glorious conquest of territories for Italian settlement under Italian rule. Luigi Einaudi's vision for an Italian Argentina had failed; Corradini questioned why the Jews of antiquity mourned their diaspora, or dispersion, while the Italians boasted of their hollow colonies in the Americas. Politicizing and condemning Italy's diaspora sharpened his critique of Liberalism. Disappointments in Argentina and the declining success of Italian cultural policies left space for Corradini's new vision: a civic religion of imperial conquest.[55]

The Return of Demographic Imperialism

Corradini's call for a revived Roman imperialism and his attacks on emigration undercut Italian support for a peaceable emigrant colonialism. His elitist doctrines reached a limited audience but won very influential converts. The small group of Nationalists was talented, well-connected, and dynamic, and seized upon Italy's feelings of inferiority reinforced by the curse of emigration. Italy had been completely overshadowed by imperial Germany, which like Italy had been united only in 1870. Could Italy compete internationally? Corradini led the nationalists in the rhetoric of imperial conquest, comparing the second-rate "present Italy" to Switzerland and hailing "the Italy of tomorrow," heir to Rome's Mediterranean empire.[56]

Not all the Nationalists agreed with Corradini. The Nationalist group in Milan, organized around the paper *La Grande Italia*, favored republicanism and irredentism over authoritarian imperialism. At the First Nationalist Congress in 1910, Corradini tried to bridge the gap, arguing that "we are the people of irredentism and emigration together. . . . Irredentism, circle of the great powers closed around us; and faraway emigration, fruit of our blood across the Ocean!"[57] With the same arguments Pasquale Villari had used for the Dante Alighieri Society to defend all Italian expatriates, Corradini linked irredentism to Italians scattered around the Mediterranean and the world, not just in Trent and Trieste. Privately, however, Corradini condemned the irredentist tradition as "sentimental," because Italy could redeem Trent and Trieste after proving itself as an imperial power.[58]

Against the irredentist nationalists of Milan, the Nationalist Association's imperialist wing founded a weekly newspaper in Rome, *L'Idea nazionale,* edited by a talented group including Enrico Corradini, Luigi Federzoni, and Roberto Forges Davanzati. They launched their first issue on 1 March 1911, to commemorate the fifteenth anniversary of the Adwa defeat. Corradini included a selection from his *La Guerra lontana,* and Federzoni wrote a long and detailed retrospective on the Adwa defeat, entitled "The duty of remembering." Careful to gloss over Crispi's mistakes, he blamed the disaster on a Socialist and Masonic conspiracy involving Turati, Rudinì, and Martini.[59] Federzoni's innovative reinterpretation of the Adwa myth associated the Nationalists' present enemies with Italy's past villainy, when Rudinì had sought peace with Ethiopia instead of revenge. Placing history on their side gave the Nationalists the conviction of inevitable success. The imperialists' newspaper became a key ideological and organizational platform, eventually overshadowing Nationalist papers that favored irredentism or Liberalism.[60]

Rewriting history was crucial for the revival of demographic colonialism in Italy. As Einaudi had substituted an imperial myth of medieval Venice for the myth of classical Rome, the Nationalists created a tragic myth around Francesco Crispi. Liberals had blamed and vilified Crispi as the cause of imperial collapse, but the Nationalists now rehabilitated his reputation as the heroic personification of Italian colonialism. The problem was not the Adwa defeat, but Italy's reaction to the defeat: "not because Italy was defeated by Abyssinia, but because Italy was defeated by the Italians . . . who threw our flag in the mud. . . . Anarchy triumphed."[61] Corradini wrote that "the tragedy of Francesco Crispi can be summarized in these words: he acted for Italy, estranged from the Italy of his time."[62] In other words, if Crispi had lived fifteen years later, the country would have followed his leadership. The Nationalist Association's secretary, Gualtiero Castellini, published a celebratory biography of Crispi in 1915, and the Nationalist leader of Turin, Mario Viana, composed a hagiographic life of Crispi in 1923.[63] Only through imperial expansion could Italians repent for the sin of Crispi's martyrdom.

The Nationalists overturned another pillar of Liberal colonialism by attacking Argentina. Giuseppe Bevione traveled to Argentina in 1910 as a correspondent for *La Stampa* of Turin, and returned disillusioned by the xenophobia and "haughty, furious jingoism" of the Argentine people.[64] Bevione, who soon converted to Nationalism, mourned that the Italian government and the Italian colony in Argentina had failed to accomplish Einaudi's vision:

> For us, latecomers to the colonial division of the globe, our true colonies, of men and not of land, are in America. . . . It was our obligation to watch the movements and developments with jealous care and infinite love: to direct the migratory flows in a shrewd and enlightened way, to ensure the maximum number of victories, and to limit the defeats to the lowest possible percentage: to defend the right and dignity of our co-nationals with inflexible energy, so not one ounce of their wealth and prestige would be unjustly sacrificed: above all to keep the name and desire of Italy alive in this million of hearts, so our country would not lose the results of their titanic effort, and the wealth and children they created would not go to the benefit of a foreign land. . . . Instead we did nothing. The emigrants, 50 percent of whom were illiterate, were left to organize themselves. . . . The most impressive and organizable of modern social phenomena was abandoned to its spontaneous and haphazard development.[65]

For Bevione, Italy's emigrant colonialism had imploded. Its climax in Argentina had been King Umberto's assassination in 1900: at the news, Italian flags had flown from practically every house, but "today foreign flags cannot be flown in the Republic without having the Argentine flag on the left." Bevione believed that the Argentines feared the display of the Italians' strength, and set out to exclude and oppress them unjustly. Yet Bevione detected a ray of hope: Italy could follow the example of Japan, another country with limited economic resources and a burgeoning population. "Japan has studied [emigration], . . . has found the solution to the problem, and now is implementing the logical measures, with an agility, a thoroughness, a vision and a determination that amaze us, grandchildren of Machiavelli, heirs of the Roman colonial wisdom." After winning their war with Russia, the Japanese had chosen to expand their empire through economic development, and "emigration policy is one of their strongest weapons."[66] Like Japan, Italy could people its own empire, instead of submitting to the caprices of foreign countries.

The Nationalists expanded the debate far beyond the fate of individual emigrants. Bevione argued that "the Italians could and should be everything in Argentina. Instead they count for nothing as a group, and as individuals they must spend their energy in an environment of constant, underhanded hostility."[67] At the First Nationalist Congress of December 1910 in Florence, Corradini paraphrased Bevione, in the language of the Communist Manifesto: "What is Italian labor in Argentina? Everything. What are the Italians? Nothing. This is exactly the same as Socialism's relationship of proletariat against bourgeoisie."[68] Bevione's study of emigration thus supported Corradini's elaboration of national socialism. Corradini's solution to Italy's dilemma, again following Marx, would be international war and revolution.

With a torrent of publications and through their personal connections, the Nationalists successfully turned Italian colonialism toward imperial conquest. The Italian Colonial Institute invited the Nationalists to the Second Congress of Italians Abroad, held under royal patronage at the fiftieth anniversary of the Kingdom of Italy. The Congress boasted representation from eighty-four cities in twenty-two countries on five continents. After visiting the newly dedicated Altar of the Fatherland in Rome, from 11 to 20 June 1911 the delegates deliberated issues surrounding Italian migration worldwide, yet controversy over Libya eclipsed all other discussions. The delegates unanimously approved Luigi Federzoni's resolution for energetic action by a strengthened military to guarantee Italy's rights in Tripolitania. The Congress's dramatic call for war was condemned by the Italian press, particularly Stefano Jacini in La Voce and a hostile editorial in prime minister Giovanni Giolitti's ally La Tribuna, although La Tribuna contradicted itself by highlighting Libya's importance for Italy.[69] Contrary to its purpose, the Congress of Italians Abroad had more effect in domestic Italian politics than in international relations with Italian emigrants. All the detailed work of the Congress, regarding emigrants' citizenship, education, and economic needs, was quickly forgotten in the rush for conquest. The outbreak of the Libyan War would wipe away the memory of Italy's American colonialism.

Libya, the New America

The Italian Nationalists created their imperialist ideology at a dangerous moment in European politics. Europe's long period of peace since 1870 had boosted the pacifist ideologies of Liberal economic competition and unlimited economic growth. Forty-three nations had agreed to the Hague Conventions of 1899 and 1907, committing themselves to the peaceful arbitration of international disputes. Wars would now be regulated by law and prevented by rational agreement. Ironically, however, the Turkish revolution of 1908 revived European aggression in the Mediterranean. The Young Turks' plans for strengthening the crumbling Ottoman Empire hastened European projects to seize its territories before new defenses could be completed. Competition for the Ottoman inheritance, among European states both small and large, provoked escalating tension between and within Europe's rival alliance blocs. Crises erupted in 1905 over Morocco and in 1908 over Bosnia-Herzegovina, with the Mediterranean balance of power at stake. Each country emerged dissatisfied from the crises' diplomatic resolutions; the long dreaded Great War between the powers of Europe seemed imminent.[70] The Second Moroccan Crisis of 1911 promised a development for the worse. The German cruiser *Panther* appeared in the Moroccan port of Agadir on 1 July 1911, demanding that France give Germany its territories in the Congo as compensation for France's unofficial ascendancy in Morocco. Backed by Britain, the French government then opened negotiations for the future of the Moroccan sultanate as a French protectorate. The status quo of the Mediterranean was changing again at the expense of its Islamic powers.

The pressures of both domestic politics and foreign diplomacy led Italy's government under Giolitti into war for Ottoman Libya. Italian diplomats had long worked toward the occupation, establishing Italian language schools and an Italian post office in Tripoli.[71] But they hoped to inherit the country without a bloody and expensive campaign, perhaps at a future diplomatic conference deciding the Ottoman Empire's final collapse. Accord between France and Germany in Morocco forced Italy's hand in 1911. The 1902 Prinetti-Barrère notes of agreement had guaranteed Italian support for France in Morocco, and French support for Italy in Libya. Italy's Foreign Minister, Antonino Di San Giuliano, could assume that once France gained its reward in Morocco, the French government would no longer be interested in endorsing an Italian Libya. The French had already tricked the Italians once in North Africa. In 1881 France had surprised Italy by marching virtually unopposed from French Algeria into Libya's neighbor, Ottoman Tunisia, after secret negotiations in Berlin. Di San Giuliano now predicted France would "Tunisify" Libya. French Tunisia, which had attracted nearly sixty thousand immigrants from southern Italy between 1881 and 1911, stood as an unrealistic comparison and inspiration for an Italian Libya. After the "loss" of Tunisia to France, Italian diplomats had informed the European powers that Italy intended to take Libya as a consolation prize. The ignominious fate of the Italian prime minister in 1881, Benedetto Cairoli, weighed heavily on Giovanni Giolitti's mind thirty years later. Giolitti knew that failure to acquire Libya after the Moroccan crisis would end his career.[72]

Well before the Second Moroccan Crisis of July 1911, Corradini and his Nationalist friends had begun an organized press campaign for an Italian conquest of Libya. In the first issue of L'Idea nazionale on 1 March 1911, the imperialist Nationalists condemned Giolitti's policy as "twisted, uncertain, weak, exhausted," and warned that Italy might lose its position in Libya to other countries. The second issue stated that Tripolitania "is the fulcrum of our foreign policy"; the Nationalist Association also voted a resolution on "the necessity of forcing upon the Italian Government an energetic action . . . to realize our aspirations in Tripolitania."[73] The imperialists worked on several other fronts. Corradini serialized his novel La guerra lontana in L'Idea nazionale and republished his observations of Latin American emigration in two collections, Il Volere d'Italia (The Will of Italy) and L'Ora di Tripoli (The Hour of Tripoli). The Nationalist Association's secretary, Gualtiero Castellini, published his book Tunisi e Tripoli in early March 1911 about his travels through North Africa. Castellini drew upon irredentist fervor by comparing fertile Libya and Tunisia with unredeemed Italian Trent and Trieste, and claimed Italy should expand southward in Africa, not eastward in the Adriatic: "I saw at El Giem a Roman stadium larger than the stadium of Pola, and at Susa I witnessed devotion to the Italian cause as great as the devotion of Zara and Gorizia."[74]

Preaching the new Nationalist gospel of imperial conquest, national unity, and the redemption of Italian emigration won important converts among the elites of Italian publishing and heavy industry. The imperialists thus enjoyed an authoritative, nationwide forum, out of proportion to their numbers. While working on the weekly *L'Idea nazionale* in Rome, Corradini's group also worked for Italy's two leading daily newspapers. Luigi Federzoni was an editor for the *Giornale d'Italia* in Rome, while Domenico Oliva, Giovanni Borelli, Roberto Forges Davanzati, and Enrico Corradini wrote for *Corriere della Sera* in Milan. Both papers were conservative opponents to Giolitti. Elsewhere, Corradini and Mario Missiroli published in *Il Resto del Carlino* of Bologna and Gualtiero Castellini wrote for the *Gazzetta di Venezia*.[75] Shortly after Giolitti returned to office as prime minister in March 1911, two of his most loyal (and heavily subsidized) newspapers began campaigns for Libya, led by Giuseppe Bevione in *La Stampa* of Turin and Giuseppe Piazza in *La Tribuna* of Rome. But the two papers pressed for war more ardently than their patron desired. According to Gaetano Salvemini, Giolitti lost control of his own press, realizing by 17 September "that the newspapers had helped him more than he had wanted, *and that public opinion had escaped his bridle.*"[76] Salvemini hypothesized that Giolitti intended to threaten an invasion of Libya a year later, in the summer of 1912. In a surge of nationalist rhetoric, however, calm preparations and rational analysis went out the window.

Even with sympathetic newspapers, how could Nationalists arouse popular fervor for the conquest of an African desert? The European Scramble for Africa, from 1881 to 1898, had fed itself on competition and speculation. Diplomats reasoned that the "light soils" of the Sahara might not actually be valuable, but they could not fall prey to rival nations. Colonies might harbor some hidden wealth for the future, like the gold mines of Victoria, Australia, discovered in 1851, or the diamond mines of South Africa, discovered in 1867. By 1911, Europeans had explored much of Africa's surface. The Scramble for Africa was dead, yet the Italians pursued its same emotional logic in Tripolitania and Cyrenaica. These desert provinces might drain the Italian economy, but they could not belong to anyone else, and they might generate money later. In fact, Libya did become one of the world's leading oil producers two decades after Italy lost control of the area in 1942. Mussolini had cut funding for mineral explorations in Libya following his conquest of the Ethiopian empire in 1936. According to his propaganda, Ethiopia held vast mineral resources that awaited discovery and development under Italian tutelage. Nonetheless, it was only a matter of time before the Italian petroleum explorations would have succeeded in Libya.[77] The region's first major oil discovery came in Algeria, near the Libyan border, in 1955; the first productive Libyan well was established in 1959, in a zone first highlighted by Italian surveyors, but developed later by big oil companies from the United States.[78]

Instead of oil, the Nationalists touted Libya's phosphates, gold, and especially its fertile lands awaiting Italian cultivation and settlement. All three were wildly exaggerated. After the fall of the Roman Empire, the Sahara Desert had expanded almost to the Mediterranean coast. Libya can boast of the hottest weather ever recorded on the earth's surface, at al'Aziziyan on 13 September 1922: 136.4 degrees Fahrenheit (58 degrees Celsius), *in the shade*. The land's mineral resources were unproven, but this did not prevent the Nationalists from claiming that in the hands of a foreign power, Libyan production would bankrupt the sulphur mines of Sicily. Corradini also hypothesized that mines would bring railroads, which would open the interior for profitable agricultural settlement.[79]

More important than the land's economy was its political significance. Italy would revisit its Roman imperial heritage in a strategic corner of the Mediterranean. The Nationalists revived the ancient Roman name *Libya*, rather than calling the Ottoman provinces "Tripolitania and Cyrenaica." No more would emigrants grovel in Latin America; as heirs of the Romans, Italians were the natural born rulers of North Africa. The Nationalists emphasized that the Arabs were inferior barbarians and deserved no pity, yet they would welcome the Italian army as liberators from the Turks. The military campaign promised to be quick, easy, and triumphal.[80]

This coordinated press campaign intimidated Giolitti's ministry. In his aide-mémoire of 28 July 1911, after the Second Moroccan Crisis, the foreign minister Di San Giuliano referred to domestic pressures within Italy as much as to the international situation in the Mediterranean. Writing the king and Giolitti, Di San Giuliano recorded, "I believe it is *probable* that, within a few months, Italy may be *constrained* to carry out a military expedition in Tripolitania," despite the dangers of sparking Austrian involvement and war in the Balkans:

> We must examine the more or less likely probabilities that such a decision will be imposed on the Government (this Ministry or another [replacement]), by Italian public opinion. Such probabilities are growing every day . . . because the feeling is widespread in Italy, though unfounded, that the Government's foreign policy is too submissive and

the interests and dignity of Italy are not respected enough; and that the national energy needs to affirm itself vigorously in some way. Every little incident in Tripoli and between Italy and Turkey is magnified by the press for diverse reasons, including the money and intrigue of the Banco di Roma.[81]

Many interests pressed for war. The Catholic Banco di Roma had invested heavily in Libya under the aegis of Tommaso Tittoni, Di San Giuliano's predecessor as foreign minister and brother to the bank's vice-president. In Tripoli the Banco established its offices inside the ancient Victory Arch of Marcus Aurelius, replacing a sausage shop as tenant, to declare Rome's renewed imperial ambition.[82] The bank also owned the Catholic paper *Corriere d'Italia,* yet another pro-war voice attacking Giolitti's policies. To resolve the matter, Di San Giuliano recommended preparing an expedition to threaten Turkey. If the Young Turks did not grant more rights to Italians in Libya, Italy should then rapidly occupy the coast, presenting the European powers with an accomplished fact. The pressure of Italian newspapers continued to wear on Di San Giuliano. Two weeks later he complained to Giolitti that Turkey would never concede peacefully, "given the attitude of public opinion in both countries and the language of our newspapers, which reflects prevailing sentiment in Italy. I already brought to your attention the consequences of words published by one newspaper, *La Stampa,* which supports our ministry in everything except foreign policy."[83] Luigi Albertini, editor of *Corriere della Sera,* boasted in his memoirs that Italian journalism dragged the government into the war: "the government was carried away in this vast and impetuous current of public opinion . . . a fact we can irrefutably prove."[84] The glare of public opinion turned secret diplomacy and dispassionate negotiation into anachronisms.

Giolitti was an unlikely warmonger. On 7 October 1911, at the start of the war, he announced Italy had invaded Libya because of "the fate of history [*una fatalità storica*]," revealing his apathy for the war's diplomatic background. Instead of war, Giolitti's speech highlighted his domestic reform proposals of extending voting rights and establishing a state monopoly over life insurance.[85] Eleven years later, after Mussolini had come to power, Giolitti confessed in his memoirs of 1922 that "we were forced, for unforeseen reasons, to disturb the peace in Europe."[86] Like his foreign minister, Giolitti referred to both foreign and domestic justifications for war. On the international field, he reasoned, "if we didn't go into Libya, another power would. . . . And Italy, so profoundly shaken by the French occupation of Tunis, would certainly not have tolerated a similar result for Libya; so we would have run the risk of a conflict with a European power, which would have been much more serious than a conflict with Turkey. Persisting in our situation, of having laid a claim on Libya to prevent others from going there without going there ourselves, would have been foolish, and would have created difficulties for us in all the other European questions, particularly in the Balkans."[87] Giolitti rationalized that a successful campaign in Libya would help Italy in all of its foreign intrigues, especially in the Balkans. By a leap of logic, war in Libya could bring peace to Europe.[88] Giolitti also noted increasing Turkish pressure on the Banco di Roma in Libya, and that a military expedition would only become more difficult once the Turks reinforced their colony. Domestically, the "Italian public was putting its nerves to the test once again, sixteen years after the disaster of the Abyssinian war."[89] Giolitti believed that he would gain conservative support through waging war. Although he preferred a diplomatic solution in Libya, Giolitti realized that a short and glorious war would strengthen his position in Italian public opinion.

Yet Giolitti's calculations were fundamentally flawed. His Liberal reforms depended upon peace, and they self-destructed under the pressure of colonial war and later world war. By entering war against Turkey, Giolitti divided the Socialist Party and undercut his own base of mass support. The founders and leaders of Italian Socialism, who for years had voted for Giolitti's policies, lost control of their party to a new generation of radicals pursuing a "maximal" program of revolution, not reform. Though the Left had given the outbreak of war a divided endorsement, the war's slow progress fed a restless alienation. Before the war's end, the Italian Socialist Party split into reformist and revolutionary factions at the Party Congress of July 1912. The fiery young Socialist Benito Mussolini entered national politics for the first time: after a heroic five-month imprisonment for his antiwar activities of September 1911, he rose in the congress to condemn the party's bourgeois leadership. The party voted overwhelmingly to expel four of its own deputies in Parliament, Leonida Bissolati, Angelo Cabrini, Ivanoe Bonomi, and Guido Podrecca, as punishment for their support for the Libyan War and their visit to the King of Italy after he escaped an anarchist's assassination attempt.[90] The four banished deputies immediately founded the splinter Reformist Socialist Party. In December 1912, at the age of twenty-nine, a triumphant Mussolini became editor of the flagship Socialist newspaper, *Avanti!* The Socialist party became increasingly violent and revolutionary, in intransigent opposition to Giolitti and any form of Liberalism.

The Nationalists also refused to enter the Liberal fold. They remained ungrateful to Giolitti and detested his lies, intrigues, and the principle of "transformism," which watered down all ideologies to favor the ruling party.[91] Corradini stated bluntly that his Nationalism "is a means for replacing the government."[92] Giolitti's wholesale adoption of the Nationalist war program threatened the new Association's survival, but the Nationalists foresaw this danger and maneuvered around it. While praising Italy's entry into war, the editors of *L'Idea nazionale* ruthlessly attacked Giolitti's leadership. It was Giolitti's fault that Italy was unprepared; that the war dragged on; that in the end, Italy paid an indemnity to Turkey instead of Turkey paying Italy.[93]

Constricted by diplomacy, Italy's campaign against Turkey did reflect uncertainty and improvisation. Italy failed to recognize the Ottoman Empire as a peer within Europe; the Italo-Turkish War was not really a colonial conflict in Africa, but a war between two of Europe's major powers, fought across the Mediterranean. The stakes and scope of the conflict were not immediately apparent. Giolitti had asked the chief of staff General Alberto Pollio how many soldiers would be required to defeat the Turks in Tripolitania and Cyrenaica. Expecting only token resistance from the Turkish garrison, Pollio estimated 22,000 men; Giolitti nearly doubled the figure to mobilize 40,000 men. In the end, 100,000 Italian troops deployed to fight in Libya, at tremendous expense. The war cost the Italian government 1.3 billion lire, nearly a billion more than Giolitti's estimate, and ruined ten years of fiscal prudence.[94]

At first the war went well for Italy. After a 24-hour ultimatum, Italy declared war on Turkey on 29 September, bombarded Tripoli on 3 October, and landed 1,700 marines on 5 October to occupy the city. The marines heroically held the city until relieved six days later by the expeditionary corps. But taking Tripoli was only the first of Italy's problems. The entire Turkish garrison of 5,000 had evacuated Tripoli, after having been reinforced on 25 September with 35,000 rifles and millions of cartridges. The war had already moved to the hinterland. So while the Italian army and navy seized Benghazi, Tubruq, Darnah, and Al Khums in October, Italy had no control beyond the coastal strip. General Carlo Caneva, the Italian commander, was careful to avoid a repeat of the

Adwa disaster. His cautious tactics led to relatively low casualties: 4,250 soldiers were wounded and 3,380 Italians died during the war, including 1,948 who died of cholera and disease. Italy used airplanes in combat for the first time in world history, both for surveillance and aerial bombardment, opening a new era in twentieth-century warfare.[95] Nonetheless, the Libyan campaign ground to a stalemate by December.

To avoid European offers of mediation and requests for concessions, Giolitti had declared the annexation of Libya on 5 November 1911. This avoided the diplomatic tangles Austria had encountered in 1908, after converting its de facto occupation of Bosnia-Herzegovina into an annexation. However, the Turks now had no incentive to stop fighting. Nor did Italy have permission from its European allies to threaten the Turks with attacks on other parts of their empire.[96] As the war dragged on, Italy seized two French ships accused of supplying the Libyan "rebels" out of Tunisia. Giolitti managed to calm a diplomatic crisis spurred by the anti-French memories of 1881, when France had humiliated Italy in Tunisia. Finally, Austria allowed Italy to attack the Ottoman Empire in the eastern Aegean Sea. In May 1912 Italy occupied the Dodecanese Islands and Rhodes and held them all for ransom. The Turks accepted Italy's offer for peace when the small independent Balkan states, Greece, Serbia, Montenegro, and Bulgaria, seized the opportunity to attack Ottoman territory in Europe. The First Balkan War began on 8 October 1912, soon followed by the Second Balkan War, with dark implications for peace in Europe. With the secret treaty of Ouchy on 15 October 1912 and the public peace treaty of Lausanne on 18 October, the Turks recognized Italy's annexation of Tripolitania and Cyrenaica, in exchange for Italy's payment of 4 percent of the Turkish national debt and recognizing the Sultan's religious authority in Libya as Caliph. Italy now had its "foothold in the Mediterranean."[97]

Despite the apparently happy ending after thirteen months of war, Giolitti had accomplished none of his domestic goals. At their Congress in December 1912, the Nationalists attacked Giolitti's mismanagement of the Libyan war and began to create their own independent political party, with Catholic support for an anti-Freemasonry platform. Italian politics were changing rapidly: the 1913 general election marked the first application of Giolitti's controversial, nearly universal male suffrage.[98] Five Nationalist leaders, including Luigi Federzoni in Rome, were elected to Parliament that year, and Giuseppe Bevione was elected as a Nationalist from Turin soon thereafter. The Nationalist-Catholic alliance defeated Ernesto Nathan's reelection campaign in Rome; Nathan was a Jewish freethinker and the former Grand Master of Italian Freemasonry who had been mayor since 1907. Enrico Corradini, however, was defeated at Marostica in the Veneto, despite his alliance with local Catholics; this began his eclipse within his Nationalist organization. At their Congress of 1914 the Nationalists expanded their ideology significantly by adopting Alfredo Rocco's ideas into their political platform. Rocco's theories of corporatist economics and politics promised an end to trade union strife. The Nationalists claimed another victory when Italy entered World War I in 1915. Four months after Mussolini's March on Rome of October 1922, the Nationalists fused with the Fascist Party, providing an established ideology and conservative prestige to the radical Blackshirt movement.[99] Rocco served as Mussolini's Minister of Justice after January 1925, while Federzoni served as Mussolini's first Minister of Colonies from October 1922 to June 1924, then as Interior Minister until November 1926. The Fascists quickly abolished many of Giolitti's reforms. Far from co-opting the Nationalists' political energy, Giolitti had displayed the fragility of his own political base.

The Libyan War brought tremendous publicity to the Nationalists and their anti-emigration rhetoric. Newspapers chose colonial experts, who had reported on Italian emigration to Argentina, as war correspondents from Libya: Giuseppe Bevione for *La Stampa*, Luigi Barzini for *Corriere della Sera*, and Enrico Corradini for *L'Illustrazione italiana*.[100] Each used his antipathy for South America to fuel a vision of Italian settlement in Italy's new territories. Libya and Argentina became two polar opposites: one craven, poor, and emasculating; the other verdant, promising, and glorious. As the Italian army fought on in Libya, Giovanni Pascoli delivered a powerful discourse or sermon, published in *La Tribuna*, building upon the ideology of the "proletarian nation": "The great Proletarian [Nation] has stirred. Before, she sent her workers elsewhere; there were too many in the Fatherland and they had to work for too little. She sent them over the mountains and over the seas, to carve canals and pierce mountains . . . to do all that was most difficult and tiring, and most humble. . . . They became a little like the blacks in America, these compatriots of America's discoverer; and like the blacks, were put beyond law and humanity from time to time, and lynched."[101] To sharpen the sting of American racism, Pascoli cited scorn for the achievements of Italian history and culture: "[Italians] were told, 'Dante? But you are a people of illiterates! Columbus? But you belong to the camorra and the Black Hand! Garibaldi? But your army was wiped out by barefoot Africans! Long live Menelik!' The miracles of our Risorgimento were forgotten, or remembered as miracles of luck and shrewdness . . . [Italians] only knew how to use a dagger. So these *laborers* returned to the Fatherland as poor as before and less content than before, or were lost obscurely in the whirlpools of other nationalities."[102] Pascoli was creating a new myth of emigration, stripped of any positive benefits for individual emigrants or for Italy. For the dignity of its emigrants, and for memory of its heroes, Italy needed a heroic and dynamic policy of imperialism.

Pascoli claimed emigration had robbed the country of its glory, exploited its people, and impoverished its people morally and materially. Only through the conquest of Libya had the Italians redeemed themselves: "the great Proletarian [Nation] has found a place for all: a vast region bathed by our sea. . . . It has responded to its duty of contributing to the humanization and civilization of the nations; to its right not to be suffocated and blockaded in its seas; to its maternal calling of providing for its willing children what they desire—labor; to this solemn commitment with the centuries of its two Histories [classical and medieval/Renaissance], that its third [the modern era] will not be lesser. . . . Ours is a defensive, not an offensive war."[103] Like Bevione, Pascoli looked to Japan as a model for Italy's imperial calling: "another nation in our time has also suddenly revealed itself. In a few years it silently transformed itself; behold, it put into action all the modern inventions and discoveries, the immense ships, the monstrous cannons. . . . Are not the conscripts and legionnaires of Italy also called *little soldiers?* Has not the new Italy in this its first great war used all the boldness of science and its ancient history? Has it not for the first time rained death from the skies upon the enemy encampments?" Pascoli went further to accuse anti-war critics of a conspiracy to exploit Italy, "the great martyr of the nations," "the *Proletarian Nation*, provider of manual labor at reduced prices": "We know why we were falsely accused. The example of Japan, which was to have been unique, has been repeated after only a short time. The *laborers* of the world proved, in their time and place, formidable *little soldiers*. The great Proletarian of the nations (industrious and populous in the west exactly as the other nation of the far east) had come to the battlefield and revealed itself on land and in the sky as a strong power, because it is more simple, more hardworking, more accustomed to suffering than enjoyment, more knowledgeable of its rights."[104] Pascoli's speech was only the most famous statement of a new Italian ideology, combining victimization, aggression, and fatal glory. The triumphant barrage of nationalist rhetoric, from every major newspaper, discredited Parliament's old Liberal policies, especially in the field of emigrant assistance. Italians were now called to a much higher destiny.

Internationally as well, the Libyan War upset the old balance of power. Editors all over Europe condemned the news of Italy's "brutality" against the Turks in Libya. On 30 September 1911, one British paper editorialized that "a nation which numbers Calabria and Apulia amongst its provinces need not go abroad for a civilizing mission. Italy has an Africa at home."[105] These comments earned a special rebuke from Di San Giuliano. European commentators worried the war could turn the Islamic world against Europe, or dissolve the ailing Turkish Empire. The European powers' overlapping claims to the Ottoman territories would surely spark the imminent pan-European war. The First and Second Balkan Wars of 1912 and 1913 only hastened the outbreak of world war in 1914.[106]

In spite of international tensions, the Libyan War proved popular with Italians across the world. In 1913 Adolfo Rossi toured Italian settlements in the Argentine countryside and wrote that "many, not only workers, but also smallholders, said they are ready to sell their possessions here, and go and live in Libya, as soon as the [Italian] Government says that some areas are ready. 'At least,' they told me, 'we will be able to contribute to the development of an Italian colony, and one day die in the shadow of our flag.'" Even Italian priests and friars put maps of Libya on display, as preparation for one day leading their parishioners to Italian Africa.[107] The radical Gaetano Salvemini opposed the Libyan campaign throughout 1912, to little effect. In 1914 he published a collection of sixteen authors' arguments against the war, with a sober preface hoping "that this will show that not everyone in Italy in 1911 and 1912 lost their heads in the deceptions of the newspapers, and that even in our generation there were men who could go against the current and be overwhelmed by it rather than support it."[108] To show the "effects of the colossal campaign of deceptions," Salvemini quoted the touching letter of an emigrant in Buenos Aires, writing home to his wife in Puglia on 3 March 1912:

You absolutely want to come here to America. I don't want that because first, things here are not like they were before, and second, when the war finishes I have to be ready to bring home some money, and we will go to beautiful Tripoli; then America will be there and no longer here; everyone here is getting ready to go to Tripoli. I know you want to come here, but I don't like this land of America and I don't want to stay here.[109]

Disappointed with Argentine America, the emigrant held faith in a new Italian America in Libya. Salvemini's frustration with this Libyan fascination contrasts with the contentment of a fellow southerner, Giustino Fortunato. Fortunato did not approve of the war; he felt Libya was useful only for its strategic location, which indeed proved true in World War II. Yet Fortunato marveled at the united support the war had stirred in the countryside: "now it is clear to me that the past fifty years of national life have not been in vain, and something new, beautiful, and promising is in the new Italy! . . . Finding myself in Gaudiano in the Ofanto valley, among the peasants of Basilicata and Puglia, for the first time in my life I saw and knew, with a joy I had never felt, that they too, at last, know they are Italians."[110] Fortunato's joy later became tragic despair with the Fascist seizure of power.

The ebullience of new conquest, however, spread even to the conscripted Italian soldiers fighting in Libya. On 17 October 1911 one soldier wrote home, "So dear father calm down and be happy because we are safe. . . . Dear father, I ask you not to worry because here we really have America [*qua abbiamo l'America addirittura*]."[111] There was no further need to emigrate to the Americas now that Italy owned Libya. The myth was complete: Libya was the new America, ripe for emigrant settlement.

The Italian Colonial Ministry

With Libya, Italy finally became a major colonial power. Unprofitable, unpopular, unheralded, and poorly funded, Eritrea and Somalia had failed to provide the "keys to the Mediterranean" as Mancini had promised in 1885. Senator Faina summarized disappointments with Eritrea by 1912: "The fact that after a quarter century of occupation and fifteen years of profound peace no migration had appeared toward Eritrea makes one doubt its suitability for labor colonization." Somalia held promise only "inasmuch as it is less well known."[112] Libya, however, added enormously to Italy's colonial portfolio. The new colony was rich in history and Roman archeology, held unexplored mineral wealth, and most important, was only 260 miles from Sicily. After months of Nationalist and colonialist propaganda, Italy expected great things from its new imperial conquest. By contrast, the prestige and political weight of emigration had been irreversibly compromised. With Libya as a settlement colony so close to southern Italy, emigrant colonialism would never again hold center stage for Italian colonialists. No more Congresses of Italians Abroad; no more plans for Italian colonies in South America; instead, the Italian Parliament relegated ethnographic colonies to an inferior legal status, separate from the new Italian Colonial Ministry.

Giolitti's government presented plans for a Colonial Ministry in 1912, long before Italy had established a semblance of control over Libya. The Senussi tribe of Cyrenaica led a long and heroic opposition to Italy's colonial rule. "Pacification" persisted past the outbreak of World War I. In 1915 Italy withdrew its troops from Libya for the Great War; Benito Mussolini ordered a renewed occupation of Libya in 1926. Senussi resistance in the interior was not completely overcome until 1932, when colonization finally began under the Fascists.[113] In promoting the Libyan War, Corradini's paper *L'Idea nazionale* had irresponsibly recommended that, in the manner of the French and British empires, "guerrilla warfare lasting several years would be an excellent school for our army, too tarnished from its duties as a [domestic] police force."[114] Libya ought to have taught the Italians how distracting and debilitating colonial wars can be, and that guerrilla warfare never improves the reputation of an army.

Despite the embarrassing chaos in North Africa, Giolitti hoped to consolidate some domestic political gains. Creating a new Italian Colonial Ministry for Libya provided an opportunity for celebration and self-congratulation. In contrast, Eritrea and Somalia had been ruled by an office in the Italian foreign ministry, and were not fully included under the colonial ministry until 1922. After Adwa, the two colonies of East Africa were forever stepchildren, not even remembered as colonies; they were omitted from the seven-volume report on Italy's colonial interests worldwide, *Emigrazione e colonie* (1903–1909). Tripolitania and Cyrenaica occupied two-thirds of Genoa's Colonial Exposition of 1914, even though the territories had not yet been conquered. The colonial ministry displayed Libya's public works, health facilities, archeology, and agriculture, dwarfing the exhibits from Somalia and Eritrea and the special pavilion from Italy's agency in Gondar, Ethiopia.[115]

With the new colony and the new ministry came fresh debate over the fundamental definition of Italian colonialism. Specifically, should Italy's vast ethnographic empire come under the legal and administrative jurisdiction of the prestigious colonial ministry? Fifteen years earlier, General Giacomo Sani had argued that a proposed colonial ministry must "direct and administer not only the Territorial Colonies (Eritrea, Benadir, etc.) but also those [colonies] that organically live in the territories of other nations. The method of direction would naturally have to be different, but the ends would be the same."[116] In Parliament, the panel evaluating the proposed Ministry of Colonies reached the opposite conclusion. Presented by Giovanni Abignente, the report of 15 June 1912 justified Italy's need for colonies by stressing the unreliability of emigration abroad: "Outlets for trade and population in countries of foreign sovereignty would be ideal, because less costly; but only if their absolute security and continuity could be assured. Where this is not true, when all it takes is the flick of a pen to disturb tremendous interests and even to destroy them, then the creation of our own colonies and protectorates becomes inescapable."[117] For many years, Italian colonialists had followed the debates in the United States over emigration restriction. It seemed only a matter of time before literacy requirements or racist quotas would cut off Italy's most important and profitable emigration outlet. The panel concluded that Italy's own interests justified the conquest and appropriation of Libya. Abignente compared Italy's pure expansionist motives with the motives of its European peers: "For peoples that suffer from the overabundance of population, or population growth fever, the necessity of having their own colonies is not, as for others, a question of ambition or imperialist tendencies, but instead is a question of life or death. They cannot wait for the coming of universal brotherhood, desired but faraway, to relieve the pressing need of means for expansion and subsistence."[118] With powerful organic metaphors, the Italian Parliament declared Italy's need for its own living space to house, feed, and support its burgeoning population. Any alternatives were naive and unrealistic. Not surprisingly, the Italian politicians ignored the interests of native Libyans while trumpeting Italy's clear need for colonies.

By stressing the instability of emigrant colonies, and the need for territorial colonies, Parliament established a clear division between the two forms of *colonie.* Of course, Italy's colonial ministry would administer only the territorial colonies. With the acquisition of Libya, Italy had become a genuine colonial power and needed to imitate closely the other European powers. The Parliamentary panel cited the examples of England, Portugal, France, Belgium, Germany, Holland, and Spain, who entrusted emigration to their diplomats. Italian emigration must likewise remain under the Ministry of Foreign Affairs, with its Directorate of Schools Abroad and its Commissariat of Emigration. The panel concluded that emigrant colonialism encompassed all of Italy's foreign policy: "because a colonial policy, understood in this sense, and especially for Italy, given the importance of its so-called *Free colonies,* is the essence, one might say, of its foreign policy."[119] If the foreign ministry gave up emigration, it would have nothing left to oversee.

Traditional, pacifist emigrant colonialism rapidly lost its appeal, supporters, and funding. The Dante Alighieri Society had previously championed emigration as a "school of the nation," supplying patriotic literature for the transatlantic voyage. But in 1912, inspired by Italy's new colonial policies after the conquest of Libya, the Society changed its message. It launched the monthly journal *La Patria,* with patriotic readings for Italian emigrants "near and far [*Ai vicini ai lontani*]."[120] The journal's cover featured an illustration of Mother Italy in a toga, holding a fasces and her child, who longs to go to the sea. This pictorial reference to emigration is flanked by symbols of war: a Roman shield and sword, the Rostrum with the prows of destroyed enemy ships, the Roman she-wolf, and broken olive branches. With the November 1912 issue, the journal changed its name to the more aggressive *Patria e colonie* (Fatherland and colonies). To assert the importance of Italian emigration abroad, the Dante Society's journal invented Italianate names for the expatriate colonies, substituting Nuova-Jork for New York.[121] According to the journal, creating the ministry of colonies in the middle of the Italo-Turkish War "was not only a gallant gesture, but an act of urgent political and administrative necessity." The journal accepted Parliament's argument that any "free colonies" in the Americas were inferior to the new conquest.[122] Contributors wrote contemptuously of "the so-called policy of Italian emigration . . . [and] all the castles in the air founded on chattering Congresses and on the Parliamentary ivory tower and on the humanitarian declarations of protection before God and man."[123] America was finished for Italians; they now needed to turn to Europe and

Africa: "The European peoples are carrying out the mission . . . of trans-
forming socially the African continent, as they have already done for the
Americas. . . . The new history of Italy is only beginning."[124] Abandoning all other interests, Italy needed to begin the settlement of Libya immediately.

Following the formation of the colonial ministry, the Italian Agricultural Colonial Institute in Florence abandoned its projects in South
America. Originally, the institute had intended to study the conditions of
Italians working in agriculture abroad. The institute's founder and secretary, Gino Bartolommei Gioli, proclaimed in 1905 that Italy must develop
expertise "to guide our best energies for the conquest of foreign markets
and the economic organization of those nuclei of *italianità* transplanted
on the soil of other countries."[125] Yet eight years later, he declared expatriate colonies a lost cause: "The contribution of Italian scholars to the
agrarian problems of foreign countries has been much less important
[than the study of Italian Africa]. Even if our extra-European emigration
since the turn of the century has succeeded in creating strong and flourishing agricultural colonies on foreign soil, [Italy's] ruling classes were
uninterested. . . . Our emigration's eminently proletarian nature, its
broad scope, and the difficulties of undertaking technical scientific studies in faraway foreign countries did not lead Italian scholars to dedicate
themselves to the questions of colonial agriculture."[126] Frustrated, Bartolommei Gioli had not found stable funding for the study of American
migration. But after Italy's conquest of Libya, his agricultural institute
drew subsidies from the new colonial ministry and government of Libya,
the foreign affairs ministry, and the ministry of education. In retrospect,
Bartolommei Gioli declared that the Institute's first seven years of activity, which had included the study of emigration, were but a prelude to its
true work in Africa. Forgetting emigrant colonialism entirely, he remarked that the Institute had achieved so much so quickly because
"Italy has very recently become a colonizing nation . . . with the extension of our dominions in Affrica [sic] our association has been able to
make great progress . . . under the impulse of new and strongly felt stim-
uli of national life."[127] By ignoring emigration, Bartolommei Gioli unwittingly tied the institute to Italy's success or failure at territorial
conquest. This would prove short-sighted. The Libyan conquest did
provide immediate opportunities, however, for assistance in the development of North Africa. Bartolommei Gioli supported an Italian army

officer's proposal for a military colonization of Libya on the model of the ancient Roman legions. On behalf of his institute, in November 1911 Bartolommei Gioli proposed to the colonial office a major research mission to investigate Tripolitania before the arrival of Italian settlers. This preliminary study might avoid "the alternating succession of enthusiasm and delusion, which distinguished our colonization in [East] African lands."[128] In 1913 the institute's president, Leopoldo Franchetti, carried out the research project in Libya, with subsidies from the ministry of colonies and also from the Nationalist Association.[129] Ferdinando Martini, one of the institute's early backers, also served as colonial minister from 1914 to 1916.

Compared with the Agricultural Institute in Florence, the Italian Colonial Institute in Rome showed more reluctance to abandon the study of free colonies in the Americas. Even in 1915, the Institute's president, Ernesto Artom, announced the Institute's twin goals of promoting Italy's "Colonies of population . . . in the great ethnographic empire" and the "Colonies of direct dominion . . . of Libya, Eritrea, and Benadir [Somalia]."[130] By upholding emigration, the Institute had earned broad political support across the spectrum of political parties. Yet in January 1913 the Italian colonial ministry upbraided the Colonial Institute for misunderstanding the word "colony." The Institute had requested a subsidy for a Colonial Information Office and library, to provide "reliable and exact news on various foreign markets, especially about consumer markets that are political dominions of [Italy] or are centers of Italian emigration."[131] Both the First and Second Congresses of Italians Abroad had encouraged the creation of such an office. The colonial ministry replied with contempt for the entire concept of emigrant colonialism: "Even if the presence of a more or less considerable group of Italian emigrants gives our economic expansion a particular importance in certain countries and in certain markets, it is evident that this does not make these places substantially different from other markets of production and consumption, in the problems they present. Despite their particular importance, these markets cannot be called colonial markets, in the exact sense of the word, and they are not considered as such by the other States that, like Italy, have [both] colonies and emigrant groups in foreign countries."[132] Italy was joining the prestigious ranks of Europe's colonial powers, and fostering emigrant colonies might breach convention and be a terrible mistake. The colonial ministry worked hard to change the Italian definition of the word *"colonia."* They contrasted the Italian Institute's proposal with other countries' "information offices that support the true colonies, that is, the territorial colonies." The governments of Britain, France, Belgium, Austria, Hungary, and the United States sponsored "information offices of a *colonial* character—in the exact sense of the word."[133] Italian colonialism now held a new political meaning.

The ministry's pressure permanently changed the Institute's focus to Africa. The Second Congress of Italians Abroad, held shortly before the Libyan War, would be the last. In 1911 the Institute produced a massive *Annuario dell'Italia all'estero e delle sue colonie* (Yearbook of Italy abroad and her colonies, 3d edition), listing all the schools, institutes, and religious orders serving Italian emigrants around the world. The Institute did not release its next yearbook until 1926, with an entirely different format and contents. Its visual symbols changed as well. The Institute replaced its original triangular monogram logo with a topless figure of Italy, crowned with a Roman helmet and carrying a fasces, presiding over migrating birds flying in formation over the sea. This confident, maternal image of imperial Italy reflected a change in mood. In 1908 the Institute had depicted royal Italy comforting the Little Italies of four continents, huddled before the newly constructed Altar of the Fatherland.[134] No longer would Italian emigrants grovel before other nations; Italy's empire was expanding in prestige, power, and influence.

Italian emigration did not shift immediately to Libya's shores. The long war against the Libyan Arabs, halted temporarily for World War I, precluded Italian settlement until after the Fascist conquest of the Libyan interior in the 1920s. Italians had already learned the lesson of establishing peace before colonization; the emigrants settled in Eritrea during the war of 1895–1897 had been evacuated at the government's expense. Furthermore, most Italian emigrants moved within established "chain migrations," back and forth to overseas communities where friends and family were already present. The Italo-Turkish War did not stop emigration from Italy; instead, as Gaetano Salvemini noted, the conflict's economic turmoil had the opposite effect. Italy's statistics for 1913 set astounding records, never again equaled, for transatlantic and continental emigration: 556,325 emigrated to the Americas and 307,627 emigrated within Europe.[135] A decade later, the stagnation of South American economies and the restriction of immigration to the United

States and Western Europe effectively closed the doors to Italian migration. Would-be migrants had to find new destinations, and Italian Libya then became an attractive choice.

On the eve of World War I, the rise of Italian Nationalism and the Libyan War forced rapid and dramatic changes within Greater Italy. The Colonial Institute, the Dante Society, and other cultural institutions turned toward the vision of Enrico Corradini: emigration must be redeemed and replaced by imperial conquest. In 1914 Roberto Michels would codify these arguments as "demographic imperialism," which guided Italian colonial policy for the next three decades.[136] Even as writers and politicians reinterpreted Italian migration under a nationalist lens, the actual conditions of emigrants abroad changed rapidly under the pressure of war and crisis. The Dante Society's correspondent in Buenos Aires, Pietro Bolzon, reported that Italian patriotism during the Libyan War met with a xenophobic backlash, revealing the futility of emigrant colonialism:

> It is not surprising that the Italians, in the very places where they work the hardest, face violent, nationalistic lockouts. Our emigrations are so large, and have spread so rapidly and overwhelmingly, as to easily provoke xenophobia; even more so when, out of a confused amalgam, they give signs of becoming conscious and effective colonies searching out their fatherland. The only remedy to the chilling and abnormal life of these *illegal colonies in someone else's house* will be to create them from now on in our conquered lands. After we transform the emigration movement into an expansionist movement, the painful contradictions will cease, and the work of those far away will be a true continuation of national greatness, free from deviations, absorptions, ingratitudes, and amputations. . . . Just wait until the end of the war [in Libya]: willing arms will not be lacking, and the experience gained in exile will be an incalculable treasure. *Today the fatherland is no longer far away.* With a new love, a new dignity is born. . . . There are no more exiles, but men intent on redeeming themselves from oblivion, transforming themselves into living, conscious transplanted branches of Rome reborn. With time, the legions of dispersed pioneers will return to the common womb.[137]

Bolzon in Argentina adopted Corradini's words as his own, envisioning the return of his compatriots to "the faraway fatherland." He argued that the spread of Nationalist ideology, combined with the circumstances of international politics, had created a new dynamic for Italian emigration.

By asserting their patriotism during the Libyan campaign, and stirring up xenophobic hatred, the Italians of Argentina only made the conquest of Africa more necessary and more pressing. In Bolzon's vision, emigrant colonialism was now obsolete. Regardless of the costs, the new Italy needed to conquer its own territorial possessions as an extended homestead for Italian settlement, not build an ethnographic empire in deference to foreign governments and host nations.

Such compelling rhetoric moved passions and events far beyond what Corradini had foreseen. The Nationalist synthesis of imperial settlement rehabilitated Crispi's policies of demographic colonialism and rallied proletarian support for a colonial war. Nationalists thus stamped Italian colonialism with their imperialist blueprint of national unity, exotic conquests, glory, and blood.

7

Earthquake, Pestilence, and World War

Natural disasters have forever plagued the Italian peninsula. Southern Italy lies in the shadow of four famous volcanoes: Mount Etna in east central Sicily; the islands of Vulcano and Stromboli just north of the Sicilian coast; and Mount Vesuvius, just south of Naples, the only active volcano in continental Europe. All of Italy is an unstable seismic zone, with irregular earthquakes, landslides, tsunamis, and floods. But early in the morning of 28 December 1908, Italy suffered the worst natural disaster in its long history. Along the margin of the African and Eurasian continental plates, between the island of Sicily and the Italian mainland, a massive earthquake shook for more than twenty seconds, only six miles below the sea's surface. Aftershocks were felt for the next five years. The quake's energy was physically visible as a brilliant flash of light. Massive waves up to twelve meters high then pummeled the coastline, tearing away buildings at their foundations and drawing cadavers far out to sea. The cataclysm destroyed cities and villages on both sides of the Straits of Messina, known in myth as Scylla and Charybdis. Messina, the largest city in northeastern Sicily with 90,000 people, was leveled. Only 2 percent of its buildings remained standing. The earthquake's movements left wave patterns in the pavement, as the city had settled more than two feet (70 cm) during the quake. Reggio Calabria, the capital of the Calabria region, was a smaller city that suffered even more thorough damage. Only two years earlier, the United States had suffered the only urban earthquake disaster in its history. The devastating San Francisco earthquake and fire of 18 April 1906 killed at least 700 people and left a quarter of a million homeless. The 1908 earthquake on the Straits of Messina, with the resulting tsunami and fire, destroyed three hundred townships and killed perhaps 120,000 people.[1]

Tremors from the disaster, both physical and emotional, were felt around the world. Hundreds of thousands of Calabrians and Sicilians in the Americas turned in desperation to the Italian-language press for news of the catastrophe. Many English-language newspapers throughout the United States also published special notices in Italian.[2] The calamity became a defining moment for the international Italian community, as the network of Italian societies and Italian-language newspapers raised millions of lire in relief funds. Unfortunately, the earthquake of 1908 was but one catastrophe in a series of deadly disasters for Italy, including the Calabrian earthquake of 1905, the Libyan War of 1911–1912, and the Great War of 1915–1918. Charitable collections for the natural disasters and for the wars' wounded provided Italians abroad with the opportunity to participate directly in the fatherland's triumphs and tragedies.

As these crises revealed, Greater Italy was not imaginary. Many Italian expatriates would support their fatherland in its hour of need, by contributing support for stricken family and friends, money for disaster relief, or military service for war. The nightmare of total warfare in Europe caused widespread anxieties long before its actual outbreak in 1914. Many envisioned that in the looming "struggle for life" between nations, each country would call upon every able soldier, whether at home or abroad. The mobilization of expatriates for the Great War became the great objective of Italy's emigration commissariat. More than three hundred thousand emigrants returned to Italy for wartime service, at the expense of the state's Emigration Fund, carefully amassed over the previous fourteen years. Emigrants' responses to Italy's troubles illustrate an enduring concern for the fatherland.

New nationalist rhetoric emphasized these international bonds of loyalty and service. Enrico Corradini and his followers preached a passionate, patriotic charity (carità di patria), linking patriotic donations and military service with divine virtues. Corradini's novel La Patria lontana (The Faraway Fatherland, 1910) features the character Lorenzo Berenga, an Abruzzese construction contractor who has earned a fortune over decades of hard work in Brazil.[3] At the end of his career, he regrets that he did not return home for the funeral of his father and mother and mourns that he has left a legacy of buildings not in Italy, but in a foreign land. The Great War begins in Europe, but Berenga is too old to return home to fight in the Italian army, as the other main characters do. Instead, he helps raise millions of lire for the fatherland. The voyage home of the expatriate volunteers marks the highest sacrifice, yet Berenga is also redeemed through his patriotic act. Rapid developments in international affairs would soon make Corradini's propaganda appear prophetic.

Italy's entrance into World War I in 1915 attracted emigrant volunteers and donors in part because of the decisive events of the previous decade, especially the regional earthquakes and colonial warfare, which had galvanized and unified Italians worldwide. The Italian state further politicized its emigrants by boycotting emigration to Argentina and Uruguay in 1911–1912. Giolitti's government pursued an activist and interventionist migration policy, under pressure and inspiration from the Nationalists. In these years the Italian state also worked to strengthen the ties of citizenship and military obligations for Italian men abroad. World War I marked a new level of patriotism and participation of expatriates in Italian affairs. Yet the postwar world, devastated and hostile, would bring Italy's international migration to an abrupt end.

The Cholera Boycott of Argentina and Uruguay

Since 1887, the Italian state had let its citizens emigrate freely, wherever they chose to go. Bilateral treaties and international conventions protected the emigrants in few cases. This Liberal approach permitted Enrico Corradini, Luigi Villari, and others to blast the government as negligent and abusive; they argued that Italy should organize and manage this precious flow of labor. Such criticisms began to sway emigration policy. In 1911 Giolitti's government broke with Liberal traditions by suspending migration to Argentina and Uruguay, in violation of emigrants' rights to travel. The fundamental emigration law of 1901 allowed for such a suspension in its first article: "Emigration is free within the limits established by law. . . . The Minister of Foreign Affairs can, in agreement with the Minister of Interior Affairs, suspend emigration toward a particular region, for reasons of public security, or when the life, liberty, or property of the emigrant may incur grave risks."[4] This article had been invoked in 1902 with regard to Brazil.[5] The newly created emigration commissariat had sent Adolfo Rossi to make a thorough inspection of conditions on the coffee plantations; on his recommendation, Foreign Minister Giulio Prinetti banned subsidized migration to Brazil. Italians wishing to travel to Brazil would have to pay their own fare. Emigration to Brazil dwindled to insignificance under these conditions. (See Appendix, Figure 1.3.) Giolitti's ban on Argentine migration, however, applied to paying passengers as well. How this drastic action was taken and implemented reveals many of the fears, hopes, and contradictions behind Italy's migration policies.

Argentina had long been the darling of Italian emigrant colonialism, hailed by Luigi Einaudi and countless others as the key to Italy's foreign affairs. With its temperate climate and extensive natural resources, the country seemed to offer unlimited potential. The Argentine government, moreover, welcomed Italian immigration; one of Argentina's founding fathers, Juan Bautista Alberdi, shaped the republican constitution of 1853 with his forcible dictum "*Gobernar es poblar* [To govern is to populate]."[6] Argentina's international standing would be measured by the size of its population and its economic development. Like the United States, the country relied upon mass immigration for economic growth and adopted accommodating regulations to attract white Europeans. Liberal Italians viewed Argentina as the most promising site for a Greater Italy, established through peaceful settlement. The number of Italians in Argentina grew to 30–40 percent of the national population. In 1907 the Italian commissioner of emigration, Leone Reynaudi, wrote the Argentine ambassador to express the long-standing Italian policy of encouraging Italian emigration to Argentina rather than to other countries: "It is superfluous to add that . . . no solution could be better accepted than to intensify the migration to the Argentine Republic, which for many years the Italians have regarded as a sister of their fatherland, across the ocean."[7] The United States, by contrast, consistently opposed the organization of foreign colonies in its midst and became notorious for the 1891 lynching of Italians in New Orleans.[8] Argentina, the star of Latin America, seemed to share more in common with Italy.

Within four years of Reynaudi's comments, Italy had changed its policy completely. The high hopes raised by Einaudi and his followers turned to deep disappointment and resentment. Italian migrants were harassed and mistreated in Argentine society, while Italy's share of the Argentine import market had peaked by 1904.[9] Argentina became a special target for Italian Nationalist invective. Giuseppe Bevione's study of 1911 called for a radical change in the two countries' unequal relationship. According to Bevione, Italy's Liberal government misunderstood and mismanaged the situation in Latin America: "Illusions are altogether useless, and it is fatal to hide the truth and prolong the deceit. The famous Italo-Argentine brotherhood does not exist. On one side, our side, there is submission, goodness, love for work, respect for law, deference, an unhealthy fever to acquire fortune, in which, sadly, memory and love of country are consumed. On the other side, the Argentine side, there is condescension, an instinctive feeling of superiority, open scorn, frequent injustice, and a real aversion to [us]."[10] Bevione could not stomach the Argentines' position that allowing Italian immigration was "charitable. . . . [This is] a colossal and fatal error." Italian workers were more valuable than gold. To demonstrate their "utility and irreplaceability" in Argentina's economy, the Italian government should bargain for their improved conditions and, if necessary, cut off the flow. "They should have received us throughout the Republic with cap in hand, as precious and desired guests. Instead we arrive like gypsies." As Bevione's rhetoric reveals, Italy's pride and even its identity as a nation and ethnicity were at stake. Was Italy part of the underdeveloped world? Who was the beggar and who the master? Italy deserved "land concessions, guarantees, preferences. . . . absolute respect for the rights, interests, and honor of its compatriots. . . . [and] the maintenance of its language."[11] Until its emigrants were protected in Argentina, the Italian government was betraying its international responsibilities.

Bevione was not alone in the campaign for an emigration boycott of Argentina. His call from the Right was balanced by calls from the Italian Left. The syndicalist Alceste De Ambris, who in Sao Paolo had campaigned to improve conditions for workers, argued that the only way to end the harassment and exploitation of Italian migrants was to organize immigration boycotts.[12] Argentine agriculture had come to depend upon tens of thousands of seasonal laborers or "swallows," who commuted for work between Italy and Argentina, harvesting the fields during summer in both the Northern and Southern Hemispheres. Still, the migrants had no protection within Argentine society. Even the Argentine Socialist Party supported a boycott of Italian immigration, which would force landowners to grant fair wages and the government to respect civil liberties.

The sense of frustration in the Americas led to new strong-arm techniques in Italy's emigration policy. Instead of quietly filling South America with Italians, while keeping excellent relations with receptive governments, the Italian government charted a new course: it would force South American governments to recognize their dependence upon Italian labor. Italy's cholera epidemic of 1910–1911 thus became the occasion for a migration boycott. Cholera, transmitted through filth and infected fecal matter, was very embarrassing to the Kingdom of Italy during its fiftieth anniversary celebrations. Italy was the only industrialized country affected by cholera's sixth worldwide outbreak. The stigma was so great that when Giovanni Giolitti returned to power as Prime Minister in March 1911, replacing Luigi Luzzatti, he conspired to keep the disease a secret, pretending that the outbreak had already run its course.[13]

But Italy's mass emigration threatened to carry the hidden plague throughout the Western world. Giolitti's concealment flagrantly violated his government's obligations under the Paris Sanitary Convention of 1903, which required all signatories to declare their epidemic infections. Diplomats from United States and France discovered the Italian government's deception in June and August 1911 but quietly agreed to the Italians' claim that their epidemic had ended in 1910. The French government worried that their own port of Marseilles would be declared unhealthy if the Italian infection were discovered. The Americans needed Italian migrant labor and agreed that publicity, with inevitable hysteria and riots, would be counterproductive in fighting cholera; they arranged for secret Italian reports on the epidemic. These two countries were crucial partners for Italian migration. France absorbed much of Italy's continental migration, with 60,956 immigrants in 1910. The United States had surpassed Argentina as an emigrant destination in 1897. By 1910, the United States received 262,554 Italians while Argentina received 104,718.[14] After resolving matters with France and the United States, Giolitti's government decided it could afford a showdown with Argentina. While compromise and discretion prevailed between Italy, France, and the United States, relations between Italy and Argentina rapidly disintegrated into a stark, brutal contest to decide who needed migration more and which economy would collapse first.

Italy refused to compromise with the Argentine inspectors who gave informal warnings, beginning in early June 1911, that they knew cholera was still present in Rome and Naples.[15] In July 1911, Argentina renewed its cholera quarantine policy of the previous year, when Italy had admitted that Naples was a contaminated port. Italian ships could either embark an Argentine health inspector at Rio de Janeiro, Brazil, or face five days of quarantine upon arrival in Argentina. Italy protested that such inspections were properly the work of the Italian emigration commissariat, and claimed Argentina was creating a new international precedent. The Italian government then laid the grounds for an international incident by ordering the Navigazione Generale Italiana steamer company not to stop in Rio for the inspection. The NGI accepted the emigration commissariat's order on 14 July, "with full faith, however, that the Commissariat has made all the necessary provisions so that the Argentine authorities will not make difficulties and that our ship *Re Vittorio* and later steamers will be free from quarantine."[16] The industrialists' faith in the Italian government was misplaced; the *Re Vittorio* was held in quarantine when it reached Buenos Aires four days later. Argentina was now publicly accusing Italy of concealing a cholera epidemic. The Italian government moved toward a diplomatic crisis on 20 July, when the Italian foreign ministry ordered the Italian naval cruiser *Etruria* to leave Argentine waters immediately, where it had harbored on a courtesy call, explaining that "Argentina, with the pretext of sanitary motives, shows it disregards the value of our emigration and the merit of our friendship."[17] A telegram from Giolitti welcomed the impending confrontation: "I fully support refusing to admit the Argentine medical inspector on Italian ships. I am in fact amazed that we complied with this indecorous demand last year. . . . The Foreign Minister can explain to our embassy that our attitude is different this year because the current prime minister considers the demand an offense against our dignity and has decided to reject it categorically and to prohibit emigration to Argentina and direct it to other countries that are more respectful of our dignity."[18] Without considering the costs to Italian migrants or Italian shippers, Giolitti had decided that the impudent Argentines must learn their place.

The Italian government contended that the twenty-day voyage from Genoa to Buenos Aires was a quarantine in itself; that the passengers' baggage was fully decontaminated with mercuric chloride; and that the Argentine inspectors infringed on Italian sovereignty. Nonetheless, the Argentine Interior Minister and Health Minister stood by their position: ships from Italy must either allow Argentine inspectors or face quarantine. On 27 July 1911 the Italian ambassador in Buenos Aires cabled Di San Giuliano, the Italian foreign minister, calling for a dramatic response: "It is necessary to defend our prestige by immediately suspending emigration to the

Plata. . . . When this crisis is overcome, I hope we can establish truly friendly and cordial relations."[19] Relations would not be friendly until Italy dominated the friendship. Giolitti's government responded by banning Italian emigration to Argentina on 30 July. Uruguay was included in the boycott six days later, as punishment for supporting Argentina. Defending Italian prestige hardly qualified as a "reason of public security," but Giolitti invoked the emigration law of 1901 anyway. Indeed, the ban had nothing to do with the best interests of Italian emigrants or shipping companies, who clamored for a rapid end to the policy. At stake was offended national pride and insulted national hygiene. Giolitti took offense at the insinuation (which was true) that the Italian government's inspectors would conceal the presence of cholera in Italy and claimed that a quarantine was not warranted under international law because the Italian ports were not infected. He hoped to wreck the economies of Argentina and Uruguay and force them to beg for a return of Italian labor. But the Argentines remembered that in 1886, during the last cholera pandemic, they had allowed a single European steamer, from Genoa, into port. This one exception resulted in infection throughout the country and the death of thousands. In 1904 Argentina had signed reciprocal health treaties with Brazil, Paraguay, and Uruguay so that such a disaster would not be repeated. Brazil and Paraguay, however, yielded to Italian diplomatic pressure and left Argentina and Uruguay to stand alone.[20]

Many Italians did not know, as Giolitti did, that their country was suffering an authentic cholera epidemic in the summer of 1911. All reports of cholera were carefully suppressed.[21] The cholera incident became instead a trial of nationalist sentiment, to decide the future of Italian migration to Argentina. Italy's patronizing rhetoric toward Latin America now became official policy. Why should Argentina dictate terms to Italy? If Italy's health precautions were good enough for the United States, should they not be good enough for Argentina? The Italian government sought support from German officials, who agreed that allowing Argentine inspectors on board would violate national sovereignty. The Imperial German Government had recently refused a similar Argentine demand to inspect German emigration hostels. In any case, Italy could hardly retreat now. The Italians of Uruguay "applauded the energetic measures taken by [Italy] against the excessive measures" taken by Argentina and Uruguay; the Italian ambassador added his opinion that the boycott came "as a providential show of force and dignity by the Royal

Government."[22] According to Italian reports, medical issues had become secondary even for Argentina; they quarantined ships with only a single Italian passenger, traveling from any port, but allowed transport ships from cholera-stricken Russia to pass without quarantine. The boycott thus took on added weight as a competitive test of national pride, economic strength, racial and ethnic health, and societal development.[23]

Italy's diplomatic corps carefully monitored Argentina's attempts to replace Italians with other ethnic groups. No alternative source of immigration seemed practical; for example, Swedes and Norwegians would be unused to the climate, and their governments opposed Argentine recruitment. The German government also blocked recruitment within its empire. Polish and Russian immigrants were considered "politically very undesirable" and were suffering more from cholera than the Italians.[24] The only workable sources were outside of Europe. In considering this option, Italian diplomats revealed their own racism, in tandem with the racial prejudices of Argentina: "Most of the new arrivals are either of inferior races or unadaptable to the social and climatic conditions of Argentina. . . . including Hindus. When these strange immigrants landed in Buenos Aires, the press raised a sensation, and public opinion worried about the future of their population's ethnic uniformity. . . . The Director of Immigration asked the steamer companies not to permit the embarkation of this category of 'undesirables'. . . . [T]he English colony is already thinking about paying for their repatriation."[25] Instead of emigrants from Italy, Italian steamers now brought replacements from Asia, still making money but at the expense of Argentina's self-image. Market competition quickly pitted Italian ethnicity against other ethnic migrant groups around the world. From the Italians' perspective, the boycott unquestionably proved their ethnic superiority.

The emigration commissariat found a new role as enforcer of the boycott, which tested Italy's control over its borders and emigrants. To thwart Argentina's hopes of recruiting Italians from neighboring countries, Italy's emigration commissioner asked the Italian press of Latin America to assist in "a patriotic work by discouraging Italians from traveling to Argentina."[26] Passenger ships could not depart from Italian ports for Argentina, but Italians might manage to embark illegally from Marseilles or from Austrian and German ports, outside of Italian regulation. The Italian company Lloyd Sabaudo reported that Austria's subsidized steamer line, the Austro Americana, was trying to lure clandestine Italian emigration to Argentina via Trieste. This friction exposed the continuing irredentist conflicts between Italy and its ally Austria. Italy also closed its Swiss border to emigrants bound for Argentina via Germany. These measures appeared successful. Italy's consul in Córdoba, Argentina, observed that Argentine newspapers "declared victory" when any Italians arrived illegally, but these numbered "several hundred at most."[27]

As the boycott dragged on, well past the peak of Italy's cholera epidemic in August 1911, Italian diplomats grinned at Argentina's growing economic distress. Italy's emigration inspector in Sao Paolo remarked, "I am happy to hear of the prohibition on emigration to Argentina . . . because it is sudden and unexpected, after the Argentine farmers had sown all available land and the temporary emigrants of last year have almost all returned to Italy; it is certain that Argentina will be badly damaged by this measure." He predicted that Argentina would lose half its wheat and oat harvest, worth 475 million lire.[28] Italy's boycott aimed specifically at Argentina's agricultural labor force. Italian children and elderly were still allowed to travel to Argentina; they would be a drain on its besieged economy. In a further blow to Argentina's agricultural base, Socialist syndicates took advantage of Italy's boycott to stage their own strikes. By June 1912, Italy's ambassador noted with pride that Argentina was racked by crises, from "the lost harvest of grain and flax, the long railroad strike, expensive transportation, the lack of money, excessive speculation, etc.; but all this has certainly been intensified, if not caused, by the end of Italian migration. This lack [of labor] has produced effects in all of Argentine agriculture, the principal source of the Republic's prosperity."[29] During Argentina's crisis of inflation and bad harvests, many Italian Argentines "who were generally thought to be rooted in Argentina" decided it was time to return to Italy. One Argentine politician saw this exodus as a sign far worse than the boycott itself.[30] The Italians no longer needed the Argentine economy; they could leave when they chose. Italy's economic ascendancy over Argentina was thus secured. The Italian ambassador recommended in November 1911 that after Argentina ended its sanctions, Italy should "immediately revoke its decree. A period of truly cordial Italo-Argentine relations will begin, which will allow us to build here a position of the first order, maybe doubling in a short time our present exports of 150 million [lire] a year."[31] In theory, the ragtag colonialism of emigrant labor would transform into the informal imperialism of industrial exports.

The end to the boycott reinforced Italy's superiority. Argentina stopped its quarantine of Italian ships on 19 December 1911 and asked for Italian emigrants to return, but Italy insisted on a diplomatic convention to resolve the matter. Negotiations between Italy and Argentina began in Rome on 5 July and ended on 17 August 1912. In the case of future epidemics, Argentina agreed not to send its inspectors aboard ship, and even renounced quarantines for all steamers without suspect cases.[32] Italy finally ended its boycott of Argentina on 24 August. However, Giolitti realized that a flood of Italians returning to the Plata region would betray Italy's dependence on migration. The surge in labor would also lower wages and expose Italian workers to abusive treatment. He arbitrarily, and illegally, decided to increase migration to Argentina slowly over a two-month period.[33] Without a public explanation, prefects and subprefects simply delayed or denied passports for Argentina until October. Prefects in Sicily and Naples pretended they did not know of the boycott's revocation, or claimed they had not received official notification. After cooperating with the long boycott, Italian steamer companies and their customers complained bitterly about Giolitti's deceit. The emigration commissioner supported the steamer companies' complaints, but Giolitti refused to budge.[34]

Italy's rising nationalism and imperialism had deeply affected the boycott's course. To celebrate Argentina's centennial in May 1910, the city of Rome had sponsored an elaborate celebration and Ferdinando Martini, the former governor of Eritrea, had traveled to Argentina as a special ambassador; Argentina, however, snubbed Italy's fifty-year anniversary exposition the following year. Argentina, with most of Europe, also condemned Italy's war in Libya in September 1911. Many Italian colonialists now saw Argentina as an enemy rather than a friend. Argentine newspapers began to worry that the temporary end to Italian immigration would become permanent, "either from the present conflict, which has made Italo-Argentine relations individually and collectively very difficult, or as a consequence of the conquest of the new African lands."[35] Italians had already begun to choose other destinations over Argentina, and soon, it seemed, Italians could settle their own "America" in Libya.[36] Einaudi's vision of a "new Italy" in La Plata was exploded by the boycott crisis and Giolitti's peremptory, deceitful tactics. After 1911, Argentina and Uruguay would never again be the cornerstone of a peaceful Greater Italy.

Succoring the Fatherland

Even as Italy's nationalistic press turned attention toward imperialism in Africa, the benefits of Italy's informal colonies grew most apparent. Tragic disasters in the early twentieth century proved the strength of the transnational Italian community. The journal *L'Italia coloniale* had observed in 1901 that whenever Italy suffered from "earthquake, flood, cholera, or any calamity, the compassionate echo of our colonizers [colonizzatori] reaches us with the most generous offers."[37] One expatriate wrote to the Dante Society that an Italian abroad "is the most assimilable individual of all. I do not mean he easily loses the love of his native land; just look at the enthusiasm with which our colonies race to aid their brothers when an epidemic, a volcanic eruption, an earthquake, or a flood desolates some part of Italy. What the Italian loses is the exterior garment of patriotism."[38] A series of wars, earthquakes, and other cataclysms gave Italian expatriates the chance to renew their inner patriotism with public demonstrations. Emigrants' donations to the Italian Red Cross for earthquake relief presaged their greater sacrifices for Italy during World War I.[39]

The whole world sympathized with Italy after the Messina-Calabria earthquake of 28 December 1908. Numbers do not convey the personal tragedies subsumed within the region's disaster. The people around Ferruzzano, Calabria, were still recovering from the relatively minor earthquake of 23 October 1907 when struck by the new calamity. The radical Gaetano Salvemini, who was teaching at the University of Messina, saw his sister, his wife, and his five children crushed in his home. Salvemini survived the quake by standing in a doorway, but was forever haunted by his tremendous loss.[40] Similarly, his colleague Benedetto Croce, the renowned philosopher, had nearly died in the earthquake of 28 July 1883 on the island of Ischia, in the Bay of Naples, when he lost both his parents and a sister. These disasters fueled regional emigration; facing broken families and collapsed economic opportunities, many attempted to build a new life abroad.

The Messina earthquake devastated Sicily's international community, as the consulates of France, Turkey, and the United States collapsed. Stuart Lupton survived as the American vice consul and on 31 December 1908 reported on the devastation: "I had not proceeded more than 50 yards [toward the consulate] when I found myself walking in water up to my knees in a place which should have been eight feet above the water level." Lupton distanced himself from survivors naked and crying for help: "without men and tools it was impossible to do anything as I kept on trying to shut my ears. Almost all the natives were hysterical, shrieking and moaning."[41] The Italian garrison of military police had collapsed, killing those troops who would have established order and distributed relief. Russia and the United States sent warships and supply ships immediately, to save the survivors from pestilence and exposure during the wintertime tragedy.[42]

As governments across Europe and the Americas organized help for Italy, the international community of Italian emigrants mobilized to succor their devastated relatives and compatriots in Sicily and Calabria. In the aftermath of the 1908 quake, Italian societies and newspapers abroad used their organizations to funnel money into relief and reconstruction. They had gained experience with recent events. *La Patria degli italiani*, the leading Italian paper of Argentina, had raised 700,000 lire for the victims of a devastating earthquake on 8 September 1905 in central Calabria. After the 1908 disaster, the paper raised more than two million lire. The Italian Chamber of Commerce in New York raised funds for the survivors of the 1905 and 1908 earthquakes, as well as the eruption of Mount Vesuvius in April 1906, which killed hundreds in the province of Naples. The Italian National Target Shooting Society of New York and the Italian community of Buffalo, New York, also collected contributions for these earthquakes, and for the floods of 1903 in Sicily.[43] Energetic fundraising displayed the latent vitality of Italy's expatriate colonies.

Appeals for disaster relief also revealed the schisms between Italy's clerical and secular institutions. While church and state collaborated in providing education for Italians abroad, neither wanted to be outdone in providing relief for the earthquake of 1908. Queen Elena presided over a secular relief effort, organized through the Italian Red Cross, but the Catholic Church launched its own charitable collection through the Vatican Secretary of State and the Vatican's Apostolic Delegate to the United States, Diomede Falconio. The divided fundraising efforts confused many donors who hoped to assist the broken families of the dead and wounded. The bishop of Providence, Rhode Island, apologized to Falconio that "a society of Italians in Bristol, R.I. collected $700 and sent that amount to the Red Cross Society. The chair of the committee engaged in this latter work assured me that he began his collection before the Pas-

tor made his announcement, and regrets that he was not able to contribute through the Church. I mention the fact only to show the good
will of the people of Bristol."[44] One Italian was disappointed to learn he
would not receive an Italian Red Cross badge for his donation through
the Apostolic Delegate. The Church raised at least $35,000 from Catho-
lics in the United States, but it seems that most of the Catholic donors
were not Italian Americans, who instead donated money directly to the
devastated towns and villages.[45]

Catholic fundraisers and the Italian Red Cross divided over the means,
management, and symbolism of disaster relief. In March 1909 the American Federation of Catholic Societies complained to the American Red
Cross, which had donated $250,000 to the Italian Red Cross, that the pres-
ident of Queen Elena's committee was Ernesto Nathan, "a Hebrew." Others on the committee included "a Socialist and Freemason, a Protestant,
and a Jewess," even though "Italy is a catholic country."[46] One American
pastor accused the Italian Red Cross of cowardice and corruption in the
relief effort. Despite negative publicity, Italian societies in the Americas
raised record amounts for the Italian Red Cross. Supporters of the Italian
Red Cross chapter in Buenos Aires received silver medals and local prestige in recognition for their efforts. Italy remained as vulnerable to earthquakes as before, and the Italian Red Cross awarded more medals to
Italian societies in Caracas, Venezuela; San Francisco, California; and
Jeanette, Pennsylvania, for their donations after the disastrous Tuscan
earthquake of 10 September 1920, which caused extensive damage in
Lunigiana and Garfagnana. This international aid for the Italian Red
Cross carried a significant economic benefit to Italy's balance of payments, along with other emigrant remittances.[47]

The Italian Red Cross coordinated relief efforts for military crises as
well. Adolfo Rossi as consul in Rosario, Argentina, coordinated contributions to the Italian Red Cross during the Italo-Turkish War over Libya. By
March 1912 the colony had raised 6,275 lire through the Pro-Patria Committee. The patriotic institutions in expatriate colonies found new missions in the new international climate. Antonino Di San Giuliano, the
foreign minister, proposed to reward such fervor by increasing subsidies
for Italian schools abroad to 650,000 lire a year: "we should support the
foundation of new [Italian] schools, in the centers of our emigration . . .
requests have recently become more numerous and more insistent because of the patriotic fervor revived in both the celebration of Italy's Fifti-

eth Anniversary and our favorable political and military situation after the conquest of Libya. . . . [I]t would be harmful, from a national point of view, to reduce the subsidies or deny new requests."[48] From the United States, Luigi Villari agreed that the Libyan War was a turning point for Italians abroad: "The show of patriotism by Italy and her colonies abroad for the war in Libya has done much for our country's international position in America. Yet the work is not yet finished, and we must never finish developing the patriotic feeling of our people."[49] Italy's newfound strength and the proven sympathy of expatriates worldwide seemed a sturdy foundation on which to continue building a Greater Italy.

Yet the challenge of World War I in 1914–1918 quickly overshadowed the triumphs of the Libyan War. The fundraising channels established for the earlier disasters allowed expatriates to help Italy in its hour of greatest need. Again, the Italian Red Cross was the funnel for patriotic aid. Italians in the United States staged patriotic dramas as benefits for the Italian wounded and donated funds for ambulances and other equipment. Just as remittances had buoyed Italy's peacetime economy, expatriate contributions were crucial to the sale of Italian war bonds. This support became even more important after October 1917, when Austrian and German units overwhelmed Italian troops at Caporetto and advanced to the outskirts of Venice and Padua. Italy was now fighting for its survival, not for ownership of Trent and Trieste. Italians abroad supplied 6.5 percent of the cash for the Italian savings bond campaign in 1917, and 10.6 percent in 1918. In 1920, expatriates again bought 7.5 percent of the treasury bonds for Italy's postwar reconstruction. Such patriotic donations faced stringent competition in the United States. The American Red Cross and the American government targeted immigrants in their propaganda campaigns, wooing them away from the Italian Red Cross and urging them to buy bonds "for the sake of the country where your children's children will be born."[50] In hindsight, World War I marked the peak of Italy's emigrant colonialism. The war would devastate Europe and forever alter international migration.

Rights and Duties for Emigrant Citizens

As strong cultural and economic ties developed among the communities of Greater Italy, the legal status of emigrants became more and more contentious. Italian writers and politicians focused on three key questions:

Could Italians abroad hold dual citizenship? Should emigrants be allowed to vote or be represented in Parliament? Any reforms were controversial because of the sheer size of Italian migration: by 1911, approximately six million Italians lived abroad, more than one-sixth of the population of the Kingdom of Italy. Expatriate citizenship was far from abstract. Beyond the appeal for monetary donations and patriotic sympathy, citizenship carried serious military obligations. Italy, like other European countries, built its military upon nearly universal male conscription at age twenty for two years of service, followed by service in the reserves until age forty-five. Because emigration drew so heavily from this age group of men, population movements became a matter of national security. In the years before the Great War, a general mobilization of all reservists seemed certain, and emigrants would inevitably play an important part.

Because of emigrants' military commitments and because most emigrants planned to return home to Italy, it seemed only fair that they participate in the political decisions of the fatherland. The Socialist Angelo Cabrini called for Italian emigrants to be given the vote, as in Norway.[51] The Italian Colonial Institute organized two Congresses of Italians Abroad, expecting them to evolve into a permanent representative body in Italy. But the Congresses of 1908 and 1911 revealed the heterogeneity and divisions within Italy's colonies abroad, from the bankers of Cairo to the miners of Pueblo, Colorado. Only wealthy expatriates could afford to represent themselves. Writing from Philadelphia, Luigi Villari argued that parliamentary representation for emigrants was impossible: "The colonial notables must be pleased by the idea because each thinks he will be among those elected to represent the Italians of America at Montecitorio [the Palace of Parliament in Rome], but one can easily see the stupidity [asinità] of this proposal. In the first place the notables are almost all American citizens, and therefore excluded, unless in the ridiculous sentimentalism toward emigration we admit foreign citizens into our Parliament."[52] Villari charged that the Italian colony was composed "90 percent of hardworking laborers with many good qualities, but ignorant, primitive nomads, and absolutely disorganized." The other 10 percent were exploiters, and these would be represented in Italy.[53] Even the Italian notables who attended the two Congresses, however, were divided by their regional concerns. The Congresses demonstrated the difficulties of a transnational Italian legislature. Notwithstanding, in 1909 Cabrini proposed a representative Council in Rome as a voice for expatriate Italian settlements, modeled on the Communal Council representing Italian towns; though supported in the Senate, the project was never realized. In 1912, when the Italian parliament voted to extend the suffrage and nearly tripled the size of the electorate, Cabrini again proposed granting emigrants an Italian vote. This vision finally became a reality with the historic election of 2006, when Italians worldwide for the first time were allowed to vote for parliamentary representation in the Italian Republic.[54]

The opposite problem, of Italians taking foreign citizenship, was also complex. Hypothetically, emigrants could become citizens of the world, with a dual loyalty to Italy and to their new homes. The emigration inspector of Messina claimed, "we do not want the children of Italians [in Brazil] to keep the nationality of their fathers . . . this would be a serious error. Through the [Italian schools abroad], we must persuade them that there is not only one great country in the world, where they were born, but that there are at least two: we want them to feel the legitimate pride of our glorious race."[55] A reinforced racial or ethnic identity could outweigh the legal status of changed citizenship. Francesco Saverio Nitti, in announcing a "new phase of Italian emigration" after the battle of Adwa, analyzed the strength of German and British expatriates and concluded that "our emigrants in the Americas must renounce their Italian citizenship and at the same time become more patriotic Italians."[56] This difficult formula reveals widespread fears in Italy that emigrants would assimilate and never be heard from again. In 1900 the second issue of *L'Italia coloniale* solicited several opinions regarding the question of emigrants voting abroad, without finding a consensus. Bishop Geremia Bonomelli and Cesare Lombroso wrote that expatriates should participate in local politics, while the emigration inspector of Genoa, Natale Malnate, believed this would imply a practical renunciation of Italian citizenship. No matter, argued the Sicilian socialist Napoleone Colajanni; emigrants must participate in their local governments to defend themselves from exploitation.[57]

What would help expatriates, however, might not help the Italian state. F. S. Nitti and other radicals proposed dual citizenship for Italian emigrants, which would have resolved many legal difficulties, particularly for those Italians who planned to return home after five or ten years. But dual citizenship was anathema for many Italian politicians. Citizenship was closely associated with universal military service. What if the emigrant's home country and host country went to war with each other? An Italian priest in Worcester, Massachusetts, tried to allay such fears in 1916: "In fact one can admire Dante without ignoring Longfellow. . . . Becoming an American citizen certainly cannot change the soul of a person. . . . America can change an emigrant's clothes, but never his heart. If we are good and loyal American citizens, when we return to the fatherland we will also be better Italian citizens. The thought of an armed conflict between Italy and the United States must not worry us, because this is impossible. These two nations share the same ideals."[58] To the chagrin of Italian Nationalists, when Fascist Italy did fight the United States twenty-five years later, Italian Americans chose to fight for their new country. Yet Italians faced enormous obstacles if they sought United States citizenship. While noncitizens could vote in many states before 1914, the state regulation of naturalization allowed a range of corrupt practices. Recently arrived Italians lacked the patronage of urban political machines, which might process the applications of Irishmen but shut out Italians. Italian efforts to organize character references were banned as citizenship fraud.[59] Only children born on American soil could be assured of their citizenship.

Ironically, by first insisting on perpetual, exclusionary Italian citizenship for emigrants and their children, the Italian state alienated hundreds of thousands of expatriates. As Attilio Brunialti had predicted in 1885, few of the second generation performed their military duties as required by Italian law. Italy viewed the children of emigrants as Italian citizens by blood (*jus sanguinis*), and liable for military service, even if they were born on American soil (*jus soli*) and thus were citizens of American governments.[60] Under this early legislation, grown children of emigrants could not return to Italy because they would be arrested as deserters and shirkers. The government of Brazil had complicated matters in December 1889 by declaring all its residents Brazilian citizens, whether born in Brazil or not, unless individuals made a contrary declaration within six months.[61] Not all the Italians of Brazil even knew of the deadline, which caused controversy among Italian politicians. Could expatriates lose their Italian citizenship by assuming a foreign citizenship unknowingly? What if Italians needed to take American or French citizenship in order to find employment, for example, in public works projects? The Italian government had to choose between enforcing a strict definition of citizenship, which would require emigrant fathers and their sons born abroad to serve in the Italian military; or a flexible definition of citizenship, without military obligations. By freeing male children of military service, with its associated penalties, more people abroad would remain Italian citizens. This policy would expand Italy's economic and cultural influence abroad, at the expense of Italy's military manpower.

The Italian Parliament resolved matters with the citizenship law of 1913. The Second Congress of Italians Abroad had recommended that Italy recognize the foreign citizenship of Italian children born abroad, but such measures were unthinkable for the Nationalists. Following a motion by Luigi Federzoni, Vittorio Cottafavi declared in 1911 that "the Italian must be able to say like the Englishman: I am alone, but I have the flag of my country behind me. The day must come when the motto 'I am an Italian citizen,' like the ancient '*civis romanus sum*,' is enough for the Italian citizen to be respected by all."[62] In June 1850, Lord Palmerston had used this Latin motto to justify before the British House of Commons his naval blockade of Greece on behalf of a single aggrieved British citizen. Could Italy do less? With Parliament's final compromise, children born of Italian fathers abroad were to be considered Italian citizens, unless they renounced their Italian citizenship as adults. Any Italian emigrant who had adopted foreign citizenship, for whatever reason, could regain his or her Italian citizenship simply by returning to Italy. The Italian state thus claimed emigrants' exclusive loyalty, unless the emigrants themselves broke ties to Italy. According to Alfredo Baccelli, who presented the legislation, "Others have tried to find a remedy in so-called 'dual citizenship.' But even saying this phrase is enough to understand its absurdity. . . . No cell in the physical world can belong to two different organisms simultaneously; and no citizen in the moral world can belong to two different political unities."[63] Italy thus upheld the duties of military service for expatriates, instead of a more diffuse political influence abroad, by rejecting dual citizenship just before the outbreak of World War I.

Blood across the Waves

As European politicians looked out to their expatriate populations, they saw opportunities for trade, political influence, and cultural expansion overseas. But most important was the resource of emigrant manpower, which could make the difference between national life or death in a cataclysmic war. In 1914, when the Great European War finally arrived, the populations of Greater Britain, Greater Germany, and Greater Italy were called upon to support their European brothers. If expatriates heeded the summons, they could leverage their nations' resources in the unexpectedly long, brutal, and total war. Italians worldwide supported Italy's war efforts to an impressive degree, as more than 300,000 reservists returned to fight.[64] Thanks to return emigration, Italy was the only combatant country in Europe to *gain population* during the war, in sharp contrast to the decimated populations of France, Britain, Germany, and Serbia, who looked abroad for help in desperation.

The British Empire's contribution to World War I stands out as the most famous example of expatriates rallying to their "home country." Five million British served in the military overseas (approximately 10 percent of the total population), joined by 458,000 Canadians (5.7 percent), 332,000 Australians (6.6 percent), 112,000 New Zealanders (10 percent), and 136,000 white South Africans (9.7 percent of the white population). This totaled 1,038,000 soldiers from the four "white Dominions," or 6.7 percent of their combined populations in 1914. The Dominions thus provided approximately one-sixth of the British Empire's troops fighting outside the United Kingdom.[65] While the Dominion governments were not legally bound to help Britain in its hour of need, there was no question of their willingness to send troops across the globe out of patriotic duty. Even if the British settlers' ancestors had left Europe a hundred years previously, the war was a chance to make a real difference for the survival of British culture, society, and political traditions. For many in the Australian New Zealand Army Corps (ANZAC), the only fear was that they would arrive in Europe after the war was over.

Germany hoped to match Britain's success by rallying the millions of Germans overseas. Young men, who were the most likely to emigrate, were responsible to register for military service through their local German consulates.[66] In 1916, an optimistic German official advised the Colonial Council to prepare for a massive return migration: "Even before the outbreak of war we heard from many who sought help to get out of the United States. We have reliable reports since then that thousands of strong German peasant families [*Bauernfamilien*] lack the means or the capital to become American citizens, through no fault of their own. Many of these families, probably most of them, desire to come back to the Motherland."[67] In fact, Germany's infamous foreign secretary, Artur

Zimmermann, threatened the U.S. ambassador that German immigrants remained loyal to their fatherland and would prevent any American military action against Germany. Ambassador James Gerard noted Zimmermann's vehemence in his memoirs: "'The United States does not dare to do anything against Germany because we have five hundred thousand German reservists in America who will rise in arms against your government. . . .' As he said this, he worked himself up to a passion and repeatedly struck the table with his fist. I told him . . . that if he could show me one person with an American passport who had come to fight in the German army I might more readily believe what he said about the Germans in America rising in revolution."[68] Gerard later confessed that he did know of one such American citizen who fought for the German Empire, but certainly not five hundred thousand. German-American legions never did materialize. Instead, the German ethnic community, the largest in the United States, fell apart. Many Germans anglicized their names to escape public persecution, as even the British Royal House changed its name from Saxe-Coburg-Gotha to "Windsor."[69]

Why did the German Americans fall so far short of imperial expectations? Germany's emigration had peaked in the mid-nineteenth century; most Germans had emigrated before the creation of a united German Empire in 1871. Scattered across the world, German emigrants participated in the empire only vicariously by reading about Bismarck in the newspapers. The resurgent Germany provoked widespread fears and xenophobic opposition in the United States, especially with the "Cahenslyism" scandal among German Catholics and Theodore Roosevelt's campaign against "hyphenated Americans."[70] And Germany was clearly fighting on the wrong side in the Great War. Submarine attacks on ships in the Atlantic, including passenger liners, could hardly rally German Americans to the imperial cause. The German politicians had lost touch with their cousins overseas.

In contrast with Germany, Italy enjoyed remarkable success in mobilizing its emigrants during World War I. Out of approximately six million Italians abroad in 1911 (no one knew for sure), the emigration commissariat paid for the return of nearly three hundred and four thousand soldiers to fulfill their military duties as reservists between 24 May 1915 and 31 December 1918.[71] This figure does not include reservists who returned to Italy at their own expense between August 1914 and May 1915, such as Vincenzo Di Francesca. The large number of soldiers, and the return rate of 5 percent, is comparable to the contribution of Australia to Britain's war effort. The Italian soldiers were not recruited by their local governments, as in the British Dominions; they were contacted by the Italian consulates, who had no legal authority to raise international armies. Like the Italians of Brazil in Corradini's *La Patria lontana* (1910), these hundreds of thousands chose to return to fight for Italy in the Great War. Reservists returned to Italy amid a large wave of return migration.[72] This dramatic expression of international solidarity was the climax of Italy's policies promoting a transnational nationalism.

Italy had nine months longer than Britain and Germany to prepare for the war. During the diplomatic crisis of July 1914, Italy was bound to Germany and Austria by a defensive alliance. But when Germany and Austria launched their offensive war against Serbia and Russia, without informing the Italian government, Italy was not required to declare war. The Italian government wisely chose not to rush to join its allies in their disastrous course. Instead, Italy opened diplomatic negotiations with both sides in the conflict.[73] The offer from Italy's friends Britain and France proved more tempting, and in May 1915 Italy declared war on Austria to redeem the Italian territories of Trent and Trieste. This "third war of the Risorgimento" promised to unify the Italians of Europe and give Italy a defensible frontier in the eastern Alps. By entering the war against Austria instead of against France, the Italian government finally embraced the long-standing tradition of irredentist subversion. Italy did not declare war against Germany until fifteen months later, in August 1916. The Italian state was more concerned with territorial irredentism than German hegemony. Interestingly, the United States took the opposite course, declaring war against Germany in April 1917 and against Austria-Hungary only in December 1917.[74]

Italy's delayed entry into the war complicated the situation for emigrants. Although Italy declared neutrality in 1914, if the war lasted long it was inevitable that Italy, as a Great Power in Europe, would enter on one side or the other. The outbreak of European war therefore marked a refugee crisis for Italian migration. In August and September 1914, nearly half a million Italian emigrants fled from France, Austria-Hungary, and Germany, abandoning everything they could not carry.[75] Fifty thousand emigrant families returned to the province of Belluno, in northeastern Italy, in the single month of August 1914. Even families who had lived abroad for twenty years were forced out of war zones without notice. Yet no employment awaited them in Italy; more than 280,000 thus became refugees in their own country.[76] Socialists appealed for impromptu public works projects at the local and national level. Transoceanic migration also faced sudden disruptions; at the announcement of war, French, German, and Austrian steamers dumped their cargo of Italian emigrants at the closest ports, including Brazil and Madagascar. The emigration commissariat addressed the refugee crisis as best it could.[77] The outbreak of war in 1915 and the resulting prospect of employment were greeted with a measure of relief.

The appeal to emigrants overseas was not meant as a call for volunteers, but rather as a required mobilization. Nevertheless, when news of Italy's war reached the Americas, tens of thousands of young men voluntarily gathered at the Italian consulates. But not everyone was wanted by the Italian military; each month the general staff called up reservists trained in different specialties. The Italian mobilization was announced on 22 May 1915 and began on 24 May. The first group called were infantrymen of ages 20 to 28. Soldiers in technical specialities, such as artillery, cavalry, engineers, mountain troops, and the naval reserve, were called over the next three years. By 1917 the Italian army was calling upon reservists ages 18 to 42, including those who had been exempt because of small stature; in 1918 they even called on soldiers suffering from trachoma. The total number of emigrants who returned as called for military service amounted to 303,919, divided as follows: 128,570 from Europe; 19,529 from northern Africa (15,130 from Algeria and Tunisia, 2,940 from Egypt, and 1,459 from Morocco); 48 from the rest of Africa; 24 from Asia; 354 from Central America; 51,774 from South America; and 103,259 from North America.[78]

Italians in South America had an economic incentive to heed the call to arms: soaring inflation had brought financial ruin. In October 1915 one Italian emigrant wrote home about critical conditions in Buenos Aires, Argentina:

> Conditions in America have become disastrous; property is now worthless, food very expensive, and salaries reduced to a minimum. . . . We live here paralyzed, close to the capital city, in such a crisis as you cannot imagine. Patience; we hope for the future. In the newspapers we read with joy about the blows that the Italian soldiers have given and are giving to those Austrian savages. Here in Argentina the generals of the Italian army are loudly praised as the best in all the world, and we

are very proud. Ever since the beginning of the Italian war, every week steamers have departed overflowing with reservists. If you saw one of these ships you would be amazed! . . . The port is full of all classes of people (except the Germans) to salute those departing. . . . We wish you health and fortune; Long live Italy, Long live the King and all the army, down with and death to all the Germans.[79]

With such serious economic problems in Argentina, the Great European War appeared as an escape, not just for the young reservists, but vicariously for the entire Italian community. Pride in "their" armies led to a series of weekly popular prints, published in Buenos Aires, to show Italian troops overcoming the Austrians in dramatic hand-to-hand combat.[80] Another Italian in Argentina wrote that many emigrants wanted to volunteer for the Italian cause but were not accepted: "they give preference to the youngest and to those due for call-up."[81] If the Italian army had accepted volunteers according to the emigrants' schedule, instead of their own rigid timetable, many more emigrants from South America would have returned to fight.[82]

The Italians of North America, however, had fewer reasons to abandon their adopted homes. As American factories produced a growing supply of wartime materiel, labor became scarce and wages soared along the neutral shores of the United States. Socialists and anarchists urged their compatriots not to fight for Italy's Liberal capitalist oppressors. Italian-language papers opined that Italians had their families in America to worry about, and urged them to donate time and money to America, not Italy.[83] Yet family ties also lured some patriots to aid the fatherland in its time of need. Out of a welter of motivations for return, from family loyalty to economic incentives to provincial nostalgia, the Italian state crafted a clear national benefit, drawing together hundreds of thousands of emigrant reservists to fight for Italy in the great crisis of World War I.

Americans wondered at the patriotism of these Italian-American reservists, some of whom had never been to Italy and did not even speak Italian. In 1916 the American journalist Gino Speranza reported on the reservists returning home to a new land in wartime: "I came over from New York with nineteen hundred of these Americani on shipboard. They were the gayest lot I have ever seen, playing and singing all the way from the North River to the Immacolatella [in the port of Naples]. They came from every point of our country; miners from the West, some wearing caps with the inscription of some flour company or the name of an express company; others decked out in American overalls, suspenders, and sweaters; there was even one Italian from Kansas in a baseball suit! Many of them had the Italian tricolor and a button of the Madonna del Carmine on one lapel and an American flag pinned to the other."[84] Technically these "Americani" had forfeited their American citizenship by taking up arms for a foreign country. Speranza hoped, however, that the United States could understand the Italians' breadth of character, and their feeling of service for their ancestral home. After the war, Speranza wrote, Congress ought to apply the "test of *character*," rather than "the new [racial] sociology," to the national immigration laws.[85] This would not happen.

Reservists were helped along their way by Italian philanthropic societies, subsidized by the Italian government. In 1916 the New York State Immigration Bureau highlighted the work of the Society for Italian Immigrants. The state government noted that the society was "highly organized and its agencies co-ordinate through the United States and Italy." Indeed, the philanthropists had prevented a crisis in the reservists' return migration: "It is obvious that the sudden influx of thousands of reservists into the city and their concentration here awaiting embarkation during the winter months would have created much hardship had not the situation been so admirably managed by this society. The fact that this Bureau has not received a single complaint in consequence of these extraordinary conditions . . . and that the Society for Italian Immigrants has cared for, housed and assisted 45,495 aliens . . . is the most remarkable achievement ever attained by an institution of this character."[86] In the New York Bureau's judgment, the pressure of wartime logistics lifted the Italian-American community to new heights.

As the war progressed, the Italian government turned to its expatriates to raise money and exert their political influence for Italy's war aims. In 1916 the Italian Colonial Institute sent representatives to North and South America "to support our national objectives, and encourage our emigrants to cooperate with the future war bond subscriptions."[87] Hopefully, the Italians abroad could boost Italy's international reputation. Antonio Salandra, the prime minister in 1915, had already compromised Italian diplomacy by bluntly announcing that Italy fought not for liberty and justice but for "sacred egoism," that is, for territorial aggrandizement. Salandra's more idealist successor, Paolo Boselli, who was also the president of the Dante Alighieri Society, hoped to use the Dante chapters as Italy's primary propaganda engine overseas. He thought this might strengthen Italy's position in the postwar negotiations. The Dante Society's board, however, rejected Boselli's bold proposal because of accompanying restrictions on funding. Nonetheless, the Dante chapters abroad helped to raise money for Italian war bonds. One lecturer told the Italians of Argentina to buy bonds as an "act of faith," and if tempted to gamble instead, they should shout "Get thee behind me, Satan!" Expatriate groups also organized financial aid for the local families of reservists fighting for Italy.[88]

Despite its contributions to the Italian war effort, however, mass migration had also tarnished Italy's international reputation. This would hurt Italy in the postwar negotiations. Woodrow Wilson, whose intervention as president of the United States won the war for the Allied powers, was prejudiced against southern Italians. In his five-volume *History of the American People* (1902), he decried the "new immigration" from southern Europe, dealing a devastating blow to Italian confidence and prestige, by stating that Chinese immigrants were preferable to Italians:

> Throughout the century men of the sturdy stocks of the north of Europe had made up the main strain of foreign blood which was every year added to the vital working force of the country, or else men of the Latin-Gallic stocks of France and *northern Italy*; but now there came multitudes of men of the lowest class from *the south of Italy* and men of the meaner sort of Hungary and Poland, men out of the ranks where there was neither skill nor energy nor any initiative of quick intelligence; and they came in numbers which increased from year to year, as if the countries of the south of Europe were disburdening themselves of the more sordid and hapless elements of their population, the men whose standards of life and of work were such as American workmen had never dreamed of hitherto. . . . the Chinese were more to be desired, as workmen if not as citizens, than most of the coarse crew that came crowding in every year at the eastern ports.[89]

On pseudo-racial grounds, Wilson welcomed northern Italians but opposed the entry of southern Italians in the United States. Such prejudice may have clouded his vision. At the Paris Peace Conference he violated his principles of ethnic self-determination at Italy's expense, while dividing the Austro-Hungarian empire. After having compromised on many points, Wilson refused to grant Italy the port of Fiume (today Rijeka, Croatia), even though the city was ethnically Italian. To explain his preference for Yugoslavia, Wilson appealed to the people of Italy directly through the press, in a futile attempt to discredit or overthrow Italy's Sicilian prime minister, Vittorio Emanuele Orlando.[90] Defying Wilson and the Allies, the poet Gabriele D'Annunzio would lead a renegade occupation of Fiume from September 1919 until Christmas 1920, creating an international incident and political spectacle with a rich legacy for fascism.[91] The issue of Fiume would poison relations between Italy, the United States, and the new country of Yugoslavia for decades.

Despite their country's disastrous politics, Italian emigrants brought back a wealth of experience and international support during the war and in the postwar period. Italians abroad stabilized the country's population and expanded its resources, thanks to return migration.[92] The migrants' unprecedented sacrifice would mark a melancholy chapter in the history of migration.

Emigration after the Great War

Wartime sacrifices on both sides of the Atlantic illustrated the ambiguities of emigrant colonialism. While many in Italy praised the patriotism of the three hundred thousand reservists, and the Emigration Fund paid for their passage to Italy, others said the emigrants were only doing their duty and deserved no thanks. From this point of view, military service was the emigrants' legal obligation, as if they had never left Italy. Politicians focused on the numbers who did not return for whatever reason, and refused to recognize the emigrants' foreign citizenship. The emigration commissariat noted with surprise that "our compatriots born in Brazil [and therefore Brazilian citizens] who returned to the fatherland for the mobilization were convinced they performed an absolutely voluntary act."[93] Considering the approximately half million Italian reservists who remained in the United States and failed to return, the commissariat blamed assimilation, vast distances to travel, and "the natural indolence of our [migrants], joined with the certainty that they would not be disturbed during their residence in America, and the hope that at the end of the war an amnesty would clear their responsibilities under [Italian] law."[94] Thus the Italian Americans received insults rather than gratitude from a government still claiming their allegiance.

Others stood by the emigrants and their sacrifice. During the war the Italian Colonial Institute contacted the emigrants who returned as reservists in order to organize a transatlantic collaboration after the war.[95] In March 1917 the Institute also established a national corporation to assist the orphans of the Italians Abroad who died in the war: "these sacred orphans of our Italians who returned to the Fatherland to fulfill the high duty of national defense, are . . . 'the martyrs of our people.' We believe that in each of these war orphans shines the image of the Fatherland and that we absolutely must save them from the shame of begging for charity and aid in a foreign land. Rather, we must raise these young paupers in the cradle of the Fatherland and family, as perpetual testimony of the fervent goodness of the Italian soul."[96] The Italian war orphans were the living victims of transnational war. Stranded in foreign countries that had disregarded or opposed their fathers' Italian service, the orphans had only an imaginary fatherland and the tenuous support of local Italian charities. Bonaldo Stringher, governor of the Royal Bank of Italy, served on the new corporation's council, together with representatives from the *Italica Gens* and *Opera Bonomelli*, the Socialists' Humanitarian Society of Milan, and the Italian Foreign Ministry, Interior Ministry, and Colonial Ministry. Tragically, amid the political and economic chaos which enveloped postwar Italy, the project soon collapsed.[97]

After the war, what would be the future of Greater Italy? Few anticipated that Liberal Italy would collapse and that the United States would finally close its gates. The war seemed to offer concrete opportunities for a truly international community. In the courtyard of the Royal Palace in Turin, the "Latin American Association" erected a monumental relief sculpture in memory of the Italian American war dead, "as heroic testimony of the vigorous union between the Latins of Italy and America." Dedicated on Columbus Day, 1923, the monument shows Columbus planning his voyage, while above him a soldier in close combat swings his rifle and strides over the body of his dead comrade (see illustrations). Many hoped that with the return of peace, the mother country would be a better guardian for her children abroad and provide loans and investments in recognition of their contributions. Eugenio Bonardelli wrote from Buenos Aires about the change among Italians overseas: "Even if patriotic sentiment—it would be foolish to deny it—used to come to life only during national festivals and during public calamities that rained upon our peninsula, now the war has awakened the energies of all the Italians in and out of the national boundaries."[98] The Italian identity now had a concrete history and international significance.

Despite these achievements, a strengthened, unified Greater Italy faced overwhelming political onslaughts after the war. The United States' strict emigration restrictions of 1921 and especially 1924 targeted the "new immigrants," including the Italians. In a triumph for racial prejudice and isolationism, Congress cut the numbers of Italian immigrants from 349,042 in 1920 to 29,723 in 1925.[99] The flood of Italian migration became a trickle. Return migration also ended: Italians could not travel back to Europe even temporarily, because they would not be readmitted into American ports. South America was locked in economic crisis and could not attract Italian emigrants. The fractured nations of Europe also opposed the return of mass migration; their own demobilized soldiers needed work. Italy's expatriate colonies could no longer be replenished from the motherland. They could be reached only through adroit propaganda.

After coming to power in 1922, Benito Mussolini scrambled to reopen the flows of migration, hosting an International Congress on Emigration in 1924.[100] Mussolini was himself a former emigrant to Switzerland, but his diplomatic initiatives were in vain. When it became clear that America's gates would remain closed, he dissolved the emigration commissariat in 1927. Even as thousands of antifascists fled from political oppression, Mussolini declared that Italy's age of migration had ceased and called for expatriates to return home.[101] The Fascist government exploited the institutions of Greater Italy, including the Italian Chambers of Commerce, the Italian schools, the subsidized cultural groups and the Italian social institutions abroad. Politicized and "fascisticized," the transnational network was nearly broken up by the spectacular devastation unleashed by Fascism and Nazism in World War II.[102]

Faced with the extraordinary crises of earthquakes and World War I, Italian emigrants' tremendous response revealed the strength of Greater Italy. The careful cultivation of cultural ties and the support for developing expatriate communities helped bring Italy not only the economic gains of trade and remittances, but tangible rewards from human resources abroad in times of challenge. The call of the fatherland resounded among Italians of all countries. The value for Italy of three hundred thousand emigrant troops in the Great War, the equivalent of fourteen full army divisions, could not be measured in money. The return of those emigrants showed the bonds of family, language, and history to be stronger than political ties in the emigrants' homes abroad. The idea of an emigrant nation had taken concrete form.

Conclusion:
Toward a Global Nation

The Kingdom of Italy celebrated its fiftieth anniversary in 1911 by dedicating the Victor Emmanuel Monument in Rome.[1] This gargantuan structure, complete with an obese statue of Italy's first king, faces Piazza Venezia astride the Capitoline Hill in the center of the city. The focal point is the "Altar of the Fatherland," where two Italian soldiers or sailors guard at all times the most sacred civic monument in Italy: the Tomb of the Unknown Soldier, lit by two perpetual flames, whose torches bear the bronze inscription, "The Italians Abroad to the Fatherland [*Gli Italiani all'estero alla madre patria*]." At the heart of Italian patriotic culture stands the contribution of Italian emigrants, with an ever-burning fire of devotion. To the west is the Janiculum Hill, central to the commemoration of Italian nationhood. Here Giuseppe Garibaldi and his troops defended the Roman Republic in 1849. Near an equestrian monument to Garibaldi, Anita Garibaldi's tomb, and a row of patriotic busts, stands another monument dedicated in 1911. It is a lighthouse atop a classical column, decorated with lions and laurel wreaths (see illustrations). At night a tricolor beacon shines from Rome's tallest hill in green, white, and red, as Italy's light shines on expatriates worldwide.

Both the lighthouse and the torches symbolize the enlightened symbiosis between Italy and Italy Abroad. The lighthouse was a gift from the Italians of Argentina "to Rome our Capital."[2] These expatriates wanted to establish a presence in the Eternal City, demonstrating not only their wealth and material success, but also their faithful ties to Italian traditions. In 1911 they had wanted to erect a memorial altar at the Victor Emmanuel Monument in the tradition of the ancient colonies of Greater

218

Greece that had sent votive offerings to the Acropolis. Although the ramps and platforms of the "Vittoriano" offered ample space, the Italian state committee rejected the idea, fearing it would inspire similar offers from every other expatriate colony across the globe. The Italian Argentines then used funds remaining from their campaign for a Christopher Columbus monument in Buenos Aires, to construct the Roman lighthouse.[3] Already in 1906 they had persuaded the City of Buenos Aires to donate equatorial hardwoods to pave Rome's Piazza Rotonda, in front of the Roman Pantheon. Buenos Aires "wanted reverently to encircle with religious silence the venerable tombs of the first two kings of Italy," buried in the ancient temple seven thousand miles away.[4] Argentina's Italians proved their piety toward the Italian king, even if they could not visit his tomb in pilgrimage, by supplying South American mahogany to quiet the clatter of Roman carriages. In a concrete, monumental way, these emigrants marked their place in a global community.

These acts of devotion illustrated the advantages of a transnational Greater Italy. Italians across the globe could exchange their local products for the benefit of all. The *golondrinas* or "swallows" who found agricultural employment year-round by harvesting crops during the summer in Italy, then crossing the equator to harvest in the Argentine summer, embodied the practical benefits of a global nation: a nation not limited to its territorial boundaries, but functioning as an international community. Ties between colonies and the metropole were manifold, as the leaders of Italian colonies abroad drew upon Italian traditions, rituals, and civic identities. Even expatriate Italian revolutionaries, who hated the Liberal Italian state, looked to the peninsula for their political leadership. Italy's leading anarchists and syndicalists, including Errico Malatesta and Alceste De Ambris, spent their years in exile in the Americas, organizing political action on both sides of the Atlantic.[5]

The Italian state set out to build upon natural emigrant affinities for their homeland with a complex and multipronged approach. Italian Liberals tied emigration to colonial expansion and international prestige. Diplomats negotiated for the rights and protection of Italian workers. Consuls helped organize patriotic festivals, schools, charities, hospitals, and cultural societies. The state promoted a nonprofit banking channel for remittances. Back in Italy, expatriates were celebrated as heroes in state-sponsored exhibitions. The transatlantic journey itself became a "school of the nation," with free pamphlets and books glorifying Italy's past and present. Italian patriots hoped to color all aspects of expatriate life abroad with a newfound national identity. Emigrant colonialism followed the model of an extended family, stretching across borders and making borders irrelevant, building bonds of loyalty to family and community back home in Italy. The president of the Dante Alighieri Society in Buenos Aires claimed that "for our colonists, Fatherland and Family blend together; for the honor of the one and the welfare of the other they work and save their hard-earned wages."[6] To reap the benefits of emigration, the Italian state put culture and tradition in the service of economics and politics.

A worldwide network of Italians abroad would have been unthinkable without the rapid technological progress which had recently collapsed the size of the world. Steamships had made transatlantic travel reliable and cheap, cutting a sea passage from months to days. Correspondence by letter traveled with unprecedented speed, while transatlantic cables carried telegrams within hours to any destination. News and information spread rapidly through international newspapers. The pace of change raised anxiety but opened new opportunities for emigrants.[7] Emigrants crossed the oceans and the equator with impunity to earn income from both the New and Old Worlds, income they planned to spend in retirement in Italy. Thanks to the chain migration of families and friends, Italian towns developed mirror communities in the Americas. Italians abroad lavishly funded the pageants and shrines of their patron saints back home. Drawing upon the experience of Italians and other groups in the United States, in 1916 Randolph Bourne put forward the vision of a "Trans-National America," where nationalism would be replaced by multiple transnational loyalties, and a new culture could be fused from immigrant contributions.[8]

In the dawn of the twenty-first century, a second wave of mass migration has begun. Communications home are instantaneous. Telephone, fax, and internet connections are cheap and readily available; print, radio, and television transmit even local news internationally. Air travel has plummeted in cost, while increasing in speed. Individuals can now shuttle between cultures and hemispheres within hours. The Italian American journalist Gino Speranza wrote in 1906 of unprecedented global migrations, and his words could well describe the world today: "commercial interests, the 'annihilation of time and space' by improved methods of transportation and the ebb and flow of travel, will render the old distinctions of nationalities and the parochial character of present-day patriotism, more and more an anachronism. The conception of citizenship itself is rapidly changing and we may have to recognize a sort of world or international citizenship as more logical than the present peripatetic kind, which makes a man an American while here, and an Italian while in Italy."[9] Speranza's prediction has been fulfilled in part: since 1990 the United States has made the acquisition of dual citizenship much easier, and Italy recognized dual citizenship in 1992. Descendants of male Italian emigrants abroad, and of females who emigrated after 1947 from the Italian Republic, may apply for Italian citizenship.[10] With the benefits of European Union citizenship and the end of the Italian military draft in 2005, more and more individuals are becoming dual citizens. Yet states continue to intervene in this transnational world, claiming their citizens' loyalties to avoid their own obsolescence and to seize opportunities. Underdeveloped countries see in emigration their chance to break from poverty. They debate the perils of mass emigration, just as the United States and Western Europe debate the implications of mass immigration. The Americas provide a salient example: transnational migrants, with one foot at home and one in the United States, are wooed for political donations and for contributions to public works at home.[11] Naturalized compatriots abroad are expected to represent their native land and influence United States foreign policy.

These tensions are not new: Italy's historical example provides an informative context. Amid all the mass migrations a century ago, Italy stood in a unique position as a sending state. Emigrants from multinational empires could not call upon a fatherland. No independent state of Israel, Poland, or Ireland existed to coordinate, support, or protect the populations of Jews, Poles, and Irish abroad.[12] Most of Germany's emigration came before the unification of the German empire in 1871, and the small German duchies lacked the resources to defend their emigrants.[13] The German Empire reached out to emigrants already departed, rather than en route. By contrast, Italian emigrants traveled from a newly united state, which worked to develop emigration as an international resource. Unlike the Scandinavian states, also experiencing mass emigration, Italy claimed to be a Great Power in world affairs. By the 1880s Italy had built the world's second largest navy, ahead of France, the United States, Germany, and Japan.[14] Although Italy did not maintain its naval advantage, it remained in the elite club of global powers, and its pioneering policies for emigration influenced Germany, France, Spain, and others. Nearly all Italian emigration traveled outside of the small Italian territorial empire, well into the 1920s, and so the Italian state had to rely upon indirect influence rather than direct administration as in the British and French empires.

The national emigration most similar to Italy's experience came from the Japanese empire. Like Italy, Japan was an ancient land undergoing national unification in the 1860s. Direct rule of the Meiji emperor, transfer of the imperial capital from Kyoto to Tokyo, and centralized administration across all regions forced political upheaval and swift modernization. Both Japan and Italy struggled to be taken seriously as global powers because of economic weakness and racist prejudices, and both were frustrated at the Paris Peace Conference following the Great War. Notably, both nations also associated the emigration of poor workers with colonialism. Hokkaido, Okinawa, and Taiwan were colonized by impoverished Japanese settlers, and Japanese emigration to Hawaii and California was viewed by government officials in the same perspective. Zentaro Otsuka, a Japanese emigrant journalist, complained in 1910 that, "Emigrants and colonialists, just like the phenomena of emigration and colonization, are often confounded. . . . Colonialists embark as imperial subjects with a pioneer spirit under the aegis of our national flag for state territorial expansion; emigrants act merely on an individual basis, leaving homeland as a matter of personal choice without the backing of sovereign power."[15] But Japanese emigration, illegal until 1884, was much more centralized than the Italians' fractured political philosophies and indirect approach could allow. Through 1894, Japan's imperial government itself recruited and contracted Japanese workers for migrant work in Hawaii. In 1900 the empire stopped the emigration of Japanese laborers to the United States, Canada, and Mexico, and this ban was strengthened in 1908 with diplomatically negotiated Gentlemen's Agreements countering racist discrimination against Japanese expatriates. Imperial subjects were expected by Japanese political elites to obey and uphold the emperor, wherever they traveled in the world, as their standing directly affected the empire's expansion. Such nationalist posturing by Imperial Japan, and later by Fascist Italy, inspired the internment of Japanese and, on a smaller scale, Italian Americans during World War II, even though nearly all of those interned were loyal to the United States. Imperial pressure on Japanese expatriates eventually proved incompatible with their individual interests on the other side of the world, and such a forced relationship was bound to collapse.[16] Liberal Italy pursued a more flexible, diverse, and open-ended policy. Emigration and its relationship to colonialism were at the center of Italy's foreign affairs but beyond the state's direct control.

Italy's efforts parallel the strategic policies of leading emigrant states in the twenty-first century. India, Russia, China, Korea, and Mexico have devoted extensive resources toward cementing the relationship between scattered expatriates and their mother country, encouraging cultural fidelity, political loyalty, and often return migration, with tangible benefits for the mother country. Intervening in emigration extended the reach of the Italian state, at home and abroad. After 1871, the Italian census numbered Italians abroad among the subjects of the King of Italy even if they had citizenship elsewhere. Italy also sponsored a series of Expositions and Congresses of Italians Abroad, who in theory were never "lost" to their fatherland. Like Italy, other states have claimed emigrants as national representatives, staking a social claim to expanded borders. The government of Haiti has declared that its emigrants comprise Haiti's "tenth province," in addition to the nine provinces on the island. One in every six Haitians lives abroad, and the government has tried to make this population an integral part of Haitian society and a crucial segment of Haiti's economy. Vicente Fox, President of Mexico, controversially declared his country "a nation of 123 million citizens," with 23 million living outside Mexico, and many of those holding United States citizenship.[17] The Office of Mexicans Abroad, under the auspices of the foreign ministry since 2002, coordinates support for Mexican citizens and voters abroad, who influence legislatures in both Mexico City and Washington, D.C. Emigration concerns both foreign and domestic politics, as the Italian Parliament recognized in 1901 by switching emigration oversight from the interior ministry, which specialized in fighting crime, to the foreign ministry, concerned with expanding influence overseas. Regulating emigration revised the limits of Italian Liberalism, greatly increasing the government's intervention in social trends, much as the British government took on more roles and more staff after the landmark Passenger Acts of 1815.[18]

In addition to its census of Italians outside Italy, the Italian state hosted Congresses of Italians Abroad in 1908 and 1911 through the Italian Colonial Institute. India followed a similar path in 2002 by launching "Pravisi Bharatiya Divas," an annual Overseas Indian Festival to bring home wealthy expatriates.[19] In its Congresses and Expositions of Italians abroad, Italy made a point of including Italians still under foreign rule in the Empire of Austria-Hungary. South Korea has similarly included Koreans from Communist North Korea under the umbrella of the Overseas Koreans Foundation.[20] Uniting Koreans abroad has proved easier than cultivating ties within the Korean peninsula itself. Likewise, it seemed easier to define *italianità* outside Italy, away from rigid religious, regional, and class divisions. As Benedict Anderson has written, it is easier for settlers outside their native lands to imagine national communities. The vision of Italian unification was forged abroad by Mazzini, Crispi, Garibaldi, and other exiles; and the young Italian state adapted to a new global era with innovative policies to "make Italians" abroad in a Greater Italy.[21]

To benefit its emigrants and profit from their labors, Italy used its influence and resources to improve the flow of money, exports, and people across borders. The Italian government won American support to establish a special nonprofit channel for emigrant remittances, with low fees for emigrants and outstanding results for the Italian state. Migrants today, by contrast, send more than $100 billion annually by commercial wire services, which have overcharged their vulnerable clients by millions of dollars. In 2004, the United States, together with the G8 and International Monetary Fund, called for greater transparency and lower fees in the channels for international remittances.[22] Perhaps the international, nonprofit work of the Banco di Napoli can serve as an example of drawing emigrant remittances into legitimate banks, with the benefits of low costs, clear accounting, and managed risks. Remittances have financed economic development at all levels, exceeding foreign aid as an outside source of capital in developing countries. Italy relied upon remittances for one quarter of its balance of payments before 1914; in the year 2004, remittances supplied US $8.5 billion to the Philippines, $16.6 billion to Mexico, and $23 billion to India. Remittances to the Dominican Republic have brought in more money than exports or foreign direct investment, supporting the most rapid growth of any economy in Latin America.[23] Likewise, remittances helped to finance Italy's crucial "industrial takeoff" in the years of peace before World War I.

Italy also relied upon exports to emigrants. As envious French investigators noted, "Most of the Italians [in South America] are manual workers. But they have become important by their sheer numbers; they have prepared the way for commerce by purchasing Italian exports and introducing Italian products to the Brazilians."[24] Being Italian abroad became associated, for example, with authentic Italian cuisine. Such food was a new creation, for mass emigration coincided with technological breakthroughs in the production of dried pasta (*pasta 'sciutta*). Only the wealthy had been able to afford fresh pasta, which requires hours of intensive labor to produce, but the industrialization of food allowed working families to eat pasta every day.[25] In 1827 Giulia Buitoni launched commercial pasta production in Sansepolcro, Tuscany, and in 1877 Pietro Barilla established a pasta factory in Parma. With the export of dried pasta and the spread of Italian American macaroni factories, emigrants could eat the new national food anywhere. Italian companies pioneered a global Italian food culture, embodied in the later slogan "Where there's Barilla, there's home [*Dove c'è Barilla, c'è casa*]."[26] Italian food emerged from an ethnic niche to provide employment across a wide range of emigrant restaurants, food markets, and distributors in many nations. Imported cheeses, tomatoes, and wines, necessary for authentic Italian cuisine, were promoted by Italian chambers of commerce worldwide. Subsidized by the Italian state, these groups campaigned vigorously for lower tariffs and better treatment of Italian workers and tenants, and promoted exports "made in Italy" as a tangible manifestation of sentimental connections with the homeland. Mexican, Chinese, Thai, and Indian foods have followed the same popular path, expanding from niche economies into lucrative markets across the United States and Western Europe.[27]

Contrasting aims guided Italy's programs for emigrants. *Italianità* meant not just a cultural identity, but a political identity. Speaking Italian in churches and schools carried an international political resonance, as Italy concentrated on teaching "the language of Dante" to adult emigrants and to their children in the second generation. Even today, language education for immigrant children remains controversial in the Americas. As the Italian government well understood, with its pioneering program for Italian schools abroad, language is the strongest and most flexible bond between migrants and their mother country.[28] Italian Liberal governments put aside ideological differences to work with Catholic and Socialist schools teaching Italian literacy. The Italian state also entrusted emigrants with celebrating patriotic holidays abroad, such as the birthdays of the King and Queen, and even establishing new

civic rites, as Italians campaigned to establish the twelfth of October as
"Columbus Day." Christopher Columbus was reborn as a mythical, pro-
totypical emigrant, whose native Italian genius established the New
World, together with the later Italian explorer Amerigo Vespucci who
gave his name to North and South America. In the twenty-first century,
ethnic and religious holiday celebrations measure the strength of cultural communities. The Indian Diwali, Irish St. Patrick's Day, Mexican
Cinco de Mayo, and Korean and Chinese New Years unite religious and
secular fervor across borders.

The reception and processing of entering emigrants drew direct Italian
state intervention, much as Mexico has negotiated with the United
States for migrants' legal entry and work permits. Immigration into the
United States between 1880 and 1915 was legal but regulated and chan-
neled. Upon arrival, immigrants were treated as a domestic concern,
completely opposed to the internationalist perspective of Italy and other
sending countries. The Italian state screened departing emigrants, structured patriotic shipboard activities for the transatlantic passage, and also
hoped to shape emigrants' experiences upon arrival at Ellis Island. Italy's
prime minister Francesco Crispi requested permission to station an Italian official at the U.S. immigration station to welcome Italians and warn
them against fraudulent exploitation. Crispi was rebuffed by American
officials and accused of interfering in American affairs. Instead, Italy
sponsored a Labor Information Office in New York City, but Ellis Island
officials did not inform immigrants of this resource. Adolfo Rossi hoped
that an international treaty would solve the impasse, but unlike in the
twenty-first century, the United States resolutely refused to treat migration as an international issue.[29] Immigrants supposedly became American upon arrival, and their uprooted background could be ignored. Like
other sending states today, however, Italy mobilized its resources to rally
expatriates as "emigrants" rather than "immigrants," representing their
native countries and their nationality abroad.[30]

Italy faced today's controversial migration issues a century ago. Like
major sending states in the twenty-first century, the Italian state had
every interest in retaining expatriates' loyalty and affection in a rapidly
changing world.[31] In 1904 the Commissioner-General for Immigration,
F. P. Sargent, accused Germany, Italy, and other countries of a cultural
conspiracy to maintain political claims over their emigrants in the
United States:

It was found expedient to colonize their subjects who come to this country, for the purpose of maintaining in them a love of their mother country. This was accomplished through agents of the home government and church, sent here to keep the colonists together, to keep them from imbibing a knowledge of and affection for the institutions of the United States, which might, and probably would, result in their purchase of homes here and final expatriation from their own country. That result meant a permanent loss to those countries of the allegiance and usefulness of such of their subjects. . . . Hence all the political and social, and occasionally religious, resources of those countries are being directed to one end—to maintain colonies of their own people in this country, instructing them through various channels to maintain their allegiance to the countries of their birth, to transmit their earnings here to the fatherland for the purchase of ultimate homes there, and to avoid all intercourse with the people of this country that would tend to the permanent adoption of American ideals.[32]

In the twenty-first century the United States encourages emigrants to send remittances and repatriate.[33] Sargent here speaks from a different assimilationist age, and the commissioner-general's claims have usually been interpreted as nativist paranoia. But Italy did encourage emigrants to buy Italian, think Italian, send money to Italy, and eventually retire there, arguing that an immigrant American identity need not be exclusive. Many aspects of mass emigration were beyond state control, yet creative policies yielded a positive outcome for the Italian *madre patria*. Rhetorically, Italy would act as both mother and father to its children (emigrants) abroad, who would help the family at home in its hour of need. By subsidizing and coordinating community activities, Italy reached out to the private sphere of Italians abroad. What Italy accomplished in the Americas is a model of state involvement which scholars may compare with other national migrations, past and present. Emigrants remained connected in a global nation, as the Italian state built upon international migration to cultivate an Italian identity.

Italy's expansion through emigration worldwide made possible a new understanding of what it meant to be Italian. Social sciences here played a key role in constructing an idea of *italianità* at home and abroad, above the regional or provincial identities that had long divided the Italian peninsula. Lamberto Loria, the founder of Italian ethnography, moved from studying exotic cultures under colonial subjugation to studying the diversity of Italian traditions, and how they could be maintained by emigrants in foreign environments outside the fatherland's political control. He conceptualized Italian ethnicity in positive terms, rather than in opposition to other peoples, and imagined emigrants as carrying a pure, though deliberately invented, national Italian ethos.

This shared idea of *italianità* beyond borders was possible because emigrants could remain in touch with their fatherland through a virtual community of letters, periodicals, and information. Revolutions in travel and communications and the mass movement of population across borders allowed a structural transformation, to adapt the term of Jürgen Habermas, of the international public sphere.[34] The free exchange of ideas in Italian newspapers abroad, for example, was outside Italy's control, yet it turned to Italy's clear benefit. Periodicals in Italy, including *L'Italia coloniale, Patria e colonie,* and *Italica Gens,* and abroad, such as *La Patria degli Italiani* in Buenos Aires and *Il Progresso Italo-Americano* in New York City, overcame conflicting regional loyalties by asserting national unity on an international stage. In the twenty-first century, with e-mail replacing telegraphs and websites replacing newspapers, the accessibility of communications makes it even easier for national communities to exist internationally.[35] One example is a website for Overseas Filipino Workers (OFW) worldwide, who write in support of their motherland from California, Scotland, Saudi Arabia, Singapore, Sudan, Tanzania, Kazakhstan, Canada, South Korea, Florida, Australia, and Italy. Their calls for greater democracy and integrity at home may be opposed by politicians there, but such transnational participants are beyond political regulation and control, and their economic influence on tourism and remittances makes them a valuable and powerful force.[36] Worldwide emigration has functioned for sending states as an idealized outlet and frontier, filled with energy and possibilities, changing the metropolitan core and redefining the nation much as the United States interacted with its expanding frontier in the West, in Frederick Jackson Turner's famous thesis.[37] Emigrants were carefully stamped as "Italian" and received as such abroad, supported by cultural, economic, diplomatic, and public health organizations in the ritual of departure, sojourn, and return home. From all its myriad impacts, abroad and at home, emigration became a defining feature of Liberal Italy.

Why did emigration become identified with Italian Liberalism? The freedom to emigrate, denied to the subjects of European states since medieval times, was one of the most fundamental liberties guaranteed under Liberal governments in the nineteenth century.[38] But in Italy, freedom of movement became much more than a theoretical principle. United Italy produced a record 26 million emigrants between 1876 and 1976, and more than half of that number emigrated before 1915. Emigration dropped radically in 1914–1918, during World War I, but no one could have predicted this in 1911. Contemporary observers imagined that emigration statistics would continue their geometric rise, or at least maintain high levels, with the continued support of Liberal policies for industrialization, urbanization, and emigration. The entire face of Italian society was changing rapidly, all the more because approximately half of the emigrants later returned home. Rural society saw the decline of patriarchal families, the end of usury, the improvement of peasant homes, and the infusion of new skills and experiences that challenged the traditional middle and upper classes. Effects ran nationwide, even as the regions of North Italy outpaced the South's development.[39]

Not all agreed with these outcomes. Formed between 1880 and 1915, amid rising Social Darwinism and at the height of Europe's Scramble for Africa, Italy's far-sighted and innovative migration policies proved extremely controversial at home and abroad. Some Italian politicians claimed that emigration could never lead to true greatness on the world stage, and that emigrant colonies would not maintain their ties to Italy. Francesco Crispi's program to settle would-be emigrants in Italian Eritrea and his attempted conquest of Ethiopia inspired popular enthusiasm, especially in the South. Although Crispi led Italy to disaster in 1896, fifteen years later Enrico Corradini resuscitated Crispi's reputation by insisting that emigration was subservient and disgraceful—that Italy's redemption would come through conquering its own empire in Africa. Corradini rebelled against the Liberal conception of spontaneous expatriate settlements, or "free colonies," as a peaceful, noble, and inexpensive form of colonial expansion: "Free colonies [*colonie libere*] for a migrating people are neither free nor colonies; they are a *form of subjection*. . . . We confuse colonies with emigration, and give emigration a rhetorical, numerical, and individual conception. . . . This is convenient and pleasant for us, but it is not serious. It is traditional, deeply rooted in the public opinion of our ruling classes, but it is not serious. . . . We must understand that emigration and colonies are two different things."[40] Corradini condemned emigrant colonialism because it diluted concepts of state, nation, and sovereignty:

a strong central government was unnecessary if sentimental *italianità* anywhere in the world sufficed as participation in the nation. He urged an immediate return to the imperial conquest of Africa and an end to Liberal government.[41]

Corradini's diagnosis of emigration as the servility of a "proletarian nation" cast a long shadow, as frustration with Liberalism's compromises, failures, and disappointments helped pave the way for Italian national socialism and Fascist rule. Luigi Villari and Amy Bernardy, two leading critics of Italy's Liberal emigration policies, became outstanding apologists for Italian Fascism, hailing Italy's "rebirth" and "awakening" under Mussolini.[42] Giovanni Preziosi represented a different threat to Italian society. Heavily involved in migration politics and as editor of *La Vita Italiana all'estero* (Italian Life Abroad), Preziosi became obsessed with challenges to Italians from other nations. Unlike Corradini, he blamed the Jews for Italy's poverty and led the campaign for anti-Semitic and racist laws in Fascist Italy. Preziosi translated into Italian the notorious libel "The Protocols of the Elders of Zion" to create fear of a Jewish conspiracy encircling the Italian people, and later became Inspector General for Race under the Nazi-occupied Italian Social Republic.[43] Emigration polemics were a political explosive, with vast, radical implications. Liberal Italy's mass migration presented an unguarded flank that attracted attacks, especially as postwar emigration became a crutch for desperate economic policies. A month before Mussolini came to power, the Liberal treasury minister Giuseppe Paratore offered a pathetic analysis: "The reality is that Italy is unable with its current resources to support 40 million inhabitants. . . . The truly practical solution of unemployment, in current conditions, is to be found in emigration. . . . The directives of Italian emigration from the Emigration Commissariat do not respond to the current and urgent needs of the Nation. . . . [the commissariat] still wants to be selective in which countries can receive our emigrant masses."[44] Paratore urged emigration even into exploitation, just to reduce population in Italy. That so many Italians left their homeland under Liberalism helped fuel demands for a replacement regime.

Some Conservatives attacked Liberalism and its migration policies as a major cause of social decline. Luigi Villari at the consulate in Philadelphia argued that the Italian government should "cut every encouragement toward emigration, whether direct or indirect (postponements of military service, tax exemptions etc.), and tax the shipping companies . . . spending the money to improve conditions in the provinces, opening schools etc. But we must announce that whoever emigrates, especially to the U.S., goes at his own risk and peril." Cutting off emigration, Villari argued, would stop the infiltration of urban influences in Italy and preserve the country's health, morals, and security.[45] Others argued for settling peasants away from cities, in agricultural colonies in Africa, under Italian rule and under the Italian flag. The Fascist state under Mussolini would eventually implement these ideas in the 1930s, with the settlement of Italians in Libya and the bloody conquest of Ethiopia.[46] Mussolini exploited emigration for new political purposes. To categorize Italians abroad, Fascists used the newer and more dynamic word *emigranti* ("emigrating") rather than the standard *emigrati* (literally, "emigrated"), and concentrated on *fascistizzazione* (Fascisticization), a singularly ugly word in the Italian language. The Fascists abroad were responsible for persecuting Italian Communists and political exiles, building support for Italy's dictatorship, and campaigning for autarky, imperialism, and racial laws. Such programs, however, were spectacularly unsuccessful, blocked by international diplomacy and eventually rejected by emigrants themselves.[47] Italians abroad refused to be associated with the totalitarian regime, especially after Fascist Italy entered World War II on the side of Nazi Germany. Three hundred thousand emigrants returned to fight for Liberal Italy in World War I; few returned for Mussolini's lost cause. Expatriates chose for themselves. Liberal Italy had practiced a more constructive policy, linking Italians abroad in a global community. Emigrant colonialism could only be a voluntary program, and collapsed when authoritarian leaders attempted to exploit expatriate resources for aggressive war.

The end of war and the fall of Italian Fascism would revive mass migration and the Liberal doctrines of peaceful colonialism by economic expansion. With the end of the monarchy and the creation of the Italian Republic after World War II, the first President of Italy to occupy the formerly royal Quirinal Palace was the prophet of emigrant colonialism, Luigi Einaudi.[48] Italy's first postwar foreign minister, Alcide De Gasperi, tried to resurrect Liberal colonial policies from before the world wars. In August 1945, as part of the postwar negotiations, he wrote to the U.S. Secretary of State in an attempt to regain possession of Libya: "Before Mussolini's invasion of Ethiopia, democratic Italy never considered colonies as a tool for imperialism, but rather as a means for absorbing

Italy's surplus manpower. Present democratic Italy considers them in this same light. . . . [A proposed] trusteeship . . . hardly corresponds to the peculiar necessities of the Italian colonies, owing to the difference between the Italian colonial conception and praxis founded on emigration, and the Anglosaxon system mainly based on raw materials and markets [sic]."[49] De Gasperi tried to convince the Americans that Italian colonialists, in contrast to the wealthy British, were trying to do something more necessary, more genuine, and more deserving. His arguments echoed Einaudi's own colonial manifesto of 1900: "On the banks of the Plata River, a new Italy is rising, a people is forming which, though Argentine, will preserve the fundamental characters of the Italian people and will prove to the world that the imperialist ideal will not remain only an Anglo-Saxon ideal. We are showing the world that Italy can create a more perfect and evolved type of colonization."[50] Instead of exploiting colonies for economic purposes, Italy supposedly pursued a nobler purpose by developing and populating colonial territories, whether in Africa or the Americas. But these two faces of Greater Italy were more different than De Gasperi implied.

Certainly the colonial conquest of foreign lands for settlement, by Britain, France, Germany, Portugal, or Italy, was a long-term disaster for both victor and vanquished. Imperial wars planted deep seeds of destruction that are still bearing fruit. The Americas, Asia, and Africa were never vacant lands awaiting European residents. The imperialist conceit of non-European lands as void and empty spawned ideologies of lasting hatred and devastation. But the Italian model of emigrant colonialism is still relevant in a post-imperial age. Exerting influence through the "informal empire" of Italians settled peaceably abroad was more humble than the British use of naval power, military force, and racial domination, but also proved more enduring and more beneficial to all involved. Italy as an "emigrant nation" used creative and innovative means to enter the global economy before the Great War. The Italian "ethnographic empire" was based on free travel, open culture, and memory, as the state worked to build social communities abroad and link them culturally and economically to the fatherland. Rather than using force, the Italian state provided emigrants with every incentive for loyalty. Free settlements beyond imperial territories laid the basis for a transnational, global network of economic, cultural, and population exchange, with Italy at its center. This flexible use of diplomacy can serve as a model for transnational influence in international affairs.

Emigration and commerce stand out as the hallmarks of globalization, whether in the nineteenth century or the twenty-first. Italy's active responses to the pressures of change spanned the spectrum from aggression to peace. Imperial wars in the name of emigration led to spectacular disasters; yet Liberal programs in support of expatriates built upon already high rates of emigrant return, strengthening ties to the mother country. The state could perform tasks which individuals could not, building international networks of communications, transport, finance, and social exchange, to shorten the distance between families across oceans. Wherever they traveled, and whatever their situation, emigrants could participate in a transnational Italian identity; and Italians on the peninsula could see emigrants' success as their own. Assisting international remittances, protecting conditions of travel, and encouraging return without prejudice were signal successes in building Italy abroad. Beyond territory, beyond borders, the nation could also provide intangible support for emigrants abroad: a sense of belonging in a harsh transnational world.

Appendix:
Maps and Figures

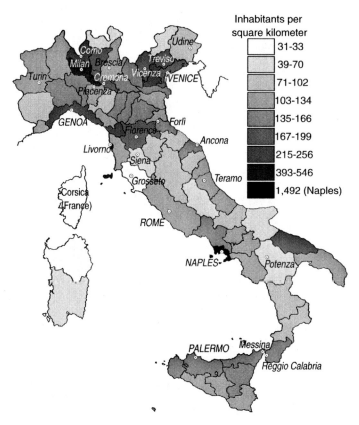

Map 1. Italy's population density by province, from the 1911 National Census

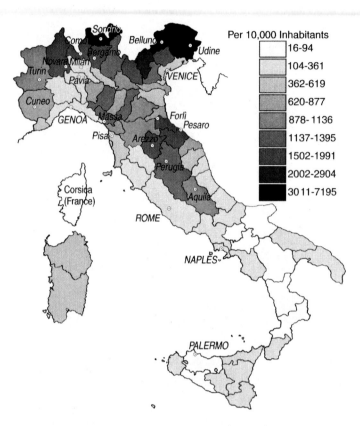

Map 2. Emigration rates by province to Europe and the Mediterranean, 1906–1911

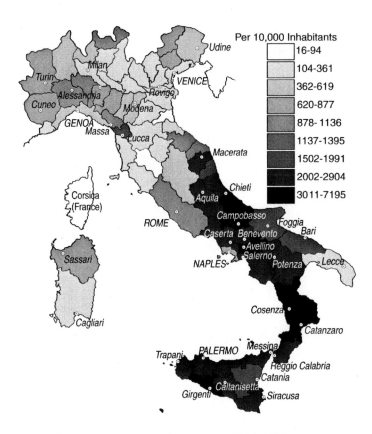

Map 3. Transatlantic emigration rates by province, 1906–1911

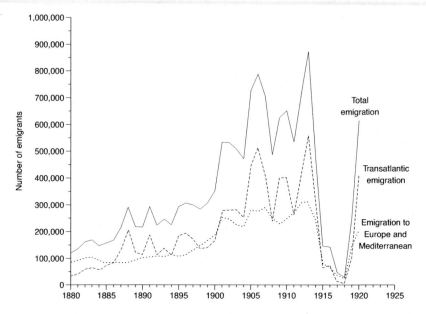

Figure 1.1. Total emigration based on number of passports, 1880–1920

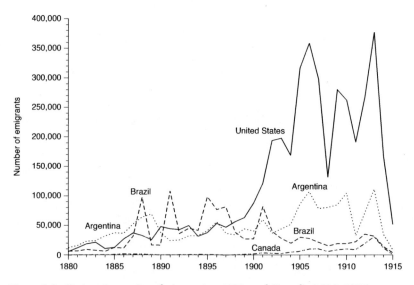

Figure 1.2. Emigration to Brazil, Argentina, USA, and Canada, 1880–1915

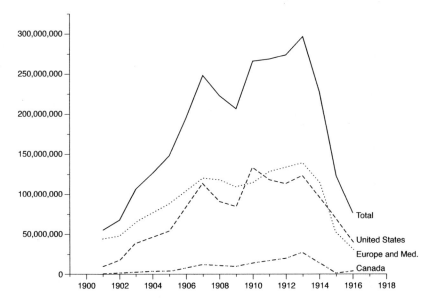

Figure 3.1. International money orders sent to Italy

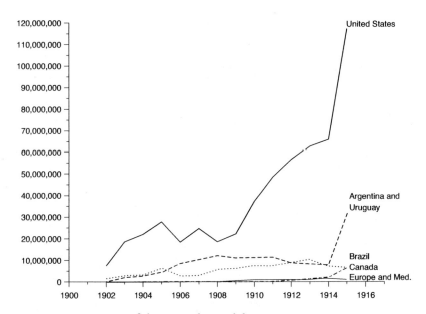

Figure 3.2. Remittances of the Banco di Napoli by country

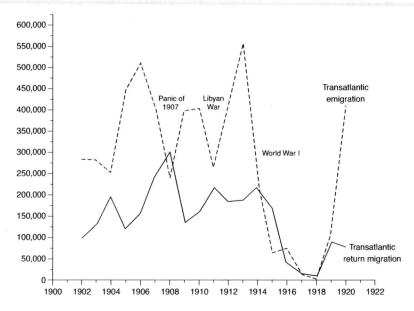

Figure 3.3. Transatlantic emigration and return migration according to passports

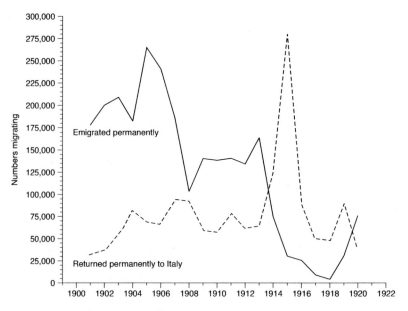

Figure 3.4. Permanent emigration and return migration according to Italian
municipal records

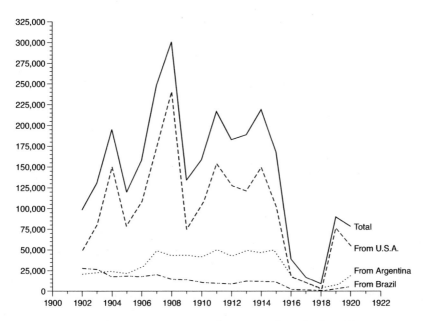

Figure 3.5. Transatlantic return migration by country from shipboard lists

Notes

Abbreviations for Archives and Sources

ACRI	Archivio della Croce Rossa Italiana, Sede via Ramazzini, Rome
ACS	Archivio Centrale dello Stato, Rome
AN	Archives Nationales, Paris
AP CD	Atti Parlamentari, Camera dei Deputati
AS Rovigo	Archivio di Stato, Rovigo
AS Venezia	Archivio di Stato, Venezia
ASBN	Archivio Storico del Banco di Napoli, Naples
ASCD	Archivio Storico della Camera dei Deputati, Rome
ASDA	Archivio Storico della Società Dante Alighieri, Sede Centrale, Rome
ASDMAE	Archivio Storico Diplomatico, Ministero degli Affari Esteri, Rome
ASMAI	Archivio Storico, Ministero dell'Africa Italiana. Held at ASDMAE, Rome
ASV	Archivio Segreto Vaticano, Vatican City
AUSSME	Archivio dell'Ufficio Storico dello Stato Maggiore dell'Esercito, Rome
BAM	Veneranda Biblioteca Ambrosiana, Milan
BArch	Bundesarchiv, Berlin-Lichterfelde
BAV	Biblioteca Apostolica Vaticana, Vatican City
CAOM	Centre des archives d'outre-mer, Aix-en-Provence
CMS	Center for Migration Studies, Staten Island, New York City
MAE	Ministère des Affaires Etrangères, Paris
MCRR	Museo Centrale del Risorgimento, Rome
NACP	National Archives at College Park, Maryland
PRO	Public Record Office, London
SAD	Sudan Archive, Durham

Note: I have used the reference and notation formats of each archive, despite contradictions. In Berlin the abbreviations *V* and *R* refer to the *front* (Vorseite) and *back* (Rückseite) of the folio page, while in the Vatican archive *v* and *r* refer to the page's *back* (verso) and *front* (recto).

Introduction

1. Italy's emigration of 26 million (1876–1976) stands as a record for international migration, exceeding Britain's and China's, but China has seen larger internal migrations. Approximately 6 million emigrated from Ireland (1815–1921). Rudolph J. Vecoli, "The Italian Diaspora, 1876–1976," in *The Cambridge Survey of World Migration,* ed. Robin Cohen (Cambridge, 1995), 114–122; Lynn Pan, *Sons of the Yellow Emperor* (Boston, 1990), 375; Cormac Ó Gráda, *Ireland: A New Economic History* (Oxford, 1994), 74, 224–225.

2. Leone Carpi, *Delle colonie e delle emigrazioni d'italiani all'estero sotto l'aspetto dell'industria, commercio, agricoltura e con trattazione d'importanti questioni sociali* (Milan, 1874).

3. By "global nation" I mean the transnational network of a "Greater Italy," centered in the Italian peninsula, and based upon transnational cultural, economic, and political ties across international borders. The phrase "global nation" has been loosely ascribed to globalization and world government: Strobe Talbott, "America Abroad: The Birth of the Global Nation," *Time,* 20 July 1992; John Richard Wiseman, *Global Nation?: Australia and the Politics of Globalisation* (Cambridge and New York, 1998). Donna Gabaccia used "diaspora nationalism" to describe patriotism and nationalism among emigrants outside Italy, in *Italy's Many Diasporas* (Seattle, 2000); Ernest Gellner, *Nations and Nationalism* (Ithaca, New York, 1983), 101–109, focuses on economic niches occupied by diaspora communities.

4. Geremia Bonomelli, "L'Emigrazione," in Esposizione Generale Italiana— Espozione delle Missioni, *Gli italiani all'estero (emigrazione, commerci, missioni)* (Turin: 1899), 17.

5. Nancy L. Green, "'Filling the Void': Immigration to France before World War I," in *Labor Migration in the Atlantic Economies,* ed. Dirk Hoerder (Westport, Connecticut, 1985), 143–161; Renè Del Fabbro, *Transalpini* (Osnabrück, 1996).

6. Calculated from ISTAT, *Sommario di statistiche storiche italiane 1861–1955* (Rome, 1958), 65; *Sommario di statistiche storiche italiane 1861–1975* (Rome, 1976), 11, 16; Commissariato Generale dell'Emigrazione, *Annuario statistico della Emigrazione Italiana dal 1876 al 1925* (Rome, 1926), 8, 44, 1533–1542.

7. Mario Isnenghi, *Il mito della grande guerra da Marinetti a Malaparte* (Bari, 1970); Daniel J. Grange, *L'Italie et la Méditerranée*, 2 vols. (Rome, 1994).

8. Brian Weinstein, "Language Planning as an Aid and a Barrier to Irredentism," in *Irredentism and International Politics*, ed. Naomi Chazan (Boulder, Colorado, 1991).

9. Silvio Lanaro, *Patria* (Venice, 1996).

10. Jan Pakulski, "Cultural Citizenship," *Citizenship Studies* 1/1 (1997): 73–86.

11. J. R. Seeley's classic study of "Greater Britain" was translated as "L'espansione dell'Inghilterra," in *Biblioteca di scienze politiche e amministrative*, ed. Attilio Brunialti (Turin, 1897).

12. Giuseppe Mazzini, *The Duties of Man* (1907. London, 1966), 9, 53. Mazzini claimed emigration manifested the problems of national disunity.

13. *Nabucodonosor*, in Piero Mioli, ed., *Giuseppe Verdi. Tutti i libretti d'opera*, 2 vols. (Rome, 1996), 1:81–82.

14. Robin Cohen, *Global Diasporas: An Introduction* (Seattle, 1997), 182, 90.

15. Enrico Corradini, "L'emigrazione italiana nell'America del Sud (1909)," in *Discorsi politici* (Florence, 1923), 73.

16. *Discorsi parlamentari di Francesco Crispi*, 3 vols. (Rome, 1915), 6 March 1890, 3:469.

17. Betty Boyd Caroli, *Italian Repatriation from the United States 1890–1914* (New York, 1973); Vecoli, "The Italian Diaspora, 1876–1976," 114–122.

18. Gianni Toniolo, *An Economic History of Liberal Italy, 1850–1918* (London, 1990), 20, 101–102; Luciano Cafagna, "Italy 1830–1914," in *The Emergence of Industrial Societies*, ed. Carlo M. Cipolla (London, 1973), 303.

19. Jonathan Friedman and Shalini Randeria, eds., *Worlds on the Move* (London, 2004); David T. Graham and Nana Poku, *Migration, Globalisation, and Human Security* (London, 2000); Myron Weiner, *International Migration and Security* (Boulder, Colorado, 1993).

20. [Commissariato Generale dell'Emigrazione], *Mobilitazione e smobilitazione degli emigranti italiani in occasione della guerra 1915–1922* (Rome, 1923).

21. Commissioner-General of Immigration, *Annual Report* (Washington, 1904), 43, 45.

22. Autobiography of Vincenzo Di Francesca, 12 March 1966. Latter-day Saint Church Historical Department, Salt Lake City, Utah, MS 9290, pp. 1–12. For the ship manifest, see www.ellisisland.org.

23. Frank Thistlethwaite, "Migration from Europe Overseas in the Nineteenth and Twentieth Centuries," in *A Century of European Migrations, 1830–1930*, ed. Rudolph J. Vecoli and Suzanne M. Sinke (Urbana, 1991), 17–57; Nina Glick Schiller, Linda Basch, and Cristina Blanc-Szanton, "From Immigrant to Transmigrant: Theorizing Transnational Migration," *Anthropological Quarterly* (1995): 48–63.

24. Adolfo Rossi, *Un italiano in America* (Milan, 1899), 4.
25. Adolfo Rossi, "Condizioni dei coloni italiani nello Stato di S. Paolo del Brasile," *Bollettino dell'emigrazione* 7 (1902): 3–88.
26. Archivio di Stato di Rovigo (AS Rovigo), Carte Rossi, n. 2, 3, and 8.
27. Richard Hakluyt, *Discourse of Western Planting* (1584. London, 1993); Klaus Bade, *Friedrich Fabri und der Imperialismus* (Freiburg, 1975); Kenji Kimura et al., *Japanese Settler Colonialism* (Cambridge, Massachusetts, 2002); Louise Young, *Japan's Total Empire* (Berkeley, 1998); Gustavo Coen, *La questione coloniale* (Livorno, 1901); Paul Leroy-Beaulieu, *De la colonisation chez les peuples modernes* (Paris, 1874); John A. Hobson, *Imperialism. A Study* (London, 1902); V. I. Lenin, *Imperialism: The Highest Stage of Capitalism* (New York, 1939).
28. Direction de l'Agriculture du Commerce et de la Colonisation, Alger, 14 November 1902. CAOM, Algerie, Department d'Alger, 5/M/6. Compare Frantz Fanon, *The Wretched of the Earth* (New York, 1963).
29. G. Perriquet, "Le rachat des terres par les Indigènes," 1903? CAOM, Algérie, Gouverment Général de l'Algérie 32/L/12.
30. Eckart Kehr, *Der Primat der Innenpolitik,* ed. Hans-Ulrich Wehler (Berlin, 1965); Wehler, *Bismarck und der Imperialismus* (Köln, 1969); Wehler, "Industrial Growth and Early German Imperialism," in *Studies on the Theory of Imperialism,* ed. Roger Owen and Bob Sutcliffe (London, 1972).
31. Pierre Milza, "Le racisme anti-italien en France. La 'tuerie' d'Aigues-Mortes (1893)," *L'Histoire* 10 (1979): 24–32; N. Lo Presti, "I fatti di Aigues Mortes e le loro ripercussioni in Italia," *Rassegna storica del Risorgimento* (1974): 282–285; Richard Gambino, *Vendetta* (New York, 1977), Marco Rimanelli and Sheryl L. Postman, eds., *The 1891 New Orleans Lynching and U.S.-Italian Relations* (New York, 1992); Donna Gabaccia, "The 'Yellow Peril' and the 'Chinese of Europe': Global Perspectives on Race and Labor, 1815–1930," in *Migration, Migration History, History,* ed. Jan Lucassen and Leo Lucassen, (Bern, 1999), 177–196.
32. Alberto Aquarone, "Politica estera e organizzazione del consenso nell'età giolittiana," *Storia contemporanea* 8/1–3 (1977): 60–61, reprinted in *Dopo Adua,* ed. Ludovica de Courten (Rome, 1989), 261; *Journal of American Ethnic History* 25, 4 (2006): 74–152.
33. Among others, Rudolph J. Vecoli, "Contadini in Chicago: A Critique of *The Uprooted," Journal of American History* 51 (1964); Anna Maria Martellone, *Una Little Italy nella Atene d'America* (Naples, 1973); John W. Briggs, *An Italian Passage* (New Haven, 1978); Dino Cinel, *From Italy to San Francisco* (Stanford, 1982); Donna Gabaccia, *From Sicily to Elizabeth Street* (Albany, 1984); Judith A. Smith, *Family Connections* (Albany, 1985); Gary R. Mormino and George E. Pozzetta, *The Immigrant World of Ybor City* (Ur-

bana, 1987); Mary Elizabeth Brown, *Churches, Communities, and Children* (New York, 1995); Samuel Baily, *Immigrants in the Lands of Promise* (Ithaca, 1999).

34. Francesco Balletta, *Il Banco di Napoli e le rimesse degli emigrati, 1914–1925* (Naples, 1972), Luigi De Rosa, *Emigranti, capitali e banche (1896–1906)* (Naples, 1980); Luciano Cafagna, *Dualismo e sviluppo nella storia d'Italia* (Venice, 1989); Mary Elizabeth Brown, *The Scalabrinians in North America (1887–1934)* (New York, 1996); Peter R. D'Agostino, "The Scalabrini Fathers, the Italian Emigrant Church and Ethnic Nationalism in America," *Religion and American Culture* 7/1 (1997); Mario Francesconi, ed., *Storia della Congregazione scalabriniana*, 5 vols. (Rome, 1973–1975); Gianfausto Rosoli, *Geremia Bonomelli e il suo tempo* (Brescia, 1999); Ronald Robinson, John Gallagher, and Alice Denny, *Africa and the Victorians,* 2d ed. (London, 1981).

35. Robert F. Foerster, *The Italian Emigration of Our Times* (1919. New York, 1968), and "The Italian Factor in the Race Stock of Argentina," *Quarterly Publication of the American Statistical Association* (1919): 347–360.

36. Gabaccia, *Italy's Many Diasporas,* 136–141.

37. Valuable, specific articles have bridged the gap between emigration and colonialism by focusing on Italian political rhetoric, particularly Gigliola Dinucci, "Il modello della colonia libera nell'ideologia espansionistica italiana. Dagli anni '80 alla fine del secolo," *Storia contemporanea* 10/3 (1979): 427–479; Fabio Grassi, "Il primo governo Crispi e l'emigrazione come fattore di una politica di potenza," in *Gli italiani fuori d'Italia,* ed. Bruno Bezza (Milan, 1983), 45–100; Daniel J. Grange, "Émigration et colonies: un grand débat de l'Italie libérale," *Revue d'histoire moderne et contemporaine* 30 (1983): 337–365; Emilio Gentile, "L'emigrazione italiana in Argentina nella politica di espansione del nazionalismo e del fascismo," *Storia contemporanea* 17/3 (1986): 355–396.

38. Emilio Franzina, "Emigrazione, navalismo e politica coloniale in Alessandro Rossi (1868–1898)," in *Schio e Alessandro Rossi,* ed. Giovanni L. Fontana (Rome, 1985), 569–621; Franzina, *Gli italiani e il nuovo mondo 1492–1942* (Milan, 1995); Romain Rainero, *I primi tentativi di colonizzazione agricola e di popolamento dell'Eritrea (1890–1895)* (Milan, 1960).

39. Federico Cresti, *Oasi di italianità* (Turin, 1996), Michelangelo Finocchiaro, *La colonizzazione e la trasformazione fondiaria in Libia* (Rome, 1968), Annunziata Nobile, "La colonizzazione demografica della Libia: progetti e realizzazioni," *Bollettino di demografia storica* 12 (1990); Angelo Del Boca, *Gli italiani in Africa Orientale,* 4 vols. (Bari, 1975–1984), Angelo Del Boca, *Gli italiani in Libia,* 2 vols. (Bari, 1986–1988); Claudio G. Segrè, *Fourth Shore* (Chicago, 1976); Denis Mack Smith, *Mussolini's Roman Empire* (Oxford, 1975).

40. Giuseppe Are, *La scoperta dell'imperialismo* (Rome, 1985).

41. A. James Gregor, *Young Mussolini and the Intellectual Origins of Fascism* (Berkeley, 1979), Gaudens Megaro, *Mussolini in the Making* (Boston and New York, 1938); Renzo De Felice, *Mussolini il rivoluzionario, 1883–1920* (Turin, 1965); Alexander Gerschenkron, *Economic Backwardness in Historical Perspective* (Cambridge, 1962); Cafagna, "Italy 1830–1914"; Vera Zamagni, *The Economic History of Italy, 1860–1990* (Oxford, 1993).

42. Simonetta Soldani and Gabriele Turi, eds., *Fare gli italiani* (Bologna, 1993); Eric Hobsbawm and Terence Ranger, eds., *The Invention of Tradition* (Cambridge, 1983).

43. Società Nazionale Dante Alighieri, Comitato di Napoli. La Commissione per l'emigrazione e le biblioteche di bordo per gli emigranti. "Relazione presentata al XX Congresso Nazionale." (Torre del Greco, 1909). ASDA, Fasc/1909 A9, pp. 9, 13–16.

1. From Africa to the Americas

1. Armando Ravaglioli, *Vedere e capire Roma* (Rome, 1980); Cesare D'Onofrio, *Gli obelischi di Roma* (Rome, 1992).

2. "Elenco numerico delle perdite subite in Eritrea," AUSSME L-7 racc. 95 f. 3.

3. Alberto Tulli, *Il "Leone di Giuda" e l'obelisco di Dogali* (Rome, 1942); Rodolfo Bonfiglietti, "Obelischi podisti e una base," *Roma* 2 (1924): 339–349; Taddesse Beyene, Tadesse Tamrat, and Richard Pankhurst, eds., *The Century of Dogali* (Addis Abeba-Asmara, 1988).

4. *Scritti editi ed inediti di Giuseppe Mazzini,* ed. Mario Menghini (Imola, 1906–1943), 86:6–7, 89:56, 92:166–70; Denis Mack Smith, *Mazzini* (New Haven, 1994), 218–221; Mazzini, *The duties of man and other essays* (1907. London, 1966); Vincenzo Gioberti, *Del primato morale e civile degli Italiani* (Turin, 1920–1932); Federico Chabod, *Italian Foreign Policy* (Princeton, 1996).

5. "Relazione sulla Colonia Eritrea negli anni dal 1902 al 1907," ACS Carte Martini b. 21; speech of Ernesto Artom, 30 May 1915, ASMAI pos. 163/2 f. 19.

6. R. J. B. Bosworth, *Italy and the Wider World 1860–1960* (London, 1996), 134.

7. Adolfo Rossi, *Un italiano in America* (Milan, 1899), 4.

8. Giuseppe Bevione, *L'Argentina* (Turin, 1911), 177.

9. John Macdonald, "Chain migration, ethnic neighborhood formation and social networks," *Milbank Memorial Fund Quarterly* 42 (1964): 82–91, and "Chain Migration Reconsidered," *Bollettino di demografia storica* 16 (1992): 35–43.

10. Betty Boyd Caroli, *Italian Repatriation from the United States 1890–1914*

(New York, 1973), 84–89; Samuel L. Baily, *Immigrants in the lands of promise* (Ithaca, 1999); Donna R. Gabaccia, *Militants and Migrants: Rural Sicilians become American Workers* (New Brunswick, 1988); Robert F. Harney, "Toronto's Little Italy, 1885–1945," in *Little Italies in North America,* ed. Harney and J. Vincenza Scarpaci (Toronto, 1981), 44.

11. Direzione Generale della Statistica, *Statistica della emigrazione italiana nel 1882* (Rome, 1883), 1–68.

12. Francesco Saverio Nitti, "I dazi di consumo in Sicilia," in *Scritti sulla questione meridionale,* vol. 1 (Bari, 1958); Giustino Fortunato, "Malaria e chinino, 30 June 1910," in *Il Mezzogiorno e lo Stato italiano,* ed. Manlio Rossi Doria (Florence, 1973).

13. Edmondo De Amicis, *Sull'Oceano* (Como, 1991), 76.

14. ASCD, Incarti di Segretaria, B. 464 (Parl. 16, 2d session, Progetto di Legge n. 85); Giovanni Florenzano, *Della emigrazione italiana in America comparata alle altre emigrazioni europee* (Naples, 1874); Giuseppe Carerj, *Il problema della emigrazione in Italia e la Società italiana per la emigrazione e colonizzazione* (Naples, 1890).

15. Direzione Generale della Statistica, *Statistica della Emigrazione Italiana Avvenuta nel 1897* (Rome, 1899), v; *Statistica della Emigrazione Italiana per l'Estero negli anni 1902 e 1903* (Rome, 1904), v–vii; *Annuario Statistico italiano, 1905–1907* (Rome, 1908), 151–152; Silvana Patriarca, *Numbers and Nationhood: Writing Statistics in Nineteenth-Century Italy* (Cambridge, 1996).

16. Vilfredo Pareto, "Il costo di produzione dell'uomo e del valore economico degli emigranti," *Giornale degli economisti* 31, series 2 (1905): 322–327; Giuseppe Prato, "Per l'emigrazione italiana nell'America Latina," *La Riforma Sociale* 10, year 7 (1900): 104–117.

17. Patrizia Audenino, "The 'Alpine Paradox': Exporting Builders to the World," in *The Italian Diaspora,* ed. George E. Pozzetta and Bruno Ramirez (Toronto, 1992); Franco Ramella, "Emigration from an Area of Intense Industrial Development: The Case of Northwestern Italy," in *A Century of European Migrations, 1830–1930,* ed. Rudolph J. Vecoli and Suzanne M. Sinke (Urbana, 1991), 261–274; David I. Kertzer, *Family Life in Central Italy, 1880–1910* (New Brunswick, 1984), 111–130.

18. Commissariato Generale dell'Emigrazione, *Annuario statistico della emigrazione italiana dal 1876 al 1925* (Rome, 1926), 92–141; Franco Vespasiano, *Contadini Emigranti Assistiti* (Naples, 1990); Pietro Borzomati, ed., *L'emigrazione calabrese dall'unità ad oggi* (Rome, 1982); Fortunata Piselli, *Parentela ed emigrazione* (Turin, 1981); Valerio Castronovo, ed., *Biellesi nel mondo* (Milan, 1986–1997); Patrizia Audenino, *Un mestiere per partire* (Milan, 1990); Paola Corti, *Paesi d'emigranti* (Milan, 1990); Mario Sabbatini and Emilio Franzina, eds., *I veneti in Brasile nel centenario*

dell'emigrazione (Vicenza, 1977); Franzina, *La grande emigrazione. L'esodo dei rurali dal Veneto* (Venice, 1977); http://dawinci.istat.it/ (accessed 4/13/07). Before World War I, the Veneto included the provinces of Udine and Belluno, with massive short-distance migration, in addition to Treviso, Vicenza, and Rovigo, with high transatlantic migration.

19. Francesco Saverio Nitti, *La nuova fase della emigrazione d'Italia* (Turin, 1896), 28–29.

20. Francesco Brancato, *L'emigrazione siciliana negli ultimi cento anni* (Cosenza, 1995); Francesco Renda, *L'emigrazione in Sicilia (1652–1961)* (Sciascia, 1989); Anna Maria Martellone, ed., *I Siciliani fuori dalla Sicilia* (Florence, 1979); John S. Macdonald, "Agricultural Organization, Migration and Labour Militancy in Rural Italy," *Economic History Review* 16/1 (1963): 61–75.

21. *Statistica della Emigrazione Italiana Avvenuta nel 1897,* v.

22. The only non-Italian port counted in Italian statistics was Le Havre, as the Compagnie Générale Transatlantique was allowed to recruit passengers from northern Italian provinces for its New York line. Commissario dell'Emigrazione, *Notizie sul movimento dell'emigrazione transceanica italiana* (Rome, 1914), 8, 13.

23. Ministero degli affari esteri, and Ministero di agricoltura industria e commercio, *Censimento degli Italiani all'estero (dicembre 1881)* (Rome, 1884), emphasis in original; [Luigi Bodio], *Sul censimento degl'italiani all'estero eseguito al 31 dicembre 1871* (Rome, 1873). Bodio estimated between 371,000 and 427,000 Italians were living abroad.

24. Direzione Generale della Statistica, *Censimento della popolazione del Regno d'Italia al 10 febbraio 1901* (Rome, 1901–1904), 5:1; Commissariato dell'Emigrazione, *Emigrazione e colonie* (Rome, 1903–1909), 2:2:331, 3:2:209. Eritrea and Somalia, as "national possessions," were excluded from this survey.

25. [Commissariato Generale dell'Emigrazione], *Notizie sulla emigrazione italiana negli anni dal 1910 al 1917 (Bozze)* (Rome, 1918).

26. Sabbatini and Franzina, eds., *I veneti in Brasile;* Luigi De Rosa, "L'emigrazione italiana in Brasile," in *Emigrazione europee e popolo brasiliano,* ed. Gianfausto Rosoli (Rome, 1987); *Annuario statistico della Emigrazione Italiana dal 1876 al 1925,* 86–91.

27. National Park Service, "Ellis Island History," www.nps.gov/stli/serv02.htm (accessed 6/16/05).

28. Commissioner-General of Immigration, *Annual Report* (Washington, 1904), 8; Alan M. Kraut, *Silent travelers* (New York, 1994), 273–276.

29. Italian Ambassador to the United States, Marquis Cusani Confalonieri, to Secretary of State William Jennings Bryan, 17 April 1914, no. 517. NACP,

Microfilm Publication M527, roll 46, Record Group 59, Records of the Department of State relating to internal affairs of Italy, 1910–1926.

30. William Henry Bishop, U.S. Consul in Palermo, to Secretary of State, n. 128, 7 May 1910, p. 1–4. NACP, Microfilm Publication M527, roll 46.

31. ASCD, Incarti di Segreteria, b. 464. Parl. 16, 2d session, Progetto di Legge n. 85 (CD). Debates 22 January–6 December 1888.

32. AP CD Leg. XVI, 2a sessione 1887, Documenti n. 85, 15 December 1887, p. 9.

33. Minister of War to Minister of Foreign Affairs, 24 January 1888 and 28 January 1888. ASMAI, pos. 34/1 f. 11.

34. Twenty Italians in Chicago tried to volunteer on 23 January, but the consul replied that many reservists had already been rejected. ASMAI, pos. 34/1 f. 11. The Italian military held a strong prejudice against volunteers.

35. AP CD Leg. XIV, prima sessione, Discussioni, tornata 7 December 1881, pp. 7587–7588, and prima tornata 27 January 1885, p. 11074. The Rubattino Steamer Company had leased Assab in 1869. Giacomo Gorrini, "I primi tentativi e le prime ricerche di una Colonia in Italia (1861–1882)," in *Biblioteca di scienze politiche e amministrative,* ed. Attilio Brunialti (Turin, 1897); Giorgio Doria, *Debiti e navi* (Genoa, 1990).

36. Enrico Serra, *La questione tunisina da Crispi a Rudinì* (Milan, 1967), 32–47.

37. Angelo Del Boca, *Gli italiani in Africa Orientale* (Bari, 1985); Raffaele Ciasca, *Storia coloniale dell'Italia contemporanea,* 2d ed. (Milan, 1940); Tullio Scovazzi, *Assab, Massaua, Uccialli, Adua* (Turin, 1996); Gennaro Mondaini, *Manuale di storia e legislazione coloniale* (Rome, 1924–1927).

38. Domenico Farini, *Diario di fine secolo,* ed. Emilia Morelli (Rome, 1961), 1:13.

39. Angelo Filipuzzi, ed., *Il dibattito sull'emigrazione* (Florence, 1976).

40. AP CD Leg. XV, prima sessione, Discussioni, prima tornata 27 January 1885, pp. 11068, 11067, 11074; Sergio Romano, "L'ideologia del colonialismo italiano," in *Fonti e problemi della politica coloniale italiana,* ed. Carla Ghezzi, vol. 1 (Rome, 1996).

41. Christopher Duggan, *Francesco Crispi* (Oxford, 2002).

42. AP CD Leg. XVI, 2a sessione 1887, Documenti n. 85, 15 December 1887, p. 9; "Il progetto di legge sull'emigrazione," *Rivista della Beneficenza Pubblica e delle Istituzioni di Previdenza* 16 (1888); Renato Mori, *La politica estera di Francesco Crispi (1887–1891)* (Rome, 1973).

43. *Discorsi parlamentari di Francesco Crispi,* 3 vols. (Rome, 1915), 3:359, 17 June 1889, emphasis added.

44. James C. McCann, *People of the Plow* (Madison, 1995).

45. *Discorsi parlamentari di Francesco Crispi,* 3:469, 6 March 1890.

46. Klaus J. Bade, *Friedrich Fabri und der Imperialismus in der Bismarckzeit*

(Freiburg, 1975); Woodruff D. Smith, *The Ideological Origins of Nazi Imperialism* (Oxford, 1986).

47. Giuseppe Prato, "L'Emigrants' Information Office' di Londra," *Riforma Sociale,* (1902); Reichskolonialamt, Kolonialrath. IV. Sitzungsperode 1895/98. No. 9, BArch, R 1001/6234, Bl. 145–151, S. 146. Unfortunately, the Emigration Office records were "destroyed on schedule."

48. Paul Leroy-Beaulieu and J. R. Seeley were translated into Italian in 1897 and published together with Attilio Brunialti, "Le colonie degli italiani," in *Biblioteca di scienze politiche e amministrative.*

49. Salvemini to Pasquale Villari, 10 February 1896, BAV, Villari 43; Valerio Castronovo, *La stampa italiana dall'Unità al Fascismo* (Bari, 1984), 83–91.

50. Pasquale Turiello, *La virilità nazionale e le colonie italiane* (Naples, 1898), 76–77; Giovan Battista Penne, *Dall'America all'Africa. La missione coloniale del popolo italiano* (Rome, 1908), 63–68; Bevione, *L'Argentina,* 164.

51. Fernando Manzotti, *La polemica sull'emigrazione,* 2d ed. (Milan-Rome-Naples-Città di Castello, 1969).

52. Emilio Franzina, "Emigrazione, navalismo e politica coloniale in Alessandro Rossi (1868–1898)," in *Schio e Alessandro Rossi,* ed. Giovanni L. Fontana (Rome, 1985), 572–590.

53. Leopoldo Franchetti, *Condizioni economiche e amministrative delle provincie napoletane* (Rome, 1985), and *Politica e mafia in Sicilia,* ed. Antonio Jannazzo (Naples, 1995); Sidney Sonnino, and Franchetti, *Inchiesta in Sicilia* (Florence, 1974).

54. Umberto Zanotti-Bianco, *Saggio storico sulla vita e attività politica di Leopoldo Franchetti* (Rome, 1950), 4–6, 71; Roberto Battaglia, *La prima guerra d'Africa* (Turin, 1958), 517–520; Alberto Aquarone, *Dopo Adua,* ed. Ludovica de Courten (Rome, 1989), 223–225.

55. Ministero per gli Affari Esteri, "Pro memoria confidenziale per Sua Eccellenza il Ministro Villari." 25 September 1891. BAV, Villari 20, 232r–233v; Franchetti to Sig. Comm. Levi, 21 July 1895, ASMAI pos. 31/2 f. 32. But French Algeria and British South Africa aimed to reduce military commitments with civilian settlements: Antony Thrall Sullivan, *Thomas-Robert Bugeaud* (Hamden, Connecticut, 1983); Anthony Kendal Millar, *Plantagenet in South Africa* (Cape Town, 1965).

56. Letter from Geremia Bonomelli, Vescovo di Cremona, 19 July 1890, AS Venezia, Carte Baratieri b. 8; letter from Oreste Baratieri, 7 May 1892, BAM, Archivio Bonomelli 10.92.94; Gianfausto Rosoli, ed., *Geremia Bonomelli e il suo tempo* (Brescia, 1999).

57. The Association had been blocked from Eritrea in 1892, as Foreign Minister Benedetto Brin attempted a compromise with resident French clerics. Ministro degli Affari Esteri to marchese L. Ridolfi, Presidente, Associazione per soccorrere i Missionari Cattolici italiani, 24 October 1892,

ASMAI pos. 33/2 f. 25; Ornella Pellegrino Confessore, "Origini e motivazioni dell'Associazione nazionale per soccorrere i missionari cattolici
italiani," *Bollettino dell'Archivio per la Storia del Movimento Sociale Cattolico in Italia* 11 (1976): 239–267.

58. I thank Andy Goldman and Kristen Needham for assisting me with the
translation of the Amharic text reproduced in Sven Rubenson, *Wichale
XVII: The Attempt to Establish a Protectorate over Ethiopia* (Addis Abeba,
1964). Carlo Giglio, *L'articolo XVII del trattato di Uccialli* (Como, 1967);
Sir Francis Clare Ford to Salisbury, 20 March 1896, PRO FO 403/239.

59. Ambassador James Rennell Rodd to the British Foreign Office, 13 May
1897, SAD 122/9. The same accusations over treacherous Amharic and
Italian versions surfaced over the Treaty of Adis Abeba of 1896. Rodd to
Salisbury, 22 June 1897, SAD 122/9.

60. Tekeste Negash, *No Medicine for the Bite of a White Snake* (Uppsala, 1986);
Abdussamad H. Ahmad and Richard Pankhurst, eds., *Adwa Victory Centenary Conference* (Addis Ababa, 1998); Yemane Mesghenna, *Italian Colonialism: A Case Study of Eritrea* (Lund, 1988).

61. Letter from Baratieri to Minister of Foreign Affairs, 5 July 1895. ASMAI
pos. 31/2 f. 34; Angelo Del Boca, "Oreste Baratieri: una parabola coloniale," in *Adwa Victory Centenary Conference,* 201–205.

62. All the dirty laundry was published as Camera dei Deputati, *Avvenimenti
d'Africa (Gennaio 1895–Marzo 1896). Documenti diplomatici presentati al
Parlamento Italiano* (Rome, 1896).

63. Asseffa Abreha, "The Battle of Adwa: Victory and Its Outcome," in *Adwa
Victory Centenary Conference,* 161. King Umberto apologized to the British
military attaché on 26 February 1896: "Had we known what was going to
happen, we should have made very different arrangements." Col. Charles
Needham, PRO FO 403/239.

64. Various figures have been gathered together in AUSSME L-7, racc. 95 f. 3.

65. Salvemini to Pasquale Villari, 10 February 1896, BAV Villari 43.

66. With the arrival of a larger force, Baratieri would be outranked as commander
by General Antonio Baldissera, yet another veteran of Garibaldi's Thousand.

67. Nicola Labanca, *In marcia verso Adua* (Turin, 1993); Angelo Del Boca, ed.,
Adua. Le ragioni di una sconfitta (Rome-Bari, 1997); British intelligence report, 14 March 1896, PRO FO 403/239.

68. AUSSME, L-7 racc. 95, f. 3; Carlo Conti Rossini, *Italia ed Etiopia dal trattato d'Uccialli alla battaglia di Adua* (Rome, 1935), 447–452; Abreha, "The
Battle of Adwa: Victory and Its Outcome," 152–158.

69. AUSSME, L-7 racc. 93, f. 9; L-7 racc. 94; letters from General Baldissera
and Major Salsa, ACS Carte Martini b. 14 f. 46.

70. Farini, *Diario,* 2:865–866. Piedmont's participation in the Crimean War
established Italy as a Great Power.

71. 265 officers had died in the wars of Unification, but 268 died at Adwa. Contrary to some historians' claims, fewer soldiers died at Adwa than in the Risorgimento. AUSSME, L-3 racc. 251 f. 7.

72. "L'Università commerciale 'Luigi Bocconi,'" *L'Italia Coloniale* 3/5 (1902): 63–69. The Bocconi University, one of Italy's finest, paralleled the foundation of Leland Stanford Jr. University in 1891.

73. Reginald Wingate to James Rennell Rodd, 12 May 1897, SAD 122/9; LTC Wingate and CPT Count Gleichen, "General Report on Abyssinia," March–June 1897, pp. 8–9, 14, SAD 122/10/1–39. The British blamed the Italians but even more the French, who had allowed the Ethiopians to import so many arms that they could attack their African neighbors with impunity.

74. Sir Francis Clare Ford to prime minister Lord Salisbury, 21 and 22 May 1896, PRO FO 403/239, citing Crispi; Comitato di soccorso delle dame romane per i prigionieri in Africa, *Diario della Missione* (Rome, 1897).

75. Franzina, "Emigrazione, navalismo e politica coloniale," 613–617; Romain Rainero, *I primi tentativi di colonizzazione agricola e di popolamento dell'Eritrea (1890–1895)* (Milan, 1960).

76. Demonstrations were also held in Varese, Florence, Sassari, Pisa, Naples, Parma, Ancona, Rome, and Arezzo. See *La Tribuna*, Rome, 4–8 March 1896; Battaglia, *La prima guerra d'Africa*, 798–800.

77. Camera dei Deputati, *Avvenimenti d'Africa.*

78. Romain Rainero, *L'anticolonialismo italiano da Assab ad Adua* (Milan, 1971). On 11 March 1897, Giustino Fortunato spoke on trading Eritrea for Tripolitania: *Il Mezzogiorno e lo Stato italiano*, 332–350; also Brunialti, "Le colonie degli italiani," 518–519.

79. See Leone Carpi, *Delle colonie e delle emigrazioni* (Milan, 1874).

80. Ercole Sori, "Il dibattito politico sull'emigrazione italiana dall'unità alla crisi dello stato liberale," in *Gli italiani fuori d'Italia*, ed. Bruno Bezza (Milan, 1983), 19–43.

81. Guglielmo Godio, *Africa e America* (Milan, 1896), 24–27, 31–32.

82. Brunialti, "Le colonie degli italiani," 358. Carlos Pellegrini, president of Argentina from 1890 to 1892, was Italian Swiss. President Juan Domingo Perón would later emphasize his Italian roots.

83. AP CD Leg. XIX, prima sessione, Discussioni, 30 June 1896, p. 6868.

84. Ibid., p. 6868–6874.

85. Francesco Saverio Nitti, *Scritti sulla questione meridionale* (Bari, 1958–1978), 1:364, 337.

86. Nitti, *La nuova fase della emigrazione d'Italia*, 4–6.

87. Farini, *Diario*, 1:13.

88. Ferdinando Martini, *Nell'Affrica Italiana* (Milan, 1891).

89. Rudinì to Martini, 30 August 1896. ACS, Carte Martini b. 20 f. 17.

90. Luciano Monzali, *L'Etiopia nella politica estera italiana 1896–1915* (Parma, 1996); Carlo Giglio, "Il trattato di pace italo-etiopico del 26 ottobre 1896," in *Studi storici in memoria di Leopoldo Marchetti* (Milan, 1969); Carlo Rossetti, *Storia diplomatica dell'Etiopia durante il regno di Menelik II* (Turin, 1910); Aquarone, *Dopo Adua*, 86, 95–98.

91. See ACS, PCM 1897 f. 50.

92. Alfredo Oriani, *L'ora d'Africa*, 2d ed. (Bologna, 1935), 135.

93. Silvana Palma, *L'Italia coloniale* (Rome, 1999), 68–69; Harold G. Marcus, *The Life and Times of Menelik II* (Oxford, 1975).

94. Rudinì to Martini, 30 January 1898, ACS, Carte Martini b. 20 f. 17.

95. Rudinì to Martini, 4 June 1898, ACS, Carte Martini b. 20 f. 17; Aquarone, *Dopo Adua*, 85.

96. Rudinì to Martini, 4 March 1898, ACS, Carte Martini b. 20 f. 17.

97. Renato Paoli, *Nella Colonia Eritrea* (Milan, 1908), 118, 288.

98. Ibid., 140–141, 292–293.

99. AP CD Leg. XXII, prima sessione, Discussioni, 13 May 1905, pp. 2784; Aquarone, *Dopo Adua*, 44–51; Martini, *Nell'Affrica Italiana*, 119–120, 153–154; Ferdinando Martini, *Cose Affricane* (Milan, 1896), 122–123.

100. "Relazione sulla Colonia Eritrea negli anni dal 1902 al 1907," ACS Carte Martini b. 21; Labanca, *In marcia verso Adua*, 150–158. By September 1900 the colonial government reached an agreement with the Società Navigazione Generale Italiana, the only steamer line that went to Eritrea, that emigrants had to make a deposit for their return fare: ASMAI, pos. 16/1 f. 8, 26 July 1901, Foreign Ministry div. 2 sez. 2, Malvano, n. 32316. In August 1900 Martini sent a circular to all Italian consulates discouraging migration to Eritrea: ASMAI pos. 16/1 f. 7

101. Paoli, *Nella Colonia Eritrea*, 96–99.

102. AP CD Leg. XXII, prima sessione, Discussioni, 13 May 1905, pp. 2784; Aquarone, *Dopo Adua*, 24, 36, 49, 218–230.

103. Alessandro Sapelli, *Memorie d'Africa (1883–1906)* (Bologna, 1935), 182; "N. P.", letter from Asmara, *L'Italia Coloniale* 3/3 (1902): 39–40; and Ferdinando Martini's speech, AP CD Leg. XXII, prima sessione, Discussioni, 15 February 1908.

104. Paoli, *Nella Colonia Eritrea*, 141–152.

105. Martini, *Nell'Affrica Italiana*, 50–51.

106. See Angelo Del Boca, ed., *I gas di Mussolini. Il fascismo e la guerra d'Etiopia* (Rome, 1996); Luigi Goglia and Fabio Grassi, eds., *Il colonialismo italiano da Adua all'impero*, 2d ed. (Rome-Bari, 1993).

107. Paoli, *Nella Colonia Eritrea*, 16–18.

108. Letter from Angelo Frau, Zaghouan, Tunisia, 27 August 1897. He sought free passage but was also willing to pay. ASMAI, pos. 16/1 f. 6.

109. ASMAI, pos. 16/1 f. 7.
110. Paoli, *Nella Colonia Eritrea,* 78.
111. Ibid., 324–325.
112. Commissariato dell'Emigrazione, *Emigrazione e colonie,* 2:4; Francesco Papafava, *Dieci anni di vita italiana (1899–1909)* (Bari, 1913), 2:693–694.
113. G. Borsa, "La crisi italo-cinese del marzo 1899 nelle carte inedite del ministro Canevaro," *Il Politico* 34/4 (1969): 618–643; Umberto Levra, *Il colpo di stato della borghesia* (Milan, 1975), 311–325; William L. Langer, *The Diplomacy of Imperialism 1890–1902,* 2d ed. (New York, 1968).
114. Guido Cora, "L'Italia in China. La Baia di San-Mun," *Nuova antologia* 164 (1899): 353.
115. V., "L'Italia in China," *Nuova antologia* 164 (1899): 749; Cesare Lombroso, "L'Italia in China. Il pericolo giallo," *Nuova antologia* 164 (1899): 338.
116. Luigi Einaudi, *Un principe mercante. Studio sulla espansione coloniale italiana* (Turin, 1900), 19.
117. Ibid., 18.
118. Ibid., 24.
119. Ibid., 14, 160–161, 16.
120. Ibid., 22–23, 12–13.
121. Ibid., 19.
122. Ibid., 146, 160.
123. Ibid., 146, 166–168.
124. Einaudi reiterated his thesis sixty years later, with a new preface: *Un principe mercante,* 2d ed. (Venice, 1995).
125. Antonio Annino, "Espansione ed emigrazione verso la America latina (*L'Italia coloniale,* 1900–1904)," *Clio* 12/1–2 (1976): 113–140.
126. Giacomo Gobbi Belcredi, "Ai lettori," *L'Italia Coloniale* 1/1 (1900): 4.
127. Gobbi Belcredi, "Che cosa è una colonia," *L'Italia Coloniale* 1/2 (1900): 50–51.
128. Paoli, *Nella Colonia Eritrea,* 19, 22. Ironically, Italian immigration to Eritrea had practically ceased, and Italian products which appealed to Eritrean tastes were now more successful: for example, Venetian cloth stamped with Menelik's portrait and an Amharic epigraph.
129. E. Pini, "Cenni storici sulla Società Italiana di Esplorazioni Geografiche e Commerciali," *Esplorazione commerciale* 16, 7 (1901): 97–136; Anna Milanini Kemény, *La Società d'Esplorazione Commerciale in Africa* (Florence, 1973), 185; Aquarone, *Dopo Adua,* 103–104; Maria Carazzi, *La Società Geografica Italiana e l'esplorazione coloniale in Africa* (Florence, 1972), 144–157, 169; Giotto Dainelli, *Gli esploratori italiani in Africa,* 2 vols. (Torino: UTET, 1960), 2:691–692; Giancarlo Monina, *Il consenso coloniale* (Roma: Carocci, 2002), 28–41; Francesco Surdich, "L'emigrazione di

massa e la Società Geografica Italiana," in *Un altro Veneto,* ed. Emilio Franzina (Abano Terme, 1983). The *Bollettino della Reale Società Geografica Italiana* featured studies of South American agriculture for emigrant colonization.

130. Relazione del Vice-Presidente [Bonaldo] Stringher al XVI Congresso della "Dante Alighieri," 21 October 1905, p. 38, ASDA Fasc/1905A8; Beatrice Pisa, *Nazione e politica nella Società "Dante Alighieri"* (Rome, 1995); Bonghi had served as Minister of Education in 1876.

131. Pasquale Villari, "Discorso, XII Congresso," *Atti della Società "Dante Alighieri"* 5, December (1901): 8.

132. Istituto Coloniale Italiano, *Atti del Secondo Congresso degli Italiani all'Estero* (Rome, 1911), 2:442–444; Patrizia Salvetti, *Immagine nazionale ed emigrazione nella Società "Dante Alighieri"* (Rome, 1995).

133. Prospectus of Istituto Coloniale Italiano, ASMAI/III p. 46 f. 13; Aquarone, *Dopo Adua,* 297–410. Antonino Di San Giuliano became President of the Italian Geographic Society and a founding vice-president of the Colonial Institute, to coordinate efforts jointly. ACS, Carte Martini b. 20 f. 18, 29 March 1906.

134. "Relazione sulla Colonia Eritrea negli anni dal 1902 al 1907," ACS Carte Martini b. 21. Contrast Daniel J. Grange, *L'Italie et la Méditerranée* (Rome, 1994), 2:1098.

135. Istituto Agricolo Coloniale, form letter dated June 1907, ASMAI pos. 163/3 f. 20; Istituto Coloniale Italiano, *Atti del primo congresso degli italiani all'estero* (Rome, 1910), and *Atti del Secondo Congresso,* 1:27–38. Originally the 1908 Congress was not labeled "the first"; compare announcements of January and June 1908, ASMAI pos. 163/2 f. 15.

136. Grange, *L'Italie et la Méditerranée,* 2:1106–1107; Michael Worboys, "The Imperial Institute," in *Imperialism and the Natural World,* ed. John M. MacKenzie (Manchester and New York, 1990); Claude Fohlen, *L'émigration française* (Paris, 1985); C. M. Andrew and A. S. Kanya-Forstner, "The French 'Colonial Party': Its Composition, Aims and Influence, 1885–1914," *The Historical Journal* 14,1 (1971): 99–128, and "The Groupe Colonial in the French Chamber of Deputies, 1892–1932," *The Historical Journal* 17 (1977): 837–866; L. Abrams and D. J. Miller, "Who Were the French Colonialists? A Reassessment of the *Parti Colonial,* 1890–1914," *The Historical Journal* 19,3 (1976): 685–725; James J. Cooke, "Eugène Etienne and the Emergence of Colon Dominance in Algeria, 1884–1905," *The Muslim World* 65,1 (1975): 39–53; Charles-Robert Ageron, *France coloniale ou parti colonial?* (Paris, 1978); John M. MacKenzie, *Propaganda and Empire* (Manchester, 1984). In contrast to the Imperial Institute, there were no women listed among the Italian Institute's 780 members in 1911.

2. The Great Ethnographic Empire

1. Ministero degli affari esteri and Ministero di agricoltura industria e commercio, *Censimento degli Italiani all'estero (dicembre 1881)* (Roma, 1884); Esposizione Generale Italiana, *Gli italiani all'estero* (Turin, 1899); Piero Barbèra, "Gli italiani all'estero all'Esposizione di Milano," *Nuova Antologia* 210/839 (1906), 440–450; Allgemeine Deutsche Schulverein zur Erhaltung des Deutschtums im Auslande, ed., *Handbuch des Deutschtums im Auslande*, 2d ed (Berlin, 1906); J. G. Bartholomew, *Oxford Economic Atlas*, 6th ed. (Oxford, 1925), map 16.

2. "The emigration law of Italy is the most paternal in its character of any legislation of its kind. . . . [it] was the first emigration law of Europe to undertake entire direction of an emigration movement, including supervision over transportation and extending protection to the Italian citizens abroad. The Italian law has since served as a foundation for the legislation of Hungary, the proposed law in Austria, and in all probability marks an era of emigration control which will influence in time the course of every European Government." James Davenport Whelpley, *The Problem of the Immigrant* (London, 1905), 238; Vincenzo Grossi, *Storia della legislazione sull'emigrazione in Italia*, ed. V. E. Orlando (Milan, 1905); Paolo Emilio De Luca, *Della emigrazione europea* (Turin, 1909–1910), 4:276.

3. Vittorio Briani, *La legislazione emigratoria italiana nelle successive fasi* (Rome, 1978); C. Furno, *L'evoluzione sociale delle leggi italiane sull'emigrazione* (Varese, 1958).

4. AP CD Leg. XXI, sessione 1900, Documenti n. 44-B, pp. 37–38.

5. See articles 21–22 and 26–27, which still affect international travel from Italy. Whelpley, *The Problem of the Immigrant*, 29–40, 238–242; Oliver MacDonagh, *A Pattern of Government Growth* (London, 1961).

6. AP CD, Leg. XXI, prima sessione, Discussioni, pp. 398–963, Senato, pp. 844–1042; Antonio Annino, "La politica migratoria dello stato postunitario. Origini e controversie della legge 31 gennaio 1901," *Il Ponte* 11–12 (1974): 1229–1268; Sabbatini and Franzina, eds., *I veneti in Brasile nel centenario dell'emigrazione (1876–1976)*.

7. Francesca Grispo, *La struttura e il funzionamento degli organi preposti all'emigrazione (1901–1919)* (Rome, 1985).

8. Giorgio Gambinossi, "Per la Colonia Eritrea," *L'Italia Coloniale* 5/7 (1904): 115–122, and editorial reply, pp. 122–123; Giovan Battista Penne, *Per l'Italia africana* (Rome, 1906), 270–280; Umberto Zanotti-Bianco, *Saggio storico sulla vita e attività politica di Leopoldo Franchetti* (Rome, 1950), 59–60. Emigrants not crossing the ocean did not pay the tax and did not benefit from the fund, until Parliament created a new law in 1910.

9. Istituto Coloniale Italiano, *Annuario dell'Italia all'estero e delle sue colonie* (Rome, 1911), 390–391; Commissariato Generale dell'Emigrazione, *Annuario statistico della Emigrazione Italiana dal 1876 al 1925* (Rome, 1926), 1637–1645; AP CD Leg. XXI, sessione 1900, Documenti n. 62-A, 2 December 1900, pp. 1–21; Vittorio Soldaini, "La raccolta delle rimesse degli emigrati italiani e l'opera del Banco di Napoli: 1902–1913," *Revue internationale d'histoire de la banque* 2 (1969): 137–188.

10. Francesco Cordasco, *Italian Mass Emigration* (Totowa, New Jersey, 1980); Grispo, *La struttura.*

11. Giovanni Preziosi, "L'emigrazione italiana negli Stati Uniti," *Rivista d'Italia* 2 (1910): 240–259; Luigi Villari, *Gli Stati Uniti d'America e l'emigrazione italiana* (Milan, 1912), 297–299.

12. Compare Naomi Chazan, ed., *Irredentism and International Politics* (Boulder, Colorado, 1991); Michael Peters, *Der Alldeutsche Verband am Vorabend des Ersten Weltkrieges* (Frankfurt, 1992); Roger Chickering, *We Men Who Feel Most German* (Boston, 1984); Mildred Salz Wertheimer, *The Pan-German League* (New York, 1971).

13. Giuseppe Mazzini, *The Duties of Man and Other Essays* (1907. London, 1966), 53.

14. Alberto Aquarone, *L'Italia giolittiana (1896–1915),* vol. 1 (Bologna, 1981).

15. Letter of 24 December 1899. ACS, Carte Martini b. 20 f. 18.

16. Luciano Monzali, *L'Etiopia nella politica estera italiana 1896–1915* (Parma, 1996).

17. Vincenzo Grossi, "L'insegnamento coloniale in Italia e nei principali paesi d'Europa," *L'Italia Coloniale* 2/11 (1901): 124–125.

18. Giuseppe Fumagalli, *La stampa periodica italiana all'estero* (Milan, 1909), 5–13. Fumagalli counted 182 periodicals (33 dailies) in Italian-speaking regions abroad; 1 periodical in Eritrea; and 289 (27 dailies) in foreign countries.

19. Ufficio Coloniale, n. gen 63188 spec. 828, Sotto Segretario di Stato to On. F. Martini R. Commissario Civile per l'Eritrea, Asmara, 22 December 1905, ASMAI/III, pacco 41 f. 5. Angelo Scalabrini, Inspector General of Schools Abroad, was in charge of the pavilion's organization.

20. Bernardino Frescura, *Diplomi e Medaglie assegnate dalla Giuria con le relative motivazioni* (Milan, 1907), 15.

21. T. Baldrati in Milan, letter to Colonial Governor, 18 May 1906, "Esito della Mostra Eritrea," ASMAI/III, pacco 41 f. 5. The King of Belgium did visit the Eritrean exhibit.

22. Istituto Coloniale Italiano, *Atti del primo congresso degli italiani all'estero (ottobre 1908),* (Rome, 1910): 1:xiv–xxii.

23. G. Caruso MacDonald, "Lo Stato di S. Caterina e la colonizzazione ital-

iana," in *Emigrazione e colonie,* ed. Commissariato dell'Emigrazione (Rome, 1903–1909): 3:1:250–251.

24. S. Coletti, "Condizioni generali della Repubblica Argentina in rapporto alla immigrazione italiana," in *Emigrazione e colonie,* 3:2:91, 133.

25. Giuseppe Capra, "La nostra guerra," *Italica Gens* 6/7–9 (1915): 145.

26. Adriano Colocci, *La crisi argentina e l'emigrazione italiana nel Sud-America* (Milan, 1892), 103–104.

27. Alfredo Cusano, *Italia d'oltremare* (Milan, 1911), 229.

28. Edward Said, *Orientalism* (New York, 1979).

29. Nicola Labanca, "'Un nero non può essere bianco.' Il Museo Nazionale di Antropologia di Paolo Mantegazza e la Colonia Eritrea," in *L'Africa in vetrina,* ed. Nicola Labanca [Paese (Treviso)], 1992).

30. Letter from the Comitato regionale della Colonia Eritrea, 4 April 1897, ASMAI/III pacco 41 f. 2; Ministero delle Colonie, *Le Mostre coloniali all'Esposizione internazionale di Torino del 1911* (Rome, 1913); Ministero delle Colonie, *La Mostra coloniale di Genova 1914,* 2d ed. (Rome, 1914).

31. Maria Carazzi, *La Società Geografica Italiana e l'esplorazione coloniale in Africa* (Florence, 1972).

32. Lamberto Loria, "Due parole di programma," *Lares* 1/1 (1912): 9–24.

33. Istituto Coloniale Italiano, *Annuario 1909* (Rome, 1909), 6, 48.

34. Lamberto Loria, "L'etnografia strumento di politica interna e coloniale," *Lares* 1/1 (1912): 73–79.

35. Lamberto Loria and Aldobrandino Mochi, *Museo di Etnografia Italiana in Firenze. Sulla raccolta di materiali per la etnografia italiana* (Milan, 1906), 7–8, 13–15; Francesco Baldasseroni, "Obituario per Lamberto Loria," *Lares* 2/1 (1912), 1–16.

36. Loria and Mochi, *Museo di Etnografia Italiana,* 13–14.

37. Loria, "L'etnografia strumento di politica interna e coloniale," 73–79.

38. Martini, *Pagine raccolte,* 813–814. The book is dedicated to the Italians of South America. Martini later was minister of colonies, 1914–1916.

39. Loria, "Due parole di programma," 10–13. The collection is now the National Museum of Popular Arts and Traditions, in the EUR district of Rome.

40. Francesco Baldasseroni, "Il Museo d'Etnografia Italiana. Ordinamento per regioni o per categorie di oggetti?," *Lares* 1/1 (1912): 44, 48.

41. Aldobrandino Mochi, "Il primo Congresso d'Etnografia Italiana," *Lares* 1/1 (1912): 25–36.

42. Francesco Baldasseroni, "Come si devono studiare gli usi e costumi dei nostri emigrati," in *Atti del Primo Congresso di Etnografia italiana,* ed. Società di Etnografia Italiana (Perugia, 1912), 179–181.

43. Amy A. Bernardy, "L'etnografia delle 'Piccole Italie,'" in *Atti del Primo Congresso di Etnografia italiana,* 173–179.

44. Donna R. Gabaccia, *We Are What We Eat* (Cambridge, Massachusetts, 1998); Franco La Cecla, *La pasta e la pizza* (Bologna, 1998); Hasia R. Diner, *Hungering for America* (Cambridge, Massachusetts, 2001); Simone Cinotto, *Una famiglia che mangia insieme* (Turin, 2001); Paola Corti, "Il cibo dell'emigrante," *Il Risorgimento* 44/2 (1992): 363–378.

45. Speech of President Hon. Ernesto Artom to Assemblea Generale dei Soci, 30 May 1915, ASMAI pos. 163/2 f. 19, emphasis added; Carla Ghezzi, "Fonti di documentazione e di ricerca per la conoscenza dell'Africa: dall'Istituto coloniale italiano all'Istituto italo-africano," *Studi Piacentini* 7 (1990): 167–192.

3. Migration and Money

1. Emphasis added. The decalogue was republished widely in Italian newspapers. Angelo Filipuzzi, ed., *Il dibattito sull'emigrazione* (Florence, 1976), 397–398; also Mirta Zaida Lobato, "La Patria degli Italiani and Social Conflict in Early-Twentieth-Century Argentina," in *Italian Workers of the World,* ed. Donna R. Gabaccia and Fraser M. Ottanelli (Urbana and Chicago, 2001), 63–78.

2. *Nel Cinquantenario della Camera di Commercio Italiana in New York* (New York, 1937), xxxix.

3. Pietro Gribaudi, *La più grande Italia. Notizie e letture sugli Italiani all'estero e sulle colonie italiane (Libia, Eritrea, Somalia)* (Turin, 1913), 199–200; emphasis in the original.

4. Ibid., 6.

5. Filipuzzi, ed., *Il dibattito sull'emigrazione,* 399.

6. Silvana Patriarca, *Numbers and Nationhood* (Cambridge, 1996); Carl Ipsen, "The Statistics of Population in Liberal Italy," *Bollettino di demografia storica* 16 (1992): 7–33; A. Cardini, *La cultura della statistica tra Italia liberale e fascismo,* Quaderni di Ricerca ISTAT 2 (Rome, 1994); www.census.gov (accessed 1/15/05).

7. Zentralauskunftstelle für Auswanderer, Bd. 1, July 1902–October 1906, BArch, R 1001/6275, Bl. 39; Walter Hazell and Howard Hodgkin, eds., *The Australasian Colonies: Emigration and Colonisation* (London, 1887).

8. Francesco Cordasco, *Italian Mass Emigration: A Bibliographical Guide to the Bollettino dell'Emigrazione 1902–1927* (Totowa, New Jersey, 1980).

9. Luciano Cafagna, *Dualismo e sviluppo nella storia d'Italia* (Venice, 1989), 297–300.

10. Donald F. Terry and Steven R. Wilson, eds. *Beyond Small Change* (Washington, D.C., 2005).

11. Luciano Cafagna, "Italy 1830–1914," in *The Emergence of Industrial Soci-*

eties, ed. Carlo M. Cipolla (London, 1973), 303; Cafagna, *Dualismo e sviluppo nella storia d'Italia,* 297–303; Vera Zamagni, *The Economic History of Italy, 1860–1990* (Oxford, 1993), 127; Gianni Toniolo, *An Economic History of Liberal Italy, 1850–1918* (London, 1990), 20, 101–102; Gino Massullo, "Economia delle rimesse," in *Storia dell'emigrazione italiana,* ed. Piero Bevilacqua, Andreina De Clementi, and Emilio Franzina (Rome, 2001–2002), 1:161–183; R. J. B. Bosworth, *Italy and the Wider World 1860–1960* (London, 1996), 159–181. The lira traded steadily at 5 lire per U.S. dollar on the gold standard, with stable prices for 1882–1914. *Sommario di statistiche storiche italiane 1861–1955,* 196–203.

12. Data from Commissariato Generale dell'Emigrazione, *Annuario statistico della emigrazione italiana dal 1876 al 1925* (Rome, 1926), 1641, 1657–1659; Direzione generale della statistica, *Annuario statistico italiano, 1895* (Rome, 1896), 697–698; *Annuario statistico italiano, 1900* (Rome, 1900), 746; Ornello Vitali, "Metodi di stima impiegati nelle serie storiche di contabilità nazionale per il periodo 1890–1970," in *I conti economici dell'Italia,* ed. Guido M. Rey, vol. 1 (Bari, 1991), 100.

13. Paquito Del Bosco, *Cartoline da Little Italy* (Rome, 1997), Compact Disc CDFO 3642; A. V. Savona and M. L. Straniero, eds., *Canti dell'emigrazione* (Milan, 1976); Ida M. Van Etten, *Vergogne italiane in America,* trans. "Umano" (Milan, 1893).

14. "300 'Fake' Banks in New York City. Hungarian and Italian emigrants fleeced out of $1,000,000 a year," *The New York Herald,* 29 October 1905, 1–2; Vittorio Soldaini, "La raccolta delle rimesse degli emigrati italiani e l'opera del Banco di Naples: 1902–1913," *Revue internationale d'histoire de la banque* 2 (1969): 137–141.

15. Francesco Balletta, *Il Banco di Napoli e le rimesse degli emigrati, 1914–1925* (Naples, 1972); *The Banco di Napoli* (Naples, 1951), 26–29.

16. The paper *L'Araldo Italiano* and the Italian consul in New York opposed the Banco di Napoli; *Il Progresso italo-americano* and the Italian Chamber of Commerce of New York supported it. Luigi De Rosa, *Emigranti, capitali e banche, 1914–1925* (Naples, 1980), 170–172; *The Banco di Napoli,* 5–8; AP CD Leg. XXI, Sessione 1900, Documenti 62A, 5–21, and Discussioni, 10 December 1900, 1290–1302; ACS, PCM 1906 2.4.858. Banco di Napoli, Direzione generale, Relazione sulla gestione 1905, 30 May 1906, pp. 2–3, 10–12, 23–24. Brazil required an especially large security deposit, which made it more difficult for the Banco to find correspondent agents.

17. De Rosa, *Emigranti, capitali e banche,* 400; Soldaini, "La raccolta delle rimesse," 147–150; Felice A. Bonadio, *A. P. Giannini, Banker of America* (Berkeley, 1994), Gerald D. Nash, *A. P. Giannini and the Bank of America* (Norman, 1992); ASBN, Banco di Napoli Servizio Emigrati Posiz. XIX, 5,

11/1, Agenzia New York to Direttore Banco di Napoli, 28 January and 10 March 1914.

18. *Notizie sulla emigrazione italiana negli anni dal 1910 al 1917* (Rome, 1918), 102; Direzione Generale della Statistica, *Statistica della emigrazione italiana per l'Estero negli anni 1902 e 1903* (Rome, 1904), 102; *Annuario statistico della emigrazione italiana dal 1876 al 1925,* 1637, 1646–1651. This compendium presents the quarterly statistics available to the Italian government in its decisions; for the most definitive statistical treatment, with the full benefit of hindsight, see De Rosa, *Emigranti, capitali e banche.*

19. *Annuario statistico della emigrazione italiana dal 1876 al 1925,* 1640, 1652–1653; *Notizie sulla emigrazione italiana negli anni dal 1910 al 1917,* 104; *Inchiesta parlamentare sulle condizioni dei contadini nelle province meridionali e nella Sicilia. Senatore Eugenio Faina, Presidente* (Rome, 1910), 8:55–58.

20. Representative Mahany of New York, quoted in Mark Wyman, *Round-Trip to America* (Ithaca, 1993), 104.

21. Renato Paoli, *Nella Colonia Eritrea, studi e viaggi* (Milan, 1908), 21–23.

22. Ibid., 78.

23. Klaus J. Bade, *Vom Auswanderungsland zum Einwanderungsland* (Berlin, 1983); Bade, ed., *Die multikulterelle Herausforderung* (Munich, 1996).

24. L. Fontana-Russo, "Emigrazione d'uomini ed esportazione di merci," *Rivista Coloniale* (1906): 26–40; Aldo Visconti, *Emigrazione ed esportazione* (Turin, 1912).

25. On the chambers within Italy: Cesare Mozzarelli and Stefano Nespor, "Amministrazione e mediazione degli interessi: le Camere di commercio," in *L'amministrazione nella storia moderna,* ed. Istituto per la scienza dell'amministrazione pubblica, vol. 2 (Milan, 1985); Elisabetta Bidischini and Leonardo Musci, eds., *Guida agli archivi storici delle camere di commercio italiane* (Rome, 1996); Jonathan Morris, *The political economy of shopkeeping in Milan, 1886–1922* (Cambridge, 1993); *I venticinque anni della camera di commercio italiana per le Americhe, 1944–1969* (Rome, 1971).

26. "La Camera di Commercio," *L'Indipendente* (Montevideo), yr. 1. n. 50, 2 October 1883. ACS, MAIC Div. Ind. e Commercio b. 477.

27. "L'Exposition de la chambre de commerce italienne," *La France* (Montevideo), n. 1119, 22 September 1885. ACS, MAIC Div. Ind. e Commercio b. 477.

28. Istituto Coloniale Italiano, *Annuario dell'Italia all'estero e delle sue colonie* (Rome, 1911), 582–591; ASBN, Banco di Napoli Servizio Emigrati Posiz. XIX, 5, 5/10, *Bollettino della Camera Italiana di Commercio* 6/9–10 (Sept–Oct 1913).

29. Camera di Commercio Italiana nel Belgio, *Atti del Secondo Congresso delle*

Camere di Commercio Italiane all'Estero (Brussels, 1913); *Nel Cinquante-nario*, 132; Camera di Commercio Italiana di Monaco di Baviera, *Relazione per il VI Congresso delle Camere di Commercio Italiana all'Estero* (Trento, 1931); MCRR, Busta 77 n. 54, Oreste Baratieri to Amalia Rossi, 17 April 1892.

30. The Chamber was formed from the older Italian Commercial Association. T. Carletti, "La Tunisia e l'emigrazione italiana," in *Emigrazione e colonie*, ed. Commissariato dell'Emigrazione (Rome, 1903–1909), 2:1:355–378.

31. Jules Saurin, *L'Invasion sicilienne et le peuplement française de la Tunisie* (Paris, [1900?]), and *Le peuplement français de la Tunisie* (Paris, 1898); Pierre Milza, *Italiens et français à la fin du XIXe siècle* (Rome, 1981); Paul Leroy-Beaulieu, *De la Colonisation chez les Peuples modernes* (Paris, 1874); Leroy-Beaulieu's articles in *L'Economiste français*, 14 July 1900, and *Le Journal des Debats*, 10 July 1900, 1–2, MAE, NS Tunisie vol. 318, p. 74.

32. MAE, NS Tunisie 385, f. 34–50.

33. "Les Italiens en Tunisie," in *La Quinzaine coloniale*, 10 June 1905. MAE, NS Tunisie 323, ff 2–3.

34. "Les Italiens en Tunisie," in *La Quinzaine coloniale*, 25 June 1905. MAE, NS Tunisie 323, ff. 4–8.

35. Ibid.

36. "Le 'Péril italien.' Les Italiens en Tunisie," in *La Quinzaine coloniale*, 25 July 1905. MAE, NS Tunisie 323, ff. 4–8.

37. Paul Cambon, Tunis, to Président du Conseil, 29 November 1884. "Chambres de commerce français à l'étranger—Tunisie,"AN, F/12/9110; J. B. Carentène, Tunis, to Ministère du Commerce et de l'Agriculture, 24 April 1884. "Chambres de commerce français à l'étranger—Tunisie," AN, F/12/9110.

38. Enrico Serra, *La questione tunisina da Crispi a Rudinì* (Milan, 1967); ISTAT, *Sommario di statistiche storiche italiane 1861–1955* (Rome, 1958), 203.

39. Ministère des Affaires étrangères. Direction des Affaires politiques. Note pour le ministre, 2 April 1906. MAE, NS Tunisie 437, f. 18–19.

40. Ministère des Affaires étrangères. Direction des Affaires politiques. Note pour le ministre, 15 October 1907. MAE, NS Tunisie 437, f. 33–34.

41. V. Wautrain Cavagnari, *La Giuria dell'Esposizione Italo-Americana* (Genoa, 1893), 373–374.

42. Ibid., 378.

43. Luigi Einaudi, *Un principe mercante* (Turin, 1900).

44. *Nel Cinquantenario*, 131–138, 199.

45. Ibid., 81, 123–128.

46. Fanny Zampini-Salazar, *L'Italia all'estero* (Rome, 1902), 23; Gribaudi, *La più grande Italia*, 200.

47. Adolfo Rossi, *Un italiano in America* (Milan, 1899); *Gli italiani negli Stati Uniti d'America* (New York, 1906), 253–256; Cafagna, "Italy 1830–1914," 300–303.

48. Gribaudi, *La più grande Italia,* 198–199; ISTAT, *Sommario di statistiche storiche italiane 1861–1975* (Rome, 1976), 118.

49. *Nel Cinquantenario,* 65–66.

50. Francesco Surdich, "I viaggi, i commerci, le colonie: radici locali dell'iniziativa espansionistica," in *La Liguria,* ed. Antonio Gibelli and Paride Rugafiori, *Storia d'Italia* (Turin, 1983), 504; Mario Enrico Ferrari, *Emigrazione e colonie. Il giornale genovese La Borsa (1865–1894)* (Genova, 1983); Paolo Longhitano, *Per la tutela della nostra emigrazione sul mare* (Messina, 1908), 6–20.

51. Ludovica de Courten, *La marina mercantile italiana nella politica di espansione* (Rome, 1989), 197–192.

52. Ferruccio Macola, *L'Europa alla conquista dell'America latina* (Venice, 1894), 97. In 1898 Macola became infamous for killing the Italian Radical leader, Felice Cavallotti, in a duel.

53. Ibid., 91–96.

54. Ambassador Rennell Rodd to Marquess of Lansdowne, "Emigration from Italy, 1903–04." PRO FO 45/903; Longhitano, *Per la tutela.*

55. de Courten, *La marina mercantile,* 178–179.

56. Ibid.; Commissioner-General of Immigration, *Annual Report* (Washington, 1904), 1–45. This form of immigration is still banned in the United States.

57. Ambassador Rennell Rodd to Marquess of Lansdowne, "Emigration from Italy, 1903–04." PRO FO 45/903.

58. de Courten, *La marina mercantile,* 185.

59. Austonio Franzoni in discussion of 19 October 1908, Istituto Coloniale Italiano, *Atti del primo congresso degli italiani all'estero* (Rome, 1910), 2:165.

60. [Andrea Cantalupi], "Il primo Congresso coloniale italiano," *Nuova antologia* 202/807 (1905): 153–154; Piero D'Angiolini and Claudio Pavone, *Guida generale degli archivi di Stato italiani* (Rome, 1981), 1:177–193.

61. Giacomo Gobbi Belcredi, "A proposito del Venezuela," *L'Italia Coloniale* 4/1 (1903): 20; Maurizio Vernassa, *Emigrazione, diplomazia e cannoniere* (Livorno, 1980).

62. *Inchiesta parlamentare . . . Faina,* 8:52.

63. ASBN Banco di Napoli Servizio Emigrati Posiz. XIX, 4, 2/1, correspondence to Director of Banco di Napoli from consul of Florianopolis, 4 November 1908; consul of Salonica, 13 August 1908.

64. Rudolph J. Vecoli, "The Italian Diaspora, 1876–1976," in *The Cambridge Survey of World Migration,* ed. Robin Cohen (Cambridge, 1995), 114–116.

65. Direzione della Statistica Generale, *Statistica della Emigrazione Italiana all'Estero nel 1881* (Rome, 1882), iii.

66. Vilfredo Pareto, "Il costo di produzione dell'uomo e del valore economico degli emigranti," *Giornale degli economisti* 31, series 2 (1905): 322–327; Alberto Beneduce, "Capitali sottratti all'Italia dall'emigrazione per l'estero," *Giornale degli economisti* 29, second series (1904): 506–518; Francesco Coletti, "Ancora del costo di produzione dell'uomo e del valore economico degli emigranti," *Giornale degli economisti* 31, series 2 (1905): 179–190.

67. *Annuario statistico della emigrazione italiana dal 1876 al 1925*, 1536–1537, 1542. While emigration statistics based on passports issued were too high, statistics from municipal records were too low. Return migration statistics are also undercounted: not all returning to Italy visited their native villages.

68. Ibid., 676–677, 688, 739–742, 791–799, 803–805; Alberto Beneduce, "Saggio di statistica dei rimpatriati dalle Americhe," *Bollettino dell'emigrazione* 11 (1911): 33–43.

69. Giovan Battista Penne, *Dall'America all'Africa* (Rome, 1908), 21; Adolfo Rossi, *Nel paese dei dollari* (Milan, 1893); Betty Boyd Caroli, *Italian Repatriation from the United States* (New York, 1973), 75–99; Wyman, *Round-Trip to America*, 75–80.

70. Commissariato dell'Emigrazione, *Emigrazione e colonie*, 3:3:89–90.

71. Luigi Villari to Pasquale Villari, 13 January 1908,Villari 58, BAV, 39v–40v.

72. B. R. Mitchell, *European Historical Statistics 1750–1993*, 4th ed. (London, 1998), 85–87; *Mobilitazione e smobilitazione degli emigranti italiani in occasione della guerra 1915–1922* (Rome, 1923); Annunziata Nobile, "Politica migratoria e vicende dell'emigrazione durante il fascismo," *Il Ponte* 30/11–12 (1974): 1333–1341; Vittorio Briani, *Il Lavoro italiano all'estero negli ultimi cento anni* (Rome, 1970), 122–124; Ornella Bianchi, "Fascismo ed emigrazione," in *La riscoperta delle Americhe,* ed. Vanni Blengino, Emilio Franzina, and Adolfo Pepe (Milan, 1992), 96–114.

73. *Statistica della emigrazione italiana 1902 e 1903*, 141; Timothy W. Guinnane, *The Vanishing Irish* (Princeton, 1997).

74. *Annuario statistico italiano, 1895*, 73–74; *Annuario statistico italiano, 1900*, 86–89.

75. *Annuario statistico italiano, 1895*, 73–74.

76. *Annuario statistico italiano, 1900*, 86–89.

77. Piedmont's population crisis was not resolved until the postwar "Economic Miracle," with massive migration from southern Italy to northern Italy.

78. Direzione Generale della Statistica, *Censimento della popolazione del Regno d'Italia al 10 febbraio 1901* (Rome, 1901–1904), 28–32.

79. Direzione Generale della Statistica, *Censimento della popolazione del Regno d'Italia al 10 giugno 1911* (Rome, 1912–1915), 82–111; http://dawinci. istat.it/ (accessed 4/13/07).

80. Emilio Sereni, *Il capitalismo nelle campagne (1860–1900)* (Turin, 1968), 351.

81. *Inchiesta parlamentare . . . Faina*, 8: 50–51.

82. Giustino Fortunato, *Pagine e ricordi parlamentari* (Florence, 1926), 2:35.

83. Michael La Sorte, *La Merica* (Philadelphia, 1985), 189–202; *Inchiesta parlamentare . . . Faina*, 8:57; Amy A. Bernardy, *Italia randagia attraverso gli Stati Uniti* (Turin, 1913), 310–337.

84. *Annuario statistico della emigrazione italiana dal 1876 al 1925*, 676–677, 791, 803, 1631–1634; Antonio Stella, "Condizioni igieniche e sanitarie degli italiani nelle città del Nord America—Il deperimento della stirpe," in *Gli italiani negli Stati Uniti d'America*, 105–125; *Sommario di statistiche storiche italiane 1861–1955*, 65.

85. Commissioner-General of Immigration, *Annual Report 1904*, 8; Alan M. Kraut, *Silent travelers* (New York, 1994), 273–276.

86. Italian Ambassador Marquis Cusani Confalonieri to Secretary of State William Jennings Bryan, 29 March 1914, no. 399, and reply by Robert Lansing, 10 April 1914, no 521. NACP, Microfilm Publication M527, roll 46, Record Group 59, Records of the Department of State relating to internal affairs of Italy, 1910–1926.

87. Luigi Villari, *Gli Stati Uniti d'America e l'emigrazione italiana* (Milan, 1912), 303–304; Stella, "Gli italiani negli Stati Uniti," 105–125.

88. *Annuario statistico della emigrazione italiana dal 1876 al 1925*, 1631–1634; Commissario dell'Emigrazione, *Notizie sul movimento dell'emigrazione transceanica italiana . . . ottobre, novembre, e dicembre 1913* (Rome, 1914), 14.

89. "L'emigrazione in Brasile," special issue, *Italica Gens* 4, no. 5–12 (1913).

90. Giorgio Sonnino, "Per il Progresso della Colonia Eritrea," *Nuova Antologia* 113, series 4 (1904): 271–279; Penne, *Dall'America all'Africa*.

91. AS Rovigo, Carte Rossi n. 3, ff. 2–11; Adolfo Rossi, "Per la tutela degli italiani negli Stati Uniti," *Bollettino dell'emigrazione* 16 (1904): 3–138.

92. ASV, Arch. Deleg. Ap. Stati Uniti II. 1b/2, f. 145–149; Michael Barone, "A Turning Point in the Italian-American Experience," in *The Columbus People*, ed. Lydio Tomasi, Piero Gastaldo, and Thomas Row (New York, 1994), 493; "Un Pioniere della colonnizzazione italiana negli Stati Uniti d'America," *Italica Gens* 1/1 (1910): 31–34; Cabrini, *Emigrazione ed emigranti*, 81–84; *Rivista di Emigrazione* 3, no. 3–4 (1910); Edward C. Stibili, "The Italian St. Raphael Society for the Protection of Italian Immigrants in the United States," in *Scalabrini tra vecchio e nuovo mondo*, ed. Gianfausto Rosoli (Rome, 1989), 469–480.

93. Jane Addams, *Twenty Years at Hull House* (New York, 1910), 372; Neil

Larry Shumsky, "'Let No Man Stop to Plunder!': American Hostility to Return Migration, 1890–1924," *Journal of American Ethnic History* 11 (1992): 56–75; Stephen Michael DiGiovanni, *Archbishop Corrigan and the Italian Immigrants* (Huntington, Indiana, 1994), 142, 193–194; Rossi, *Nel paese dei dollari.*

4. The Language of Dante

1. "pur troppo s'è fatta l'Italia, ma non si fanno gl'Italiani." Massimo d'Azeglio, *I miei ricordi,* 2 vols. (Florence, 1867), 1:7. His original manuscript reads differently: "Italy's greatest need is to create Italians who know to fulfill their duty" ("il primo bisogno d'Italia è che si formino Italiani che sappiano adempiere al loro dovere"), *I miei ricordi,* ed. Massimo Legnani (Milan, 1963), 6; Simonetta Soldani and Gabriele Turi, eds., *Fare gli italiani* (Bologna, 1993); Albert Russell Ascoli and Krystyna Von Henneberg, eds., *Making and Remaking Italy* (Oxford, 2001).
2. Giuseppe Prato, "Per l'emigrazione italiana nell'America Latina," *La Riforma Sociale* 10, year 7 (1900): 109.
3. Ferdinando Martini, *Pagine raccolte* (Florence, 1912), 811.
4. Edmondo De Amicis, *Cuore* (Turin, 1972), 290–316.
5. *La Patria* 1/6 (1912): 565.
6. Giorgio Floriani, *Scuole italiane all'estero. Cento anni di storia* (Rome, 1974), 7–47; Patrizia Salvetti, "Le scuole italiane all'estero," in *Storia dell'emigrazione italiana,* ed. Piero Bevilacqua, Andreina De Clementi, and Emilio Franzina (Rome, 2001–2002), 2:535–550.
7. Alain Dubosclard, *Histoire de la Fédération des Alliances Françaises aux États-Unis* (Paris, 1998); Maurice Bruézière, *L'Alliance française* (Paris, 1983).
8. Bericht des Ausschußes des Kolonialraths zur Berathung des Entwurfes eines Gesetzes über das Auswanderungswesen, 28 January 1896, BArch, R 1001/6234, Bl. 107, emphasis added; *Denkschrift des Auswärtigen Amtes über das deutsche Auslandsschulwesen* (Berlin, [1913?]), Lichterfelde Archiv-Bibliothek, AA Bibliothek, RD 16/5.
9. Nancy Mitchell, *The Danger of Dreams* (Chapel Hill, 1999); H. H. Herwig, *Germany's Vision of Empire in Venezuela, 1871–1914* (Princeton, 1986).
10. See Pasquale Villari's speeches of 1897 and 1903, and the Central Council's report of 1907: *Atti della Società "Dante Alighieri"* n. 13, December (1903): 9–10; n. 7, February (1898): 10–13; n. 28, January (1908): 8–18; ASDMAE Serie P, pacco 726 posiz. 1090.
11. Luigi Barzini, *L'Argentina vista come è* (Milan, 1902), 166.
12. Angelo Filipuzzi, ed., *Il dibattito sull'emigrazione* (Florence, 1976), 169–172.
13. "Cronaca: Noticine sulla Prima Esposizione italiana," published by *L'Operaio Italiano.* ACS, MAIC Div. Ind. e Commercio b. 83.

14. *L'Eco dell'Esposizione Industriale—Artistica—Operaia Italiana nella Repubblica Argentina,* 24 April 1881, p. 3. ACS, MAIC Div. Ind. e Commercio b. 83.

15. Società Unione Operai Italiani. Comitato dell'Esposizione. Rendiconto, 1881. ACS, MAIC Div. Ind. e Commercio b. 83.

16. *Catalogo Descrittivo della Mostra Storico-Artistica* (Milan, 1907); *Guida ufficiale della Esposizione Nazionale e della Mostra di Arte Sacra* (Turin, 1898).

17. Luciano Trincia, *Per la fede, per la patria* (Rome, 2002).

18. "L'italiano? No grazie, io parlo dialetto," *Corriere della Sera,* 20 April 2007.

19. Manzoni's revision was a financial failure, but he became a Senator of Italy in 1860 and chaired a national study of the Italian language in 1868. Compare with Polish, Greek, and Hungarian patriotic linguists: Roy Porter and Mikul Teich, eds., *Romanticism in National Context* (Cambridge, 1988); Denis Mack Smith, ed., *The Making of Italy, 1796–1870* (New York, 1968); *Vocabolario degli Accademici della Crusca* (Venice, 1612), the first of its kind; Luca Serianni and Pietro Trifone, eds., *Le altre lingue,* vol. 3, and *I luoghi della codificazione,* vol. 1, *Storia della lingua italiana* (Turin, 1993–1994); Luigi Peirone and Claudio Marchiori, *Storia linguistica e storie della lingua italiana* (Genova, 1990). On Italo-Romance, Rhaeto-Romance, and Gallo-Romance language subgroups in Italy, see www.ethnologue.com (accessed 3/8/07).

20. Stephen Michael DiGiovanni, *Archbishop Corrigan and the Italian Immigrants* (Huntington, Indiana, 1994), 148–149; Luigi Rava, "L'insegnamento dell'italiano nella Repubblica Argentina," *La Patria* 1/4 (1912): 282; Eugen Weber, *Peasants into Frenchmen* (Stanford, 1976).

21. Tullio De Mauro, *Storia linguistica dell'Italia unita,* 2d ed. (Bari, 1970), 53–63, 292; Martin Clark, *Modern Italy, 1871–1995,* 2d ed. (London and New York, 1996), 34–39.

22. Rudolph J. Vecoli, "The Formation of Chicago's 'Little Italies'," *Journal of American Ethnic History* 2 (1983): 5–20.

23. Pasquale Villari, "I dialetti e la lingua. Discorso per l'Accademia della Crusca," *Nuova antologia* (1909): 388, 385–395.

24. Relazione del Vice-Presidente Stringher al XVI Congresso della "Dante Alighieri," 1905, p. 8, ASDA Fasc/1905A8.

25. Giosué Notari, "La Provincia di Córdoba e alcune delle sue colonie agricole," in *Emigrazione e colonie,* ed. Commissariato dell'Emigrazione 3/2 (Rome, 1903–1909), 3:2:91.

26. Comitato della Camera Italiana di Commercio ed Arti, *Gli Italiani in Tunisia* (Tunis, 1906), 101–103.

27. Comitato della Camera Italiana di Commercio ed Arti, ed., *Gli Italiani nella Repubblica Argentina* (Buenos Aires, 1898), 11, 503–511.

28. Ministero delle Colonie, *Le Scuole italiane in Tripoli* (Rome, 1914), 16.

29. *Gli italiani negli Stati Uniti d'America* (New York, 1906), 438. The Society still exists, as the Tiro a Segno Foundation in Greenwich Village.

30. Tania Regina De Luca, "Inmigracion, mutualismo e identidad: São Paulo (1890–1935)," *Estudios Migratiorios Latinoamericanos* 10/29 (1995): 191–208; Luigi Tomassini, "Mutual Benefit Societies in Italy, 1861–1922," in *Social Security Mutualism*, ed. M. van der Linden (Bern, 1996), 225–271; John W. Briggs, *An Italian Passage* (New Haven, 1978), 15–37.

31. T. Carletti, "La Tunisia e l'emigrazione italiana," in *Emigrazione e colonie*, 2:1:375–378.

32. *Gli italiani negli Stati Uniti d'America* (New York, 1906), 438.

33. Ibid.

34. Many societies exempted their members from paying dues while in Italian military service. MAE, NS Tunisie 385, f. 107–117.

35. Letter to Italian workers' associations from the Dante committee in Bologna. ASDA, Fasc/1904 A9.

36. ASDA, Fasc/1904 A9.

37. Società Nazionale Dante Alighieri, Comitato di Napoli. La Commissione per l'emigrazione e le biblioteche di bordo per gli emigranti. "Relazione presentata al XX Congresso." ASDA, Fasc/1909 A9, pp. 9, 13–16, and A15.

38. ASDA, Fasc/1909 A9, p. 16.

39. Request by the Italian consul in Patras, Greece, 2 April 1886, ASDMAE Archivio Scuole 1868–1888 b. 218.

40. Istituto Coloniale Italiano, *Annuario dell'Italia all'estero e delle sue colonie* (Rome, 1911), 415, 437.

41. Pasquale Villari, "Discorso, XIV Congresso," *Atti della Società "Dante Alighieri"* 13, December (1903): 2, citing Visconti-Venosta, Minister of Foreign Affairs.

42. The Italian government did not provide pensions until the law of 18 December 1910. Floriani, *Scuole italiane all'estero,* 32–47. Teresa Di Chiara of Patras, Greece, requested a pension in 1887, but the Foreign Minister replied that Italian municipalities provided pensions, not the central government. ASDMAE Archivio Scuole 1868–1888 b. 218.

43. Villari, "Discorso, XIV Congresso," 6–7.

44. Bonaldo Stringher, "Relazione, XV Congresso," *Atti della Società "Dante Alighieri"* no. 17, December (1904): 11.

45. Giuseppe Gentile, "Dei modi più convenienti per organizzare e condurre la scuola e tutti gli altri mezzi di cultura italiana nell'America del Nord," in *Atti del Secondo Congresso degli Italiani all'Estero,* ed. Istituto Coloniale Italiano (Rome, 1911), 1102.

46. Villari, "Discorso, XIV Congresso," 2.

47. Enrico Serra, *La questione tunisina da Crispi a Rudinì* (Milan, 1967), 428–430.

48. Stringher, "Relazione, XV Congresso," 7.

49. Pasquale Villari, "Discorso, XII Congresso," *Atti della Società "Dante Alighieri"* 5, December (1901): 9.

50. Istituto Coloniale Italiano, *Annuario dell'Italia all'estero e delle sue colonie,* 395–437.

51. The relevant telegrams were intercepted and are translated into French in MAE, NS Tunisie 385, f. 285–415.

52. The preference for funding Mediterranean over American schools continued into Fascism. Floriani, *Scuole italiane all'estero,* 79.

53. Villari, "Discorso, XII Congresso," 9.

54. Comitato di Tunisi, Società Dante Alighieri, to Pres. Prof. Villari in Firenze, 7 February 1902. ASDA Fasc/1902 B12.

55. "Dibattito, XV Congresso," *Atti della Società "Dante Alighieri"* no. 17, December (1904): 17–19; Napoleone Colajanni, *La Dante e gli emigrati analfabeti* (Rome, 1904).

56. Beatrice Pisa, *Nazione e politica nella Società "Dante Alighieri"* (Rome, 1995), 266–267.

57. "Dibattito, XV Congresso," 17–19.

58. Giovan Battista Penne, *Dall'America all'Africa. La missione coloniale del popolo italiano* (Rome, 1908), 22–23; Paquito Del Bosco, *Cartoline da Little Italy* (Rome, 1997), Compact Disc CDFO 3642.

59. "Cronaca dei Comitati," *Atti della Società "Dante Alighieri"* 14 (1904): 8, emphasis in the original.

60. Gentile, "Dei modi più convenienti," 2:1092–1093.

61. Half of the printed program for the New York City celebrations of 20 September 1893 was filled by advertisements for local Italian shops, wholesalers, insurers, importers, dentists, druggists, bankers, etc. "Programma della grande Festa Campestre sotto gli auspici delle Società Italiane Unite . . . ," CMS, Italian Miscellany, b. 11 f. 150.

62. Yves Déloye, *Ecole et citoyenneté* ([Paris], 1994).

63. Gordon A. Craig, *Germany, 1866–1945* (Oxford, 1978), 73–78, 186–192.

64. "Report of the Committee on State Schools: Compulsory Education" NEA, *Journal of Proceedings and Addresses* (New York, 1891), 295, 298; Cecilia Elizabeth O'Leary, *To Die For* (Princeton, 1999), 173.

65. John Higham, *Strangers in the Land,* 2d ed. (New Brunswick, 1988), 247–248.

66. O'Leary, *To Die For,* 150–152, 161–162; Louise Harris, *The Flag over the Schoolhouse* (Providence, 1971), 177; John Bodnar, *Remaking America* (Princeton, 1992); Desmond S. King, *Making Americans* (Cambridge, Massachusetts, 2000).

67. Harris, *The Flag over the Schoolhouse,* 175–180, 187, 191–196.

68. Quoted in O'Leary, *To Die For,* 177.
69. Istituto Coloniale Italiano, *Atti del Secondo Congresso degli Italiani all'Estero* (Rome, 1911), 2:562–563.
70. Ranieri Venerosi, "I sussidi alle scuole italiane in America," *Italica Gens* 5/1–2 (1914): 1–3.
71. Bonaldo Stringher, "Relazione del Consiglio Centrale, XVI Congresso," *Atti della Società "Dante Alighieri"* no. 21, December (1905): 9–10.
72. Ranieri Venerosi, "Per gli Scambi commerciali colle Colonie italiane del Brasile Meridionale," *Italica Gens* 5/3–8 (1914): 65–68; Francesco Surdich, "I viaggi, i commerci, le colonie: radici locali dell'iniziativa espansionistica," in *La Liguria,* ed. Antonio Gibelli and Paride Rugafiori, *Storia d'Italia. Le regioni dall'Unità a oggi* (Turin, 1983), 490–498.
73. Pasquale Petrone, "Immigranti italiani in Brasile: identità e integrazione," *Altreitalie* 13 (1995): 27–42; Arnd Schneider, *Future Lost* (Oxford, 2000).
74. Stringher, "Relazione," 32.
75. Piero Barbèra, "Impressioni argentine. Da un recente viaggio," *Nuova Antologia* 167/667 (1899): 440–464; Samuel L. Baily, *Immigrants in the Lands of Promise* (Ithaca, New York, 1999), 191–216.
76. Tancredi Castiglia, "Paranà, Brasile," in *Emigrazione e colonie,* 3:1:190.
77. Pasquale Villari, "Discorso, X Congresso," *Atti della Società "Dante Alighieri"* 9, March (1900): 12.
78. James Crawford, *Bilingual Education,* 4th ed. (Trenton, New Jersey, 1999); William G. Ross, *Forging New Freedoms* (Lincoln, Nebraska, 1994).
79. Theodore Roosevelt, "True Americanism" [1894], in *American Ideals and Other Essays* (New York, 1897), 26, 28.
80. Ibid., 29.
81. Ibid., 28–29. The periodical *L'Italia coloniale* and *Nuova antologia* regularly quoted Roosevelt, and Giuseppe Di Stefano-Napolitani cited him on the floor of Parliament: AP CD, leg. XXIII, prima sessione, Discussioni, 7 June 1912, pp. 20536–20537.
82. Sidney Sonnino, Foreign Affairs Minister, Direzione Generale delle Scuole italiane all'Estero, to President of the Società Nazionale "Dante Alighieri" Roma, 22 May 1916, ASDA Fasc/1916 A25.
83. Pietro Gribaudi, *La più grande Italia. Notizie e letture sugli Italiani all'estero e sulle colonie italiane (Libia, Eritrea, Somalia)* (Turin, 1913), 8.
84. V. Wautrain Cavagnari, *La Giuria dell'Esposizione Italo-Americana, Genova 1892. Relazione* (Genova, 1893); *Guida ufficiale della Esposizione Nazionale e della Mostra di Arte Sacra* (Turin, 1898); *Gli Italiani all'Estero (Esposizione internazionale di Milano 1906),* 5 vols. (Milan, 1907).
85. Istituto Coloniale Italiano, *Atti del primo congresso,* and *Atti del Secondo Congresso.*

86. United States Immigration Commission [Senator William S. Dillingham, chair], *Dictionary of Races or Peoples,* vol. 5, *Reports of the Immigration Commission,* 41 vols. (New York, 1970); Robert F. Foerster, "The Italian Factor in the Race Stock of Argentina," *Quarterly Publication of the American Statistical Association* (1919), 347–360.

87. Fumagalli, *La stampa periodica italiana,* 129, lxxix–lxxx.

88. Ibid., xxxv–lxxviii, 12–13, 89–95; Leonardo Bettini, *Bibliografia dell'anarchismo, periodici e numeri unici anarchici in lingua italiana pubblicati all'estero (1872–1971),* vol. 1 (Florence, 1976); Carlos Rama, "La stampa periodica italiana nell'America Latina," *Movimento Operaio* 5 (1955), 802–805; Angelo Trento, "'Wherever We Work, That Land is Ours': The Italian Anarchist Press and Working-Class Solidarity in São Paulo," in *Italian Workers of the World,* ed. Donna R. Gabaccia and Fraser M. Ottanelli (Urbana, 2001), 102–120.

89. Fumagalli, *La stampa periodica italiana,* 80; Vittorio Briani, *La stampa italiana all'estero* (Rome, 1977); Sally M. Miller, *The Ethnic Press in the United States* (New York, 1987); Robert E. Park, *The Immigrant Press and Its Control* (New York, 1922); Bénédicte Deschamps, "Echi d'Italia. La stampa dell'emigrazione," in *Storia dell'emigrazione italiana,* 2:313–334.

90. Quoted in "Il Progresso Italo-Americano. Per la Mostra del Lavoro degl'Italiani all'Estero. Esposizione Internazionale di Torino pel Cinquantenario dell'Unità nazionale, 1911." CMS, Italian Miscellany, b. 11 f. 144.

91. Giovanni Verrazano was vindicated with the Verrazano Narrows Bridge, dedicated in 1964; but Antonio Meucci was forgotten. Italians nationwide campaigned for Columbus Day as a state holiday, and it became a federal holiday in 1971. Bernardino Ciambelli, "Columbus Day," in *Gli italiani negli Stati Uniti d'America* (New York, 1906), 153–55.

92. "Il Progresso Italo-Americano . . ." CMS, Italian Miscellany, b. 11 f. 144; Fumagalli, *La stampa periodica italiana,* 131–132.

93. Carletti, "La Tunisia e l'emigrazione italiana," 377.

94. Fumagalli, *La stampa periodica italiana,* lxxix–lxxx.

95. Giovanni Preziosi, "L'emigrazione italiana negli Stati Uniti," *Rivista d'Italia* 2 (1910): 253–254, quoting Villari.

96. Gentile, "Dei modi più convenienti," 1088–1089.

97. Gian Piero Brunetta, *Cinema perduto* (Milan, 1981), 41–44, and *Cent'anni di cinema italiano* (Bari, 2004), 1:50–62; Giuliana Bruno, *Streetwalking on a Ruined Map* (Princeton, 1993), 122–146; Giorgio Bertellini, "Italian Imageries, Historical Feature Films, and the Fabrication of Italy's Spectators in Early 1900s New York," in *American Movie Audiences,* ed. Melvyn Stokes and Richard Maltby (London, 1999), 29–45; Riccardo Redi, *Cinema muto italiano* (Venice, 1999).

98. President of the Dante Alighieri Society Luigi Rava to prime minister Sonnino; received 10 April 1906, ACS, PCM 1906 2.3.345.

99. Luigi Rava, "L'insegnamento dell'italiano nella Repubblica Argentina," *La Patria* 1/4 (1912): 284.

100. Rava, "L'insegnamento dell'italiano nella Repubblica Argentina," 282–284.

101. Francesco Netri, Comitato di Rosario di Santa Fé della Società Dante Alighieri di Roma, "La tutela dell'italianità negli emigrati," 20 July 1901, ASDA, Fasc/1901 A7Bis.

102. Vilfredo Pareto, "Il costo di produzione dell'uomo e del valore economico degli emigranti," *Giornale degli economisti* 31, series 2 (1905): 322–327.

103. Pasquale Villari, "L'emigrazione e le sue conseguenze in Italia," *Nuova antologia* 128 (1 January 1907): 33–56; Villari, "Le conseguenze della emigrazione italiana giudicate da un cittadino americano," *Nuova antologia* 215/131 (1907): 3–8.

104. Giovan Battista Penne, *Per l'Italia africana* (Rome, 1906), 703–704.

105. Vincenzo Grossi, *Tedeschi e Italiani nel Brasile meridionale* (Città di Castello, 1904); John Gallagher and Ronald Robinson, "The Imperialism of Free Trade," *The Economic History Review* 2d series, 6 (1953): 1–15; D. C. M. Platt, ed., *Business Imperialism* (Oxford, 1977).

106. ASDA, Fasc/1901 A7Bis; Ulisse Infante, "La circoscrizione consolare di Rosario di Santa Fé," in *Emigrazione e colonie*, 3:2:209.

107. Luigi Barzini, *L'Argentina vista come è* (Milan, 1902), 145–152.

108. This argument favored local interests, as shipping to South America was monopolized by Genoa and shipping to North America was controlled by Naples. Paolo Longhitano, *Relazioni commerciali fra l'Italia ed il Brasile* (Genova, 1903), 13–14.

109. See the debates of 19 October in Istituto Coloniale Italiano, *Atti del primo congresso*, 2:148–149.

110. Quoted in Gribaudi, *La più grande Italia*, 52.

111. Memoria "Il Congressso 'Gli Italiani all'Estero'." [1908] BAV, Villari 58, f. 76; Luigi Villari, *Gli Stati Uniti d'America e l'Emigrazione italiana* (Milan, 1912), 290; preface to *Gli italiani negli Stati Uniti d'America* (New York, 1906).

112. Luigi Villari to Pasquale Villari, 13 January 1908. BAV, Villari 58, ff. 39v–40v. The Italians of Philadelphia did not participate in the Congress, even though Boston, Buffalo, Chicago, New York City, San Francisco, Hoboken (New Jersey), Stamford (Connecticut), and Pittsburg (*sic*) all sent representatives.

113. Ibid., ff. 39r–40v.

114. "Quello che ha fatto l'Italica Gens nel primo biennio ed i suoi propositi per l'avvenire," *Italica Gens* 3/1 (1913): 5.

115. See the lists of organizations, divided by consular district, in Istituto Coloniale Italiano, *Annuario dell'Italia all'estero e delle sue colonie*, 469–507.

116. Barzini, *L'Argentina vista come è*, 166.

5. For Religion and for the Fatherland

1. Giovanni Spadolini, *L'opposizione cattolica da Porta Pia al '98* (Florence, 1976); Arturo Carlo Jemolo, *Church and State in Italy 1850–1950* (Oxford, 1960); David I. Kertzer, *Prisoner of the Vatican* (Boston, 2004).

2. Esposizione Generale Italiana, ed., *Gli italiani all'estero* (Turin, 1899), 18.

3. Ibid.

4. Peter R. D'Agostino, "The Scalabrini Fathers, the Italian Emigrant Church and Ethnic Nationalism in America," *Religion and American Culture* 7/1 (1997): 121–159.

5. Kristen Petersen Farmelant, "Trophies of grace: Religious conversion and Americanization in Boston's immigrant communities, 1890–1940" (Ph.D. dissertation, Brown University, 2001).

6. Mario Francesconi, *Giovanni Battista Scalabrini vescovo di Piacenza e degli emigrati* (Rome, 1985).

7. Giovanni Battista Scalabrini, "L'emigrazione italiana in America. Osservazioni," in *Scalabrini e le migrazioni moderne*, ed. Silvano Tomasi and Gianfausto Rosoli (Turin, 1997), 35; Tomasi, "Scalabriniani e mondo cattolico di fronte all'emigrazione italiana," in *Gli italiani fuori d'Italia*, ed. Bruno Bezza (Milan, 1983), 145–161.

8. Carlo Marcora, ed., *Carteggio Scalabrini Bonomelli (1868–1905)* (Rome, 1983), 282–283.

9. Francesconi, *Giovanni Battista Scalabrini*, 1004, 689.

10. "Delle condizioni religiose degli emigrati italiani negli Stati Uniti d'America," *La Civiltà Cattolica*, yr. 39 n. 918 (15 September 1888): 646, 641, 647. In ASV, Arch. Deleg. Ap. Stati Uniti II. 1b/1, f. 3.

11. Ibid., 653.

12. Francesconi, *Giovanni Battista Scalabrini*, 1026.

13. Claudia Carlen, ed., *The Papal Encyclicals 1740–1981* ([n. p.], 1990), 3:191–193.

14. Bernard J. Lynch, "The Italians in New York," *The Catholic World*, April 1888, 70–71, 72.

15. D'Agostino, "The Scalabrini Fathers," 125–126; Robert J. Wishes, "The Establishment of the Apostolic Delegation in the United States of America" (Ph.D. thesis, Pontificia Università Gregoriana, 1981); Robert A. Orsi, *The Madonna of 115th Street* (New Haven, 1985).

16. Giovanni Battista Scalabrini, "L'Italia all'estero," in *Gli italiani all'estero*, 39.

17. Silvano M. Tomasi, "Scalabrini e i vescovi nordamericani," in *Scalabrini tra vecchio e nuovo mondo,* ed. Gianfausto Rosoli (Rome, 1989), 453–467, and "Americanizzazione o pluralismo?," in *Gli Italiani negli Stati Uniti* (Florence, 1972), 389–422; Francesconi, *Giovanni Battista Scalabrini,* 966–974.

18. Stephen Michael DiGiovanni, *Archbishop Corrigan and the Italian Immigrants* (Huntington, Indiana, 1994), 68–69; Colman J. Barry, *The Catholic Church and German Americans* (Washington D.C., 1953), 183–236; Robert Emmett Curran, *Michael Augustine Corrigan* (New York, 1978).

19. Francesconi, *Giovanni Battista Scalabrini,* 1006.

20. Barry, *The Catholic Church and German Americans,* 136–182. By 1884, of the seventy-two Catholic bishops in the United States, only twenty-five were native. Though Germans had the largest Catholic population, there were eight German-born bishops and twenty Irish-born bishops. DiGiovanni, *Archbishop Corrigan,* 68–75, 102–103.

21. Barry, *The Catholic Church,* 156–157, 313–316.

22. Scalabrini to Corrigan, Piacenza 10 August 1891: *Scalabrini e le migrazioni moderne,* 279.

23. Francesconi, *Giovanni Battista Scalabrini,* 1160.

24. Silvano M. Tomasi, *Piety and Power* (New York, 1975).

25. Mary Elizabeth Brown, ed., *A Migrant Missionary Story: The Autobiography of Giacomo Gambera* (New York, 1996).

26. DiGiovanni, *Archbishop Corrigan and the Italian Immigrants,* 173–194; Mary Louise Sullivan, *Mother Cabrini* (New York, 1992), 379–382; Francesconi, *Giovanni Battista Scalabrini,* 1050–1070.

27. Angelo Filipuzzi, ed., *Il dibattito sull'emigrazione* (Florence, 1976), 224–246. The Columbus Hospital merged with the Italian Hospital in the 1970s to form the Cabrini Medical Center in New York City.

28. Sullivan, *Mother Cabrini,* 157–158.

29. Ibid., 380; Rudolph J. Vecoli, "Prelates and Peasants: Italian Immigrants and the Catholic Church," *Journal of Social History,* (1969): 217–268; D'Agostino, "The Scalabrini Fathers."

30. *Scalabrini e le migrazioni moderne,* 13.

31. Bonomelli to Baratieri, 19 July 1890. AS Venezia, Carte Baratieri b. 8, Fasc. B.

32. Francesconi, *Giovanni Battista Scalabrini,* 1032.

33. Scalabrini to Cardinal Simeoni, Prefect General of Propaganda Fide, 18 July 1891, cited in ibid.; Patrick J. N. Tuck, ed., *French Catholic Missionaries and the Politics of Imperialism* ([Liverpool], 1987); Francois Renault, *Cardinal Lavigerie* (London, 1994); Joseph Dean O'Donnell, *Lavigerie in Tunisia: The Interplay of Imperialist and Missionary* (Athens, 1979); Ornella

Pellegrino Confessore, "Origini e motivazioni dell'Associazione nazionale," *Bollettino dell'Archivio per la Storia del Movimento Sociale Cattolico in Italia* 11/2 (1976): 239–267.

34. Baratieri to Bonomelli, 17 July 1893, BAM, Carte Bonomelli, 11.93.186.

35. Baratieri quoting Bonomelli in a letter to Bonomelli, 19 August 1893, BAM, Carte Bonomelli, 11.93.216.

36. Marcora, ed., *Carteggio Scalabrini Bonomelli*, 313; Francesconi, *Giovanni Battista Scalabrini*, 1032.

37. Istituto Coloniale Italiano, *Annuario dell'Italia all'estero e delle sue colonie* (Rome, 1911), 508.

38. Ornella Pellegrino Confessore, "L'Associazione Nazionale per soccorrere i missionari cattolici italiani," in *Scalabrini tra vecchio e nuovo mondo*, 524–531.

39. Bonomelli to Scalabrini, 25 June 1900. Marcora, ed., *Carteggio Scalabrini Bonomelli*, 362.

40. Bonomelli to Scalabrini, 23 April 1900. Ibid., 358.

41. *Scalabrini e le migrazioni moderne*, 139–149; Francesconi, *Giovanni Battista Scalabrini*, 1006.

42. Scalabrini to Bonomelli, 24 April 1900. Marcora, ed., *Carteggio Scalabrini Bonomelli*, 359.

43. *Bollettino Bimensile dell'Opera di Assistenza*, 1, n. 3 and 4 (July–October 1901); Raniero Paulucci di Calboli, *Lacrime e sorrisi dell'emigrazione italiana* (Milan, 1996).

44. St. Pius X, canonized in 1954, was personal friends with Bonomelli and Scalabrini when he was bishop of Mantua from 1884 to 1893. Gianfausto Rosoli, "La problematica dei patronati cattolici di emigrazione sotto Pio X," in *Un altro Veneto*, ed. Emilio Franzina (Abano Terme, 1983): 175–189; Gianfausto Rosoli, "L'emigrazione italiana in Europa e l'Opera Bonomelli," in *Gli italiani fuori d'Italia*, 163–201; Gino Rocca, "L'opera di assistenza degli operai italiani emigrati in Europa e nel Levante (l'Opera Bonomelli)," *Affari sociali internazionali* 1–2/3, 1 (1973–1974): 90–91.

45. Confessore, "L'Associazione Nazionale," 535–536; Silvano M. Tomasi, "Fede e patria: The 'Italica Gens' in the United States and Canada, 1908–1936," *Studi Emigrazione* 28/103 (1991): 319–331.

46. Prospectus of 9 December 1909. ASV, Arch. Nunz. Argentina 44 fasc. 2, ff. 34–36. Emphasis in the original.

47. Circular of Opera di Assistenza degli Operai Italiani emigrati in Europa e nel Levante, November 1900. BAV, Villari 1, ff. 256–258; Peter R. D'Agostino, "Italian Ethnicity and Religious Priests in the American Church," *The Catholic Historical Review* 80/4 (1994): 714–740.

48. "L'Italica Gens," *Italica Gens* 1/1 (1910): 11.

49. Giuseppe Gentile, "Dei modi più convenienti per organizzare e condurre la scuola e tutti gli altri mezzi di cultura italiana nell'America del Nord," in *Atti del Secondo Congresso degli Italiani all'Estero*, ed. Istituto Coloniale Italiano (Rome, 1911), 2:1096.

50. "Notizie Italiane. Il Secondo Congresso degli Italiani all'Estero," *Italica Gens* 2/3 (1911): 142–143.

51. "La Italica Gens nel terzo anno dalla sua fondazione," *Italica Gens* 3/12 (1912): 357; Mary Elizabeth Brown, *Churches, Communities, and Children: Italian Immigrants in the Archdiocese of New York, 1880–1945* (New York, 1995).

52. "La Nostra Marina," *Italica Gens* 1/1 (1910): 45–46.

53. "L'emigrazione in Brasile," *Italica Gens* 4/5–12 (1913): 405–407.

54. Ranieri Venerosi, "La Libia Italiana," *Italica Gens* 2/10 (1911): 362.

55. ASV, Arch. Deleg. Ap. Stati Uniti II. 127/1–4; ACRI, busta "Benemerenze. Rilevate nello Schedario Grande (Rilegato) 1888–1931."

56. Letter of 24 August 1899 from Arturo Galanti to Pasquale Villari, ASDA, Fasc/1899B17.

57. Sullivan, *Mother Cabrini*, 171, 213.

58. Istituto Coloniale Italiano, *Annuario dell'Italia all'estero e delle sue colonie*, 395–437.

59. Giuseppe Fumagalli, *La stampa periodica italiana all'estero* (Milan, 1909), 91.

60. Stephanos Zotos, *Hellenic Presence in America* (Wheaton, Illinois, 1976).

61. Error 37. Ernesto Rossi, ed., *Il "Sillabo." Gli errori del secolo*, 3d ed. (Florence, 1957), 40.

62. Casimir J. Wozniak, *Hyphenated Catholicism* (San Francisco, 1998); Bernard Wielewinski, *Polish National Catholic Church* (Boulder, Colorado, 1990).

63. Jemolo, *Church and State in Italy 1850–1950*; Mario Viglione, ed., *Rapporti Stato e Chiesa dall'unità d'Italia ad oggi*, 2d ed. (Brescia, 1987); John F. Pollard, *The Vatican and Italian Fascism, 1929–32: A Study in Conflict* (Cambridge, 1985).

64. Philip Cannistraro and Gianfausto Rosoli, *Emigrazione, chiesa e fascismo. Lo scioglimento dell'opera Bonomelli* (Rome, 1979); Peter R. D'Agostino, "The triad of Roman authority: Fascism, the Vatican, and Italian religious clergy in the Italian emigrant church," *Journal of American Ethnic History* 17/3 (1998): 3–38.

65. Francesco Baldasseroni, "Come si devono studiare gli usi e costumi dei nostri emigrati," in *Atti del Primo Congresso di Etnografia italiana*, ed. Società di Etnografia Italiana (Perugia, 1912), 179–182.

6. Emigration and the New Nationalism

1. Francesco Netri, Comitato di Rosario di Santa Fé della Società Dante Alighieri, "La tutela dell'italianità negli emigrati," 20 July 1901, ASDA Fasc/1901 A7Bis, p. 3; Luigi Barzini, *L'Argentina vista come è* (Milan, 1902), 145; Luigi Einaudi, *Un principe mercante. Studio sulla espansione coloniale italiana* (Turin, 1899); A. Di San Giuliano, "L'emigrazione italiana negli Stati Uniti d'America," *Nuova antologia* 202/805 (1905): 98–102.

2. Enrico Corradini, *La Patria lontana* (Milan, 1910), 1–2, 7–8. Corradini does not mention emigration in *La vita nazionale* (Siena, 1907).

3. MacGregor Knox, "Il fascismo e la politica estera italiana," and Claudio G. Segrè, "Il colonialismo e la politica estera," in *La politica estera italiana,* ed. R. J. B. Bosworth and Sergio Romano (Bologna, 1991), 287–330, 127–146; Zeev Sternhell, Mario Sznajder, and Maia Asheri, *The Birth of Fascist Ideology* (Princeton, 1994).

4. R. J. B. Bosworth, *Italy, the Least of the Great Powers* (London, 1979), 135–138.

5. Alexander De Grand, *The Hunchback's Tailor* (Westport, Connecticut, 2001); Alberto Aquarone, *L'Italia giolittiana (1896–1915)* (Bologna, 1981); Gaetano Salvemini, *Il Ministro della Mala Vita* (1909. Milan, 1962), 73–141. After Mussolini, however, Giolitti's reputation improved: Giovanni Ansaldo, *Il ministro della buona vita* (Milan, 1949), and Salvemini's own second thoughts, "Introductory Essay," *Italian Democracy in the Making,* ed. Arcangelo William Salomone (Philadelphia, 1945), vii–xviii.

6. Denis Mack Smith, *Modern Italy* (Ann Arbor, 1997), 103–105; Paolo Alatri, *Gabriele D'Annunzio* (Turin, 1983), 189–199.

7. "Alle batterie siciliane" (1899), *Odi e Inni,* in Giovanni Pascoli, *Poesie,* ed. Mario Pazzaglia (Roma: Salerno Editrice, 2002), 653–660; Carlo Salinari, "Le origini del nazionalismo e l'ideologia di Pascoli e di D'Annunzio," *Società* 14 (1958): 459–486; Claudio Varese, *Pascoli politico* (Milan, 1961), 241–254; Pasquale Verdicchio, *Bound by Distance* (Madison, 1997). At Carducci's death the University of Bologna offered the chair to Gabriele D'Annunzio as a successor "national poet," but D'Annunzio refused the offer. Paolo Alatri, *Gabriele D'Annunzio* (Turin, 1983); Mario Biagini, *Il poeta solitario,* 2d ed. (Milan, 1963).

8. "A Ciapin" (1899), *Odi e Inni,* in Pascoli, *Poesie,* 558–561. The word ghebì means "an Ethiopian palace."

9. "Una sagra," Messina, June 1900, in *Pensieri e discorsi* (1907), Giovanni Pascoli, *Prose,* vol. 1 (Milan, 1946), 170–171. The "perpetual flame" [*fuoco inconsumabile*] also refers to the burning bush seen by Moses.

10. "Coloni africi" (1901), Giovanni Pascoli, *Carmina/Poesie Latine,* 2d ed. (Milan, 1954), 520–525; "L'eroe italiano," Pascoli, *Prose,* 207.

11. Giovanni Pascoli, *Poesie* (Milan, 1939), 275–296, 420–431; "Gli emigranti nella luna," ibid., 388–406.

12. "Inno degli emigrati italiani a Dante" (1912), *Odi e Inni,* in Ibid., 920, 947–948; "Una festa italica," Pascoli, *Prose,* 316–323; "Nota a 'Italy,'" Giovanni Pascoli, *Nuovi Poemetti,* 6th ed. (Bologna, 1914), 219.

13. "In morte di Giosuè Carducci," published in *Il Resto del Carlino,* Bologna, 17–18 February 1907, and *Patria e umanità* (1914); Pascoli, *Prose,* 407–408.

14. Barzini, *L'Argentina vista come è,* 155–156, 214, 217–218.

15. Angelo Scalabrini to Pasquale Villari, 30 December 1899, BAV, Villari 43, ff. 447r–446v.

16. Donato Sanminiatelli to Senator Pasquale Villari, 22 March 1899, ASDA, Fasc/1899 B33. Villari's comments do not appear in the *Atti parlamentari.*

17. Istituto Coloniale Italiano, *Italia e Argentina. Opuscolo-ricordo della commemorazione in Campidoglio del primo Centenario dell'indipendenza Argentina* (Rome, 1911).

18. Robert Lumley and Jonathan Morris, eds., *The New History of the Italian South* (Exeter, 1997); Salvatore Lupo, *Il giardino degli aranci* (Venice, 1990); Aliza Wong, *Race and the Nation in Liberal Italy* (New York, 2006).

19. Gaetano Salvemini, *Il Ministro della Mala Vita* (Milan, 1962).

20. Massimo Livi-Bacci, *A History of Italian Fertility* (Princeton, 1977); Rudolph M. Bell, *Fate and honor, family and village* (Chicago, 1979), 193–200; Sidney Sonnino and Leopoldo Franchetti, *Inchiesta in Sicilia* (1877, 2d ed., 1925. Reprint, Florence, 1974); Franchetti, *Condizioni economiche e amministrative delle provincie napoletane,* ed. Antonio Jannazzo (Rome, 1985).

21. *Inchiesta parlamentare sulle condizioni dei contadini nelle province meridionali e nella Sicilia. Senatore Eugenio Faina, Presidente* (Rome, 1910), 8:72–73; John S. Macdonald, "Agricultural Organization, Migration and Labour Militancy in Rural Italy," *The Economic History Review* 16/1 (1963): 61–75; Donna R. Gabaccia, *Militants and Migrants: Rural Sicilians become American Workers* (New Brunswick, New Jersey, 1988); Frank Snowden, *Violence and Great Estates in the South of Italy: Apulia, 1900–1922* (Cambridge, 1986).

22. Giustino Fortunato, "La XIX Legislatura e la politica coloniale, 11 March 1897," in *Il Mezzogiorno e lo Stato italiano,* ed. Manlio Rossi Doria (Florence, 1973), 2:342.

23. Francesco Saverio Nitti, *L'emigrazione ed i suoi avversari* (Turin, 1888), and "La nuova fase della emigrazione d'Italia," *La Riforma sociale* 3/2 (1896): 745–771.

24. Di San Giuliano, "L'emigrazione italiana," 97; Dino Cinel, *The National Integration of Italian Return Immigration* (Cambridge, 1991). Nitti served on the Parliamentary inquest of 1910, which concluded that "emigration is a temporary relief, and can be the start of a solution, but is not the solution of the southern problem." *Inchiesta parlamentare . . . Faina,* 8:55.

25. *Reports of the Immigration Commission* (New York, 1970), 81–82.

26. Cesare Lombroso, *L'uomo delinquente,* 5th ed. (Turin, 1896); Gina Lombroso-Ferrero and Cesare Lombroso, *Criminal Man* (New York, 1911); Mary Gibson, *Born to Crime: Cesare Lombroso and the Origins of Biological Criminology* (Westport, Connecticut, 2002); Gian Antonio Stella and Emilio Franzina, "Brutta gente. Il razzismo anti-italiano," in *Storia dell'emigrazione italiana,* 2:283–312.

27. *Annuario statistico della Emigrazione Italiana dal 1876 al 1925,* 1639; John Dickie, *Darkest Italy* (New York, 1999).

28. Luigi Bodio to Pasquale Villari , 9 July 1911, BAV, Villari 6, 222v; Giustino Fortunato, *Il Mezzogiorno e lo Stato italiano* (Florence, 1926), 2:497–500; Vera Lutz, "Alcuni aspetti strutturali del problema del Mezzogiorno: la complementarità dell'emigrazione e dell'industrializzazione," in *Nuova antologia della questione meridionale,* ed. Bruno Caizzi (Milan, 1975); Franco Vespasiano, *Contadini Emigranti Assistiti* (Naples, 1990); Francesco Barbagallo, *Lavoro ed Esodo dal Sud* (Naples, 1973); Sereni, *Il capitalismo nelle campagne; Inchiesta parlamentare . . . Faina,* 8:55–56; Francesco P. Cerase, "Expectations and Reality: A Case Study of Return Migration from the United States to Southern Italy," *International Migration Review* 8/2 (1974): 245–262.

29. Luigi Aldrovandi, preface to *Gli italiani negli Stati Uniti d'America* (New York, 1906), v.

30. Pasquale Villari, *Lettere meridionali* (Turin, 1972); Villari, *Scritti sull'emigrazione* (Bologna, 1909).

31. Villari, *Gli Stati Uniti d'America e l'emigrazione italiana,* 306–307.

32. Wilbert C. Blakeman, *The Black Hand* (New York, 1908); John E. Zucchi, *Little Slaves of the Harp* (Montreal, 1992); Salvatore Lupo, "Cose nostre: mafia siciliana e mafia americana," in *Storia dell'emigrazione italiana,* 2:245–270.

33. Letter of Luigi to Pasquale Villari, 1908. Villari 58, BAV, f. 61, 64, 67.

34. *Inchiesta parlamentare . . . Faina,* 8:57–58, 51.

35. Angelo Cabrini, *Emigrazione ed emigranti* (Bologna, 1911), 265–266; Linda Reeder, *Widows in White* (Toronto, 2003); Emiliano Lanciano, *Cara moglie,* ed. Eide Dedicato Iengo (Editrice R. Carabba, 1984); Augusta Palombarini, *Cara Consorte* (Ancona, 1998).

36. Fabio Filippi, *Una vita pagana* (Florence, 1989).

37. Enrico Corradini, "To Benito Mussolini, Duce of Victorious Italy," preface, *Discorsi politici* [1923], in Enrico Corradini, *Scritti e discorsi 1901–1914*, ed. Lucia Strappini (Turin, 1980), 4–5; "Introduzione" by Strappini, vii–lxii; compare Franco Gaeta, *Il nazionalismo italiano* (Naples, 1965).

38. Filippi, *Una vita pagana*, 136–138; Monique de Taeye-Henen, *Le nationalisme d'Enrico Corradini* (Paris, 1973); Richard Drake, "The Theory and Practice of Italian Nationalism, 1900–1906," *Journal of Modern History* 53/2 (1981): 213–241.

39. See Enrico Corradini's "La penetrazione pacifica degli altri," in *L'ora di Tripoli* (Milan, 1911), 159; "L'emigrazione italiana nell'America del Sud," in *Discorsi politici (1902–1923)* (Florence, 1923), 73; and "I nostri connazionali in Tunisia," *Atti della Società Nazionale "Dante Alighieri"* 33, July (1910): 6–7, 35–36.

40. *La patria lontana* is "a work of art, among the most beautiful and important of the last several years . . . a breath of fresh air." *Atti della Società Nazionale "Dante Alighieri"* 33, July (1910).

41. Corradini, *La Patria lontana*, 256; Mario Isnenghi, *Il mito della grande guerra* (Bari, 1970), 9–21.

42. Enrico Corradini, *La Guerra lontana* (Milan, 1911), x–xi; Corradini, *Scritti e discorsi 1901–1914*, 196.

43. Corradini, *La Guerra lontana*, xi; Alfredo Oriani, *Fino a Dogali* (Bologna, 1912) and *L'ora d'Africa*, 2d ed. (Bologna, 1935).

44. Enrico Corradini, *Il volere d'Italia* (Naples, 1911), 178.

45. Enrico Corradini, *Le vie dell'Oceano* (Milan, 1929).

46. Enrico Corradini, *L'ora di Tripoli* (Milan, 1911), viii–ix. Compare with Pascoli, *Prose*, 414.

47. "Le nazioni proletarie e il nazionalismo," speech of January 1911, in Corradini, *Scritti e discorsi 1901–1914*, 184–185.

48. Speech of 11 May 1909 at the Dante Alighieri Society in Milan: Corradini, "L'emigrazione italiana nell'America del Sud," 76; Oscar Handlin, *The Uprooted*, 2d ed. (Boston, 1973); John Bodnar, *The Transplanted* (Bloomington, 1985); Giuseppe Prezzolini, *I trapiantati* (Milan, 1963).

49. Corradini, "L'emigrazione italiana nell'America del Sud," 80, 85–86.

50. "Le nazioni proletarie e il nazionalismo" (1911), in Corradini, *Scritti e discorsi 1901–1914*, 188–189.

51. Corradini, "L'emigrazione italiana nell'America del Sud," 87; R. A. Webster, *Industrial Imperialism in Italy, 1908–1915* (Berkeley, 1975).

52. Giulio Barni et al., *Pro e contro. La Guerra di Tripoli. Discussioni nel campo rivoluzionario* (Naples, 1912); Alexander J. De Grand, *The Italian Nationalist Association and the Rise of Fascism in Italy* (Lincoln, 1978), 51.

53. *La Perseveranza*, 13 July 1911. BAV, Villari 6, f. 222v.

54. Enrico Corradini, "Proletariato, Emigrazione, Tripoli," in *L'ora di Tripoli*, 221–222; Francesco Coletti, "Dell'emigrazione italiana," in *Cinquanta anni di storia italiana*, ed. Accademia dei Lincei, vol. 3 (Milan, 1911).

55. Corradini, "L'emigrazione italiana nell'America del Sud," 73; Emilio Gentile, "L'emigrazione italiana in Argentina nella politica di espansione del nazionalismo e del fascismo," *Storia contemporanea* 17/3 (1986): 355–396.

56. Corradini, "L'emigrazione italiana nell'America del Sud," 74; Enrico Corradini, *Sopra le vie del nuovo impero. Dall'emigrazione di Tunisi alla guerra nell'Egeo* (Milan, 1912); Emilio Gentile, *La grande Italia* (Milan, 1997).

57. Enrico Corradini, *Il nazionalismo italiano* (Milan, 1914), 58; De Grand, *The Italian Nationalist Association*, 32–36.

58. Letter from Corradini, 9 April 1909, in Antonio Todisco, *Le Origini del Nazionalismo Imperialista in Italia* (Rome, [1925?]), 25; compare Pasquale Villari, "Discorso, X Congresso," *Atti della Società "Dante Alighieri"* 9, March (1900): 6–21, and "Discorso, XII Congresso," *Atti della Società "Dante Alighieri"* 5, December (1901): 8.

59. Luigi Federzoni, *A.O. il "posto al sole"* (Bologna, 1936), 33–52.

60. De Grand, *The Italian Nationalist Association*, 17–40.

61. Enrico Corradini, "Commemorazione della battaglia d'Adua. Discorso letto a Bologna, Teatro del Corso, 1 marzo 1914," *Il nazionalismo italiano*, 245, 254.

62. Corradini, *La Guerra lontana*, vii.

63. Gualtiero Castellini, *Crispi* (Florence, 1915); Mario Viana, *Crispi: L'eroe tragico* (1923).

64. Giuseppe Bevione, *L'Argentina* (Turin, 1911), 138.

65. Ibid., 123–124.

66. Ibid., 99–100, 159, 166.

67. Ibid., 137.

68. Corradini, *Il nazionalismo italiano*, 53–54.

69. Stefano Jacini, "Il secondo congresso degli italiani all'estero," *La Voce* n. 26, 29 June 1911; *La Tribuna*, 16 June 1911, quoted in Raffaele Molinelli, "Il nazionalismo italiano e l'impresa di Libia," *Rassegna storica del Risorgimento* 53/2 (1966), 295–296; De Grand, *The Italian Nationalist Association*, 32; Istituto Coloniale Italiano, *Atti del Secondo Congresso degli Italiani all'Estero* (Rome, 1911), 1:27–38.

70. Isnenghi, *Il mito della grande guerra*; Anne Louise Antonoff, "Almost War: Britain, Germany, and the Bosnia Crisis, 1908–1909" (Ph.D. dissertation, 2006, Yale University).

71. The Italian postal bank blocked the Banco di Napoli from establishing correspondents in Libya. ASBN Banco di Napoli Servizio Emigrati Posiz. XIX, 5, 4bis/2, Ministero del Tesoro, Ispettorato Generale, no. 2131, to Direttore Generale, Banco di Napoli, 15 July 1905.

72. "France's interest will end once it has Tunisihed [*tunisificato*] Morocco, that is, when the part of the Franco-Italian accord favorable to France has exhausted its purpose and only the part favorable to Italy remains." Di San Giuliano, 28 July 1911, in Claudio Pavone, ed., *Dalle carte di Giovanni Giolitti* (Milan, 1962), 3:53; Giolitti, *Memorie della mia vita* (Milan, 1922), 2:328–329; Francesco Malgeri, *La guerra libica (1911–1912)* (Rome, 1970), 15–17.

73. *L'Idea nazionale,* 1 March, 8 March 1911; cited in Molinelli, "Il nazionalismo italiano e l'impresa di Libia," 291.

74. Today, an Italian name only applies to Gorizia. The other cities are Al Khums, Libya; Pula, Croatia; Susah, Tunisia; and Zadar, Croatia. Gualtiero Castellini, *Tunisi e Tripoli* (Turin, 1911), xiii.

75. Daniel J. Grange, *L'Italie et la Méditerranée (1896–1911)* (Rome, 1994), 1104; De Grand, *The Italian Nationalist Association,* 26–32; Valerio Castronovo, *La stampa italiana dall'Unità al Fascismo* (Rome, 1984), 172–174; Paolo Maltese, *La terra promessa* (Milan, 1968), 33–34. See also the collected articles, Giuseppe Bevione, *Come siamo andati a Tripoli* (Turin, 1912); Giuseppe Piazza, *La nostra terra promessa* (Rome, 1911).

76. Gaetano Salvemini, "Perchè siamo andati in Libia," in *Come siamo andati in Libia* (Florence, 1914), xxi; emphasis in original. Salvemini notes that shortly after Giolitti returned to office, all Italian military officers were issued Italian-Arabic vocabularies: xviii–xix.

77. The Italians found oil while drilling for water in 1913–1917, and the state petroleum company, AGIP, began systematic research for petroleum in 1936. AGIP was directed instead to explore in Ethiopia, and had to sell its stake in Iraqi oil explorations as well. Matteo Pizzigallo, *La "politica estera" dell'AGIP (1933–1940)* (Milan, 1992), 1–35, 73–93.

78. Esso (Standard Oil of New Jersey) struck oil in June 1959, drawing upon Italian research. Frank C. Waddams, *The Libyan Oil Industry* (Baltimore, 1980), 28–30.

79. Enrico Corradini, "L'esempio di Tunisi: Le miniere," in *L'ora di Tripoli* (Milan, 1911), 56; *Guinness World Records 2001* (London, 2000), 172.

80. Ranieri Venerosi, "La Libia Italiana," *Italica Gens* 2/10 (1911); Piazza, *La nostra terra promessa;* Corradini, *L'ora di Tripoli.*

81. Di San Giuliano, Fiuggi, 28 July 1911, in Pavone, ed., *Dalle carte di Giovanni Giolitti,* 3:52, 54–55. Emphasis in the original.

82. Castellini, *Tunisi e Tripoli,* 78; Malgeri, *La guerra libica (1911–1912),* 17–36.

83. Di San Giuliano, Vallombrosa, 9 August 1911, in Pavone, ed., *Dalle carte di Giovanni Giolitti,* 3:57–58.

84. Luigi Albertini, *Venti Anni di Vita Politica* (Bologna, 1950–1953), 2:123;

Marcella Pincherle, "La preparazione dell'opinione pubblica all'impresa di Libia," *Rassegna Storica del Risorgimento* 56 (1969); Salvatore Bono, "La guerra libica," *Storia contemporanea* 3 (1972): 65–83.

85. Albertini, *Venti Anni di Vita Politica,* 2:205–206.

86. Giolitti, *Memorie della mia vita,* 2:362.

87. Ibid., 2:334.

88. Di San Giuliano made the same specious argument: Pavone, ed., *Dalle carte di Giovanni Giolitti,* 3:52–55; Webster, *Industrial Imperialism in Italy,* 4–5.

89. Giolitti, *Memorie della mia vita,* 2:238, 362.

90. Podrecca had not visited the King but was expelled anyway. Leone Iraci, "Idee e dibattiti sull'imperialismo nel socialismo italiano," *Studi Piacentini* 7 (1990): 125–165; Maurizio Degl'Innocenti, *Il socialismo italiano e la guerra di Libia* (Rome, 1976).

91. See Corradini's speeches of 1913, "Nazionalismo e democrazia" and "Liberali e nazionalisti" in *Discorsi politici (1902–1923)*. But Bevione, writing for the pro-Giolitti *La Stampa,* dedicated *Come siamo andati a Tripoli* to Giolitti "with admiration and gratitude as an Italian."

92. Corradini, "Proletariato, Emigrazione, Tripoli," 29.

93. Gianpiero Turati, "Il movimento nazionalista in Italia e il Congresso di Roma," *Patria e Colonie* 1/12 (1912): 490–492.

94. Giolitti, *Memorie della mia vita,* 2:357–358; Albertini, *Venti Anni di Vita Politica,* 2:124–126; Mack Smith, *Modern Italy,* 248; Segrè, "Il colonialismo e la politica estera," 133–138, and *Fourth Shore* (Chicago and London, 1976); Martin Moore, *Fourth Shore* (London, 1940); Sergio Romano, *La quarta sponda* (Milan, 1977); Angelo Del Boca, *Gli italiani in Libia* (Rome-Bari, 1986–1988); Giovanni Roncagli, *Guerra Italo-Turca* (Milan, 1918).

95. Albertini, *Venti Anni di Vita Politica,* 2:122; Vincenzo Lioy, *L'opera dell'Aeronautica. Eritrea-Libia (1888–1932)* (Rome, 1964); see aerial photography in Stato Maggiore del Regio Esercito, Ufficio storico, *Campagna di Libia* (Rome, 1922–1927), vol. 2.

96. Albertini, *Venti Anni di Vita Politica,* 2:149–153.

97. Ibid., 2:118–204; William Askew, *Europe and Italy's Acquisition of Libya, 1911–1912* (Durham, North Carolina, 1942), 237–245.

98. The electorate jumped from 3 million to 8.5 million. All males over thirty could vote, and males under thirty who had served in the military could vote; there was no literacy or taxpayer requirement. Christopher Seton-Watson, *Italy from Liberalism to Fascism: 1870–1925* (London, 1967), 281–283.

99. De Grand, *The Italian Nationalist Association;* Francesco Perfetti, ed., *Il nazionalismo italiano* (Bologna, 1977); Emilio Gentile, *Storia del Partito*

fascista (Rome, 1989); Renzo De Felice, *Il fascismo e i partiti politici italiani* (Bologna, 1966).

100. Bevione, *Come siamo andati a Tripoli;* Corradini, *Sopra le vie del nuovo impero.* Federzoni was the war correspondent for *Il Giornale d'Italia* and Castellini for *Gazzetta di Venezia.*

101. "La grande proletaria si è mossa," speech given at Teatro di Barga (near Bologna) on 26 November 1911, "while the Italian army advanced on Ain Zara in Libya," as a benefit for the dead and wounded of the war. Pascoli, *Prose,* 557–558. Pascoli and Corradini were enemies: in 1899, as editor of *Il Marzocco,* Corradini published two pieces of Dantean literary criticism which offended Pascoli. He demanded that Corradini be fired, and indeed Corradini soon left the magazine. Filippi, *Una vita pagana,* 136–138.

102. "La grande proletaria si è mossa," Pascoli, *Prose,* 557–558. Emphasis in original.

103. Ibid., 558, 560, 564.

104. Ibid., 559, 560–561, 566–567. Emphasis in original.

105. Askew, *Europe and Italy's Acquisition of Libya,* 69–70.

106. Giolitti, *Memorie della mia vita,* 472–473; James Joll, *The Origins of the First World War,* 2d ed. (London, 1992).

107. "Gli italiani nella provincia di Santa Fè. Colloquio col console Adolfo Rossi," reprint from *La Patria degli Italiani,* Buenos Aires, September 1913. AS Rovigo, Carte Rossi n. 6.

108. Salvemini, "Perchè siamo andati in Libia," x.

109. "La grande illusione," in Gaetano Salvemini's newspaper *L'Unità* 1, n. 21, 4 May 1912. Salvemini, *Come siamo andati in Libia e altri scritti dal 1900 al 1915,* ed. Augusto Torre (Milan, 1963), 180.

110. Giustino Fortunato, *Pagine e ricordi parlamentari* (Florence, 1926), 58–59.

111. Salvatore Bono, *Morire per questi deserti* (Catanzaro, 1992), 57.

112. Eugenio Faina, *Congresso Agrario in Roma Aprile 1912. Relazione sul tema Il ritorno dell'emigrante,* ed. Società degli Agricoltori Italiani (Rome, 1912), 17–19.

113. Annunziata Nobile, "La colonizzazione demografica della Libia: progetti e realizzazioni," *Bollettino di demografia storica* 12 (1990): 173–188; Federico Cresti, *Oasi di italianità* (Turin, 1996); Michelangelo Finocchiaro, *La colonizzazione e la trasformazione fondiaria in Libia* (Rome, 1968).

114. Molinelli, "Il nazionalismo italiano e l'impresa di Libia," 303.

115. Ministero delle Colonie, *La Mostra coloniale di Genova 1914,* 2d ed. (Rome, 1914); Carlo Giglio, "Cenno sui successivi ordinamenti burocratici e archivisitici del Ministero degli esteri dal 1861 al 1922 e del Ministero delle colonie dal 1912 al 1953," in *Inventario delle Fonti manoscritte relative alla storia dell'Africa del Nord esistenti in Italia,* ed. Carlo Giglio,

vol. 1 (Leiden, 1971), xxi–xxiii; Commissariato dell'Emigrazione, *Emigrazione e colonie* (Rome, 1903–1909), 2:4.

116. F. Fabbri, "Il dicastero delle colonie," *Rivista politica e letteraria* 1/2 (1897): 58–59.

117. Relazione della Giunta Generale del Bilancio, 15 June 1912. AP CD, leg. 23 Documenti, n.1165-A, p. 8. The commission cited Marcel Dubois and Paul Leroy-Beaulieu as authorities.

118. AP CD, leg. 23 Documenti, n.1165-A, p. 8.

119. Ibid., 30, 1–7.

120. After the closure of *L'Italia coloniale* (1901–1904) and *Rivista di emigrazione* (1908–1911), the major journals addressing expatriate colonies were *Italica Gens* and *La patria*. Istituto Coloniale Italiano, *Atti del primo congresso degli italiani all'estero* (Rome, 1910), 2:343–344.

121. "Corrispondenze," *La Patria* 1/9 (1912), 267.

122. A. Alemanni, "Il Ministero delle Colonie," *La Patria* 1/7 (1912): 4, 7–8.

123. Agostino De Biasi, "Corrispondenze," *La Patria* 1/7 (1912): 81–82.

124. Errico De Marinis, "La Patria," *La Patria* 1/1 (1912): 1–2.

125. Gino Bartolommei Gioli, *Come l'Italia debba promuovere lo sviluppo agricolo delle colonie* (Florence, 1905), 8; Attilio Mori, "Il problema dell'emigrazione e l'Istituto Agricolo Coloniale," *Nuovi Doveri* 3/64–65 (1909): 342–344.

126. Gino Bartolommei Gioli, *Gli studi di agricoltura coloniale in Italia* (Rome, 1913), 5.

127. Ibid., 4–5; Gino Bartolommei Gioli, *Relazione morale dell'attività dell'Istituto nell'esercizio 1914–1915* (Florence, 1916), 2, 12–13, and *Relazione morale dell'attività dell'Istituto nell'esercizio 1913–1914* (Florence, 1914), 20.

128. "Progetto di Missione di Studio in Tripolitania," 14 November 1911, p. 4, Archive of the Istituto Agronomico per l'Oltremare, Florence, Fasc. 2400; *La Patria* 1/3 (1912): 278–279.

129. Molinelli, "Il nazionalismo italiano e l'impresa di Libia," 315n; Società italiana per lo Studio della Libia, *La Missione Franchetti in Tripolitania* (Florence, 1914), 1–4. Immediately after World War II, the Colonial Agricultural Institute returned to its expert advisement of Italian agricultural migration in South America. In 1959 the Institute was renamed the Overseas Agronomic Institute, sponsored by the Italian Ministry of Foreign Affairs, and continues to organize scientific projects for agricultural development in Europe, Africa, and South America.

130. Speech of President On. Ernesto Artom to the General Assembly of Members, 30 May 1915, ASMAI pos. 163/2 f. 19.

131. Letter of G. Bettolo, president of the Italian Colonial Institute, to the Foreign Affairs Minister, 4 November 1912 n. 2320, ASMAI pos. 163/2 f. 18.

132. Ministero delle Colonie, Relazione a S.E. il Sottosegretario di Stato per le Colonie, 9 January 1913, ASMAI pos. 163/2 f. 18.

133. Ibid.; original emphasis.

134. Istituto Coloniale Italiano, *Annuario dell'Italia all'estero e delle sue colonie* (Rome, 1911); Regolamento e Programma dei Lavori del Secondo Congresso degli Italiani all'Estero, 1910, ASMAI pos. 163/2 f.16; letter of 5 April 1918, ASMAI pos. 163/2 f. 19; Ticket for the First Congress of Italians Abroad, "under the high patronage of His Majesty Vittorio Emanuele III," Roma-Torino 1908, ASMAI, pos. 163/2 f.15. The Italian Colonial Institute's offices were in the Palazzo delle Assicurazioni Generali, next to the Altar of the Fatherland.

135. Commissariato Generale dell'Emigrazione, *Annuario statistico della Emigrazione Italiana dal 1876 al 1925* (Rome, 1926), 8, 44; Salvemini, *Come siamo andati in Libia e altri scritti*, 291; Segrè, *Fourth Shore*, 42–56; John S. Macdonald, "Chain migration, ethnic neighborhood formation and social networks," *Milbank Memorial Fund Quarterly* 42 (1964): 82–91.

136. Roberto Michels, *Il imperialismo italiano* (Milan, 1914).

137. Pietro Bolzon, "Corrispondenze," *La Patria* 1/8 (1912): 176–177, 180–181; emphasis added.

7. Earthquake, Pestilence, and World War

1. Estimates of deaths ranged from 60,000 to 120,000. This tragic toll has been superseded only by the Tokyo-Yokohama earthquake of 1 September 1923 (140,000); the Tangshan, China earthquake of 28 July 1976 (240,000); and the Indian Ocean tsunami of 26 December 2004 (283,000). By comparison, perhaps 20,000 or 30,000 died in the Mount Vesuvius eruption of 79 A.D. over Pompeii, Herculaneum, and Stabiae. A. Bottari et al., "The 1908 Messina Strait Earthquake in the regional geostructural framework," *Journal of Geodynamics* 5 (1986): 275–302; F. Barberi et al., "Volcanism of the Southern Tyrrhenian Sea and its Geodynamic Implications," *Journal of Geophysical Research* 78/23 (1973): 5221–5232; John Dickie, John Foot, and Frank M. Snowden, *Disastro!* (New York, 2002); F. Mulargia and E. Boschi, "The 1908 Messina earthquake and related seismicity," in *Earthquakes* (Oxford, 1983), 497–500, 514; Stuart K. Lupton, U.S. Vice Consul in Palermo, to Assistant Secretary of State, 31 December 1908, p. 4. NACP, Microfilm Publication M862, roll 985, Record Group 59, Department of State, Minor file 1906–1910. The island of Iceland also has active volcanoes. In 1971 the capital of Calabria was moved to Catanzaro.

2. Giuseppe Fumagalli, *La stampa periodica italiana all'estero* (Milan, 1909), 134.

3. Enrico Corradini, *La Patria lontana* (Milan, 1910).

4. AP CD Leg. XXI, prima sessione, Discussioni, 3 December 1900, 952; Luciano Tosi, "Italy and International Agreements of Emigration and Immigration," in *The World in My Hand* (Rome, 1997).

5. João Fábio Bertonha, "A migração internacional como fator de política externa. Os emigrantes italianos, a expansão imperialista e a política externa da Itália, 1870–1943," *Contexto Internacional* 21/1 (1999): 143–164; Alfred Crosby, *Ecological imperialism*, 2nd ed. (Cambridge, 2004).

6. Lucía Piossek de Zucchi, ed., *Alberdi* (S. M. de Tucumán, Argentina, 1986); Juan Bautista Alberdi, *Escritos*, ed. Oscar Terán (Buenos Aires, 1996).

7. L. Reynaudi, Commissario Generale dell'Emigrazione, Riservato to Ministro della Repubblica Argentina, 9 December 1907; approved by Tittoni at the Foreign Ministry, 14 December 1907. ASDMAE, CGE Archivio Generale b. 23.

8. Marco Rimanelli and Sheryl L. Postman, eds., *The 1891 New Orleans Lynching and U.S.-Italian Relations* (New York, 1992); David A. Smith, "From the Mississippi to the Mediterranean: The 1891 New Orleans Lynching and its Effects on United States Diplomacy and the American Navy," *The Southern Historian* 19 (1998): 60–85.

9. Eugenia Scarzanella, *Italiani Malagente* (Milan, 1999); Laura Randall, *An Economic History of Argentina in the Twentieth Century* (New York, 1978), 212–217.

10. Giuseppe Bevione, *L'Argentina* (Turin, 1911), 137.

11. Ibid., 164–165.

12. *Avanti!*, 7 August 1911, cited in Frank Snowden, *Naples in the Time of Cholera, 1884–1911* (Cambridge, 1995), 342.

13. Giolitti also knew that quarantines threatened Italy's export of perishable foods and citrus fruits. Ibid., 247–248, 293–296, 345.

14. Ibid., 321–328, 333–338; Commissariato Generale dell'Emigrazione, *Annuario statistico della Emigrazione Italiana dal 1876 al 1925* (Rome, 1926), 86–91. Migration from Italy to Argentina fell to 32,719 in 1911 and 72,154 in 1912. These numbers include Italian women and children, who were not restricted by the boycott. Italian migration to France rose to 63,370 in 1911 and 74,089 in 1912. Migration to the United States fell to 191,087 in 1911 and rose to 267,637 in 1912 and 376,776 in 1913. ISTAT, *Sommario di statistiche storiche italiane 1861–1955* (Rome, 1958), 66.

15. On 3 June 1911 the Navigazione Generale Italiano informed the Commissioner General of Emigration, Pasquale Di Fratta, that the Argentine

Health Inspector, Dr. Castillo, had told them he had found cholera present in Naples and Rome but had made no official report; the NGI then asked for an unofficial report of Italy's precautions. Di Fratta forwarded this to the Interior Ministry, Direzone Generale di Sanità on 5 June 1911. ASDMAE, CGE Archivio Generale b. 23, f. 84.

16. Direzione, Navigazione Generale Italiano, to Commissariato dell'Emigrazione, 14 July 1911. The Italian ambassador claimed that his government's duplicity cost the NGI Company only "a few thousand lire." Viganotti to Di San Giuliano, ciphered telegram from Italian Legation, Buenos Aires, 16 November 1911. ASDMAE, CGE Archivio Generale b. 23, f. 84.

17. Telegrams of 20 and 21 July 1911 between Undersecretary of State for Foreign Affairs Di Scalea and Admiral Leonardi Cattolica. ASDMAE, CGE Archivio Generale b. 23, f. 84.

18. Telegram of 21 July 1911 from Giolitti to Comm. Peano, Capo Gabinetto Ministero Interno, intended for Di San Giuliano, Minister of Foreign Affairs. ASDMAE, CGE Archivio Generale b. 23, f. 84.

19. Viganotti to Di San Giuliano, ciphered telegram from Italian Legation, Buenos Aires n. 3567, 26 July 1911. ASDMAE, CGE Archivio Generale b. 23, f. 84.

20. ASDMAE, CGE Archivio Generale b. 23; Snowden, *Naples in the Time of Cholera,* 338–343.

21. Snowden, *Naples in the Time of Cholera,* 345–359.

22. Report from Regia Legazione Montevideo, n. 2179/179, 10 August 1911, to Ministro Affari Esteri; Correspondent in Berlin of the Emigration Commissariat, Prof. A. F. Labriola, Riservata n. 1050, to the Commissar, 2 August 1911. ASDMAE, CGE Archivio Generale b. 23, f. 84.

23. *Corriere Mercantile* (Genoa) v. 87 n. 168, 22 July 1911; Consul Dallaste Brandoli, Liverpool, to Emigration Commissariat, n. 87.0/78 p. M/25, 14 August 1911. ASDMAE, CGE Archivio Generale b. 23, f. 84.

24. A. F. Labriola reporting from Berlin, n. 1940, 27 December 1911; Ferrante in Stockholm, conf. n. 252/124, 12 August 1911. ASDMAE, CGE Archivio Generale b. 23, f. 84.

25. Italian Legation, Buenos Aires, "L'emigrazione in relazione al conflitto sanitario italo-argentino," to Ministro degli Affari Esteri, 30 June 1912, p. 4. ASDMAE, CGE Archivio Generale b. 23, f. 82.

26. Emigration Commissioner Di Fratta to the Italian Consul of Sao Paolo on 22 September 1911, Telegram n. 6992, ASDMAE, CGE Archivio Generale b. 23, f. 84.

27. Italian Consulate Córdoba, Argentina, n. 2470, 3 October 1911; Lloyd Sabaudo to Commissariato Generale dell'Emigrazione, 10 August 1911. ASDMAE, CGE Archivio Generale b. 23, f. 84.

28. Umberto Tomezzoli, Ispettore dell'emigrazione in Brazil, Sao Paolo, to Ministro degli Affari Esteri, 1 August 1911. ASDMAE, CGE Archivio Generale b. 23, f. 84.

29. Italian Legation, Buenos Aires, "L'emigrazione in relazione al conflitto sanitario italo-argentino," 30 June 1912, p. 3. ASDMAE, CGE Archivio Generale b. 23, f. 82.

30. Ibid., pp. 3–4. The Commissariat allowed the reunification of families and the return of expatriates who were visiting Italy only briefly. Commissario Generale dell'Emigrazione, *L'Emigrazione Italiana dal 1910 al 1923* (Rome, 1926), 1:653–655; Randall, *Economic History of Argentina*, 89–96.

31. Viganotti to Di San Giuliano, encrypted telegram, 16 November 1911. ASDMAE, CGE Archivio Generale b. 23, f. 84. Viganotti's hopes were not fulfilled.

32. Uruguay did not capitulate until 10 May 1914. Commissario Generale dell'Emigrazione, *L'Emigrazione Italiana dal 1910 al 1923*, 1:655; Telegram by Primo Levi, 26 December 1911. ASDMAE, CGE Archivio Generale b. 23, f. 84.

33. The decree revoking Italy's boycott was signed by Di San Giuliano and Giolitti on 24 August 1912. Under the same date, express telegram n. 15972 ordered prefects to diffuse emigration to Argentina over two months. ASDMAE, CGE Archivio Generale b. 23, f. 85.

34. Angelo Cabrini and others in Parliament referred complaints to the Emigration Commissariat; see telegrams dated 10 September and 23 September 1912. Emigration Commissioner Giovanni Gallini noted the protests of La Veloce and Lloyd Sabaudo, which had canceled second class berths on the first voyage to Argentina after the boycott; telegrams dated 29 August and 2 September 1912. ASDMAE, CGE Archivio Generale b. 23, f. 85.

35. *La Razon,* 10 June 1912. Cited in "L'emigrazione in relazione al conflitto sanitario italo-argentino," Italian Legation, Buenos Aires to Ministro degli Affari Esteri, 30 June 1912, p. 4, in ASDMAE, CGE Archivio Generale b. 23, f. 82; Pietro Bolzon, "Corrispondenze," *La Patria* 1/8 (1912): 177; G. Borghetti, "Rassegna," *La Patria* 1/9 (1912): 183–184.

36. The prefect of Trapani in Puglia explained that "many emigrants have set out for the other states of the Americas." Prefettura di Trapani, Ufficio di PS n. 5883, 12 December 1912. ASDMAE, CGE Archivio Generale b. 23, f. 85; Istituto Coloniale Italiano, *Italia e Argentina* (Rome, 1911); Ferdinando Martini, *Lettere [1860–1928]* (Milan, 1934), 449–450; Donato Sanminiatelli, "Nel primo centenario dell'indipendenza argentina," *Atti della Società "Dante Alighieri"* 33, July (1910); Snowden, *Naples in the Time of Cholera,* 341–342.

37. Il dragomanno [pseud.], "Programmi e colonie," *L'Italia coloniale* 2/3 (1901): 34.

38. Consiglio Centrale, "Relazione, XVII Congresso," *Atti della Società "Dante Alighieri"* 26, January (1907): 11.

39. Citations in ACRI, busta "Benemerenze. Rilevate nello Schedario Grande (Rilegato) 1888–1931"; in Montevideo alone, 91 diplomas of recognition were awarded after World War I. Donations to the Red Cross were also significant in Italy's balance of payments. Guido M. Rey, ed., *I conti economici dell'Italia* (Bari, 1991), 1:100–101.

40. Gaspare De Caro, *Gaetano Salvemini* (Turin, 1970), 149–150.

41. Stuart K. Lupton, U.S. Vice Consul in Palermo, to Assistant Secretary of State, 31 December 1908, p. 4. NACP, Microfilm Publication M862, roll 985, Record Group 59, Department of State, Minor file 1906–1910.

42. Ibid., pp. 1–8; Giovanni Giolitti to the U.S. Ambassador, 4 January 1909, NACP, Microfilm Publication M862, roll 985, Record Group 59, Department of State, Minor file 1906–1910. The U.S. Congress approved $500,000 in cash in addition to $300,000 in supplies delivered in Messina, and President Theodore Roosevelt coordinated the aid through diplomatic channels. The funds were spent in barracks for the homeless.

43. *Gli italiani negli Stati Uniti d'America* (New York, 1906), 179, 438; *Nel Cinquantenario della Camera di Commercio Italiana in New York* (New York, 1937), 134; Fumagalli, *La stampa periodica italiana*, 148–150; Mario Baratta, *I terremoti in Italia* (Florence, 1936), 139–142.

44. Letter of Bishop Matthew Starkins, 23 January 1909. ASV, Arch. Deleg. Ap. Stati Uniti II. 127/1–4, f. 162.

45. ASV, Arch. Deleg. Ap. Stati Uniti II. 127/1–4, ff. 12, 62, 252–253, 261; and letter to the Apostolic Delegate, 15 February 1909, by Ferdinando Faga of Florence, Alabama, who had lived in the United States for twenty-two years, f. 273.

46. ASV, Arch. Deleg. Ap. Stati Uniti II.127/1–4, ff. 324–325, 336; Peter R. D'Agostino, *Rome in America* (Chapel Hill, 2004). The American Catholics quoted the Jesuit journal *Civiltà Cattolica*'s false charges regarding Elena's committee.

47. ACRI, "Benemerenze. Rilevate nello Schedario Grande (Rilegato) 1888–1931"; ASV, Arch. Deleg. Ap. Stati Uniti II.127/1–4, f. 302; Baratta, *I terremoti in Italia,* 67; Rey, ed., *I conti economici dell'Italia,* 1:100.

48. Di S. Giuliano, Ministro Affari Esteri, 3 April 1913 to Giolitti. ACS, PCM 1913 f.14.3.352. L200,000 annually came from the national budget, and the Minister of the Treasury approved Di San Giuliano's proposal to replace the Emigration Fund's annual L450,000 with additional state expenditures.

49. Luigi Villari, *Gli Stati Uniti d'America e l'Emigrazione italiana* (Milan, 1912), 305.

50. Quoted in Christopher M. Sterba, "'More Than Ever, We Feel Proud to Be Italians': World War I and the New Haven *Colonia,* 1917–1918," *Journal of American Ethnic History* 20/2 (2001): 93; Nancy Gentile Ford, *Americans all!: Foreign-born soldiers in World War I* (College Station, Texas, 2001); Paola Corti, *L'emigrazione* (Rome, 1999), 136–137, 141; Francesco Balletta, "Il Banco di Napoli e le rimesse degli emigrati, 1914–1925," *Revue internationale d'histoire de la banque* 1 (1968): 44–45; Marzia Miele and Cesarina Vighy, eds., *Manifesti illustrati della Grande Guerra* (Rome, 1996), 92–95; Bonaldo Stringher, *Su le condizioni della circolazione e del mercato monetario* (Rome, 1920), 114, 123.

51. Angelo Cabrini, *Il Partito Socialista Italiano e la politica dell'emigrazione* (Rome, 1908), 23.

52. Memoria Il Congressso "Gli Italiani all'Estero," 1908, BAV, Villari 58, f. 85.

53. Ibid., f. 76/3.

54. The neofascist Mirko Tremaglia proposed the bill, and became Italy's first Minister for Italians Abroad, 2001–2006. "Il voto degli italiani all'estero è legge," *Corriere della Sera,* 20 December 2001; www.ministeroitalian inelmondo.it (accessed 5/10/05); Istituto Coloniale Italiano, *Atti del primo congresso degli italiani all'estero* (Rome, 1910), 2:11–114, 332–333; ASCD, Incarti di Segreteria, index 1909–1913, s.v. "Colonie Libere": discussion in Chamber of Deputies 22 June 1909, in Senate 30 June–1 July 1909; in Chamber 22 May 1912.

55. Paolo Longhitano, *Relazioni commerciali fra l'Italia ed il Brasile* (Genova, 1903), 6; Cesarina Lupati, *Vita Argentina* (Milan, 1910), 269–274.

56. Francesco Saverio Nitti, *La nuova fase della emigrazione d'Italia* (Turin, 1896), 17.

57. Vitaliano Rotellini, "Il Pregiudizio Elettorale," *L'Italia Coloniale* 1/2 (1900): 13–20.

58. Gioachino Maffei, "Il dovere degl'Italiani d'America," *Italica Gens* 7/7–12 (1916): 142. H. W. Longfellow was the United States' first great poet, and made a seminal translation of Dante.

59. Dorothee Schneider, "Naturalization and United States Citizenship in Two Periods of Mass Migration: 1890–1930, 1965–2000," *Journal of American Ethnic History* 21/1 (2001): 53–55; Mark Wyman, *Round-Trip to America* (Ithaca, 1993), 65. By law, aliens had to live in the United States for five years before naturalization, and after the federal Naturalization Act of 1906 they were required to pass an English speaking test.

60. Pasquale Villari lobbied unsuccessfully for a change in this policy. Minister of Justice Gianturco to Villari, 14 January 1901, ASDA, Fasc/1901 A1bis; Attilio Brunialti, *L'Italia e la questione coloniale* (Milan, 1885).

61. The Italian government reacted by denying state protection to those who

voted in Brazilian elections. Commissariato dell'Emigrazione, *Emigrazione e colonie* (Rome, 1903–1909), 3:1:364, 393; "L'emigrazione in Brasile," *Italica Gens* 4/5–12 (1913): 395–397.

62. Istituto Coloniale Italiano, *Atti del Secondo Congresso degli Italiani all'Estero* (Rome, 1911), 2:308–309; G. Borghetti, "Rassegne 'Italiani all'Estero'," *La Patria* 1/7 (1912): 90–91; Ranieri Venerosi, "Il 2o Congresso degli Italiani all'estero," *Italica Gens* 2/6–7 (1911): 253–258.

63. AP CD Leg. XXIII, prima sessione, Discussioni, 11 June 1912, pp. 20700, 20701–20702, 20704–20716. The law required two years of residence to reactivate Italian citizenship, but the law's sponsors explained that emigrants could apply for citizenship immediately upon their return. Gaetano Salvemini, who adopted U.S. citizenship as an exile from fascism, returned to postwar Italy and decided in 1954 to renounce his American citizenship to get back his Italian passport. He was surprised to learn that he had already regained his Italian citizenship by living in Italy for two years. De Caro, *Gaetano Salvemini*, 417–419.

64. [Commissariato Generale dell'Emigrazione], *Mobilitazione e smobilitazione degli emigranti italiani in occasione della guerra 1915–1922* (Rome, 1923).

65. Robert Holland, "The British Empire and the Great War, 1914–1918," in *The Oxford History of the British Empire* (Oxford, 1999), 4:117–118. The British empire's total mobilized forces at home and abroad were 9.5 million, while Italy mobilized 5.6 million.

66. "Regelung des Auswanderungswesens, Allgemeines," Bd. 2, 4 December 1895–February 1896. BArch, R 1001/6234, Bl. 65.

67. Fürsorgevereins für deutsche Rückwanderer. Geschäftsbericht. Vorschläge zur Besiedlung der deutschen Kolonien Bd. 5, May 1916–July 1919. BArch, R 1001/6267, Bl. 51.

68. James W. Gerard, *My Four Years in Germany* (New York, 1917), 236–237.

69. Ibid., 237; Frederick C. Luebke, *Bonds of Loyalty: German Americans and World War I* (DeKalb, Illinois, 1974).

70. Cecilia Elizabeth O'Leary, *To Die For* (Princeton, 1999); David M. Reimers, *Unwelcome Strangers* (New York, 1999).

71. In 1911, Italians abroad were numbered at 5,805,100, or 16.74 percent of the population of the Italian peninsula. *Annuario statistico della Emigrazione Italiana dal 1876 al 1925*, 1533–1542; ISTAT, *Sommario di statistiche storiche italiane 1861–1975* (Rome, 1976), 11, 16; *Mobilitazione e smobilitazione degli emigranti italiani*, 22. Consulates were responsible for keeping the current addresses of male emigrants, but were hopelessly understaffed for this task. Istituto Coloniale Italiano, *Atti del primo congresso*, 2:162–165.

72. Wyman, *Round-Trip to America,* 111–112. Wyman notes that 38,108 Polish Americans enlisted in an army under Gen. Joseph Haller; 20,720 arrived in France, but only a month before the armistice.

73. Luigi Albertini, *The Origins of the War of 1914,* trans. Isabella Massey (Oxford, 1952–1957), 2:217–253, 3:296–363.

74. René Albrecht-Carrié, *Italy at the Paris Peace Conference* (Hamden, Connecticut, 1966), 52–56, 236–242.

75. Roberto Michels, "Die wirtschaftlichen Wirkungen des Völkerkrieges auf Italien in den ersten Monaten," *Archiv für Sozialwissenschaft und Sozialpolitik* 40 (1915): 592–619; Michels, "Cenni sulle emigrazioni e sul movimento di popolazione durante la guerra," *La Riforma sociale* 24 (1917): 1–60; Renè Del Fabbro, *Transalpini* (Osnabrück, 1996), 277–282; Deputazione Provinciale di Ascoli Piceno to Segretariato per gli emigranti in Ascoli Piceno, 14 September 1914, ACS MinInt Comuni b. 838.

76. Direzione generale della statistica, *Annuario Statistico italiano, 1914* (Rome, 1914), 300; Municipio di Feltre (provincia di Belluno), Relazione, Prefect of Belluno to Interior Ministry, September 1914, ACS MinInt Comuni b. 838.

77. *L'Emigrazione Italiana dal 1910 al 1923,* 1:670–678, 680–685.

78. *Mobilitazione e smobilitazione degli emigranti italiani,* 18–22; *L'Emigrazione Italiana dal 1910 al 1923,* 1:726–729.

79. Augusto Cicconi, writing from Villa Ballester (near Buenos Aires), 10 October 1915, in Augusta Palombarini, *Cara Consorte* (Ancona, 1998), 106.

80. "Italia Redenta. Fatti storici della Guerra Italo-Austriaca," F.lli Scotti, Buenos Aires, in Miele and Vighy, eds., *Manifesti illustrati della Grande Guerra,* 63–64.

81. Abele Sola, Buenos Aires, 10 June 1915, in Samuel L. Baily and Franco Ramella, eds., *One family, two worlds* (New Brunswick, 1988), 163.

82. *L'Emigrazione Italiana dal 1910 al 1923,* 1:733–738.

83. Humbert S. Nelli, "Chicago's Italian-Language Press and World War I," in *Studies in Italian American Social History,* ed. Francesco Cordasco (Totowa, New Jersey, 1975), 69–70; Sterba, "'More Than Ever, We Feel Proud to Be Italians,'" 74–77; Fiorello B. Ventresco, "Loyalty and Dissent: Italian Reservists in America During World War I," *Italian Americana* 4/1 (1978).

84. Gino C. Speranza, "The 'Americani' in Italy at War," *The Outlook* (New York City) 112 (12 April 1916): 861. Speranza later served as an attaché at the American Embassy in Rome. He estimated that at least sixty or seventy thousand reservists had left the United States.

85. Ibid., 863.

86. New York State Department of Labor Industrial Commission, *Fifth Annual Report of the Bureau of Industries and Immigration (1915)* (Albany, 1916),

28–29. Of the 81,000 reservists who had already passed through New York City, 58,000 embarked at New York and the rest departed from New England.

87. Meeting of General Assembly, Italian Colonial Institute, 27 November 1915. ASMAI, pos. 163/2 f. 19, pp. 1–2.

88. Gualtiero Raffaelli, *La Patria nell'anima dei nostri emigrati* (Cingoli, Marche, 1924), ix, 21, 74, 79; Miele and Vighy, eds., *Manifesti illustrati della Grande Guerra,* 61–63; *Mobilitazione e smobilitazione degli emigranti italiani,* 69–102; Patrizia Salvetti, *Immagine nazionale ed emigrazione nella Società "Dante Alighieri"* (Rome, 1995), 164–176; Luciano Tosi, *La propaganda italiana all'estero nella prima guerra mondiale* (Trieste, 1977), 66–68.

89. Emphasis added. Woodrow Wilson also praised Jim Crow: "The southern States were readjusting their elective suffrage so as to exclude the illiterate negroes and so in part undo the mischief of reconstruction; and yet the rest of the country withheld its hand from interference. Sections began to draw together with a new understanding of one another": *A History of the American People* (New York, 1902), 5:212–214, 300; O'Leary, *To Die For,* 220–222. Wilson was elected president of the American Historical Association in 1924. Italian anarchists had a notorious political reputation in Wilson's state of New Jersey, having sponsored the assassination of King Umberto I.

90. Albrecht-Carrié, *Italy at the Paris Peace Conference,* 146–147; H. James Burgwyn, *The Legend of the Mutilated Victory* (Westport, Connecticut, 1993), 277–281, 301; Thomas A. Bailey, *Woodrow Wilson and the Lost Peace* (New York, 1944), 268–270; August Heckscher, *Woodrow Wilson* (New York, 1991), 564, 624, 627.

91. Mark I. Choate, "D'Annunzio's Political Dramas and His Idea-State of Fiume," *Forum Italicum* 31/2 (1997): 367–388; Paolo Valesio, *Gabriele d'Annunzio* (New Haven, 1992).

92. B. R. Mitchell, *European Historical Statistics 1750–1993,* 85–87; Wyman, *Round-Trip to America,* 111–112.

93. *L'Emigrazione Italiana dal 1910 al 1923,* 1:740.

94. Ibid., 733.

95. Meeting of General Assembly, Italian Colonial Institute, 17 December 1916. ASMAI, pos. 163/2 f. 19, p. 4 .

96. Meeting of General Assembly, Italian Colonial Institute, 24 June 1917. ASMAI, pos. 163/2 f. 19, pp. 6–7.

97. The ASMAI papers cited above are the only reference I have found to this charitable corporation.

98. Eugenio Bonardelli, "Corrispondenze," *Italica Gens* 6/10–12 (1916):

266–267. See also Eugenio Bonardelli, *La cooperazione economica tra i nostri emigrati* (Turin, 1911).

99. *Annuario statistico della Emigrazione Italiana dal 1876 al 1925,* 86–91; Pellegrino Nazzaro, "L'Immigration Quota Act del 1921, la crisi del sistema liberale e l'avvento del fascismo in Italia," in *Gli italiani negli Stati Uniti* (Florence, 1972).

100. Note Mussolini's preface to Commissario Generale dell'Emigrazione, *L'Emigrazione Italiana negli anni 1924 e 1925* (Rome, 1926), vii–viii; Maria Rosaria Ostuni, "Il fondo archivistico del Commissariato generale dell'emigrazione," *Studi emigrazione* 15/51 (1978): 411–440; Ornella Bianchi, "Fascismo ed emigrazione," in *La riscoperta delle Americhe,* ed. Vanni Blengino, Emilio Franzina, and Adolfo Pepe (Milan, 1992), 96–114; Monte S. Finkelstein, "The Johnson Act, Mussolini and Fascist Emigration Policy, 1921–1930," *Journal of American Ethnic History* 8/1 (1988): 38–55; and the Italian government's propaganda piece: Antonio Stella, *Some Aspects of Italian Immigration to the United States* (New York, 1924).

101. Carlo Levi, *Christ Stopped at Eboli,* trans. Frances Frenaye (New York, 1947), 124–132; Ernesto Ragionieri, "Italiani all'estero ed emigrazione di lavoratori italiani," *Belfagor* 17/6 (1962): 640–669.

102. Stefano Luconi, *La "diplomazia parallela"* (Milan, 2000); Philip Cannistraro, "Per una storia dei Fasci negli Stati Uniti (1921–1929)," *Storia Contemporanea* 26/6 (1995): 1061–1044.

Conclusion

1. Vittorio Emanuele II, the king of Piedmont-Sardinia, was crowned King of Italy in 1861; the Italian capital was moved from Turin to Florence in 1864, and then to Rome in 1871. Catherine Brice, *Monumentalité publique et politique à Rome: Le Vittoriano* (Rome, 1998); Bruno Tobia, *L'altare della patria* (Bologna, 1998); Marcello Venturoli, "Il monumento a Vittorio Emanuele II," *Capitolium: Rivista di Roma* 40/4 (1965): 219–223.

2. The monument's inscription reads "Gli italiani in Argentina MCMXI A Roma Capitale."

3. Franco Borsi and Maria Cristina Buscioni, *Manfredo Manfredi e il classicismo della Nuova Italia* (Milan, 1983), 181–186.

4. See the commemorative plaque, placed by the Commune of Rome on Piazza Rotonda in February 1906 in thanks to Buenos Aires. Ironically, only two kings are buried in the Pantheon: Vittorio Emanuele II (1878) and Umberto I (1900).

5. Michael Topp, "The Transnationalism of the Italian American Left," *Jour-*

nal of American Ethnic History 17 (1997): 39–63; Leonardo Bettini, *Bibliografia dell'anarchismo,* vol. 1 (Florence, 1976).

6. Gualtiero Raffaelli, *La Patria nell'anima dei nostri emigrati* (Cingoli, Marche, 1924), 128.

7. Nina Glick Schiller, "Transmigrants and Nation-States: Something Old and Something New in the U.S. Immigrant Experience," in *The Handbook of International Migration,* ed. Charles Hirschman, Philip Kasinitz, and Josh De Wind (New York, 1999), 94–119; Glick Schiller and Georges Fouron, "Transnational Lives and National Identities: The Identity Politics of Haitian Immigrants," in *Transnationalism from Below,* ed. Michael Peter Smith and Luis Eduardo Guarnizo (New Brunswick, 1998), 130–61.

8. Randolph S. Bourne, "Trans-National America," *Atlantic Monthly,* July 1916, 86–97; Leslie J. Vaughan, "Cosmopolitanism, Ethnicity, and American Identity: Randolph Bourne's 'Trans-National America'," *Journal of American Studies* 25/3 (1991): 443–59; Nina Glick Schiller, Linda Basch, and Cristina Blanc-Szanton, eds., *Towards a Transnational Perspective on Migration* (New York, 1992).

9. Gino C. Speranza, "Political Representation of Italo-American Colonies in the Italian Parliament," in *The Italians,* ed. Francesco Cordasco and Eugene Bucchioni (Clifton, New Jersey, 1974), 310.

10. http://www.ambwashingtondc.esteri.it, and http://travel.state.gov/law/citizenship/citizenship_778.html, accessed 4/21/2007.

11. Robert C. Smith, "Migrant Membership as an Instituted Process: Transnationalization, the State and the Extra-Territorial Conduct of Mexican Politics," *International Migration Review* 37/2 (2003): 297–343; Nancy Foner, *From Ellis Island to JFK* (New Haven, 2000); Pamela M. Graham, "Reimagining the Nation and Defining the District: Dominican Migration and Transnational Politics," in *Caribbean Circuits,* ed. Patricia R. Pessar (New York, 1997), 91–125; Susan Stanton Russell, "Remittances from International Migration," *World Development* 14/6 (1986): 677–696; Douglas S. Massey, "International Migration at the Dawn of the Twenty-First Century: The Role of the State," *Population and Development Review* 25/2 (1999): 303–322.

12. Matthew Frye Jacobson, *Special Sorrows* (Cambridge, Massachusetts, 1995).

13. Mack Walker, *Germany and the Emigration, 1816–1885* (Cambridge, 1964); Klaus J. Bade, "Labour, Migration, and the State," in *Population, Labour and Migration in 19th- and 20th-Century Germany,* ed. Bade (Hamburg, 1987), 59–85; Steve Hochstadt, "Migration and Industrialization in Germany, 1815–1977," *Social Science History* 5/4 (1981): 445–468; Dieter Langewiesche, "Wanderungsbewegungen in der Hochindustrialisierungsperiode," *Vierteljahrschrift für Sozial- und Wirtschaftsgeschichte* 64/1 (1977): 1–40.

14. David A. Smith, "From the Mississippi to the Mediterranean: The 1891 New Orleans Lynching and Its Effects on United States Diplomacy and the American Navy," *The Southern Historian* 19 (1998): 60–85; Paul M. Kennedy, *The Rise and Fall of the Great Powers* (New York, 1987), 198–206; Martin Clark, *Modern Italy 1871–1995* (London, 1996), 26.

15. Eiichiro Azuma, *Between Two Empires* (Oxford, 2005), 17.

16. Ibid., 17–31; Louise Young, *Japan's Total Empire* (Berkeley, 1998), 307–341; Akira Iriye, *Pacific Estrangement* (Cambridge, Massachusetts, 1972), 133–136; Roger Daniels, *Prisoners without Trial*, 2d ed. (New York, 2004); Lawrence DiStasi, *Una storia segreta* (Berkeley, 2001); Stephen Fox, *The Unknown Internment* (Boston: Twayne Publishers, 1990).

17. Tim Steller, "Mexico Is Courting Its Citizens Abroad," *The Arizona Daily Star*, April 18 2002; Douglas S. Massey et al., *Return to Aztlan* (Berkeley, 1987); Robert C. Smith, "Reflections on Migration, the State, and the Construction, Durability and Newness of Transnational Life," *Soziale Welt. Sonderband* 12 (1998): 197–217, and "Transnational Localities: Community, Technology and the Politics of Membership within the Context of Mexico and U.S. Migration," in *Transnationalism from Below*, 196–238; Jorge Durand, Emilio A. Parrado, and Douglas S. Massey, "Migradollars and Development," *International Migration Review* 30/2 (1996): 423–444; Michael Jones-Correa, *Between Two Nations* (Ithaca, 1998); Patricia R. Pessar, ed., *When Borders Don't Divide* (New York, 1988); Maria Elena Muñoz, *Las relaciones dominico-haitiana* (Santo Domingo, 1995).

18. Oliver MacDonagh, *A Pattern of Government Growth* (London, 1961); P. Dunkley, "Emigration and the State, 1803–1842," *The Historical Journal* 23 (1980): 353–80.

19. *The Independent* (London), 11 January 2003, p. 14.

20. C. Fred Bergsten and Inbom Choi, eds., *The Korean Diaspora in the World Economy* (Washington, DC, 2003).

21. Benedict Anderson, *Imagined Communities,* 2d ed. (London, 1991); Donna R. Gabaccia, *Italy's many diasporas* (Seattle, 2000).

22. U.S. Department of State Bureau of International Information Programs, "Global Poverty Action Plan Approved by G8 Leaders," (http://usinfo. state.gov, 2004, June 9).; José de Luna Martínez, "Workers' Remittances to Developing Countries," in *World Bank Policy Research Working Paper 3638* (Washington, DC, 2005); International Monetary Fund, *World Economic Outlook* (Washington, DC, 2005); United Kingdom Department for International Development (DFID), *Sending Money Home?* ([London], 2005); "International Money Transfer Class Action Settlement," Canada NewsWire, 20 October 2003.

23. "Meeting the Challenge," *LatinFinance,* November 2002, p. 7; Patricia R.

Pessar, *A Visa for a Dream* (Boston, 1995), 76–79; "Vajpayee invites Indian diaspora to cash in on Indian economic boom," Agence France Presse, 9 January 2003; Miguel Moctezuma Longoria and Hector Rodriguez Ramirez, *Impacto de la migracion y las remesas en el crecimiento economico regional* (Mexico City, 1999); Francesco Balletta, *Il Banco di Napoli e le rimesse degli emigrati, 1914–1925* (Naples, 1972).

24. "Les possibilités du Commerce Français dans l'Amérique du Sud. Un entretien avec M. Charles Wiéner," *Bulletin de l'Union des Associations des anciens élèves des Écoles Supérieures de Commerce* 10 (5 July 1908), 391–392. Archives Nationales (AN), F/12/9199.

25. Hasia R. Diner, *Hungering for America* (Cambridge, Massachusetts, 2001), 21–83; Piero Bevilacqua, "Emigrazione transoceanica e mutamenti dell' alimentazione contadina calabrese fra Otto e Novecento," *Quaderni storici* 47 (1981): 520–555; Vito Teti, "La cucina calabrese: un'invenzione americana?," *I viaggi di Erodoto* 5/13–15 (1991): 58–73; Franco La Cecla, *La pasta e la pizza* (Bologna, 1998).

26. Barilla launched its slogan in 1985: www.barilla.it and www.buitoni.com.

27. Donna R. Gabaccia, *We Are What We Eat* (Cambridge, Massachusetts, 1998); Alejandro Portes and Leif Jensen, "What's an Ethnic Enclave? The Case for Conceptual Clarity," *American Sociological Review* 52 (1987): 768–771; George J. Borjas, *Heaven's Door* (Princeton, 1999); Peggy Levitt, "Social Remittances: Migration Driven Local-Level Forms of Cultural Diffusion," *International Migration Review* 32 (1998): 926–948; Pierre Bourdieu, "Le capital social: notes provisoires," *Actes de la recherche en sciences sociales* 31 (1980): 2–3.

28. "L'italiano e le grandi communità italiane nel mondo," in *La lingua italiano nel Mondo*, ed. Ignazio Baldelli (Rome, 1987); Alejandro Portes, "Children of Immigrants," in *The Economic Sociology of Immigration* (New York, 1995), 248–279; Joel Perlmann, "Immigrants, Past and Present," in *The Handbook of International Migration*, 223–238.

29. Clipping from 1902, AS Rovigo, Carte Rossi n. 10, p. 16; Laura Pilotti, *L'Ufficio di informazioni e protezione dell'emigrazione italiana di Ellis Island* (Rome, 1993); Barry R. Chiswick, "Are Immigrants Favorably Self-Selected?," *American Economic Review* 89/2 (1999).

30. Peter B. Evans, "Transnational Linkages and the Economic Role of the State," in *Bringing the State Back In*, ed. Peter B. Evans, Dietrich Rueschemeyer, and Theda Skocpol (Cambridge, 1985), 192–226; Barbara Schmitter Heisler, "Sending Countries and the Politics of Emigration and Destination," *International Migration Review* 19/3 (1985): 469–484; Barbara Schmitter, "Sending States and Immigrant Minorities—the Case of Italy," *Comparative Studies in Society and History* 26 (1984): 325–334; Luis

Eduardo Guarnizo, "The Rise of Transnational Social Formations: Mexican and Dominican State Responses to Transnational Migration," *Political Power and Social Theory* 12 (1998): 45–94.

31. Hilary Pilkington, *Migration, Displacement, and Identity in Post-Soviet Russia* (London, 1998); Deepak Nayyar, *Migration, Remittances, and Capital Flows: the Indian Experience* (Delhi, 1994); Sergio Diaz-Briquets and Sidney Weintraub, eds., *Migration, Remittances, and Small Business Development: Mexico and Caribbean Basin Countries* (Boulder, 1991); Hein Mallee and Frank N. Pieke, *Internal and International Migration: Chinese Perspectives* (Richmond, Surrey, 1999); Sucheng Chan, "European and Asian Immigration into the United States in Comparative Perspective, 1820s to 1920s," in *Immigration Reconsidered,* ed. Virginia Yans-McLaughlin (New York, 1990), Prasenjit Duara, "Nationalists Among Transnationals: Overseas Chinese and the Idea of China, 1900–1911," in *Ungrounded empires,* ed. Aihwa Ong and Donald M. Nonini (New York, 1997), Aihwa Ong, *Flexible Citizenship* (Durham, North Carolina, 1999).

32. Commissioner-General of Immigration, *Annual Report* (Washington DC, 1904), 43, 45.

33. P. Parameswaran, "Remittances to developing nations to jump from 100 billion dollars," Agence France Presse, 8 April 2005.

34. Jürgen Habermas, *The Structural Transformation of the Public Sphere,* trans. Thomas Burger (Cambridge, Massachusetts, 1989).

35. Contrast Andreas Wimmer and Nina Glick Schiller, "Methodological Nationalism, the Social Sciences, and the Study of Migration," *International Migration Review* 37/3 (2003): 575–611.

36. www.inq7.net/globalnation/sec_ofw/ 2004/dec/index.htm (accessed 7/15/05).

37. John Mack Faragher, *Rereading Frederick Jackson Turner* (New York, 1994).

38. The Russian Empire and Kingdom of Prussia altogether prohibited emigration (as opposed to expulsion). Vicenzo Grossi, *Storia della legislazione sull'emigrazione in Italia e nei principali Stati d'Europa* (Milan, 1901); Mack Walker, *Germany and the Emigration, 1816–1885* (Cambridge, 1964).

39. Rudolph J. Vecoli, "The Italian Diaspora, 1876–1976," in *The Cambridge Survey of World Migration,* ed. Robin Cohen (Cambridge, 1995), 114–122; Mark Wyman, *Round-Trip to America* (Ithaca, 1993), 10–12.

40. Enrico Corradini, *Il volere d'Italia* (Naples, 1911), 189, 197–199; emphasis in the original.

41. Ibid., 190–191; James Sheehan, "The Problem of Sovereignty in European History," *American Historical Review* 111/1 (2006): 1–15.

42. Luigi Villari, *The Awakening of Italy: The Fascist Regeneration* (London, 1924), and *The Fascist Experiment* (London, 1926); Amy Bernardy, *Ri-*

nascita regionale (Rome, 1930), and *Fascismo sanmarinese. Pubblicato in francese dall'annuario 1930 del Centre international d'études fascistes di Losanna* (San Marino, 1931).

43. Renzo De Felice, *Storia degli ebrei italiani sotto il fascismo,* 4th ed. (Turin, 1988). Preziosi launched *La Vita Italiana all'estero. Rassegna mensile di Politica Estera, Coloniale e di Emigrazione* in 1913.

44. Treasury Minister Giuseppe Paratore to Prime Minister Luigi Facta, 28? September 1922, ACS, PCM 1922 f.2.9.2732.

45. Luigi Villari to Pasquale Villari, 29 January 1908, BAV Villari 58, pp. 44r–45v.

46. Annunziata Nobile, "La colonizzazione demografica della Libia: progetti e realizzazioni," *Bollettino di demografia storica*/12 (1990): 173–188; Carlo Giglio, *La colonizzazione demografica dell'Impero* (Rome, 1939).

47. Stefano Luconi, *La "diplomazia parallela". Il regime fascista e la mobilitazione politica degli italo-americani* (Milan, 2000).

48. Carlo Sforza also served in the prewar and postwar Italian Foreign Ministry. Alessandro Brogi, *L'Italia e l'egemonia americana nel Mediterraneo* (Scandicci, Florence, 1996).

49. "Exchange of Correspondence Concerning Italian Peace Treaty," *The Department of State Bulletin* (Washington, D.C.) 13/333 (1945): 764; see De Gasperi's 1949 speech on emigration, Zeffiro Ciuffoletti and Maurizio Degl'Innocenti, eds., *L'emigrazione nella storia d'Italia* (Florence, 1978), 2:234–235. Despite De Gasperi's efforts, the new United Nations made Libya immediately independent in 1951.

50. Luigi Einaudi, *Un principe mercante. Studio sulla espansione coloniale italiana* (Turin, 1900), 12–13; Francesco Nobili-Vitelleschi, "Politica coloniale. Espansione coloniale ed emigrazione," *Nuova Antologia* 99 (1902): 106–109.

Index

tions, 4, 23, 40, 58, 92, 108, 112, 115, 149, 158, 169, 196, 197–198, 203, 231; colonies, 12, 13, 31, 33, 48, 58, 75, 164, 165, 183, 232; economy, 50, 74, 89, 117, 125, 147; Colonial Council follows Italian example, 103; anti-Germans, 135–136; lack of expatriate support, 208–210
Giannini, A. P., 79
Gini, Corrado, 75
Gioberti, Vincenzo, 22, 106, 147
Giolitti, Giovanni, 49, 102, 149, 150, 152, 168–177, 181, 191–192, 194–196, 199
Global nation, 2, 5–6, 14, 16, 62, 100, 226–228, 233, 235, 239–241
Globalization, 1, 18, 20, 51, 229–230, 232, 240–241; internet, 220
Gobbi Belcredi, Giacomo, 52
Godio, Gugielmo, 41
Gratteri, Sicily, 10
Greece, Greeks, 81, 93, 113, 134, 144, 176, 207, 219
Gribaudi, Pietro, 74, 89, 120
Grisons, Switzerland, 64

Habermas, Jürgen, 228
Haiti, Haitians, 223
Hakluyt, Richard, 12
Harrison, Benjamin, 136
Hartford, Connecticut, 24
Hoboken, New Jersey, 24
Hobson, John A., 12
Holidays, ethnic, 73, 85, 104, 116, 117, 225–226
Holland, 183
Humanitarian Society, 126, 141, 216
Hungary, Hungarians, 3, 4, 7, 26, 54, 57–58, 62, 63–66, 149, 186, 210, 214, 224, 269

Illinois, 11. *See also* Chicago
Illiteracy, 4, 19, 50, 107, 110, 113–114, 125–127, 158, 167, 178
Immigration, 14–16, 18; Argentina, 9, 27, 50, 73, 118, 124–125, 187–199; Australia, 4, 125; Brazil, 11, 27, 50, 117–118, 127, 187; Eritrea, 45–47, 81; France, 112, 194; Germany, 112; Italy, 221; Switzerland, 112; Tunisia, 84–87, 170; U.S., 9–11, 16, 24, 27–28, 50, 70, 73–74, 77–78, 80–81, 85, 88–89, 91, 94, 97–100, 101, 107, 112, 115–119, 125–127, 131–146, 152, 156, 187, 194, 203, 209, 213–214, 217, 220–221, 225–227
Imperial Institute, 55
Imperialism theory: new vs. old, 12; "social," 13; Anglo-Saxon, 51, 232; informal, 198; demographic, 187; and Nationalism, 148–149, 159, 161–166, 169–170, 199–200; and Fascism, 231–232. *See also* Empire; Scramble
Incentives for emigrant loyalty, 15, 71, 72, 211–212, 232
India, Indians, 17, 50, 81, 197, 223–224, 225–226
L'Inferno (1911), 123
Interior Ministry, Italian (police), 22, 44, 49, 149, 177, 191, 216; loses emigration oversight, 59–62, 223
Internal colonization, 14, 42
International Monetary Fund, 224
Ireland, Irish, 24, 95, 131, 133–134, 135, 206, 221, 226
Ireland, John, Archbishop, 135
Irredentism, 5, 19, 54, 57–58, 62–66, 112, 128, 143, 150, 165–166, 170, 198, 210
Isandhlwana, Battle of, 37